WHITE WINE ENOLOGY

ADVANCED WINEMAKING STRATEGIES FOR FINE WHITE WINES

Optimizing Shelf Life and Flavor Stability of Unoaked White Wines

---

VOLKER SCHNEIDER

WINE APPRECIATION GUILD PRESS

SAN FRANCISCO

White Wine Enology

Text copyright © 2019 Volker Schneider

No part of this book may be reproduced or transmitted in any form or by any means, electronic or mechanical, including photocopying, recording, or by any information storage and retrieval system, without permission in writing from the copyright holder.

Wine Appreciation Guild Press
an imprint of
Board and Bench Publishing
www.boardandbench.com

Editorial direction by Annika LD Imelli
Design and composition by PerfecType, Nashville, TN

ISBNs
978-1-935879-14-5 (print)
978-0-932664-61-7 (ePub)

Library of Congress Cataloging-in-publication is on file with the Library of Congress

Although all reasonable care has been taken in the preparation of this book, neither the author nor the publisher can accept liability for any consequences arising from the information contained herein, or from use thereof.

Preface

The enological literature tends to put emphasis on red wines; comprehensive treatises on the enology of white wines are scarce. When such treatises appear, they tend to focus upon maximizing aroma and quality in the widest sense. This book takes a different approach. It deals with the preservation of quality. And it is dedicated exclusively to fruity white wines regardless of their sugar content. Ultimately, it shows that the enology of white wines is quite different from that of red wines in many aspects.

Wines of this type are commonly unoaked and not intended for barrel aging. They constitute the largest share of the global white wine market. However, their rapid and often premature aging in one or another way is a problem almost all wineries are concerned with. This applies despite the fact that some of these wines might undergo what is considered graceful aging. In an innovative approach to address these concerns, this book deals with flavor preservation rather than with vinification strategies aiming at obtaining short-lived quality benefits. In doing so, it addresses one of the key issues of white wine enology, which is the limited shelf life and poor flavor stability of most of these wines.

By definition, wine aging is not related to common wine faults of microbial origin, which might accidentally arise during aging or be detected only after some time of storage. In contrast, it is based on chemical reactions occurring at variable rates. As will be shown in chapter 4, these rates and their sensory outcome can be affected by global climate change, which introduces new challenges past generations did not experience.

As a chemical process, white wine aging comprises much more than the commonly known oxidative aging, frequently referred to as premox. Thus, talking about adverse aging means, firstly, differentiating the various kinds of aging according to sensory criteria, specifying the flavor-active compounds responsible for them, and identifying the chemical mechanisms of their formation. That's why this book has a strong sensory focus. In a second step, there are clear definitions of enological measures to be taken or avoided in order to mitigate the aging reactions and to improve flavor stability. These measures start as early as on the crush pad and continue throughout all phases of juice processing, wine stabilization, bottling, and storage.

In response to these complex challenges, this book covers one of the key areas of enology hardly ever embraced in a single volume. It aims at providing a valuable inside into the inherently cross-disciplinary nature of fine white wine making, unifying knowledge scattered across chemistry, technology, and microbiology. All issues it raises are traced back to their scientific fundamentals and illustrated by original data, most of them obtained under commercial winemaking conditions. The listing of comprehensive bibliographical references allows for deepening up-to-date expertise on specific subject areas.

Nevertheless, this book is not intended to be a purely academic one. Whilst it is aimed at readers with basic knowledge of winemaking and chemistry, it particularly addresses practitioners in search of food for thought. Against the background of their questions, it also suggests solutions to typical engineering issues. Thus, numerous practical hints and technical details of hands-on winery work round up the picture and provide a holistic view of one of the most fascinating fields of contemporary winemaking.

However, winemaking is more than process technology. After decades of a tendency to technocracy and even over-processing, a growing number of winemakers embrace a trend toward minimal or non-interventionist winemaking in an attempt to respect consumer expectations and traditions. Recent research has allowed us to understand why some traditional techniques, evolved through experience, can be beneficial. It has provided knowledge, insights, and carefully selected techniques that can even improve the fine heritage of traditional winemaking. Examples such as the utilization of oxygen in must, working with yeast lees after fermentation, and winemaking without added sulfites are discussed in detail.

As a guidance for readers and in order to make reading easier, each major chapter designated by a two-digit number is preceded by a short introduction summarizing the contents. Cross-references within the text provide additional guidance.

The author has many friends and colleagues to thank for being willing to critically review and comment the manuscript of this book before publication. He accepts liability for any errors it might contain. Their disclosure will be taken into account in a future edition.

The author

Table of Contents

1. Introduction..7

2. **Typical and oxidative aging**..9

2.1. Chemical pathways, reaction products, and sensory results....................9

2.2. Influence of the phenolic composition and heavy metals......................17
2.2.1. Oxidation of phenols in wine..17
2.2.2. Total phenols and importance of flavonoid phenols................................20
2.2.3. Measurement of flavonoid phenols...30

2.3. Influence of grape processing...33
2.3.1. Skin contact time...33
2.3.2. Pressing..34

2.4. Influence of juice treatment..37
2.4.1. Effect of fining agents on phenolic compounds.....................................37
2.4.2. Importance and methods of juice clarification.......................................43
2.4.3. Effects of sulfur dioxide and oxygen before fermentation.....................50
2.4.4. Passive and active must oxidation..56
2.4.5. Chemical and analytical effects of must oxidation.................................60
2.4.6. Sensory effects of must oxidation...61

2.5. Effect of reducing agents in the wine...66
2.5.1. Effect of sulfur dioxide on oxygen-related reactions.............................66
2.5.2. Wines without added sulfites..79
2.5.3. Effect of ascorbic acid...80
2.5.4. Effect of ellagitannins...86
2.5.5. Effect of sulfur-containing amino acids..88
2.5.6. Oxygen consumption by post-fermentation yeast lees...........................94
2.5.7. Working with yeast lees in practice..101

2.6. Impact of oxygen uptake post-fermentation..106
2.6.1. Oxygen uptake through container materials..107
2.6.2. Oxygen uptake through the wine surface and headspace inertization...108
2.6.3. Oxygen uptake upon wine treatments..112
2.6.4. Importance and measures of gentle white wine treatment...................114
2.6.5. Sensory assessment of oxygen uptake in filtered wines......................122
2.6.6. Oxygen uptake during and after bottling and its sensory impact........126

2.7. Effect of storage temperature...137

3. **Reductive aging and post-bottling reduction flavor**........................143

3.1. Volatile sulfur compounds eliciting aging off-flavor..........................143
3.1.1. Definitions, causes, and important key compounds.............................143
3.1.2. Differentiation between reductive taints and minerality......................148

3.2. Reactions and evolution of volatile sulfur compounds.......................151

3.2.1. The importance of precursors..151
3.2.2. Variability and reactivity of volatile sulfur compounds.............................153

3.3. Identification and removal of reduction flavor pre-bottling...................157
3.3.1. Practical identification of reduction flavor...157
3.3.2. Determination of copper requirements for treatment................................158
3.3.3. Removal of reduction flavor in practice..162

3.4. The role of bottle closure and oxygen in reductive aging......................169
3.4.1. Importance of the gas tightness (OTR) of bottle closures.........................169
3.4.2. Screw caps using liners with variable OTR...173

3.5. Measures to prevent post-bottling reductive aging..............................176
3.5.1. Assessing wines' proneness to post-bottling reduction flavor....................176
3.5.2. Copper management pre-bottling...179
3.5.3. Stability and toxicity of copper..181
3.5.4. Screw cap liners scavenging reduction flavor...186

4. Atypical aging (ATA)..191

4.1. Sensory identification and compounds involved...................................191

4.2. Limited significance of microbial formation...194

4.3. Chemical formation of 2-aminoacetophenone.......................................195

4.4. Viticultural causes and countermeasures..198

4.5. Enological measures against ATA..201

4.6. Assessing the wines' proneness to ATA..204

5. Petrol flavor..207

5.1. Sensory characteristics and causes..207

5.2. Viticultural countermeasures...209

5.3. Enological countermeasures..210

6. Epilog..213

7. Literature..215

Index...235

1. Introduction

The quality and market value of fruity white table wines strongly depend on their distinctive flavor, which may be varietal, origin-related, or fermentation-derived to a variable degree. Much effort and enological knowledge is dedicated to its production, but much less attention is paid to its preservation. However, white wines are sensitive products. They are subject to a far more dynamic aging than red wines. In the majority of cases, the sensory outcome of this aging process is opposed to current understanding of quality; white wines aged in a positive way are rare exceptions. The limited shelf life of white table wines after bottling is a global problem.

All wines change during storage. These changes are driven by intrinsic and extrinsic factors. A gradual decay of fruity aroma attributes, particularly of those produced by the fermentation metabolism of yeast, is common to all kinds of wine and considered unavoidable. This process is referred to as maturation. In a second phase, distinctive aging flavors appear in white wines, usually after bottling. Their occurrence adversely affects the sensory profile and quality patterns initially intended by the winemaker.

In order to take targeted measures for optimizing white wine shelf life and flavor stability, it is indispensable to differentiate the various kinds of aging flavor according to their sensory characteristics and chemical pathways. For this purpose, there is a need of specific terms applied in descriptive sensory analysis. Their precise use depends on sensory training, experience, and linguistic expertise of the tasters involved. Unfortunately and much to the disadvantage of wine quality control, sensory terms are frequently misused, abused, or exchanged among themselves. The term "oxidized" is a good example of linguistic confusion. It gives no information about whether there is the typical smell of free acetaldehyde involved in the aroma pattern as it might only occur in the absence of free sulfur dioxide, or whether the smell is elicited by other oxidation products generated despite the presence of free sulfur dioxide. Misunderstandings caused by imprecise language use often lead to erroneous decisions when it comes to choose enological countermeasures for preventing or remedying premature aging flavors.

According to prevailing sensory criteria, there are four different kinds of white wine aging:

- Typical and oxidative aging giving rise to a wine commonly called maderized or simply oxidized. It is reminiscent of cooked vegetables, boiled potatoes, wet soil, black tea, honey, nuts, hay, and straw. Additionally, the odor of free acetaldehyde reminding one of bruised apples may appear and mask these olfactory descriptors when free sulfur dioxide has been decreased to nil by oxygen uptake. An intensification of color and an increase of astringency on the palate may occur simultaneously, but must not do so.

- Reductive aging leading to the formation of volatile sulfur compounds, particularly thiols and hydrogen sulfide, whose stinky smell is reminiscent of burnt rubber, cooked cabbage, rotten eggs, and garlic. Its appearance is fostered when wines prone to produce it are stored under anoxic conditions or bottled using bottle closures with a low oxygen ingress rate. Therefore, it is also known as post-bottling reduction flavor.

- Atypical aging resulting essentially from the conversion of a phytohormone called indole-3-acetic acid into 2-aminoacetophenone and some by-products reminiscent of mothballs, soap, floor polish, acacia blossom, and laundry in wines produced from stressed or unripe fruit.

- Petrol flavor calling to mind gasoline, kerosene, and dry apricots. It is related to an acidic hydrolysis of grape-derived precursors found in wines obtained from a very limited number of grape varieties, Riesling in particular. It is not affected by reactions of oxidation or reduction.

Oxidative aging with its familiar sensory pattern has always been known and is still the most common form of aging of white wines. Therefore, it is also called typical aging or aging per se. The other variants of aging are considered abnormal or faulty deviations from typical white wine evolution. The frequently encountered confusion between typical and atypical aging is a particularly serious problem in enology with far reaching consequences.

As a matter of principle, any white wine is subject to one or another kind of aging. The only question is which specific form of aging will arise, and how fast it will do so. It is also possible that two forms of aging appear simultaneously. Combinations of aging flavors that are frequently observed include:

- typical aging + atypical aging,

- petrol flavor + typical aging,

- atypical aging + reductive aging,

- reductive aging + petrol flavor.

The sensory identification of these combinations of simultaneously occurring types of aging places high demands on sensory training and expertise of tasters.

2. Typical and oxidative aging

2.1. Chemical pathways, reaction products, and sensory results

Introduction: As a beginning, chapter 2.1 describes the flavor-active compounds generated during what is considered typical aging, the odor profile they elicit, their precursors, and some of the reaction pathways responsible for their formation. It distinguishes between products always formed under oxygen-free conditions and those relying on oxygen uptake. To understand these issues, we will make a small excursion into the broad field of organic chemistry responsible for what we smell in white wines.

Under standard winery conditions, wine picks up oxygen before, during, and after bottling. The amounts picked up are highly variable and hardly ever checked.

Based on a given amount of oxygen picked up by the wine, oxidation of white wines leads to a substantially different outcome than that of red wines. It is standard knowledge that a certain amount of oxygen is required for maturation of red wines. Oxygen uptake, however, rarely improves the sensory quality of white wines that are produced to display fruity, floral, vegetative, or mineral aromas considered prerequisite for the sensory expression of their cultivar or origin.

From a chemical point of view, wine aging is a complex process. Before going into details about how typical aging can be mitigated by enological measures, an up-to-date overview of the underlying reactions and compounds is useful.

Non-oxidative aging reactions in any wine

While the major part of aging is driven by oxygen-related reactions in most wines, it is obvious that there are also non-oxidative reactions taking place simultaneously. They occur in any wine regardless of its oxygen exposure. For a better understanding of what is oxidative aging as the very traditional problem in white winemaking, they are covered at first.

Every winemaker is familiar with the rather unspecific decay of fruity aroma attributes of any kind of wine during the very first weeks and months after alcoholic fermentation. It is basically related to a gradual loss of fermentation-derived aromatics, which are not specific to the grape variety the wine originated from but rather to the yeast strain it was fermented with. The hydrolytic breakdown of acetic acid esters with higher alcohols resulting from fermentation metabolism plays a major role in this process (Rapp and Mandery 1986, Garofolo and Piracci 1994). Depending on the storage temperature, this reaction comes to a complete halt after some years, when hydrolysis achieves an equilibrium between esters and their corresponding alcohols. It is unavoidable in very young wines, but not necessarily considered as a kind of aging detrimental to quality.

However, there is more. In an early work, several lactones produced by multifarious reaction mechanisms have been identified as partially responsible for the typical off-odor of white wines aged under anoxic aging conditions (Muller et al. 1973). At a later stage, the formation of odor-active compounds by reactions between amino acids on one hand and dicarbonyl compounds (as diacetyl) or ketones (as acetoin) on the other hand was proven. In the presence of sulfur-containing amino acids and in particular cysteine, numerous pyrazines, thiazoles, thiazolidines, and oxyzoles are produced by the Maillard and Strecker reactions at relatively low temperature and wine pH. These strong-smelling compounds display odors of corn, roasted hazelnuts, popcorn, sulfur, and ripe fruits (Marchand et al. 2000, Pripis-Nicolau et al. 2000). As might be expected, the synthesis of these compounds increases with temperature.

It will be shown further on that the aroma attributes referred to above are not very different from those produced under conditions of oxidative aging. Therefore, it can be fairly difficult to distinguish by sensory means whether typical aging has been caused by oxidation, by mere thermal load under anoxic conditions, or by both. Clearly, oxidation accelerates typical aging as perceived by smell, but exclusion of oxygen does not totally prevent it.

The relative share of non-oxidative reactions leading to what is perceived as typical aging has gained in importance since almost air-tight metal-lined screw caps (Chapter 3.4) are used in certain countries for sealing bottled wines. These seals are able to create an anoxic environment excluding oxidative aging reactions, but cannot avoid a rapid decay of fruity varietal aromatics and the appearance of a roasted or nut-like aging aroma when the storage temperature is inadmissibly high. In certain wines, they can even generate a very particular kind of aging called reductive aging (Chapter 3).

Sensory studies upon the temperature impact on the rate of typical aging are available (Chapter 2.7). These studies and their practical implications deserve much more attention than they presently do. Further work in this field should try to assess the relative proportions of oxygen-dependent and non-oxidative reactions in the overall rate of typical aging.

Oxidative aging

Traditionally, oxygen pickup has been poorly controlled in the wine industry. As a consequence, typical aging is closely associated with oxidation. The sensory characteristics of oxidative aging are widespread and have always be observed by any winemaker.

During a long time, there was only limited knowledge about the chemical reactions and reaction products responsible for oxidative spoilage. Only after the advent of more sophisticated analytical tools over the last quarter of a century, knowledge about typical aging has become more extensive.

2. Typical and oxidative aging

Formation of malodorous carbonyls by oxidation

Under storage conditions allowing for oxygen uptake, the coupled oxidation of vicinal di- and tri-hydroxyphenols leads to the formation of acetaldehyde and higher aldehydes, which substantially contribute to the aroma of Sherry wines (Wildenradt and Singleton 1974) and, at lower concentrations, also to that of other wines. While the enzymatic generation of acetaldehyde during alcoholic fermentation is common to all wines, its non-enzymatic formation by oxidation can severely compromise the quality of white wines under certain conditions (Baro and Quiros Carrasco 1977). For Riesling wines, it was shown that under conditions of aerobic storage a large array of compounds is produced that is not observed when storage takes place under anoxic conditions. These odor-active compounds include benzaldehyde, furfural, and acetaldehyde (Simpson 1978).

When wine was stored in wooden barrels allowing for oxygen uptake, an increase of saturated and unsaturated carbonyl compounds as well as methyl ketones was observed. Under these conditions, the typical smell of the oxidized wine was tentatively ascribed to 2-nonanon and 2-undecanone (Ferreira and Bertrand 1996).

In another study on white wines undergoing barrel-aging, 2,5-furandicarbaldehyde, furyl hydroxymethyl ketone, and hydroxymaltol have been identified as further chemical markers of oxidative aging, especially of the honey descriptor resulting therefrom. However, it is not known to which extent these compounds are derived from wood. Their concentration decreases by post-fermentation yeast lees stirring (Lavigne-Cruege et al. 2000). It is not clear whether the latter effect is due to adsorption of these compounds by yeast lees or to consumption of dissolved oxygen by post-fermentation yeast cells (Schneider et al. 2016).

The role of higher aldehydes produced upon oxidation

Under conditions of accelerated aging, 22 new odor-active compounds were identified for the first time after oxidation of six different white wines. Four of them were present in all wines and 14 in more than half of them. Several of these compounds displayed a repulsive, oxidized smell. Using methods of sensory profiling analysis and multivariate statistics, 15 of the discriminated odor attributes proved to be affected by oxidation, whereby the overall aroma pattern changed by 60 %. There was a sensory oxidation pattern common to all oxidized wines (Escudero et al. 2000 a).

The aroma profile of oxidized wines was primarily ascribed to higher aldehydes as methional, a strong odorant displaying an off-flavor reminiscent of cooked vegetables. It was assumed to be produced by coupled oxidation of methionol with ethanol, or via Strecker degradation of the amino acid methionine mediated by ortho-quinones formed during wine oxidation (Escudero et al. 2000 b, Ferreira 2003 a).

Both alcohols and amino acids act as precursors

Strictly speaking, the Strecker degradation of amino acids involves the interaction of sugar-derived α-dicarbonyl compounds with free amino acids. The amino acid in the presence of α-dicarbonyl compounds is decarboxylated and deaminated, forming an aldehyde with one carbon atom less than the amino acid and known as "Strecker aldehyde".

In a wider sense, many other dicarbonyl compounds including ortho-quinones can be used. Indeed, in wine conditions, Strecker degradation was shown to occur preferentially via the reaction of ortho-quinones with the amino acids when metals are present (Monforte et al. 2018). Quinones are generated by oxidation of phenols, which act as primary oxygen acceptors in wine (Chapter 2.2.1.). Under comparable oxidation conditions, catechin, a flavonoid phenol, yields more phenylacetaldehyde from phenylalanine than nonflavonoid phenols (Oliveira et al. 2017).

After the role of the above-mentioned methional being unrevealed, subsequent work showed that the intensity of the cooked vegetables odor correlates positively with the concentrations of 2-nonenal, benzaldehyde, furfural, and eugenol, while acetaldehyde levels are not significantly influenced by oxidation (Escudero et al. 2002). Further research groups confirmed the importance of methional as a key compound in the aroma pattern of oxidized white wines, altogether with phenylacetaldehyde, 3-(methylthio)-propionaldehyde, and sotolon (4,5-dimethyl-3-dihydroxy-2(5H)-furanone) (Ferreira et al. 2002, 2003 a, 2003 b, Ferreira 2007), benzaldehyde, furfural, and other higher aldehydes resulting from oxidation of unsaturated fatty acids (Ferreira et al. 1997, Culleré et al 2007) or amino acids (Bueno et al. 2016).

As a summary of compositional data, it can be stated that the typical aroma of oxidative aging is caused by a large variety of carbonyls, among which higher aldehydes are the most important compounds, and sotolon as a volatile lactone. For simplifying the analytical quantification of that kind of aroma, 2-phenylacetaldehyde, methional, sotolon, and 3-methylbutanal can be used as chemical markers (Pons et al. 2015, Mayr et al. 2015).

Variable acceptance threshold of oxidative aging

It is not yet clearly established whether the main pathway of the formation of all these aldehydes is the Strecker degradation of the respective amino acids or direct oxidation of the respective alcohols. However, from a practical point of view, the conditions of their generation and their sensory impact are much more important: Their concentration strongly correlates with oxygen uptake, temperature, and the intensity of odor descriptors referred to as boiled potatoes, farm-feed, hay, straw, wood, and honey.

Obviously, under comparable oxidation and storage conditions, the relative concentrations of these aroma-active compounds also depend on the respective amounts of precursors and further intrinsic factors of each wine. This explains why oxidative aging displays somewhat variable aroma profiles. It might explain furthermore why some tasters perceive oxidative aging as less repulsive in wines made from very ripe fruit than in wines made from less ripe grapes. Fruit quality, consumers' expectations, traditions, and cultural environment determine to what extent the flavor of typical aging is accepted.

2. Typical and oxidative aging

Figure 1 gives an extreme example of typical aging in an unoaked white wine intended to be fruity. The aroma profile changed completely during the first year of bottle storage. As a side effect, astringency and bitter rating also increased. The reason for this are explained in chapter 2.2.1.

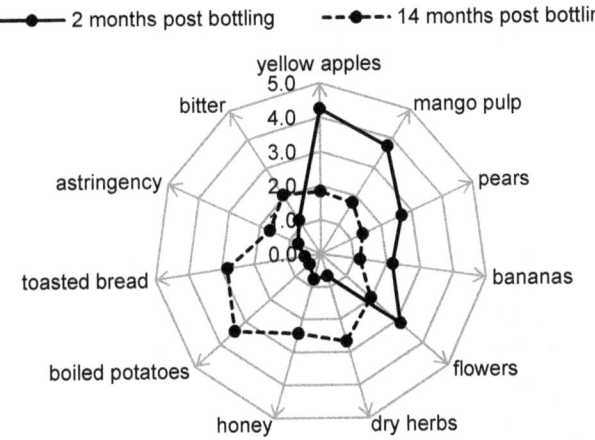

Figure 1: Typical aging of an unoaked Chardonnay during 12 months of bottle storage with cork at 18° C (65 F).

Effect of sulfur dioxide on higher aldehydes

In red wines, it has been shown that the formation rates of these oxidation-derived higher aldehydes as methional and phenylacetaldehyde are linear but strongly dependent on the individual wine for a given amount of oxygen consumed. Most of them display a formation rate that correlates positively with the level of combined SO_2 and the concentration of their corresponding amino acids, but not with their corresponding alcohols. Indeed, they are to a large extent complexed as bisulfite adducts at the free SO_2 levels usually found in wines. Cleavage of the bound forms occurs during the first steps of oxidation as a consequence of equilibrium shifts caused by SO_2 depletion. As the free SO_2 level decreases, the concentration of the free odor-active fraction increases. At low levels of free SO_2, *de novo* formation can also be observed with amino acids as the most important precursors (Grant-Preece et al. 2013, Ferreira et al. 2015, Bueno et al. 2016).

The entirety of research results shows that higher aldehydes responsible for the smell of oxidative aging are generated by several pathways altogether:

- oxidation of higher alcohols,
- Strecker degradation of amino acids,
- release from SO_2-bound forms.

All three reactions are promoted by oxygen uptake as it can occur before or after bottling.

The data obtained on the relationship between higher aldehydes and SO_2 in red wines cannot be used to remedy white wines affected by oxidative aging. Practical experience shows that increasing the free SO_2 level from for example 30 to 60 mg/L only marginally improves their aroma. This observation suggests that higher aldehydes are less reactive with SO_2 than acetaldehyde, which disappears entirely upon SO_2 addition. This behavior has a simple explanation:

Indeed, it has been shown that the dissociation constant of the SO_2-adduct with higher aldehydes is much higher than that with acetaldehyde. In other words, higher aldehydes have a lower potential to be bound by SO_2. As a result, it is difficult to decrease their concentrations below the detection threshold by adjusting free SO_2 to levels typically used in wine (Grant-Preece et al. 2013). Higher aldehydes and free SO_2 can co-exist.

Oxidation accelerates the breakdown of fruity aroma compounds

Alongside with the production of new odor-active compounds, oxidative aging can lead to a breakdown of existing molecules contributing to fruity aroma attributes of young wines. The hydrolysis of fermentation-derived esters is the major factor of changes in the aroma profile during the first months after alcoholic fermentation. Eventually, it proceeds until the equilibrium between esters and their corresponding alcohols is achieved (Garofolo and Piracci 1994). Theoretically, this equilibrium is not directly influenced by oxygen. However, research upon the impact of oxygen on the concentration of these esters led to conflicting results.

Variable oxygen permeation through different bottle closures (Chapter 2.6.6.) did not affect the concentration of the esters at least over the range of mild oxidation conditions obtained by the use of standard closures (Ugliano et al. 2015). In contrast, bottling with air-containing bottle headspace resulted in lower ester concentrations than bottling under inert conditions (Patrianakou and Roussis 2013). This effect is explained by a degradation of esters via the Fenton reaction (Waterhouse et al. 2016), which ultimately leads to a nonspecific oxidation by oxygen radicals (Chapter 2.2.1.).

Sensory consequences also occur when oxygen uptake during wine storage causes modification or decrease of terpenols and norisoprenoids, both compound groups conveying a floral-fruity smell (Rapp and Mandery 1986, Ferreira et al. 2002). However, greatest losses of fruity attributes observed upon exposure to oxygen should be primarily due to oxidative degradation of sulfur-containing compounds, for example polyfunctional thiols which can significantly add to the varietal character of some wines. They can even be predominant in wines obtained from Sauvignon blanc and some other varieties, where they are also known as varietal thiols.

Breakdown of fruity compounds enhances the effect of off-flavor

The whole bulk of research shows that oxidative aging comprises, besides the synthesis of new molecules known for their off-flavor, also the degradation of fruity-

2. Typical and oxidative aging

floral aroma compounds that are expected and looked for in young wines. Furthermore, it reveals that some reactions causing the sensory perception of typical aging are able to occur under anaerobic conditions. However, it also emphasizes the importance of oxygen uptake and subsequent oxidation reactions, which cause the formation of multifarious carbonyls like higher aldehydes as new odor-active compounds.

At a low concentration level, the compounds responsible for typical aging can be considered to contribute to aroma complexity. When their concentration increases, they adversely affect wine quality more and more until they become ultimately responsible for the aroma feature of typically aged wines.

How far a white wine should be aged primarily depends on personal preference. If a consumer accepts so-called mature wines with a touch of astringency despite their having lost much of their original fresh-fruity varietal character, typical aging is of less concern. Contrariwise, if one prefers the wine possessing a fruity elegance and freshness or showing a distinctive varietal or stylistic character, then flavor stability is a key issue.

Difference between oxidative aging and the smell of free acetaldehyde

In the worst case, the odor of the multifarious carbonyls produced upon oxidative aging can be accompanied and partially masked by free acetaldehyde with its typical smell reminiscent of bruised apples and sherry. Acetaldehyde is the principal aldehyde present in wine and primarily produced as a secondary product of alcoholic fermentation in a concentration range of 5 to 100 mg/L. In addition, a few mg/L can be produced as a result of oxidation of ethanol during oxidative wine storage (Chapters 2.2.1 and 2.5.1). High acetaldehyde levels are largely responsible for high bound SO_2 levels.

Acetaldehyde binds almost spontaneously with free SO_2 at a ratio of 1 mg acetaldehyde to 1.45 mg SO_2 as long as free SO_2 is available. The resulting hydroxysulfonate addition product is non-volatile and odorless. The small dissociation constant of $K_D = 5 \times 10^{-6}$ for this reaction explains why the equilibrium favors the formation of product. Furthermore, it explains why a wine containing 100 mg/L acetaldehyde displays only 0.00002 mg/L acetaldehyde in the unbound, odor-active form as long as free SO_2 is not limited. In other words, free acetaldehyde and free SO_2 exclude one another. Therefore, the smell of free acetaldehyde disappears as soon as sulfites are added in an amount large enough to bind it entirely and to ensure some free sulfur dioxide in excess. The reaction is completely reversible.

In this context, it is crucial to correctly interpret acetaldehyde concentration data. Headspace measurements by gas chromatography only record free acetaldehyde, which does not occur in the presence of free SO_2, while photometric and enzymatic measurements record both the free and the bound form.

Only free acetaldehyde is odor-active

There is considerable confusion in the literature concerning the sensory threshold of acetaldehyde, which is reported to be somewhere between 10 and 100 mg/L, depending on the source and without specifying SO_2 levels. In actual fact, most winemakers and many consumers are able to sensorially detect concentrations as low as 1 mg/L free acetaldehyde in model solution or after removal of SO_2 from wine. The presence of free acetaldehyde is a common wine fault related to the absence of any free SO_2 as it might occur after its depletion by oxygen ingress or in wines without added sulfites. When wine without added SO_2 is to be produced (Chapter 2.5.2), it is paramount to minimize acetaldehyde levels for sensory reasons since no SO_2 can be supplied to bind it.

Free acetaldehyde can cause a sensory bias: Oxidative aging proceeds in the presence of free SO_2 used as the traditional antioxidant in the wine industry, but it is strongly accelerated in its absence. It is imperative to distinguish the sherry-like smell of free acetaldehyde from that of oxidative, typical aging, even though both of them might occur simultaneously. Unfortunately, there are not yet any analytical means to quantify free acetaldehyde for routine control. Most acetaldehyde measurements provide total acetaldehyde regardless of the extent to which it is bound or free. Instead, a screening procedure for free acetaldehyde can be used. It is based on its SO_2 binding.

Screening test for free acetaldehyde

A stock solution containing 10,000 mg/L SO_2 is prepared by dissolving 18 g/L potassium metabisulfite ($K_2S_2O_5$) in one liter of water. Adding 0.5 mL of that solution to 100 mL wine sample provides 50 mg/L SO_2. After five minutes, wine odor is evaluated and compared to an untreated control. The reduction or disappearance of a bruised apple/sherry like odor is indicative of free acetaldehyde.

This approach can be upgraded to test how much SO_2 must be added to achieve a desired level of free SO_2. For that purpose, increasing amounts of SO_2 stock solution are added to wine samples and SO_2 levels measured the following day.

Oxidative aging is difficult to remedy

In contrast to the smell of free acetaldehyde which is easy to deal with in wine stabilization by addition of SO_2, the higher aldehydes responsible for the smell of oxidative aging are much less reactive. Theoretically, they do bind to sulfur dioxide to produce an odorless addition product, but the extent of this reaction is not satisfactory in remedying white wines affected by oxidative aging (Grant-Preece et al. 2013). The reactions leading to their formation are sparsely reversible under practical winemaking conditions. This is the reason why the smell of oxidative aging cannot be effectively reversed by addition of the commonly used reducing agents as sulfur dioxide or ascorbic acid.

Because of the diversity and low reactivity of the compounds involved, they are difficult to remove from wine. Since they do not carry any phenolic groups in the molecule, they cannot be removed by fining agents as PVPP or caseinates. Such fining agents are only able to lower phenols acting as catalysts in the formation of oxidative aging and the astringency they cause (Chapters 2.2 and 2.4.1).

Some minor improvement of wines affected by the odor of typical aging can be achieved by fining with activated charcoal or yeast lees obtained from young wines. Charcoal has well-known side-effects feared for unspecifically stripping out any aroma compounds. However, more specific fining agents are not available, nor do other fining materials commonly used in the wine industry show any effect on oxidative aging as perceived by smell.

2.2. Influence of the phenolic composition and heavy metals

Introduction: Phenolic substances are strongly involved in oxygen-related aging reactions as they are the primary oxygen acceptors even in the presence of free sulfite. The underlying chemical reactions, the sensory significance of the variable phenolic composition of white wines for shelf life and aging, and its analytical assessment in quality control are outlined.

2.2.1. Oxidation of phenols in wine

There are countless organic compounds in wine that are potential targets for oxidation processes, but only a few of them are accessible to direct oxidation by molecular oxygen. These are phenolic substances and heavy metal ions like iron and copper. When wine picks up oxygen, phenols are the primary reactants that are oxidized and able to bind large amounts of oxygen. Their oxidation initiates the oxidation of other compounds, including SO_2, in a downstream reaction called coupled oxidation.

Phenolic compounds possess a common structure comprising at least one aromatic benzene ring with one or more hydroxyl (-OH) substituents. The most important wine phenols are presented in chapter 2.2.2. Those containing a 1,2-dihydroxyl or a 1,2,3-trihydroxyl substitution pattern are the most easily oxidized. This process is more rapid at higher pH due to a higher percentage of dissociated phenolate anions that react with oxygen.

Phenols (PhOH) are weak acids, and their dissociation yielding phenolate anions (PhO$^-$) can be written according to the general formula

$$PhOH \rightarrow PhO^- + H^+$$

However, as their dissociation constant is very low with pKa = 9-10, only a small proportion of phenolate ions occur in wine, but much more will be present in a pH 4 wine than in a pH 3 wine. This is consistent with higher pH wines being more prone to oxidation (Chapter 2.5.1).

The oxidation of phenols leads to their corresponding quinones. As a result, phenolic hydroxyl (-OH) substituents are replaced by quinoid (=O) substituents. This oxidation is promoted by transition metal ions such as iron and copper, which are always present at trace concentrations at least. It initiates a cascade of chemical transformations. Figure 2 depicts the reaction schema in a very simplified way.

When phenols oxidize, hydrogen peroxide (H_2O_2) is also generated in one of the first steps. In the competitive scenario of wine with the simultaneous presence of free SO_2 (shown as H_2SO_3) and divalent iron (Fe^{2+}), the major part of hydrogen peroxide is scavenged by SO_2 which, in turn, is oxidized to sulfate (shown as H_2SO_4). Free SO_2 is also able to partially reduce quinones back to the phenols they originated from.

Figure 2: Oxidation of phenols, formation of hydrogen peroxide, and oxidation of alcohols by the Fenton reaction.

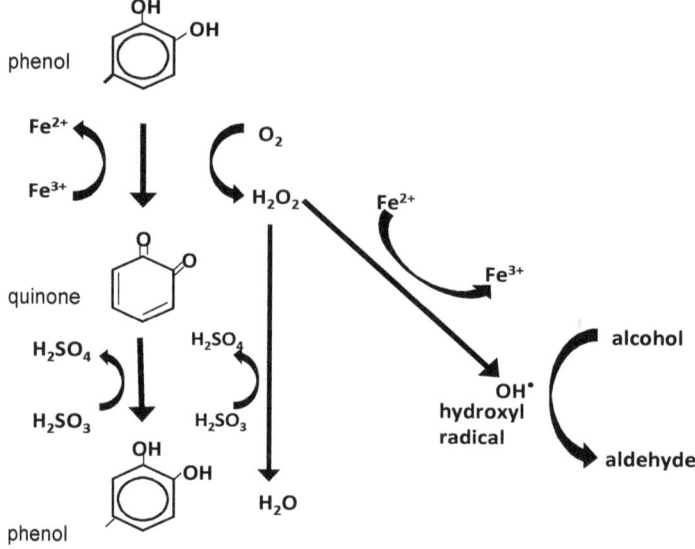

Reactions of hydrogen peroxide produced upon phenol oxidation

A minor fraction of the peroxide is converted into hydroxyl radicals through a chain reaction that is catalyzed by heavy metals. The hydroxyl radicals are able to oxidize any kind of wine constituents not accessible to direct reaction with oxygen. This reaction is known as the Fenton reaction. It leads to an unspecific oxidation of wine components at rates that are proportional to their concentrations, thus oxidizing ethanol to acetaldehyde, glycerin to glyceraldehyde, tartaric acid to glyoxylic acid, etc.

In the broadest sense, this reaction is also responsible for the oxidation of higher alcohols to the corresponding higher aldehydes as soon as hydrogen peroxide is generated by oxidation of phenols (Wildenradt and Singleton 1974, Singleton 1987, Waterhouse and Laurie 2006, du Toit et al. 2006, Danilewicz 2007, Elias and Waterhouse 2010, Oliveira et al. 2011, Danilewicz 2012). Thus, it explains to a large extent the involvement of higher aldehydes in the aroma profile of wines affected by oxidative aging.

2. Typical and oxidative aging

The direct reaction of sulfite with molecular oxygen (O_2) is very slow. Free sulfur dioxide protects wine against oxidation only in an indirect way by trapping intermediate peroxide and, thus, impeding the Fenton reaction. Wanting to protect wine against oxidation means first and foremost controlling the Fenton reaction (Elias and Waterhouse 2010). Under practical conditions, this undertaking is barely achievable because it would require the total absence of heavy metal ions.

The heavy metals required to catalyze the reaction are present in sufficient concentrations in all wines. Under winery conditions, it is impossible to entirely prevent or remove them. For that reason, control and limitation of oxygen uptake after primary fermentation and particularly after filtration (Chapter 2.6) is of major importance to protect white wine against oxidative aging.

Reactions of quinones produced upon phenol oxidation

The quinones generated upon phenol oxidation deserve further consideration. They are unstable and react in different ways:

1. As mentioned before, they are partially reduced back by SO_2 to their corresponding phenols they stem from. Thereby, sulfite is oxidized to sulfate. However, this reaction is not complete. Its extent depends on the initial level of free SO_2. In the absence of SO_2, it does not occur at all. The incompleteness of this reaction is one of the reasons why a part of the oxygen remains irreversibly bound to the wine matrix instead of being scavenged by SO_2, and why a given amount of dissolved oxygen in wine oxidizes less SO_2 than expected by stoichiometric calculations (Danilewicz 2016, Waterhouse et al. 2016). The extent to which SO_2 protects wine against oxidation is discussed in detail in chapter 2.5.1. Likewise SO_2, ascorbic acid is also able to convert quinones back to the original phenols when it is added to the wine (Chapter 2.5.3).

2. A quinone combines spontaneously with a remaining phenol, and in the process the produced dimers can rearrange their structure through an enol-like conversion reaction to form a new diphenol. For example, a quinone-phenol dimer can be converted into a new diphenol dimer. Thus, the original phenolic hydroxyl (-OH) groups are regenerated, and the quinoid state is abolished. Several reaction pathways of this kind have been postulated (Singleton 1987); one of them is represented in figure 3. It is a particular case in chemistry in which oxidation is reverted without the action of a reducing agent.

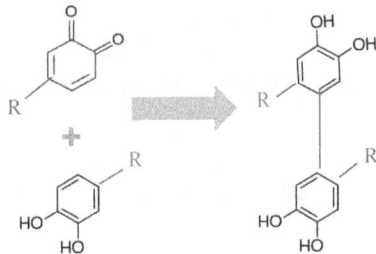

Figure 3: Regeneration of a phenolic OH-group through polymerization of a quinone with a phenol.

When the quinone is already a dimer, the same reaction generates the trimer of a phenol, a trimer of a quinone generates the tetramer of a phenol, etc. The regenerated phenolic hydroxyl groups are available for further oxidation. Therefore, this reaction pattern is called regenerative polymerization. It explains why more oxygen can be taken up than would be expected from the stoichiometric possibilities of the original number of phenol molecules present.

3. Nucleophilic addition reaction with sulfur-containing amino acids and peptides, in particular with glutathione, which is an important thiol in wine and musts. The resulting addition product is colorless (Chapter 2.4.3).

4. Nucleophilic addition reaction with amino acids according to a pathway called Strecker degradation, leasing to the formation of Strecker aldehydes participating in the off-flavor of oxidative aging (Chapter 2.1).

5. Nucleophilic addition reaction with sulfite, leading to a sulfonate addition product. This reaction is not to be confounded with the reduction of quinones back to the original phenols, in which sulfite acts as a reducing agent.

6. Nucleophilic addition reaction with hydrogen sulfide (H_2S) involved in the reduction flavor (Chapters 3.1) of wines affected by that defect. This reaction possibly explains the effectiveness of oxygen additions sometimes used to remove the off-aroma.

7. Nucleophilic addition reaction with desirable aromatic thiols that are responsible for the distinctive varietal aroma of some cultivars as Sauvignon blanc, explaining the sensitivity to oxygen uptake of wines obtained from these cultivars.

In the competitive reaction scenario of wine, the aforementioned quinone reactions are in an equilibrium, which depends on concentrations and relative reaction rates of the initial compounds (Nikolantonaki and Waterhouse 2012). The addition of reducing agents used in winemaking, in general SO_2 but also ascorbic acid and glutathione in some cases, has the purpose to shift the equilibrium towards reactions 1 and 3, thus diverting quinones from undergoing reactions 2, 4, and 7 that are responsible for the sensory perception of oxidative aging. Chapters 2.5.1, 2.5.3 and 2.5.5 cover in detail to what extent this is possible.

2.2.2. Total phenols and the importance of flavonoid phenols

Phenolic chemistry of grapes and wine can be quite daunting for the winemaker not only because of its complicated reaction mechanisms but also because of the chemical nomenclature. However, phenols are important in defining wine style and predicting aging.

The broad class of phenols originating from the grapes are composed essentially of two groups – a flavonoid and a nonflavonoid fraction. They are summed up to the total phenol content. In standard white wines, total phenols are around 200 mg/L.

Nonflavonoid phenols

In grapes, most of the nonflavonoid phenols are dissolved in the berry pulp, with some of them also present in the skins. Because of their easy extractability from grape pulp, their levels are relatively constant in white and red wines regardless of skin contact prior to pressing. They comprise mainly derivatives of hydroxybenzoic acids based on the C6-C1 structure of benzoic acid, and derivatives of hydroxycinnamic acids based on the C6-C3 structure of cinnamic acid (Figure 3). The various acids are differentiated by the substitution pattern of their benzene ring. Furthermore, most of them are esterified with sugars or organic acids like tartaric acid.

The derivatives of hydroxycinnamic acids, particularly caftaric acid, and their oxidation products are the most abundant class of phenolics in white juices and wines with concentrations of 100 to 200 mg/L. They are also called hydroxycinnamates.

Figure 4: General structures of benzoic acid and cinnamic acid.

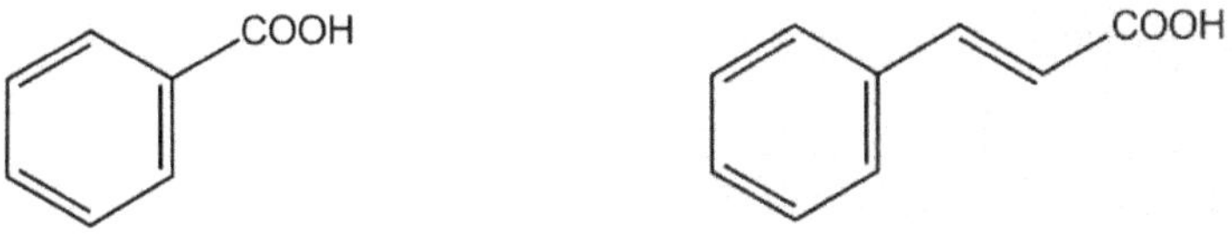

benzoic acid   cinnamic acid

Basically all grape-derived nonflavonoid phenols can display a bitter taste and elicit a sensation of astringency. However, they are hardly able to do so in wine to an appreciable extent because their concentration is close to their sensory threshold (Smith and Waters 2012). Therefore, they must not be confounded with tannins. They do not play a direct role in the taste of wine. At best, they collectively contribute to weight and volume on the palate. This is demonstrated when specific phenol-absorbing fining agents are inadvertently used on white wines whose phenolic make-up consists nearly solely of nonflavonoids; the wines become thin and meager since there are no other phenols able to react with the fining material. Besides, the involvement of nonflavonoids in the aging process of white wines is without practical importance for taste and color (Singleton and Noble 1976, Arnold et al. 1980, Vérette et al. 1988).

Only when wines are aged in wooden barrels, treated with oak alternatives or certain commercial tannins, they can contain a second group of nonflavonoid phenols, which are not grape-derived and commonly called hydrolysable tannins. They include ellagitannins and gallotannins, which release ellagic acid and gallic acid after hydrolysis, respectively. They display astringency frequently perceived as distractingly strong directly after their addition, but tending to decrease during aging due to their breakdown caused by oxidation and hydrolysis. However, their chemical structure and properties differ from grape-derived tannins. Despite not being naturally present in grapes, they are the main commercial tannins legally authorized as wine additives. One of the reasons for this is their putative action as a reducing agent, which is covered in chapter 2.5.4.

Flavonoid phenols

Flavonoid phenols possess a common C6-C3-C6 skeleton composed of three rings (A, B, and C) according to the general structure

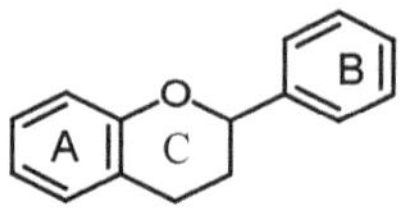

They are constituted by different sub-categories differing by the insaturation degree and substituents of the lateral B-ring. Almost solely one category of them, the flavan-3-ols, can be found in white wines. Although flavan-3,4-ols and flavonols are also present in the skins of grapes grown under sunny conditions, they are only detected in trace amounts in finished white wine.

The flavan-3-ols consist essentially of isomers of catechin and epicatechin. Both of them occur partially as gallate esters, i.e. esterified with gallic acid (Figure 5). Furthermore, a part of them occurs as polymers, which vary in their monomeric composition, linkage configuration, and chain length.

Figure 5: Structure of catechin, epicatechin, and their gallates.

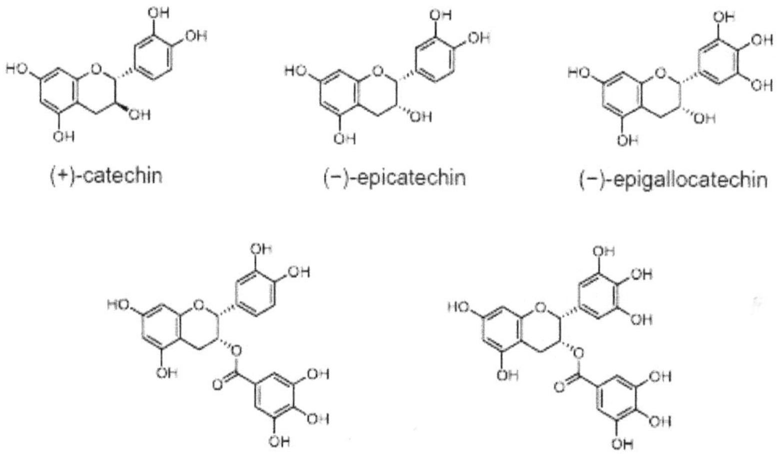

(+)-catechin   (−)-epicatechin   (−)-epigallocatechin

(−)-epicatechin gallate   (−)-epigallocatechin gallate (EGCG)

In the grape, flavonoid phenols occur in the firm tissues of skins, seeds, and stems, where they are extracted from during skin contact and by mechanical impact on the must during transport and pressing. Depending on grape processing and juice treatment, they are present in white wines at highly variable concentrations ranging from approximately 1 to 30 mg/L. In young white wines, they comprise mainly colorless monomers of catechin and epicatechin, which are able to elicit some sensation of bitterness and astringency on the palate.

Astringency is not a basic taste as is sweet, sour, or bitter, but rather a tactile or haptic sensation on the mucous membranes in the oral cavity and pharynx evoking

2. Typical and oxidative aging

a feeling of desiccation, scouring, shrinking, and friction. This sensation is caused by the precipitation of salivary proteins, which leads the saliva to lose its effect as a lubricant. Often but not always astringency is accompanied by a bitter basic taste (Noble 1998). For the purpose of sensory training, pure astringency is best represented by aqueous solutions of potassium aluminum sulfate (alum).

During wine aging, flavonoid phenols undergo polymerization, which can be either oxidative or nonoxidative. This means that many small molecules combine to fewer dimeric or even larger molecules. Polymerization is accelerated by a previous oxidation of the phenolic compounds (Chapter 2.2.1). It proceeds the faster the higher the initial concentration of the flavonoids. The reason is easy to explain: To make two molecules react one with another, they must first collide in the three-dimensional space according to the law of chance. The probability that this happens increases as their number grows.

Figure 6 displays how the polymerization rate of catechin depends on its initial concentration, shown as the decrease of its monomeric form. In this case, the absolute concentrations have less importance than the curve slopes (a). At an initial concentration of 60 mg/L (a = –0.0777), polymerization proceeds 14.7 times faster than starting at an initial concentration of 5 mg/L (a = –0.0053). In the concentration range of less than 5 mg/L, corresponding to that of white wines with optimal shelf life, almost no polymerization can be observed. In this context, optimal shelf life is to be understood as a wine's resistance to the effect of oxidative aging and the appearance of astringency.

Figure 6: Polymerization of catechin as affected by its initial concentration, measured as the decrease of its monomeric form during exposure to air (10 % ethanol; pH 3,7; 21°C).

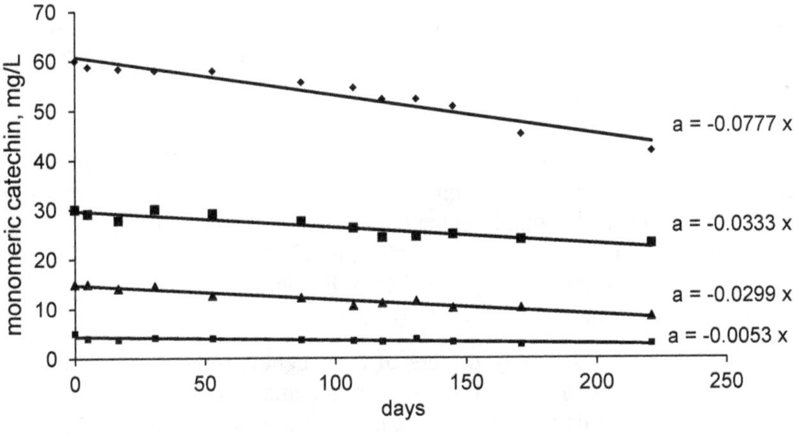

The role of flavonoid phenols in browning and mouthfeel

White wines without significant amounts of flavonoid phenols are stable in color and not able to produce significant browning under conditions of aerobic aging (Rossi and Singleton 1966, Simpson 1982, Lee and Jaworski 1988, Fernández-

Zurbano et al. 1995, 1998, Schneider 1998 a). Figure 7 depicts the browning rate of young filtered white wines kept under air without any SO_2 additions. Browning was measured as absorbance at 420 nm (A 420).

Figure 7: Browning (A 420) of filtered white wines exposed to air without SO_2 additions as affected by their content of flavonoid phenols (F).

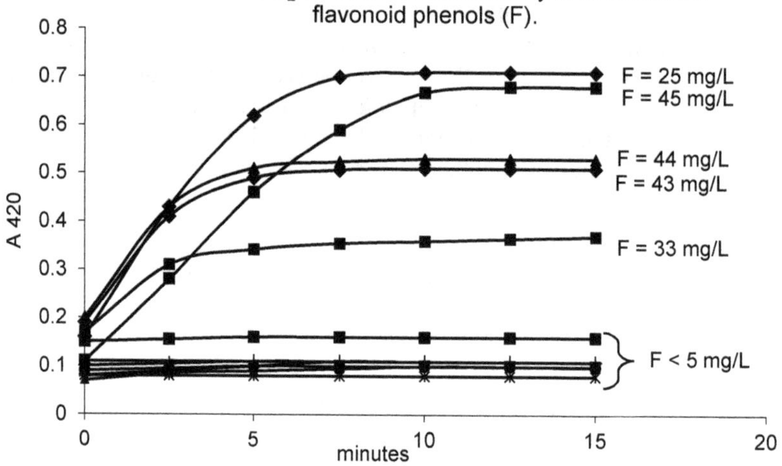

The higher the flavonoid content, the more intensive is the browning achieved. This browning potential is nothing else than the visible evidence of a wine's proneness to undergo drastical chemical changes upon oxygen uptake. Under the same conditions, white wines containing less than 5 mg/L of catechins remain almost stable in color.

The underlying reaction of browning is the polymerization of flavan-3-ols. A 100 mg/L catechin solution in 13 % ethanol at pH 3.5 is almost colorless. Exposed to air, it browns. The polymerization rates referred to in figure 6 were associated with increasing browning.

In research and quality control, the increase of browning (A 420) is often used as a measure to quantify oxidation of white wine under specific conditions in a given period of time. The undisputable dependence of browning on flavonoid content strongly limits the informative value of that approach. There is no direct correlation between browning and the degree of oxidation. Browning is more driven by flavonoids than by oxygen uptake.

Whilst phenols are not the only drivers of astringency, bitterness and 'phenolic taste', they are the most important. Flavonoid phenols and the polymers they are able to form are the primary grape-derived phenols causing astringency. However, increased flavonoid contents in very young white wines are not necessarily detectable by taste (Arnold and Noble 1979). The reason is that at the very early stage of white wines, they occur predominantly as colorless monomers, i.e. as single molecules. Their relatively low taste intensity explains why potential astringency is perceived as less aggressive in young white wines.

When light bodied white wines displaying low flavonoid levels (< 5 mg/L) are spiked with increasing amounts of monomeric catechin, winemakers used and dedicated to the production of that kind of wine style are able to detect an increase of 10 ± 5 mg/L, depending on the wine matrix. This difference threshold in white wine is much lower than the catechin detection threshold reported for water (Delcour et al. 1984).

The more flavonoids polymerize during aging, the more their astringency, their bitter taste, and their yellow color increase at an identical concentration (Noble 1994). The dimer, consisting of two single molecules, already shows noticeable astringent properties, which further increase as polymerization proceeds towards longer molecule chains (Lea 1978, Lea et al. 1978, 1979, Arnold et al. 1980, Robichaud and Noble 1990, Delcour et al. 1984). As a consequence, the difference threshold of these polymers is expected to be lower than 10 mg/L as observed for monomeric catechin.

The higher the initial concentration, the faster this flavor development proceeds (Figure 6). Insofar, astringency in white wines is also dependent on storage and aging (Schneider 2006 b). Its sensory perception inevitably presents a snapshot. The increasing astringency of white wines displaying relatively high flavonoid levels is a phenomenon widely known by practitioners. When it occurs, it is usually noticed long before any visible browning can be observed.

The afore-mentioned behavior is fundamentally different from what happens when flavonoids undergo polymerization in red wines. In such wines and in the presence of anthocyanins, they polymerize by differing reaction pathways, thus forming different products and achieving different and often softer forms of sensory expression. In wines containing no anthocyanins as white grape and apple wines, astringency steadily increases with polymerization.

Comparable with red wines, however, are masking and reinforcing effects by other wine constituents. White wine matrix parameters such as pH, total acidity, alcohol, sugar, polysaccharides etc. affect the sensory response stimulated by flavonoids. As pH decreases, astringency is enhanced (Fontoin et al. 2000). pH as a factor for astringency is generally underestimated. When wine phenols and ethanol are added to white wine, both additions enhance astringency and bitterness in an additive way, suggesting that also alcohol directly contributes to these attributes in white wines. On the other hand, taste and texture produced by addition of wine phenols are more pronounced in wines with lower alcohol levels (Gawel et al. 2013).

Describing mouthfeel requires precise terms

Strong matrix effects make it impossible to stipulate universally valid flavor threshold concentrations in wine for any given phenol or to predict concentration on the basis of perceived astringency. Even so, winemakers focusing upon light bodied, lean, fruity and elegant white wines such as those typically represented by Riesling, Sauvignon blanc, unwooded Chardonnay etc. are quite able to identify astringency and bitterness associated with elevated flavonoid levels. When doing so, they use fining for phenol reduction (Chapter 2.4.1) or take steps to minimize phenol uptake prior to fermentation (Chapter 2.4.2 and 2.4.4). Their perception of phenol-derived astringency seems a very specific one suggesting the use of more precise terms such as mouth drying or roughening rated independently (Kallithraka et al. 2007).

On the other hand, the level of astringency which is accepted, rejected, or desired depends on personal preference, sensitivity, and cultural context. Thus, some winemakers have recently shown an increasing willingness to incorporate more phenolics into their white wine as a way to improve what they consider palate structure, texture, and individuality. The addition of commercial tannins is one way to achieve this goal. In most extreme cases, these attempts lead to fermenting white grapes on the skins with intent to produce so-called orange wines (Chapter 2.3.1). The outcome can be seen as a fault in contemporary winemaking circles since it detracts from the fresh varietal characters sought in fruity white wines dominating the market. Hence, they are considered niche products.

Whenever a sensory attribute is evaluated, there is a need for clear definitions and agreed terminology. Some of the terms used to describe the sensory responses stimulated by red wine phenolics include mouth-drying, velvet-like, puckering, harsh, viscous, hot, etc., but it is questionable whether the less diverse phenolics in white wines justify sensory terms going beyond the basic notions of astringency and bitterness most winemakers are able to interpret.

Tannin additions have become a widespread tool in modern winemaking. Some commercial preparations of grape-derived tannins are also recommended for white wines and promoted for improving structure, adding volume, emphasizing finesse etc. These appealing terms cannot distract from the fact that adding these tannins equates to enhancing astringency and shortening shelf life of fruity white wines when oxygen is taken up. Moreover, it invalidates all efforts of soft grape processing (Chapter 2.3.2). The simultaneous use of tannin additions and phenol-reducing fining agents for palate softening (Chapter 2.4.1) by not a few winemakers is one of the contradictions in a poorly understood enology.

The role of flavonoid phenols in aroma stability

The odor changes occurring during oxidative aging appear long before any taste and chromatic changes can be observed. Any increase in color as measured spectrophotometrically at 420 nm indicates that profound modifications of taste and odor have already taken place. The browning potential is closely associated with a wine's predisposition to undergo premature oxidative aging.

Furthermore, there is a close relationship between the content of flavonoid phenols and oxidative aging as perceived by smell when wines are aged under conditions of mild oxygen uptake as it can occur through the bottle closure. Figure 8 shows this effect on two white wines supplemented with flavonoid phenols extracted from grape seeds and the same amount of pure catechin. Similar results must be expected when commercial grape tannins are added to white wines.

This behavior is systematic, though flavonoid phenols are non-volatile and odorless. When it was documented for the first time (Schneider 1989 a), it was hypothesized that flavonoids would act as a sort of catalyst in the formation of oxidative

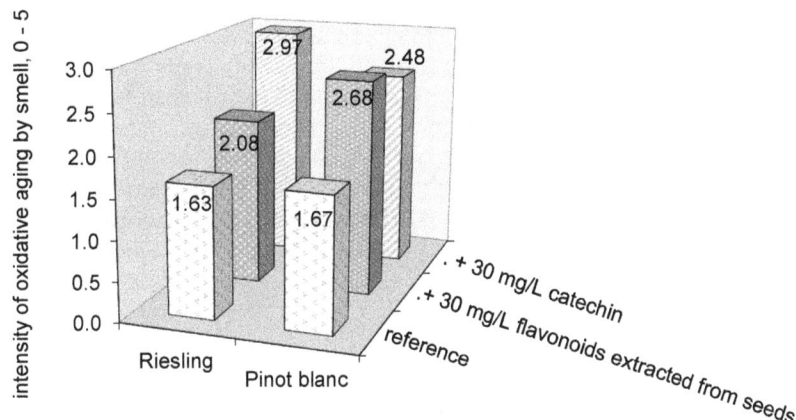

Figure 8: Impact of flavonoid phenols on oxidative aging as perceived by smell of two bottled white wines sealed with cork after eight months' bottle storage. n = 18 tasters.

aging perceived by smell to an extent not known from nonflavonoids. It would take another quarter of a century before this phenomenon was substantiated by analytical data:

For three chemical markers of oxidative aging – methional, phenylacetaldehyde, and sotolon - an increased formation was shown in the presence of elevated contents of catechin. Oxidation products of catechin such as acetaldehyde and quinones (Chapter 2.2.1) were supposed to be responsible for that formation. Out of 54 white wines bottled with cork closures, those displaying less than 3 mg/L flavonoids showed the lowest levels of sotolon, methional, and phenylacetaldehyde, while there was a strong effect of the winery and winemaking techniques (Pons et al. 2015).

The aforementioned critical concentration limit requires a classification of its magnitude: In a survey on 37 Austrian white wines, total flavonoids ranged from 3 to 35 mg/L (Schneider 2009), while another survey on 57 French white wines reported mean concentrations of 9.8 mg/L catechin and 5.3 mg/L epicatechin (Carando et al. 1999). In Czech white wines, catechin ranged from 7 to 13 mg/L and epicatechin from 5 to 9 mg/L (Lampíř et al. 2013). Similar concentrations were reported for white wines from South Africa (de Villiers 2005). These data show that in many wineries there is much room for improvement regarding shelf life, and most probably also for reducing astringency, just by lowering flavonoid levels.

As a conclusion, it can be stated that flavonoid phenols in concentrations found in most white wines do not only contribute to astringency, but also adversely affect their aroma stability. Besides their direct gustatory effect, they influence smell in an indirect way. Therefore, their evaluation, prevention or removal is of crucial enological interest if the purpose is producing fruity white wines with satisfactory aroma stability and without propensity for browning and tannin formation. This leads to the question of how to evaluate flavonoid phenols by simple analytical means. It is addressed in chapter 2.2.3.

The special case of pinking and its difference to browning

Pinking is the term used to describe a troublesome salmon-red blush color appearing in a few white wines produced exclusively from white grape varieties. In contrast to browning, aroma and flavor are usually not affected when pinking occurs. The responsible compounds are anthocyanins synthesized by white grapes under certain climatic conditions. Their minimum amount in wine for pink color visualization is 0.3 mg/L. The appearance of pinking after bottling is due to the lowering of free SO_2 upon oxidation, which leads to an increase of the relative amount of the anthocyanins' red flavylium form and subsequent polymerization products that are resistant to SO_2 bleaching (Andrea-Silva et al. 2014). If the oxidation process continues, the wine begins to brown.

A common feature of pinking wines is their relatively high flavonoid level originating from careful protection of must against oxidation (Chapter 2.4.3). Indeed, the proneness of wine to develop pinking is facilitated by reductive fruit and juice treatment leading to the preservation of the anthocyanins. Conversely, all technical means during juice processing aiming at reducing flavonoid phenols act in the opposite way. Wine treatment with PVPP (Chapter 2.4.1) and ascorbic acid (Chapter 2.5.3) has been explicitly reported to prevent or cure pinking (Lamuela-Raventós et al. 2001).

As a test to check wines for pinking susceptibility, addition of approx. 75 mg/L H_2O_2 followed by storage at 25° C for 24 hours was proposed (Simpson 1977). This test corresponds to an accelerated aging test under oxidative conditions also used to check for flavonoid phenols and browning potential (Chapter 2.2.3). The red color produced is indicative of the amount of pinking precursors and whether treatment with PVPP is advisable. Laboratory trials should be performed to establish the amount of PVPP required to reduce the pinking precursors to a level where the wine passes the pinking test.

Total phenol content of white wines is almost meaningless

Fundamentally, it makes a great difference if 200 mg/L total phenols in a white wine consist of 200 mg/L nonflavonoids or 180 mg/L nonflavonoids + 20 mg/L flavonoids. There is no relationship between the total phenol content and the stability of fruity flavor during aging (Schneider 1989 a, Schneider 2000). This behavior is in contrast to familiar observations made on red wines. The ability of their several orders of magnitude higher flavonoid levels to strongly undergo regenerative polymerization, to consume large amounts of oxygen without any harm in doing so, and to interact with anthocyanins is a possible explanation.

Despite the importance of flavonoid phenols in particular, total phenol content is an analytical figure still measured in many wineries with the purpose of evaluating shelf life, tannins, and browning potential of white wines. It is usually measured by means of the Folin-Ciocalteu reagent (Singleton and Rossi 1965) and expressed as gallic acid or catechin equivalents, or more quickly as ultraviolet absorbance at

280 nm after appropriate sample dilution. Electrochemical methods are under development but require more experience to ensure reproducible results.

While the high levels of total phenols in red wines can be approximately assessed by measuring the absorption in the UV range at 280 nm, there is a wide variability in the spectral features of white wines (Somers and Ziemelis 1972) and total phenol levels often too low to be precisely evaluated by direct absorbance measurements. Therefore, colorimetry in the visible range using the Folin-Ciocalteu reagent is commonly used for that purpose. It is based on the reduction of a mixture of phosphotungstic and phosphomolybdic acid to a blue colored complex by phenolic compounds in alkaline solution. However, this method is not specific and has serious drawbacks when used on white wines.

It has been established since the 1960's that measuring total phenols with the Folin-Ciocalteu reagent yields results strongly affected by variable levels of reducing sugars, sulfur dioxide, ascorbic acid, and other reducing wine compounds (Singleton and Rossi 1965, Somers and Ziemelis 1980, Schneider 1993). Results obtained are falsely high. The distorting effects of the various interfering compounds add up in a synergistic way (Moutounet 1981). Furthermore, about 30 % of the results obtained on white wines is attributable to the amino acid tyrosol containing a phenolic hydroxyl (-OH) group plus nucleic derivatives (Myers and Singleton 1979). These errors remain when the Folin-Ciocalteu reagent assay is replaced by reaction with iron salts (Danilewicz 2015). They also continue to occur when total phenols are assessed by more recent methods of infrared spectroscopy like FT-NIR since their calibration is based on total phenols as measured with the widely used and accepted Folin-Ciocalteu reagent assay.

Methods to eliminate the error caused by SO_2 have been proposed (Scholten and Kacprowski 1992, Schneider 1993), but they do not eliminate other interfering factors as sugars and nucleic derivatives. Thus, measuring total phenols in white wines by this method is unspecific, of low reproducibility, and an analytical anachronism, though it might be useful for red wines with around ten times more total phenols, which make analytical interferences lose importance. The most crucial drawback is, however, that it does not provide any information about the level of flavonoid phenols in white wines, which is decisive for sensory and technical reasons.

Figure 9 depicts schematically how total phenols in white wines can be composed. Nonflavonoid phenols resulting from the grape pulp juice make up the larger part with some 100 to 200 mg/L. In addition, variable but always much smaller amounts of flavonoid phenols extracted from grape solids are present. Both fractions constitute total phenols.

The crucial point is that white wines with identical total phenol content can display quite different amounts of flavonoid phenols. Therefore, a low total phenol level does not necessarily indicate a low flavonoid concentration. There is no useful correlation between both parameters.

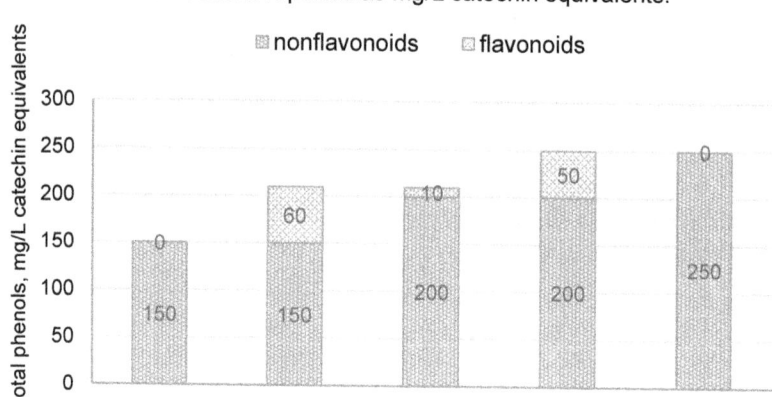

Figure 9: Variable concentrations of flavonoid phenols at identical levels of total phenols in different white wines. All concentrations reported as mg/L catechin equivalents.

2.2.3. Measurement of flavonoid phenols

Since the importance of flavonoid phenols for taste, odor, color, and shelf-life has become known, different analytical approaches have been developed for specifically measuring them, aiming at identifying wines prone to undergo premature oxidative aging. Under a more practical point of view, these methods come out to assess tannin content. They are based on the following principles:

1. Accelerated browning tests (de Villiers 1961, Caputi and Peterson 1965, Singleton and Kramling 1976, Simpson 1982, Müller-Späth 1992, Haigerov 1996): Under conditions of enhanced temperature, oxygen exposure, addition of hydrogen peroxide and/or increased pH, flavonoids are induced to produce browning within a short spell of time. Measurement value is the intensity of brown color. The most simple and traditional version of these tests consists in leaving the wine overnight in an open glass and evaluating the brown color produced the next day. The result is affected by free SO_2, suspended yeast lees, and heavy metals.

2. Precipitation or subtractive methods calculating flavonoids as the difference in total phenols before and after flavonoid precipitation. They require precipitation agents commonly used for flavonoid precipitation in the course of tannin quantification in red wines such as gelatin (Blouin et al. 2000), methyl cellulose (Sarneckis et al. 2006), bovine serum albumin (Harbertson et al. 2003), PVC/trichloroacetic acid (Burckhardt 1976), or methanal/HCl (Kramling and Singleton 1969). Except for methanal/HCl, all these reagents are not able to completely precipitate the relatively low amounts of lowly polymerized flavonoids in white wines if they affect them at all. Furthermore, even if they do so, total phenol

measurements are not sensitive enough to reliably quantify the differences generated by precipitation steps in contemporary white wines with low flavonoid concentrations.

3. Various chromatographic methods (HPLC) enable identification and quantification of individual phenolic compounds. However, they are rarely available to wineries for routine measurements and yield results difficult to interpret. They are inappropriate for measuring flavonoids as a sum comparable to the common measurement and significance of total acidity as the sum of individual acids.

4. Indirect spectrophotometric measurement in the UV-area (Puisais et al. 1968, Somers and Ziemelis 1972, Somers and Ziemelis 1985, Somers and Pocock 1991). This analytical approach is available to more wineries, quick and easy to use with very little sample preparation. Simple measurements of the absorbances at 280 nm and 320 nm on the clarified juice or wine and the use of some correction factors allow for assessing total phenols, nonflavonoids (hydroxycinnamates) and calculating flavonoids by subtraction. The major drawback of this indirect measurement is that is lacks specifity since the formula and correction factors provided do not apply to all juices and wines. This is clearly demonstrated by negative results obtained on some wines.

5. Direct spectrophotometric measurements in the VIS-range relying on the formation of colored products from the reaction of flavonoids with cyclic aldehydes as chromophores. These chromophores are vanillin (Rebelein 1965, Pompei and Peri 1971) or 4-dimethylaminocinnamaldehyde (DAC) (Zironi et al 1992) in either sulfuric or hydrochloric acid. The reaction with vanillin yields inflated results not following sample dilution in a linear way (Schneider 1989 b). In contrast, the reaction with DAC is very specific to flavan-3-ols in white wines, where it yields linear results without any interferences.

Spectrophotometric measurement of flavonoid phenols in routine control

The colorimetric measurement of flavonoids using the 4-dimethylaminocinnamaldehye (DAC) reagent according to Zironi et al. (1992) is poorly known in winery quality control settings. However, it has proven its suitability for routinely and very specifically assessing flavonoid phenols in white juices and wines over the last two decades. It is easy and rapid to perform, robust, sensitive, and without interferences by non-phenolic wine constituents. It can also be performed by less trained lab staff. The only prerequisite is a simple spectrophotometer operating in the VIS-range and a filter or centrifuge for sample clarification if required. Results are easy to interpret (Schneider 1995).

DAC reacts with the electron-rich 8 and 6 positions of the A ring of flavonoids. These positions are involved in polymerization reactions and less available for reaction with DAC when polymerization proceeds, though DAC is also sensitive to terminal flavonoid units on the polymers. Thus, polymers are included in the measurement to a lesser extent than monomers. Ultimately, this means that when the degree of polymerization increases, measured values have to be expected to decrease. However, flavonoid concentration in white wines is far too low to give results significantly affected by polymerization. Results strongly correlate with perceived astringency and long-term behavior of wines.

Since the original papers (McMurrough and McDowell 1978, Zironi et al. 1992) are difficult to access, the measurement procedure is reproduced hereinafter:

Measurement of flavonoid phenols in white wines using the DAC-reagent

– Dissolve 100 mg 4-dimethylaminocinnamaldehyde (DAC) in 75 mL methanol 100 % and adjust to 100 mL with HCl 37 %. Fresh reagent should be prepared every two days and stored in the dark.

– Add 1 mL filtered wine sample to 5 mL reagent and read absorbance at 640 nm and 10 mm path length when it reaches its maximum after 3 to 5 minutes.

– Obtain the concentration from a calibration curve. To construct the calibration curve, 10 mg (+)-catechin are dissolved in 100 ml ethanol (corresponding to 100 mg/L) and diluted to 50 – 25 – 12.5 – 5 – 0 mg/L catechin using ethanol 13 %.

– Results are reported as mg/L catechin.

Flavonoid concentrations of less than 5 mg/L catechin as measured by the DAC-reagent do not contribute to typical aging or to astringency in white wines. In blush and rosé wines with light color, levels of up to 30 mg/L can be considered optimal since anthocyanins are also included to some extent. Under these conditions, wines can be considered practically free of tannins and their monomeric precursors. Accordingly, in the use of fining agents aiming at reducing astringent phenols doesn't make any practical sense. This analytical approach is superior to sensory evaluation for two reasons:

- It detects flavonoid phenols which for lack of polymerization or due to masking effects do not yet display astringency at the moment of sensory assessment, although they are prone to do so during aging. Thus, they can be reduced by specific fining agents subsequently as a preventive measure before bottling.

- It prevents useless and wearing fining procedures aiming at removing tannins in wines in which poor sensory judgment makes one believe that one has detected them, though they are not actually present. Other sensations able to feign astringency are frequently evoked by the burning sensation of high alcohol contents, the pungent and scratching aftertaste of volatile acidity, or the grinding-gluey taste of elevated calcium levels.

All flavonoid concentration data referred to hereinafter have been obtained by this method.

2.3. Influence of grape processing

Introduction: The previous sections have shown the impact of the phenolic make-up of white wines on their flavor stability. This chapter describes how it is affected by technical variables on the crush pad. A very practical approach is adopted dealing with gentle grape processing.

2.3.1. Skin contact time

As mentioned earlier, flavonoid phenols are extracted from the solid grape tissues as soon as they are exposed to a liquid phase in the form of juice. Mechanical harvesting has often been made responsible for enhanced flavonoid extraction, but in the meantime harvesters have been improved in a way they are able to deliver almost undamaged berries without extraneous matter as leaves or pieces of bark.

Most commonly, flavonoid extraction starts when berries are damaged after harvest in the course of downstream grape processing. There are many critical points able to yield excessively high flavonoid levels in the must. Extraction on the truck is one of them and frequently observed when vineyards are located long distances from the winery. Older crusher-destemmer devices cracked seeds and chopped stems, thus creating a large surface area for flavonoid extraction. Modern crushers are available with adjustable rollers to minimize this effect.

When contemporary crusher-destemmer equipment is used, skin contact is one of the primary sources of flavonoid uptake. On-site measurements on industrial scale have shown the major factors affecting it:

Skin contact of crushed grapes over 24 hours at 15° C results in the extraction of some 15 to 20 mg/L flavonoids in the presence of SO_2, depending on cultivar and fruit ripeness. This effect is enhanced at higher temperature, in the presence of elevated sulfur dioxide levels or an inert atmosphere (Singleton et al. 1980, Marais 1998), and after mechanical disintegration of the must by upstream pumping cycles. If no SO_2 is present during the skin contact period, flavonoid accumulation in the liquid phase is largely offset by their precipitation due to the effect of must oxidation (Chapter 2.4.3).Therefore, it is not feasible to relate skin contact duration to flavonoid concentrations in the freshly pressed juice, nor to relate these concentrations to those in the finished wines.

Skin contact is frequently performed to enhance extraction of grape-derived aroma compounds. Taking into account the adverse impact of simultaneously extracted flavonoid phenols on taste properties and aroma stability, the effect of aroma enhancement by this means can thus be readily cancelled out or even reversed by typical aging during storage. In order to limit flavonoid extraction, skin contact for increasing grape-derived aroma is frequently run as 'cold soak' after cooling the must. Temperatures above 15° C strongly boost flavonoid extraction (Ramey et al. 1986, Marais 1998).

When skin contact is limited to a couple of hours, previous destemming has only limited impact on flavonoid uptake since seeds continue to be present as a potential source of flavonoids (Williams et al. 1995). Selective extraction of stems, skins, and seeds of grapes from several cultivars showed that approximately half of total flavonoids originate from the seeds (Schneider 1992).

The other way round – orange wine or skin contact extreme

Orange wines represent a singular kind of wine and even the first wines humankind ever made some 7,000 years ago in the area between the Black and the Caspian Sea, which is considered the birthplace of winemaking. They are also referred to as amphora wines, though their storage in clay amphorae was only a technical need since no other storage vessels were available by that time. Contemporary containers do the job as well. In contrast, the key element of their production is an extended skin contact period of white cultivars including fermentation on the skins and several months of post-fermentation maceration. This ancient way of winemaking has been resumed in the Western World more recently as a way to create an alternative wine style as opposed to fruity white wines.

The extended skin contact imparts typical orange wines flavonoid phenols in concentrations ranging from 1,500 to 2,500 mg/L (as catechin equivalents), a brown to amber color, and levels of astringency and bitterness close to those of light red wines. The flavonoid extraction rate ranges between 8 to 35 mg/L per day at ambient temperature, depending on cultivar and the presence of alcohol. Furthermore, the catalytic role of flavonoid phenols on aroma modulation (Chapter 2.2.1) reaches extreme levels and explains why these wines inevitably present the aroma pattern of oxidative aging accompanied by a total loss of fruity attributes at a very early stage (Schneider 2018).

The production of orange wines from white grapes is an enological option illustrating in the most extreme way the impact of flavonoids on both taste and smell. Orange wines are the antipodes of fruity white wines from both a sensory and an enological point of view.

2.3.2. Pressing

In most wineries, presses are fed using pumps. However, each pumping cycle of grapes, especially of heavily crushed fruit or after longer skin contact, can be considered one too many. Any pressure resistance on the pump discharge side caused by pipe deflections, valves, small cross sections, and large differences in height exacerbates mechanical tearing and grinding of the fruit tissue. As a result, flavonoids are extracted more easily. Conveying grapes and must using dumping devices or gravity flow is much gentler than pumps and screws. Pumping of crushed fruit after tissue disruption and initial flavonoid extraction by skin contact boosts flavonoid levels even more. Slowly running pumps with large cross sections are preferable for that purpose when gravity flow cannot be used.

Press technology has considerably evolved over the last decades. For quality reasons, continuous presses have been largely abandoned in favor of gentler batch presses minimizing the extent of tearing and scouring of skins and seeds, thus delivering juices with less suspended solids, potassium, pectines, and phenols. However, there are also significant differences between the various types of batch presses with regard to juice quality.

In batch pressing, the number of times the pomace cake is broken up by depressurizing and rotation has more impact on flavonoid extraction and overall juice quality than the pressure applied. Each time the grapes are moved and crumbled in the press, mechanical impact on skins and seeds facilitates the release of flavonoids.

Figure 10 depicts how juice flavonoid levels increase with increasing number of pressing fractions in two kinds of batch presses. One of them is an old-style horizontal head press with chains connected between the two moving heads, and the other one is a modern membrane press with the membrane mounted on one side of the press horizontally between the two ends. Data refer to fruit pressed right after crushing and destemming. While there were no clear differences between presses for free-run juice and the first two pressings (cycling blocks), flavonoid levels sharply increased in further pressings produced by the head press, while they did so much less in the pressings delivered by the gentler membrane press.

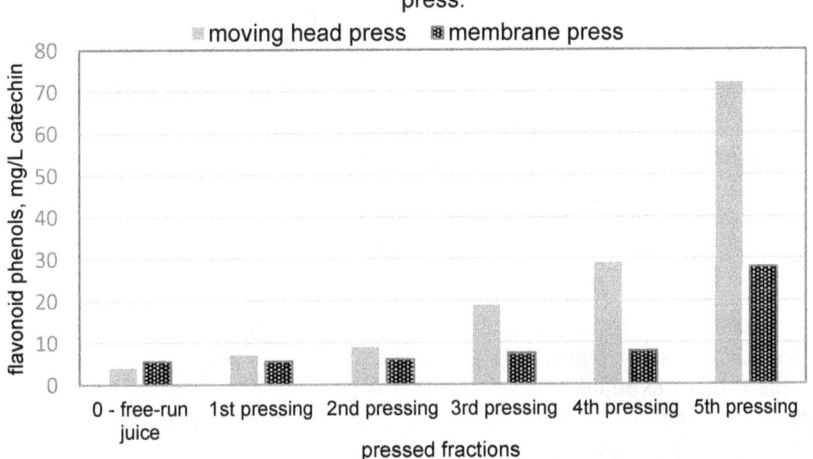

Figure 10: Impact of pressing fractions on flavonoid phenols. Comparison between a membrane press and a moving head press.

Many winemakers are aware of the lower quality of heavy juice pressings, keeping the last pressings separated with the options to improve them by additional enological treatments, blend them back later according to the desired wine style, or bottle them under different labels. It depends on the individual winery, operating situation, fruit quality, the pressing system and its handling if such an approach is beneficial. It might be worth reconsidering separating the pressings when modern membrane presses are used and basic requirements of juice treatment (Chapter 2.4) met. The way a press is operated is as least as important as its design.

Measuring flavonoid phenols in the juice by use of the DAC-method described in chapter 2.2.3 is a fast and easy approach to assess pressing quality. When flavonoids exceed some 50 mg/L in the last 10 % of juice leaving the press or 10 mg/L in the blend of free-run plus all pressing fractions, the pressing process should be rethought or pressings treated separately. Oxidative juice treatment might (Chapter 2.4.3) might be another option.

When no skin contact takes place, free-run juice reflects the phenolic composition of the pulp, which varies among varieties and comprises essentially the nonflavonoid hydroxycinnamates from the pulp juice. It is the preferred juice for sparkling wine production since it also meets other requirements for that kind of wine such as low pH, low potassium level, and higher acidity. Juices obtained from whole-bunch pressing show similar properties.

Stems are a source of flavonoids, but destemming is not a reliable means to lower flavonoid uptake upon pressing. The presence of stems in the must facilitates the release juice draining through the pomace cake. In contrast, destemmed fruit requires more mechanical load and more pressure acting in the press to extract the juice. As a result, pressing destemmed fruit can actually result in even higher flavonoid levels.

The outcome will be quite different when longer skin contact takes place. During that period, stems would act as an additional source of flavonoids and other undesirable compounds, besides of seeds and skins. This is one of the reasons for destemming. Hence, destemmers are usually incorporated into the crusher.

Each variety has a distinct pattern of phenolic composition in the grape skins and seeds, which is further impacted by fruit ripeness. Therefore, there is also a noticeable influence of cultivar and fruit ripeness on flavonoid release (Somers and Pocock 1991). Under comparable conditions of grape processing, Chardonnay and Pinot gris display higher flavonoid levels than Riesling. These differences might contribute to explain the lightness and longevity of Riesling vs. the body and volume of Chardonnay wines.

There is also a trend towards higher flavonoid levels in wines obtained from very ripe fruit, but pressing-induced flavonoid extraction and juice treatment still modulate the actual flavonoid release even if it is potentially higher due to ripeness. Bitterness in wines obtained from high Brix fruit is more frequently related to high alcohol than to high flavonoid levels.

The significance of flavonoid phenols in modern white wines

Strictly speaking, elevated concentrations of flavonoid phenols and the concomitant drawbacks for sensory appreciation and shelf life of fruity white wines are the consequence of deficiencies in grape and / or juice processing. Over decades of industrial winemaking, mechanical stress of the grapes and the subsequent disintegration of the firm fruit tissues by frictional and shearing forces have been the major reason for an increased extraction of flavonoid phenols from seeds, skins, and stems. In the meantime, the overwhelming majority of white wines around the world display much lower flavonoid levels than those observed at the end of the last century. As a consequence, flavonoids have lost a great deal of their former importance as a factor contributing to premature oxidative aging and as a carrier of astringency. Highly scored white table wines rarely display more than 5 mg/L flavonoid phenols. In case where they do so, their fruitiness will be called into question in their near future.

This positive development is largely due to technical progress having led to the emergence of more gentle techniques of grape processing, which have become widely disseminated. Thus, devices for fruit transportation within the winery, crushing, and pressing have achieved a level of technical perfection that can reduce flavonoid extraction to a minimum. Substantial improvement cannot be expected, though exceptions confirm the rule.

However, this general tendency does not prevent issues with elevated flavonoid levels in particular cases, for example in typical problem wineries, after long skin contact, hard pressings, very reductive juice treatment, or poor juice clarification. These problem are winery-specific in the majority of cases. Stage-to-stage controls of flavonoid phenols, for example by means of the DAC reagent (Chapter 2.2.3), are able to rapidly identify the shortcomings along the production chain.

While adequate equipment for gentle grape processing is available without limits, further potential for reducing flavonoid pick-up and improving general quality can rather be found in juice processing.

2.4. Influence of juice treatment

Introduction: Proper juice treatment is a neglected issue in many wineries and countries, but it has an overwhelming effect on white wine quality and longevity. SO_2 additions and oxygen uptake play a crucial role. Oxidation of juice must not be confounded with oxidation of wine. It improves long-term flavor stability post-bottling. In contrast to popular beliefs and some official doctrines, is not necessarily detrimental to wine aroma. Thus, the following chapter also presents results from 40 years of the author's practical experience with both oxidative and reductive juice handling. Furthermore, the effects of finings are discussed. The most important question, however, is the outcome of juice clarification in terms of residual turbidity.

2.4.1. Effect of fining agents on phenolic compounds

It is widely known in the wine industry that phenol-derived astringency can be lowered by fining. For that purpose, there is a plethora of fining agents offered by the supply industry. These preparations are applied when an elevated flavonoid level threatens to compromise wine's shelf life, when it elicits an astringency already considered distracting, or just under the pressure of advertising, emotions, or collective reflexes. Bentonite, a mineral clay commonly used for protein stabilization, does not have any effect on phenols in white musts and wines.

Basically, the reaction mechanism of all fining agents lowering phenols are identical in juice and wine. However, since there are more extensive data on their action on wine, results on wine fining are also presented in this context.

When phenol reducing fining agents are applied on juice, the amount added is generally not based on any objective criteria. In contrast, when they are used on wine, their appropriate application rate is frequently determined by sensory evaluation of bench scale trials with the given wine at a given point of time. This is the traditional approach of remedying wines with excessive astringency, bitterness, or 'phenolic taste'. However, when the application rate is determined by the sensory outcome at a given moment, only the most polymerized, most astringent, and most reactive flavonoids are removed. Less astringent flavonoid fractions remain in solution, able to reproduce astringency at a later moment by means of their subsequent polymerization during aging. It is important to remember that phenol-derived astringency is a snapshot in a wine's lifetime.

In contrast, the analytical determination of flavonoid phenols (Chapter 2.2.3) also includes monomeric precursors of more astringent compounds that would be formed later. This allows for adjusting the amount of fining agent to remove them in a preventive way and achieving more sensory stability in the long term.

What is also important in this regard is that phenols may not be the only cause of astringency and bitterness in white wines, and that elevated alcohol levels also play an important role (Smith and Waters 2012). Measuring flavonoids provides a secure basis for deciding whether fining makes any sense at all. When there are no substantial amounts of flavonoids, fining to reduce astringency make no sense and is rather counterproductive.

Low impact of gelatin

Gelatins are widely used for clarification and reducing astringent tannins in red wines. The precipitation of tannins with added gelatin is based on a mutual discharge of oppositely charged colloidal micelles and their subsequent flocculation. Gelatin at wine pH carries a positive charge, but when no negatively charged micelles are available, excessive gelatin remains in solution.

The effectiveness of gelatin strongly depends on its specification (Cosme et al. 2008, Cosme et al. 2012), but also on the kind of wine to be fined. It is expected to remove phenols by precipitation and flocculation. However, in most contemporary white wines with their relatively low phenol levels, it tends to show little effectiveness in reducing flavonoid phenols and astringency. These wines lack flavonoids on a level of concentration and polymerization required to generate micelles able to interact with gelatin. This can easily be found out when no haze is produced upon addition of gelatin to the wine. The same is true for fresh egg white and egg albumin. They only have affinity for polymerized tannins with a high number of phenolic groups and do not precipitate with simple low molecular phenols.

This behavior is in contrast to the effectiveness of gelatin and egg white fining of red wines, which display two to three orders of magnitude higher flavonoid concentrations, thus reaching a degree of polymerization high enough to flocculate with these protein fining agents. However, what works out pretty nicely in red wines cannot be expected in contemporary whites. Used without colloidal silica, better known as 'Kieselsol'' for counter-fining, gelatins pose a serious risk of remaining in the wine, causing overfining and thus increasing the possibility of the wine throwing a protein haze. Overfining means that that the flocculation of the gelatin is incomplete as both phenols and gelatin may temporarily be present in clear solution until the system becomes instable at a later point of time.

Considering the effect of gelatin on flavonoid phenols in the specific case of must, it is slightly more noticeable than in wine. Figure 11 shows results for various kinds of gelatin and other treatments on two musts. These musts contain relatively low concentrations of flavonoid phenols, which are frequently encountered after gentle grape processing. In this specific case, their targeted reduction was not even necessary.

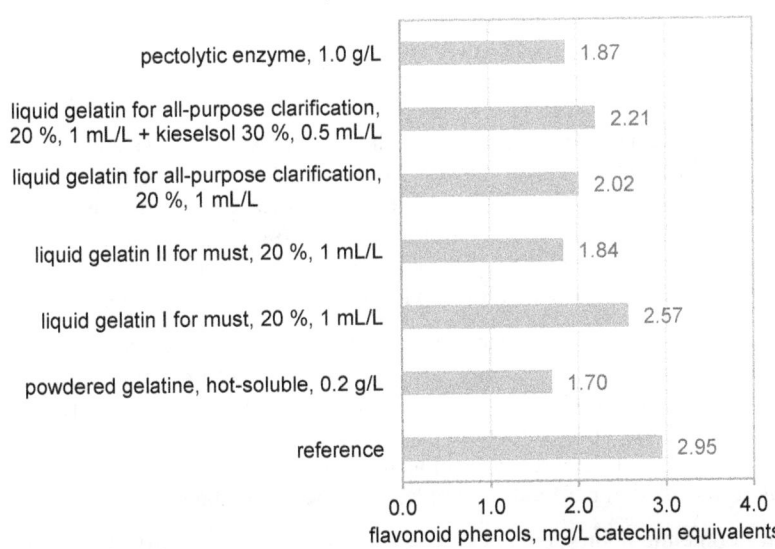

Figure 11: Effect of various gelatins on flavonoid content in white must (means of two musts).

As will be shown in Chapter 2.4.2, the absence of significant amounts of phenols able to react with gelatin results in elevated gelatin residues in such musts.

The traditional theory on the action of gelatin may hold true for white musts and wines obtained from very heavy pressings or archaic and inadequate grape processing from long past times. It needs to be revised and adapted to current conditions.

PVPP

PVPP (polyvinylpolypyrrolidone) is a synthetic, powdered, and insoluble polymer with "protein-like" characteristics that prevents residues and overfining. It has been shown to be the most effective phenol absorbent for removing both monomeric and polymeric flavonoids (Sims et. al. 1995, Barón et al. 1997). Unlike the soluble protein fining agents that preferentially remove larger phenols, it finds its major application in binding with and removing small and monomeric phenolic species such as catechins occurring in white musts and wines. It can be used both as a preventive measure and as a means to remove astringency and browning already existing as well as pinking precursors. However, its careless use in high amounts on low-flavonoid wines can severely reduce flavor and color.

There are two types of PVPP available. The first is designed for single use, this is in the form of a micronized powder with a very large surface area. To make handling easier, in more recent times this powder is processed into granulates, which easily disintegrate in contact with the liquid. The second one is designed to be regenerated and has a larger particle size able to withstand repeated recycling, but less surface area able to absorb phenols.

Generally, the wine supply industry provides micronized PVPP for single use. It can be used in conjunction with other treatments and does not require previous hydration, but prolonged mixing after addition for a minimum of a quarter of an hour.

Casein and caseinates

Casein, potassium caseinates and even swim bladder isinglass take an intermediate position regarding their reactivity with flavonoids. Comparable with gelatins, their effectiveness depends on their molecular weight distribution and surface charge density (Braga et al. 2007, Cosme et al 2009). However, from a more practical point of view, they completely precipitate even in low-phenol white wines apart from residues at trace concentrations with potentially allergenic effect.

Pure casein has largely disappeared from the market since it flocculates exclusively and immediately due to the acidity of the medium before reaction with phenols takes place. Hence, it must be rapidly distributed through the entire mass of wine before it flocculates, thus ruling out batch processing. The only solution is to feed it continuously in the product stream using an injection pump, making it possible to avoid flocculation before it is completely dispersed in the wine.

To overcome the poor solubility of casein, it is frequently modified by treatment with potassium bicarbonate. The resulting potassium caseinates are widely applied for white wine fining because they are readily soluble and easy to use.

Of particular interest is the action of mixed commercial preparations generally recommended by the supply industry for lowering phenols and astringency. They consist mostly of caseinates, silicates, isinglass, gelatin, and PVPP, though their composition is highly diverse.

Plant proteins

In response to concerns about fining agents of animal origin, extensive research has started to replace them by plant proteins. This research is in full progress and has achieved some useful results for red wine fining, but not yet for lowering phenols in white musts and wines.

Figure 12 depicts the average effects of various common fining agents on flavonoid phenols in a range of commercial white wines with variable initial flavonoid contents. Six different gelatin brands did not show any significant effect on these wines, though they might show some effect when applied to wines with extremely high flavonoid levels. In contrast, commercial mixtures of protein-based fining agents give workable results, though decreasing with increasing application rates. Their action tends to be limited to flavonoids displaying astringency at the moment. Hence, they provide sensory effects on the short term, but are not able to resolve problems with high contents of flavonoids interfering in aging on the long term. A thorough impact was only achieved by PVPP and hot-soluble casein.

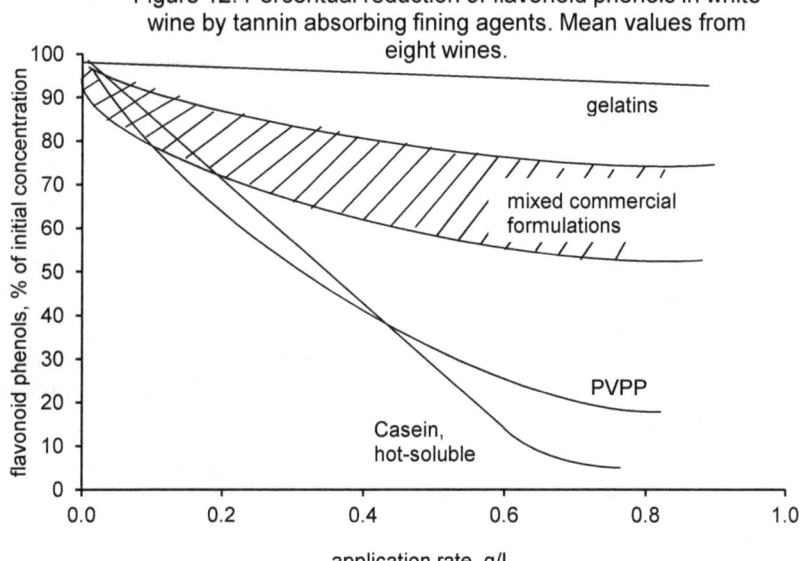

Figure 12: Percentual reduction of flavonoid phenols in white wine by tannin absorbing fining agents. Mean values from eight wines.

Practical considerations

In general, the larger the amount of fining agent added, the more flavonoids are removed. However, this reaction is non-stoichiometric. Its extent depends on the initial flavonoid concentration and their degree of polymerization. Low amounts of fining agent usually induce a sharp decrease of high flavonoid levels, but reducing low flavonoid concentrations requires disproportionately high amounts of fining agent.

The fining effect also depends on details of technical application. Fining involves a reaction taking place on the surface of the fining agent. Therefore, the method of its dissolution, hydration and mixing is important.

Moreover, there are different proprietary formulations consisting of a mix of various fining agents in proportions and purity that are often not disclosed. Such products promise easy solutions at one stroke but do not take into account the specific circumstances of a given must, winery, or vintage. Since their effectiveness is barely predictable, it is advisable to conduct bench tests and check the sensory and/or analytical outcome. Analytical data on flavonoid phenols help to back up sensory evaluation.

It is recommended to use fining agents diluted in a small amount of water. Thorough mixing of the wine is essential. The difficulty of this operation varies according to the volume to be treated. The fining agent must be added uniformly and slowly and dispersed throughout the entire mass of wine immediately. Otherwise, it risks to finish coagulating before it is completely mixed with the wine, thus reducing its effectiveness. Mixing of the wine volume should start before the fining material is added.

For mixing the wine volume, pumping over or injecting compressed gas are the least suited ways of working. When used on sensitive white wines, they cause severe aroma stripping (Chapter 2.6.4). Propeller mixers are quite useful for fining volumes up to 50,000 liters (13,000 gal.) provided they start working before uniform and slow addition of the fining agent slurry starts. For larger volumes, sucking the slurry through a "Y" on the suction side of a pump while transferring or using a proportioning dosing pump is more adequate for optimal homogenization.

It is important to emphasize that none of all the phenol reducing fining agents is specific to flavonoid phenols since they also remove nonflavonoids (Cosme et al. 2012). The nonflavonoid phenol fraction is considered positive as it contributes to body and weight on the palate (Chapter 2.2.2). Thus, it is easy to understand that the excessive use of these fining agents can severely impair flavor and color. Furthermore, they are reputed to strip aromatic compounds from wine by adsorption onto the fining agent (Voilley et al. 1990, Moio et al. 2004) or by volatilization or oxidation during the fining procedure (Schneider et al. 2005 a).

It should be one of the primary tasks of future enological research to help winemakers improve fruit and juice handling and thus make these finings superfluous instead of promoting their use.

Last not least, there is a rule of thumb: Musts forgive strenuous treatments much better than wines. One of the reasons is that most aroma of sensitive white wines is only produced during primary fermentation. Hence, it cannot be stripped out by fining the must.

Heavy metals promote oxidative aging, but only when oxygen is picked up

Elevated contents of heavy metal ions, particularly iron and copper, can cause turbidity. Copper is even subject to legal limits. Heavy metals are also known to promote oxidation since they act as catalysts in the transfer of dissolved oxygen to oxidizable compounds (Chapter 2.2.1). Nevertheless, their decrease by any kind of fining is not a suitable way to improve resistance of wine against oxidative aging.

Under usual storage conditions in tanks of stainless steel or in bottles, wine binds oxygen faster than it can be picked up (Chapter 2.6.3 and 2.6.5). Under these conditions, the oxidation rate is rather controlled by the available oxygen than by the amount of heavy metal ions or other catalysts present. An often cited statement in the wine industry is that elevated copper levels after copper fining against reduction flavor would accelerate oxidative aging. They can actually do so, but do not under conditions of limited oxygen supply. Only when oxygen is available without restrictions as it happens when accelerated aging tests are run (Chapter 2.2.3), in containers not thoroughly topped, or during barrel aging (Chapter 2.6.1 and 2.6.2), heavy metals gain importance as a decisive factor in promoting oxidation.

2.4.2. Importance and methods of juice clarification

Juice clarification is a crucial step towards optimizing clean varietal aroma expression, fruitiness, and shelf life of white wines (Singleton et al. 1975, Houtman and du Plessis 1981, Bach and Hess 1982, Bach and Nobis 1985). The demands on the level of juice clarification are still widely underestimated in the wine industry. Quality losses caused by poor juice clarification irreversibly shape wine quality and cannot be compensated for by any means during the subsequent stages of winemaking.

Compounds detrimental to wine quality that are eliminated by juice clarification to a greater or lesser extent comprise residues of soil and vineyard sprays, parts of insects and molds, grape tissue debris, precursors of off-flavors like astringency, oxidative aging, reduced aromas, or atypical aging occurring at later stages during aging. Furthermore, juice clarification decreases bacteria and indigenous yeasts, but also survival factors for yeasts required to prevent sluggish fermentations. It lowers flavonoid phenols bound to grape tissue fragments and those already precipitated during juice processing. Otherwise, they would redissolve in the alcoholic medium after the onset of fermentation and increase flavonoid levels in the wine.

For a long time, the level of juice clarification has been the mere result of chance, mostly obtained by static settling overnight. Only the dissemination of modern pectolytic enzymes and the advent of appropriate filter and flotation units helped many wineries to achieve a reproducible and satisfactory degree of juice clarity. In a very few cases, juice clarity is even exaggerated to an extent that causes fermentation problems. Nonetheless, filtration or flotation are not mandatory for a perfect juice clarification. Cold settling continues to be a viable method for that purpose, though requiring separate processing of the bottoms to recover the appreciable amount of juice they still contain.

The more recent but very effective technique of flotation is addressed in chapter 2.4.4.

Not the technique but the level of clarification is decisive

When a winemaker is asked about outcome and level of his juice clarification, the usual response is how he executes it. This kind of reply demonstrates that the kind of technical implementation is considered paramount, while little attention is given to the result. However, what is really decisive is the result obtained, expressed as juice limpidity. It can be measured and quantified as the amount of juice solids remaining in suspension, i.e. as cloudiness or residual turbidity.

Many winemakers try to assess residual solids simply by eyeballing. The standard conclusion is that the clarified juice looks more or less milky or opalescent, like the appearance of an opal. However, as long as the level of clarification is evaluated by visual assessment, winemakers have a quite individual judgment of what they consider a satisfactorily clarified juice. This complicates communication. In order to create a standardized assessment basis for decision making, the use of hard figures one can measure in a reproducible and objective way has a major benefit.

Measurement of must turbidity

For measuring the degree of juice clarification or residual turbidity, there are two methods available:

- Gravimetric measurement of residual solids after a defined volume or weight of juice is centrifuged for a few minutes. The supernatant must become absolutely clear. After centrifugation, the volume or weight of the sediment is determined and results given as % vol./vol. or % wt./wt. The major drawback of this approach is that the dryness or compactness of the sediment highly depends on the individual juice and the operating conditions of the centrifuge, thus complicating comparability of results.

- Photoelectric measurement of suspended solids by means of a turbidity meter, also known as nephelometer, which measures the scattering of a beam of light as it gets reflected off the suspended particles. No sample preparation is required. This approach is characterized by high resolution, reproducibility, and comparability. Results are expressed as NTU (nephelometric turbidity units) of the juice.

Under both commercial and research conditions, direct turbidity measurements are beneficial. They are readily accessible since there are inexpensive turbidity meters available. They provide easily reproducible results in a short spell of time. Therefore, this method has become the preferred one around the world. In contrast, gravimetric measurements require more elaborate sample preparation using previous separation of the solids by centrifugation, their drying and weighing, all steps involving possible sources of error.

Both methods, of course, depend on careful collection of the samples to be tested. Juice from the top of the settling tank will always have fewer solids than juice at the bottom, but since the point is to settle the lees, there is no interest in mixing them up all over again. Samples should be collected from the center of the vessel, right after racking, or during the course of any other means of clarification.

It is desirable that more importance should be attached to residual juice turbidity, and that the visual assessment of its level should be replaced by instrumental measurements offering greater objectivity and reproducibility.

Effect of juice clarification level on wine quality

From a sole quality point of view, juice can never become clean enough when hyper-fruity white wines with long-lasting varietal aroma are to be produced. The sensory effect of residual juice turbidity is overwhelming. When one and the same juice is clarified to a variable extent in a way that four different juices are obtained and fermented under comparable conditions, one will obtain four different wines.

2. Typical and oxidative aging

Generally speaking, wine quality and purity increase with increasing juice clarity in a linear way.

The level of juice clarification is sometimes deliberately used as a means to fine-tune the style of wine. High solids promote flavonoids and astringency, providing a more rustic wine. Any other contribution of juice solids to mouthfeel and volume has not yet been shown. What has been proven for sure is that poor juice clarification compromises aroma purity, varietal expression, and flavor stability. Dirt does not promote quality. A residual turbidity of 80 to 100 NTU (Schneider 2005 b, Nicolini et al. 2011) is deemed to be the acceptable upper limit for fruity white wines. More solids depress the fruit. They yield considerable amounts of methionol, a compound that smells like meat or potato peels.

Effect of juice clarification level on fermentation

Clarification also alters the nutritional status of the must, but care must be taken to grasp individual effects. Yeast assimilable nitrogen (YAN) essential for yeast growth consists of amino acids and ammonium, which are small molecules fairly well dissolved in the liquid. Thus, YAN levels are not substantially affected when insoluble solids are removed by juice clarification, but they are decreased by bentonite fining.

On the other hand, juice solids contain sterols and fatty acids essential for yeast cell membrane integrity and acting as yeast survival factor towards the end of fermentation. These compounds decrease the better the juice is clarified. Solids are also helpful in the release of carbon dioxide, which hampers yeast metabolism at excessively high concentrations. Thus, when residual turbidity is lower than 20 NTU, sluggish or stuck fermentations are much more likely to occur. For that reason, exaggerated juice clarification is as questionable as poor clarification.

In summary, it can be stated that the optimum level of juice clarification is in the range from 20 to 100 NTU before inoculation. The techniques used to achieve this objective comprise sedimentation by cold settling, flotation, centrifugation, and filtration. However, the procedure used is much less important than the outcome, measured as residual solids and expressed as NTU. What really matters is reaching the goal, though there are different techniques to get there.

Each of these techniques is able to achieve a satisfactory level of juice limpidity, though the expense can be excessive in some cases. Centrifuges are usually over-extended to achieve the currently required clarification levels without an unworkably low flow output. Filtration provides most often excessively clean juices tending to sluggish fermentations. By use of appropriate clarifying agents, especially pectolytic enzymes, both traditional cold settling and flotation can yield juice with a high level of clarification, frequently below 10 NTU of residual turbidity and almost comparable to that of filtration.

When residual turbidity is too low to allow for a smooth fermentation, it can be corrected by judiciously adding back some of the sludge removed. This is the typical situation when a turbidity meter becomes most beneficial. Another solution would be the addition of high amounts of yeast nutrients or some bentonite.

Enzymes promote juice settling more effectively than gelatin and bentonite

Liquid preparations of highly hydrolyzed gelatin are easy to handle and widely commercialized to promote juice clarification by settling. However, they are largely ineffective for that purpose, and the same applies to most of the bentonite brands. Only powdered high-bloom gelatin requiring previous dissolution in hot water can improve settling to a measurable extent. This kind of gelatin becomes indispensable when flotation is used for clarification.

In contrast to fining agents, the use of pectolytic enzymes is paramount in most juices regardless of the technique used for their clarification. Fining agents are hardly able to provide the level of clarification they achieve. Dispensing with enzymes only makes sense in a very few juices obtained from very ripe and sound fruit having undergone far-reaching pectin degradation on the vine. It is difficult to predict if this has happened when the fruit arrives to the crush pad. An additional advantage is the easier and less exhausting filtration of the future wine. Therefore, pectinase addition has become a standard in current commercial practice.

Enzyme activity is a function of temperature and contact time. Recommended dosage rates are available from the manufacturer and vary considerably, depending on the activity of the product. Bentonite irreversibly inhibits pectolytic enzymes. Therefore, bentonite additions must be postponed by some 3-5 hours from the moment of enzyme addition. Enzyme addition as early as upon crushing helps to gain time and facilitates juice extraction.

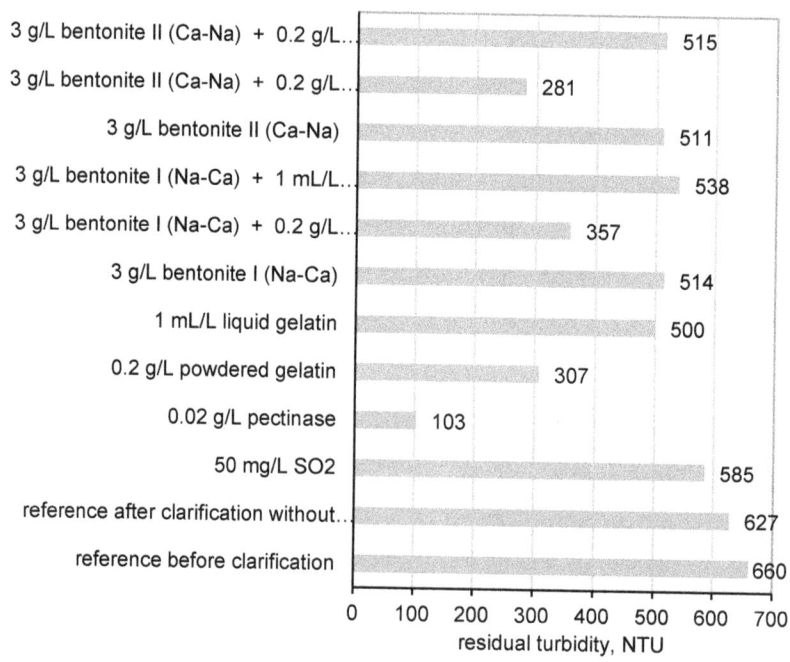

Figure 13: Action and interaction of gelatins, bentonites, and pectinase on juice clarification by cold settling. Means of two juices.

Figure 13 illustrates the effect of the above-mentioned clarifying agents on settling of juices obtained from sound fruit grown under cool-climate conditions. Dosages were on the higher side. Two brands of bentonite (I and II) had only a marginal effect on residual juice turbidity despite the high amounts used, and this effect was not substantially improved by simultaneous addition of liquid gelatin. A high-bloom powdered gelatin improved clarification both with and without bentonite, but did not achieve the impact of the pectolytic enzyme, which was the only clarifying agent yielding satisfactory results.

Details on bentonite fining

It is vital to understand the role of bentonite in this context. It is a key issue in white and rosé winemaking. All white must/wines contain unstable proteins, and bentonite fining is the most reliable treatment to eliminate them. In commercial advertising and older textbooks, it is sometimes also recommended for clarification of must and wine. However, bentonites are bad clarification agents regardless of their type, pre-treatment by swelling in water, addition and mixing protocols, and sedimentation time. Most often, they make the must/wine more turbid than before. Hence, they are used primarily for protein removal in white musts and wines.

Sodium bentonites are the most effective for protein stabilization, but they are relatively difficult to mix into suspension and produce excessive and loose compaction of lees. Sodium-calcium (Na-Ca) bentonites are a good compromise between effectiveness and lees volume.

The amounts of bentonite used in these trials (Figures 13 and 14) might appear excessively high, but it is crucial to understand that there are cultivars and growing areas that frequently require such high amounts for protein stabilization. Riper grapes, mechanical harvesting, and changes in pressing techniques have considerably increased bentonite requirements in white wines all over the world as compared to some 0.5 g/L additions half a century ago. Methods to evaluate protein stability and bentonite requirements are outlined in Zoecklein et al. (1995).

On the other hand, bentonite treatment (>1 g/L) of wine sometimes detracts from aroma intensity via absorption and oxidation. Therefore, its use is recommended in must to avoid excessive interventions on the wine. Yeast-derived aroma compounds only produced during fermentation cannot be removed by must treatments. Moreover, fewer operations are required and wine losses are reduced, as the bentonite settles out with the yeast after fermentation is completed. Undoubtedly, this approach causes some losses of yeast assimilable nitrogen, which can easily be overcome by yeast nutrient additions whenever necessary. What matters is reducing interventions on delicate, fruit-driven wines to the absolute minimum (Chapter 2.6.4).

Most wineries remove bentonite added to must before fermentation, while others choose to add it after must clarification. Its presence during fermentation stimulates the fermentation by acting as a support for yeast and facilitating CO_2 release. Furthermore, it reduces the amount of bentonite needed to stabilize the wine by approximately 30 to 50 %. A major drawback of fermenting in contact with bentonite is the need of early racking post-fermentation as most bentonites would release too much iron causing iron instability on the long-term. Thus, a prolonged aging on the yeast lees (Chapter 2.5.7) is ruled out. On the other hand, aging on the lees is known to improve protein stability and reduce bentonite requirements.

The effect of pectolytic enzymes and silica dioxide

Figure 14 shows further results obtained after settling of juices from another harvest with special regard to the limited effect of various gelatins and the benefits of auxiliary silica dioxide (kieselsol) additions.

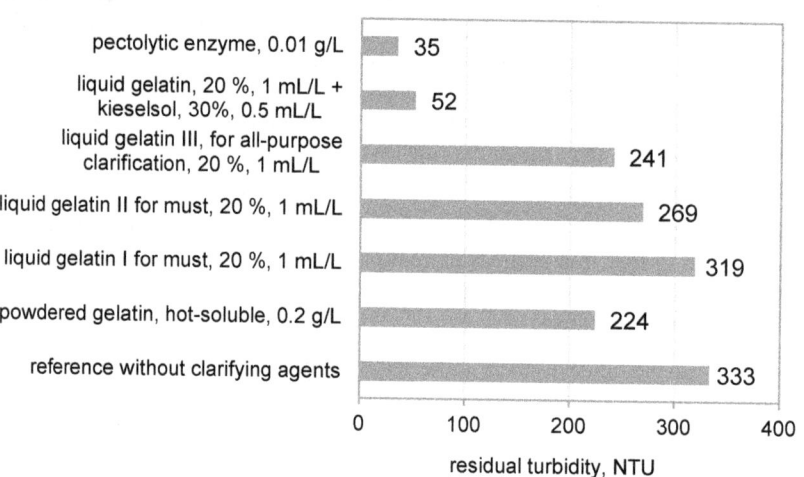

Figure 14: Residual turbidity of of settled juice after treatment with various gelatins and pectolytic enzyme. Means of two juices.

In particular liquid gelatin preparations that are frequently supplied for juice settling and are easy to handle hardly serve the purpose they are sold for. This behavior changes completely when they are used in conjunction with an equivalent amount of silica dioxide, more commonly known as kieselsol, which ensures their precipitation and flocculation. The gelatin reaction with the kieselsol forms a fine granular suspension that attracts suspended must particles that become a mass heavy enough to settle quickly.

Kieselsol is a replacement for tannins added in former times for the same purpose. It produces faster sedimentation and superior clarity, while it does not affect the palate. A typical addition for promoting must clarification is 0.5 mL/L of kieselsol 30 % in combination with 0.2 g/hl powdered gelatin. The order of addition is not really important, but it is essential that both compounds are added one directly after the other under continuous stirring.

Without the use of kieselsol, liquid gelatin formulations remain in solution in contemporary white juices, behave as an unstable protein, and require higher amounts of bentonite for protein stabilization. This is shown in figure 15. In comparison with figure 14, it can be seen that the gelatins that least contribute to juice settling are the ones which most enhance bentonite requirements for protein stabilization.

2. Typical and oxidative aging

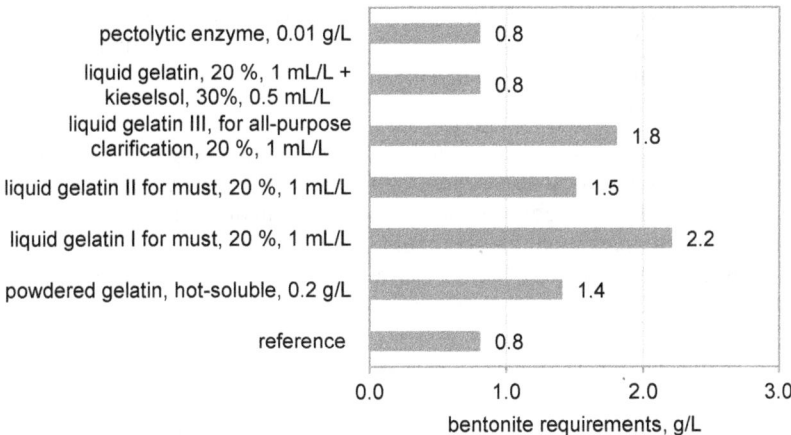

Figure 15: Requirement of bentonite for protein stabilization of settled juice after treatment with various gelatins and pectolytic enzyme. Means of two juices.

Invariably, juices obtained from rotten fruit are much harder to clarify than those from sound fruit. This is because they also contain ß-glucan, a colloidal fungal polymer produced by botrytis which can only be broken down enzymatically after addition of an exogenous ß-glucanase. This enzyme is not present in the grape but industrially prepared and commercially available, frequently in a mix with pectinase. With the quantities usually added under industrial conditions, it requires more waiting time than pectinase, often more than one week.

Standardized work plans are hardly viable

It is well known that juices display variable amounts of solids with differing compositions. Thus, their behavior upon clarification is also different even when completely healthy fruit is processed. Cultivar and fruit ripeness, but even more so mechanical tearing and grinding during conveying of crushed fruit by pumps and screws plays a role in that. Pumps and screws produce more embarrassing fine lees than gravity flow. Hence, there cannot be any standardized work plan but just general guidelines.

Let's recap: Most juices require the addition of pectolytic enzymes to achieve an economically viable and qualitatively satisfactory degree of clarification indispensable to meet consumer expectations on fruity white wines. While this is widely accepted for cold settling, it is even more important when flotation (Chapter 2.4.4) is used. The clarifying effect of fining agents is widely overestimated. Most of those used to promote cold settling do not provide the level of juice clarification required for contemporary fruity white wines rather regardless of their dosage. Only the combination of gelatin plus silica gel provides excellent clarification when both compounds are used in the right proportion. However, it is not a means to reduce the volume of the must bottoms. When sedimentation is used for must clarification, the amount of bottoms increases proportionally with solids settled and juice clarity, and finings hardly contribute to make them more compact.

Use of the must bottoms

When must is clarified by flotation, the bottoms obtained are rather compact, do not necessarily justify any further treatment, and are often discarded. On the other hand, bottoms obtained from settling still contain an appreciable amount of liquid requiring recovery. For that purpose, filter presses and vacuum rotating filters, both working with diatomaceous earth or perlite, are widely employed.

There is much practical interest in processing the bottoms before primary fermentation starts. In this way, the juice obtained can be blended back with the clarified juice the bottoms stem from without losses of quality. After the onset of fermentation, a wide array of undesirable compounds contained in the solids start dissolving in the alcohol-containing medium; flavonoid phenols are only a part of them. Thus, wines obtained from fermented bottoms suffer heavy quality losses justifying supplementary treatments, frequently with charcoal, before they can be used for blending into low-tier brands.

2.4.3. Effects of sulfur dioxide and oxygen before fermentation

The solubility of flavonoid phenols and the extent to which they remain dissolved in the juice largely depends on the redox regimen before the onset of fermentation. The term 'redox' refers to the interaction between reactions of oxidation and reactions of reduction.

When freshly pressed grape juices are entirely left to themselves without any addition of sulfur dioxide, they undergo browning. The cause of browning is an enzymatic oxidation of phenols by polyphenol oxidase (PPO) (Dubernet and Ribéreau-Gayon 1974). It requires dissolved oxygen.

Oxidation of juice

The first step of this enzymatically induced reaction is the oxidation of caftaric acid, a nonflavonoid phenol, by PPO. The reaction product is the quinone of caftaric acid. This quinone is quite unstable and able to oxidize flavonoid phenols in a second step. As a consequence, the oxidized flavonoids undergo polymerization to larger molecular aggregates, which are insoluble in the aqueous environment of juice and precipitate as brown, solid particles (Cheynier and Ricardo-da-Silva 1991). The final result is a strong decrease of all kinds of phenols. When flavonoid phenols precipitated in juice are removed by means of juice clarification, they are no longer available for oxidation in wine.

Traditional enology teaching erroneously associates juice oxidation with wine oxidation. Therefore, it impedes juice oxidation by the addition of sulfur dioxide, thus preventing it from browning. The basic role of SO_2 in this context is to inactivate PPO. It registers a 90 % decrease in activity when 50 mg/L SO_2 is added to the juice. When this happens, phenols are protected against oxidation, remain soluble in the juice, and find themselves in the resulting wine. Concomitantly, the juice remains green.

2. Typical and oxidative aging

Thus, adding SO_2 to must has become one of the central dogmas of enological doctrine for generations of enologists. Here and there, the effect of SO_2 is complemented by addition of ascorbic acid and the use of inert gases during fruit processing and pressing. Both of them are known to remove dissolved oxygen indispensable for oxidation. In doing so, one obtains wines with higher levels of total and flavonoid phenols (Cáceres-Mella et al. 2013).

Different levels of juice oxidation

At the other end of the extreme is a deliberately oxidative juice processing going as far as to actively oxidize the juice. Between both extremes of the scale, there is a broad range of gradual differences between reductive and oxidative juice processing. This is illustrated in table 1. All variants and extremes shown therein find practical application. Nonetheless, depending on country, regionally predominant school of thought, and zeitgeist, the tendency is more into one direction or the other. The implications on wine quality and shelf life can be profound, though they may not necessarily be so. They require a more detailed discussion.

Table 1: Reductive vs. oxidative juice processing in white wine production. Impact of SO_2 and oxygen prior to fermentation on the sensory stability of white wine during aging.

oxidation prior to fermentation ↓	hyper-reduction	Extreme protection against oxidation by use of SO_2, ascorbic acid, and inert gas on fruit, upon pressing, and during juice processing. No oxidation.
	reductive vinification	Addition of SO_2 and perhaps ascorbic acid, limited oxygen uptake during juice processing. No oxidation.
	standard vinification	Addition of SO_2 to fruit or juice without special measures to avoid oxygen uptake. Some oxidation.
	oxidative vinification	No addition of SO_2 prior to fermentation, no measures to impede oxygen uptake. Passive oxidation.
	active juice oxidation (hyper-oxidation)	No addition of SO_2 prior to fermentation, deliberate supply of air or pure oxygen to juice. Actively promoted oxidation.

(susceptibility of oxidative aging ↑)

The term 'juice hyperoxidation' as it is generally used to refer to oxidative juice processing does not meet the needs to precisely describe the gradual differences outlined in table 1. Rather, it means the active oxidation of juice by deliberate injection of air or pure oxygen. However, a certain level of juice oxidation is also achieved by passive oxygen uptake during grape and juice processing. For that purpose, it's just sufficient to forego any SO_2 additions prior to juice clarification. Under these conditions, PPO activity is preserved so that it transfers dissolved oxygen to phenols.

Differences between juice and wine oxidation

Many winemakers are appalled by the browning of juice and associate it with browning of wine. However, dispensing with SO_2 additions prior to fermentation and the subsequent juice browning are by no way associated with oxidation phenomena known from wine. It's about two totally different reactions, whose long-term effects are diametrically opposed. The basic differences can be summarized as follows:

- The oxidation of juice is an enzymatic one, specific, and induced by grape-derived polyphenol oxidase as long as it is not inactivated by SO_2. In contrast, the oxidation of wine is a chemical one, unspecific and only partially inhibited by SO_2 (Chapters 2.2.1 and 2.5.1),

- The by-product of enzymatic oxidation in juice is only water. The non-enzymatic oxidation of wine, however, generates hydrogen peroxide and oxygen radicals, both of them extremely reactive (Chapter 2.2.1) and with far-reaching consequences for wine aroma.

- In both cases, phenols oxidize. In juice, the oxidation products precipitate as brown solids, while they are soluble and thus sensorially active in the alcoholic environment of wine. This is easy to verify when a brown must is filtered through a lab filter, which yields a filtrate of normal green-yellow color known from standard white wines.

The deliberate oxidation of white grape must has become disseminated to some extent in cool-climate growing areas where low harvest temperatures make SO_2 additions pre-fermentation unnecessary for microbial control. The reasons are traced to sensory results and shelf life of the wines obtained. Therefore, it is useful to deepen the understanding of the reactions involved. However, when must oxidation in the absence of SO_2 is performed under hot harvest conditions, effective must cooling must be ensured to avoid microbial spoilage.

Polyphenol oxidases

The enzymatic oxidation of juice obtained from sound fruit is induced by an enzyme called tyrosinase. This kind of polyphenol oxidase occurs in all grapes. As mentioned before, it is largely inhibited by SO_2 and bentonite, and completely inactivated by pasteurization and alcohol. At the latest, it is totally broken down by the end of primary fermentation. This is the reason why the oxidation of white wines obtained from sound fruit is of chemical instead of enzymatic nature.

2. Typical and oxidative aging

In musts from rotten grapes, there is a further polyphenol oxidase produced by Botrytis cinerea and called laccase. This enzyme has a much broader spectrum of possible phenolic substrates than tyrosinase. Furthermore, its inactivation by SO_2, bentonite and alcohol is very limited (Dubernet and Ribéreau-Gayon 1974). Hence, it remains partially active in the wine.

Both kinds of polyphenol oxidase induce the oxidation of phenols to their corresponding quinones. Subsequent reactions generating insoluble brown pigments are non-enzymatic.

Reaction mechanism of juice oxidation

In white musts, the by far dominant part of total phenols are nonflavonoids, especially derivatives of hydroxycinnamic acid (Chapter 2.2.2). Caftaric acid is the most important of them. Besides, musts contain highly variable amounts of glutathione, a strongly reducing amino acid compound involved in non-enzymatic reactions (Chapter 2.5.5) following enzymatic oxidation of caftaric acid.

Tyrosinase oxidizes preferentially caftaric acid, which is converted into its corresponding quinone during the first phase of juice oxidation. This quinone is the primary oxidation product. Due to its high concentration and reactivity, it is also the starting product of three subsequent reactions of purely chemical nature (Singleton et al. 1985, Lee and Jaworski 1988, Moutounet et al. 1989, 1990, Rigaud et al. 1990, 1991, Cheynier et al. 1990 a, 1990 b, 1991 a, 1991 b):

a) It combines with glutathione to a colorless reaction product called 2-S-glutathionyl-caftaric acid or simply 'grape reaction product' (GRP), which is not brown.

b) After glutathione is exhausted, it oxidizes other phenols including GRP and flavonoids. Thereby, it is reduced back to the original caftaric acid. This partial regression of caftaric acid enables it to be oxidized again by PPO. Thus, the must is able to consume more oxygen.

c) It can react with its own precursor, caftaric acid. Thereby, it is reduced to the original phenolic structure without the intervention of an exogenous reducing agent. After that, it is available to be oxidized again.

Figure 16 depicts the structural formulas of caftaric acid and GRP.

Figure 16: Structural formulas of caftaric acid and 2-S-glutathionyl-caftaric acid *(grape reaction product, GRP)*.

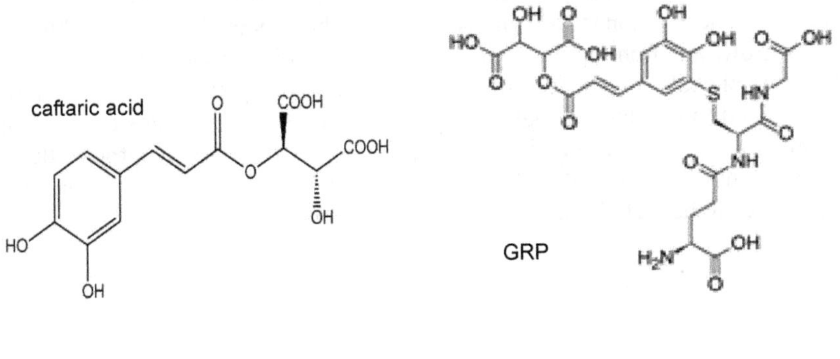

All three reactions (a, b, and c) occur simultaneously and independently one from another. But when the quinone of caftaric acid is scavenged by elevated concentrations of glutathione or reduced by bisulfite (SO_2), its subsequent reactions including the oxidation of flavonoids are restrained or completely cancelled. As a consequence, the oxygen demand for precipitation of flavonoids increases.

The total oxygen consumption capacity of grape musts without SO_2 is highly variable; it depends on the initial concentration of caftaric acid. However, their oxygen consumption rate depends on the molar ratio of caftaric acid and glutathione. This ratio is specific to each grape variety (Rigaud et al. 1990).

When flavonoids are oxidized by the caftaric acid quinone (b), they start polymerizing and precipitate as a brown flocculation. However, when there are elevated levels of caftaric acid (c), their oxidation requires more oxygen before oxidation and polymerization of flavonoids can start.

When flavonoids are protected from oxidation, they remain in solution and are able to form brown pigments by chemical oxidation of the wine, which are fairly soluble in the alcoholic medium post fermentation.

Kinetics of oxygen consumption rate during juice oxidation

Under conditions of unlimited oxygen availability, the average amount of oxygen bound by grape musts without SO_2 is 50 mg/L O_2 during the first three hours of oxygen supply. The values fluctuate between 30 and 65 mg/L O_2 in 95 % of musts (Crapisi et al. 1995). The reaction rate on a per-hour basis ranges from 4 to 200 mg/L O_2 in the broadest sense (Neradt 1970, Dubernet and Ribéreau-Gayon 1974, Moutounet et al. 1990, Gétaz and Fabre 1990, Schneider 1991, Koch and Baumgarten 1995).

This considerable range of variation can be explained by differing juice composition, different reaction kinetics, and partial exhaustion of phenolic substances already during pressing. Oxygen uptake during whole-cluster pressing without protection by inert gas has been estimated at 10 to 15 mg/L O_2 when no SO_2 was added before pressing (Cheynier et al. 1993). To classify these amounts, one must bear in mind that musts can take up and dissolve approximately 8 mg/L O_2 at standard pressure and ambient temperature, according to one oxygen saturation concentration. As dissolved oxygen (DO) is lowered by binding, more oxygen can be taken up.

Oxidation of must decreases the concentrations of all phenolic compounds, but caftaric acid concentration is particularly affected (Cheynier et al. 1989, Nicolini et al. 1991). However, from an enological and sensory point of view, the decrease of flavonoid phenols is the effect looked for. For their complete precipitation, musts are required to consume oxygen during a time span of 15 minutes to two hours (Crapisi et al. 1995, Koch and Baumgartner 1995). For the same purpose, the uptake and binding of 10 to 30 mg/L DO is required when initial must flavonoid levels are deemed to be high. Figure 17 gives some examples.

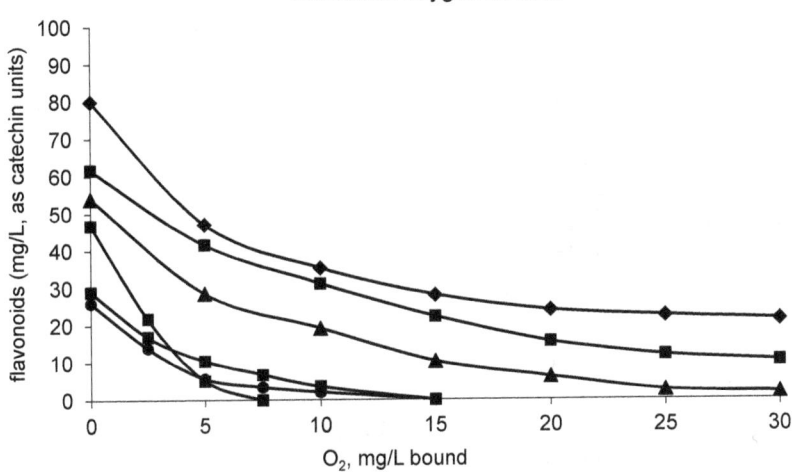

Figure 17: Precipitation of flavonoid phenols in the course of oxygen uptake by six different musts as affected by the amount of oxygen bound.

In untreated juices without SO_2, the consumption of 1 mg/L DO can lead to a precipitation of as much as 8 mg/L of flavonoid phenols, expressed as catechin units. The amounts of oxygen bound at the beginning of the process bring about the highest losses of flavonoids.

Addition of SO_2 strongly reduces tyrosinase activity and oxygen consumption rate. Therefore, SO_2 addition is the traditional means to prevent must oxidation. Bentonite additions also reduce tyrosinase activity, but lower glutathione acting as a reducing agent at the same time. Taken together both effects, the impact of bentonite on flavonoid precipitation is fairly limited (Schneider 1994).

Tyrosinase activity is also influenced by temperature according to basic rules of enzyme kinetics, but that effect has shown to be hardly relevant when must oxidation is pursued under commercial winemaking conditions. Natural tyrosinase activity is not a limiting factor as long as no SO_2 is present.

In contrast to popular expectations, the browning intensity of oxidized musts does not give any information on the amount of oxygen consumed and the extent of flavonoid precipitation achieved. Similarly, there is no way to reliably predict the extent of flavonoid precipitation based on the amount of oxygen consumed. The reason is that the effect of a given amount of oxygen depends on various compositional factors of the must (Moutounet et al. 1989, Moutounet et al. 1990, Schneider 1991). Therefore, the performance of deliberate must oxidation is assessed by measuring residual flavonoid phenols after clarification (Chapter 2.2.3). For fresh and lean white wines, levels of less than 5 mg/L are sought after fermentation. Even though total phenols are decreased by must oxidation, their content does not allow any conclusions to be drawn about flavonoid levels achieved (Chapter 2.2.2).

Here and there, the supply industry offers equipment for assessing the amount of oxygen required for every single must. They are based on the measurement of the oxygen consumption rate of the must. Their aim is to provide only as much oxygen as the must is able to enzymatically bind within a given period of time. In practice, they are useless and superfluous since there is no close connection between that rate and the total amount of oxygen consumed on one hand, and flavonoid precipitation on the other hand.

Last but not least, the dissemination of gentle grape processing techniques attenuating mechanical stress on fruit has resulted in a substantial decrease of average flavonoid levels over the last quarter of a century. As a consequence, there is much less need of deliberately and actively adding oxygen to must. In many wineries, active must oxidation by injecting oxygen can be advantageously replaced by passive must oxidation to obtain the desired result. This is achieved by just doing nothing to protect must against oxidation, especially not adding any SO_2.

2.4.4. Passive and active must oxidation

Active must oxidation means the aimed and targeted supply of oxygen to must. Regarding flavonoid removal, it is much more effective than passive must oxidation, a feature becoming important when flavonoid levels are expected to be high. It can be performed by various technical approaches, using either air or pure oxygen:

– Pumping-over the juice filling the vessel from the top. Each pumping cycle provides 2 to 3 mg/L DO.

– Pumping-through loosening the hose at the suction side of the pump allows for sucking 3 to 8 mg/L DO in the form of air.

– Using a porous, sintered pipe made of stainless steel fitted onto the suction side of the pump allows for sucking up to 8 mg/L DO as long as that pipe is not clogged by slimy must dirts on the inside.

– Using a porous sparging stone (2 to 10 µ pore width) made of sintered stainless steel or ceramic suspended into the must for adding pure oxygen in a batch process: After the sparger is hooked to a O_2 cylinder via a hose, the cylinder valve is opened smoothly in a way that just a slight release of bubbles can be observed on the liquid surface. The amount of oxygen supplied cannot be controlled because insoluble surplus oxygen will be released through the liquid surface. Thus, more oxygen is used than dissolved. In typical small-scale winery settings, a typical concentration of some 10 mg/L DO is achieved after one hour. The process can be repeated when most of the dissolved oxygen has become depleted by reactions of enzymatic oxidation. No mixing is required during the operation since the gas disperses almost evenly in the must.

– Using a gas-injection unit with an in-line sparger comparable to those employed for supplying carbon dioxide to still or effervescent wine. These carbonater-like devices usually include a Venturi gas injector and a carbonating stone providing an almost molecular dispersion of the gas. The amount of oxygen they actually provide depends on the working pressure and the ratio of product flow to gas flow. A working pressure of 5 bar allows for providing up to 40 mg/L DO when air is used. The gas flow may be adjusted to match the product flow.

- Devices for micro-oxygenation of red wine, provided that they are freely adjustable to the range of macro-oxygenation required for must oxidation. They work with pure oxygen and allow for a precise oxygen dosage without heavy losses.
- Within the scope of the procedures cited before, the oxygen used can be technical grade. The small amounts of other gases it contains do not interfere in the process.
- Flotation is a more recent technique of juice clarification that can also be used for active oxygen supply. It can be considered as a kind of revere settling since suspended solids move upward and thus against gravity. The process requires the injection of bubbles of gas into a pressurized (5 to 6 bar) chamber where the juice is pumped through. When this mixture arrives to the bottom of the flotation tank, the bubbles expand, adhere onto the surface of the solids, make them lighter than the juice, and cause them to rise to the surface where they can be removed leaving the clarified juice below the surface.

Flotation can be used in either a continuous or batch mode, but more decisive is the choice of the gas. According to Henry's law, the amount of DO or any other dissolved gas is proportional to its partial pressure in the gas phase. Thus, it is tempting to hypothesize that a flotation unit run with air at typically 5 bar and 20° C would dissolve some 40 mg/L O_2 in the juice since oxygen solubility at standard pressure and the same temperature is 8 mg/L. However, in practice, DO increase in the must while passing through the flotation plant is only some 1 to 2 mg/L. This observation confirms that only a minute part of the oxygen supplied by flotation with air is effectively absorbed into the liquid. Its major part occurs as undissolved gas bubbles rising up with the juice solids before escaping at the surface. Therefore, flotation using air is comparable to other methods of active juice oxidation and supplies much less DO to the must than could be expected from the pressure it works at. The issue is bubble size and time between injection and arrival at the surface.

The flavonoid flocculation produced upon flotation with air is removed concomitantly in the same single working step since flotation is a highly efficient technique for must clarification. Thus, the use of this double action - must oxidation and clarification - yields very fruity and delicate white wines. It has found early acceptance in some traditional white wine growing areas of the Old World. The resulting wines usually display not more than 3 mg/L flavonoid phenols and excellent resistance against oxidative aging.

All of the aforementioned oxygenation techniques add oxygen, of which a hardly quantifiable portion is released as insoluble and ineffective into the atmosphere. Therefore, one must differentiate between the amount of oxygen added, and the amount of oxygen actually dissolved and able to react. Most literature references refer to the amount of oxygen added without taking into account losses caused by incomplete absorption of the added gas. This is one of the reasons why sensory and analytical results of active must oxidation (Chapters 2.4.5 and 2.4.6) have always been highly variable, inconsistent, and poorly reproducible.

These techniques of active must oxidation, also referred to as juice hyperoxidation, are an invention of the 1970's (Müller-Späth 1977, Müller-Späth et al. 1977, 1978, Guerzoni et al. 1981). After surprisingly positive results, it was further developed in the 1980's to resolve problems caused at that time by mechanically aggressive grape processing resulting in high flavonoid levels and astringent wines with poor shelf life. In the meantime, it has lost nothing of its usefulness for treatment of musts obtained after strenuous fruit conveyance, long skin contact periods, or strong pressings. The same is true for wineries pursuing the production of fruity white wines without added sulfites. They need to impose exceptionally high demands on their wines' stability against oxidative aging.

On the other hand, improved grape processing and juice clarification techniques have led to lower flavonoid levels making active juice oxidation less important. Passive must oxidation suffices for improving shelf life of wines obtained from most contemporary musts. Its advantage is that it lowers less total and nonflavonoid phenols able to scavenge oxygen radicals, which would otherwise foster the appearance of the so-called atypical aging (Chapter 4) in white wines obtained from stressed fruit.

Practical application of passive must oxidation

Passive must oxidation means dispensing with all active additions of oxygen as well as of SO_2 and inert gases prior to primary fermentation. As a result, there is no interference with the natural redox-balance of must. The first SO_2 addition only takes places after fermentation. Thus, must picks up and enzymatically reacts with 10 to 20 mg/L O_2, a large portion of which being already picked up during pressing (Cheynier et al. 1993).

Under these conditions, tyrosinase activity is not inhibited by SO_2 and able to transfer the oxygen onto phenols. As a result, one obtains a satisfactory precipitation of flavonoids. Low levels of residual flavonoids are absorbed during fermentation by yeast cells (Schneider 1991). Ultimately, passive must oxidation is not more than standard procedure but dispensing with SO_2 additions, all other steps being as usual.

Musts obtained from rotten fruit display laccase activity (Chapter 2.4.3) expected to be still present post-fermentation and available for enzymatic phenol oxidation in the wine. When this happens, laccase reinforces the effect of must oxidation and facilitates early removal of oxidizable phenolic substrate by must clarification. Even the targeted implementation of laccase-induced oxidation for phenol removal from must has been proposed (Servili et al. 2000).

The degree of must clarification (Chapter 2.4.2) is decisive for the result of must oxidation, perhaps more than the amount of oxygen consumed and browning intensity of the must. Oxidized musts are brown to a variable degree. When such brown juices are filtered, the filtrate displays the normal green-yellow color of young white wines. This observation proves that the compounds responsible for must browning are already flocculated as solids and susceptible to removal by mechanical means. Since they tend to produce a sediment, this happens during standard cold settling or, alternatively, when they rise up upon flotation.

Flavonoids that are precipitated and remain in the must after clarification start redissolving after fermentation by the effects of alcohol and sulfur dioxide. In practice, this behavior translates as follows: The effect of must oxidation will be cancelled out when fermentation starts in poorly clarified musts. The residual turbidity obtained after must clarification should by no means exceed 100 NTU.

Even after thorough clarification, oxidized musts continue displaying a brownish color and an oxidized aroma reminiscent of bread and nuts. Given the extremely reductive conditions of primary fermentation, these characteristics completely disappear within the first two or three days of fermentation. After utilization of initial oxygen present, fermentations become absolutely anaerobic. Young white wines right after fermentation display the usual fruity aroma pattern.

Microbiological considerations

Microbial risks are a serious concern impeding grape and must processing without SO_2 additions in many if not most wineries. They increase when temperature increases. Thus, temperature is a determining factor deciding about the possibility of running must oxidation. Harvest at low temperature, short fruit transportations, and efficient must cooling are the tools making it possible. Cooling is also the way to gain time for achieving flavonoid precipitation and must clarification before fermentation starts. Winemaking under cool-climate conditions makes oxidative must handling much easier.

On the other hand, must oxidation and SO_2 additions do not completely exclude one another when SO_2 is deemed indispensable for microbiological reasons. When must already contains low levels of free SO_2 of less than 20 mg/L, its inhibitory effect on must oxidation can be overcome by correspondingly higher oxygen additions using active oxygen supply. SO_2 can also be added after precipitated flavonoids have been removed by must clarification. However, it must be taken into account that while enzymatic oxidation of phenols is a fast reaction, their subsequent polymerization and precipitation require 5 to 12 hours. When SO_2 is added too early, polymerization and precipitation steps are inhibited.

As soon as yeast starts fermentation, it consumes DO (Chapter 2.5.6) and hence it is not any more available for fostering the growth of oxygen-dependent microorganisms. This applies in particular to bacteria and wild yeasts producing volatile acidity and ethyl acetate. Thus, a quick start of fermentation induced by inoculation immediately after clarification is the best way of creating microbial protection in musts without SO_2. However, if for whatever reason spontaneous fermentation is envisaged, SO_2 addition is highly recommended to avoid microbial spoilage, to comply with hygiene standards, and to ensure commercial viability.

No impact on fermentation kinetics

Oxygen is well known as a survival factor for yeast during fermentation. In order to avoid sluggish fermentations and ensure complete dryness, additions of 5 to 10 mg/L O_2 during active fermentation are recommended and successfully employed. They are most efficient after the lag phase of yeast has come to an end, i.e. during the second or third quarter of fermentation (Sablayrolles et al. 1996). The oxygen supplied is spontaneously and almost completely consumed by yeast. It is not available for oxidation reactions and pursues exclusively microbiological objectives in fermenting white musts.

Oxygen picked up before fermentation is not any more available for that purpose. It is totally depleted by the enzymatic reactions taking place in must before fermentation starts. Hence, oxidative must treatment cannot replace oxygen additions during fermentation. It has no impact on fermentation kinetics, the production of acetaldehyde, or bound SO_2 levels in the future wine.

2.4.5. Chemical and analytical effects of must oxidation

From the viewpoint of aroma chemistry, active must oxidation was shown to decrease volatile phenols (Dubourdieu and Lavigne 1990, Nicolini et al. 1991) and malodorous volatile sulfur compounds (Müller-Späth 1977, Müller-Späth et al. 1977, 1978, Guedes de Pinho et al. 1994). Wines obtained from oxidized musts are less prone to develop reduction flavor since SO_2 added prior to fermentation is one of its precursors (Chapter 3.2.1).

Under the same conditions, an increase of free terpenols, acetates, fatty acids and their esters (Artajona et al. 1990, Cejudo-Bastante et al. 2013) as well as higher aldehydes and alcohols (Cordonnier and Bayonove 1982, Valero et al. 2002) was observed. The analytical data presented suggest that must oxidation has some impact on aroma composition, but not necessarily in a negative way. A stronger formation of higher aldehydes, especially C6-aldehydes, was associated with a slightly higher intensity of green-vegy aroma by smell, though the differences were not significant (Guedes de Pinho et al. 1994).

The numerous cultivars used in these studies did not include Sauvignon blanc, whose wines are known for their high and sensorially relevant contents of varietal thiols. These thiols are reminiscent of tropical fruits and known to be sensitive to oxygen. They are decreased by must oxidation (Coetzee et al. 2013) in an indirect way that is outlined in chapter 2.4.6.

From the viewpoint of phenolic composition, must oxidation induces a decrease of all kind of phenolic compounds (Cejudo-Bastante et al. 2011), slight losses of total phenols, and a strong decrease of flavonoid phenols and wine browning potential extending to their complete removal (Müller-Späth et al. 1977, 1978, Schneider 1991, 1998 b, 2005 b). Caftaric acid is degraded to a large extent (Nicolini et al. 1991) and converted into GRP (*grape reaction product*). Based on this reaction, the ratio of light absorbance at 320 nm and 280 nm has been proposed as an analytical marker for must oxidation. It is less than 0.5 in wines obtained from oxidized musts (Zironi et al. 1997).

The levels of total or flavonoid phenols in wine do not give any information about whether must oxidation has taken place. Flavonoids precipitated upon must oxidation will redissolve in the alcoholic environment of wine when they are not thoroughly removed by must clarification. Or they are not even incorporated into the must when grape processing is sufficiently gentle.

2.4.6. Sensory effects of must oxidation

To the extent that oxidation is prevented before fermentation, the disposition to oxidize shifts to the stage of wine with all sensory consequences derived therefrom (Table 1). Phenols are the primary oxygen acceptors in wine, and the phenols that are removed by oxidation and clarification of must are not any more available for oxidation in the wine. The basic outcome is a better resistance of wine to oxidative aging. The proponents of oxidative must handling make use of that advantage.

Furthermore, the entire range of fining agents commercialized for decreasing phenols, astringency, and bitterness (Chapter 2.4.1) becomes superfluous. Wines made from oxidized musts do not display astringent phenols, also known as tannins. Their level of flavonoid phenols does not exceed 5 mg/L, provided that must clarification has been performed to less than 80 NTU residual turbidity. Furthermore, astringent and burning sensations resulting from high acidity or alcohol levels are partially suppressed by the oily mouthfeel of GRP produced during must oxidation (Gawel et al. 2014).

Better flavor stability and resistance to oxidative aging of wines obtained from oxidized musts has long been acknowledged. The reason for this is the removal of flavonoid phenols, whose oxidation in wine would give rise to the formation of higher aldehydes responsible for the typical aroma pattern of oxidative aging (Chapter 2.1). From this point of view, flavonoid levels of less than 5 mg/L are considered desirable (Pons et al. 2015). They can always be achieved when must oxidation and proper clarification are performed.

The major and ever-lasting argument invoked against must oxidation is that it adversely affects wine aroma. This is certainly true for Sauvignon blanc. More often, however, there are psychological barriers when the oxidation of must is falsely associated with the oxidation of wine, and when current doctrines are not critically scrutinized. Decision-making in winemaking is largely driven by emotions. The less hard facts are known, the more emotions get the upper hand. Brown juices can indeed be frightening for people. Thus, the most vehement opponents of must oxidation are indeed to be found among those who have never employed it.

The special case of Sauvignon blanc

There is no doubt about irreversible aroma losses brought about by must oxidation on cultivars with sensorially significant levels of oxygen-sensitive aroma thiols. These cultivars comprise first of all Sauvignon blanc (Nicolini 1992, Coetzee and du Toit 2012), followed at some distance by some other varieties of regional importance.

In musts obtained from these cultivars, aroma thiols occur as bound to glutathione and cysteine. Only when they are released from these odorless precursors by a specific enzymatic activity of certain yeast strains, they become odor-active. Interestingly, the concentration of precursors is not affected by must oxidation since they are not sensitive to oxygen. However, addition of glutathione to the must induces an increase of the production of odor-active thiols in the resulting wine. The other way round, they are lowered when glutathione is removed by oxidation (Roland et. al. 2010). In other words, losses of aroma thiols due to oxidative must processing of these varieties are not caused by their oxidation in the must, but rather by the decrease of glutathione levels required to protect them from oxidation in the wine (Chapter 2.5.5).

As a practical consequence, oxidation of Sauvignon blanc musts appears feasible without affecting varietal aroma when the initial glutathione levels are reconstituted afterwards. Addition of specific glutathione-rich dry inactivated yeast preparations is a means to achieve this purpose (Gabrielli et al. 2017). There is a need of more research under commercial winemaking conditions.

A global survey

The adverse effect of must oxidation on Sauvignon blanc aroma is widely acknowledged, but also frequently generalized and recklessly transferred to all cultivars. However, sensory results of must oxidation on other cultivars are diverse, conflicting, and thus justifying a close look at the results obtained from studies across the world:

– A sensory comparison of wines obtained from oxidized vs. SO_2-protected must showed stronger varietal aroma and higher overall quality in the lots from oxidized musts of Chardonnay from France (Cheynier et al. 1989, 1991 a), of Parellada, Muscat and Chardonnay from Spain (Artajona et al. 1990), Riesling and Seyval blanc from Ontario (Wilson et al. 1993), and Riesling and Gewürztraminer from Alsace (Bailly 1990).

– Under similar conditions, must oxidation resulted in lower aroma intensity and less fruitiness of Sauvignon blanc from South Africa (Marais 1998), of Grenache (Cheynier et al. 1989) and Pinot noir (Blanck 1990) from France, various other varieties from California (Singleton et al. 1980, Ough and Crowell 1987) and diverse European countries (Guedes de Pinho et al. 1994, Dubourdieu and Lavigne 1990), as well as in wines affected by atypical aging (Chapter 3) from Germany (Burkert et al. 2011).

– Lower aroma intensity but softer mouthfeel was obtained by must oxidation of Riesling, Müller-Thurgau, and Gewürztraminer from Germany (Schmidt et al. 2003).

– Changes in the aroma pattern without losses of aroma intensity were observed after must oxidation of Chardonnay from Spain (Cejudo-Bastante et al. 2011, Riesling from Germany (Schneider 1996) and various other varieties (Müller-Späth et al. 1977, 1978).

2. Typical and oxidative aging

- No significant differences in aroma were obtained by must oxidation of Riesling in Germany (Perscheid and Zürn 1977, Bach and Nobis 1985) and of a range of other varieties from Italy (Nicolini et al. 1991), Alsace (Meistermann 1990), and Washington (Nagel and Graber 1988).

- Losses of total phenol content brought about by must oxidation cause inevitably a decrease of oxygen radical scavengers, which would be able to counteract the formation of atypical aging (Chapter 4.3). When passive must oxidation is employed, this effect is not significant (Köhler et al. 1996). However, active must oxidation results in a stronger decrease of total phenols and, thus, in a higher susceptibility of wine to develop atypical aging, provided it is predetermined by the fruit. When this is a concern, flotation of must should be run with nitrogen instead of air (Lipps 2005).

In simple terms, the whole bulk of comparative trials on must oxidation carried out worldwide yielded sensory results that were positive for one third, negative for another third, and without difference for the remaining third of the wines obtained from oxidized musts. In the light of these findings, it is difficult to understand why traditional enology teaching unilaterally rejects must oxidation on the basis of alleged aroma losses in the resulting wines. Nevertheless, results are indeed conflicting, and the contradictions they contain can be explained by a series of enological and sensory variables. They lead to the following

Best practice for implementation of trials and evaluation of results

- Variable boundary conditions including residual turbidity after must clarification, yeast strain, fermentation kinetics, temperature, post-fermentation treatment and storage of the wine can easily affect sensory results more than the redox regimen of the must (Bach and Nobis 1985). Must clarification is of particular importance. Its quality of execution, measured as residual turbidity, has more influence on the extent of flavonoid removal than the amount of oxygen picked up and bound by the must. In many cases, it affects general quality more than the decision for oxidative or reductive must processing. The importance of must turbidity is generally underestimated. Poor must clarification makes all enological efforts useless.

- When the initial concentration of flavonoid phenols is low, must oxidation does not provide significant sensory differences on the palate.

- Variable levels of protection against oxidation in the control must: The more the efforts made to keep it reductive by additions of SO_2, ascorbic acid, or the use of inert gases, the more the resulting wine will be different from that obtained from the oxidized must.

- Variable oxygen supply to the oxidized must: Passive must oxidation entails less oxygen turnover than active must oxidation.

- Diverging concepts of quality: In sensory evaluation, tasters are frequently asked for a quality ranking. Quality is a hedonic concept. Thus, the result inevitably reflects the personal preference of the tasters for one or another style of wine. In most cases, they prefer the style they are used to. Flavonoid phenols are tannins that impart a kind of flavor that cannot be found in wines made from oxidized musts. Thus, in comparison with a control wine containing flavonoids, the lot obtained from oxidized must can display less mouthfeel. This may be interpreted as lean, elegant, supple and soft in one case, but also as thin and dull in another case. A white wine high in flavonoids can be full-bodied and expressive for one taster, while it appears harsh, aggressive and rustic to another taster. It will be short-lived in any case. The still widespread use of fining agents aiming at softening astringent white wines is the proof that flavonoids are considered to detract from quality in the majority of cases.

- Sensory evaluation is carried out at different time points and development stages of the wines. In particular astringency must not occur a priori in a young white wine, but may appear during aging (Chapter 2.2.2).

- Aroma as perceived by smell also depends on the time point of evaluation. In many cases, wine obtained from oxidized must displays somewhat less aroma intensity than that made with SO_2 added to must when it is very young. These relations are reversed with advancing age. This happens the faster the more SO_2 has been added to the must, the higher its flavonoid content, and the more oxygen the wine picks up during aging (Chapter 2.6).

Figure 18 gives an example of how the aroma profile of a Riesling changes during aging as a result of must oxidation vs. SO_2 to the must (Schneider 1996). Sixteen months after the end of primary fermentation, the intensities for the fruity attributes 'pear', 'peach', and 'lemon' in the wine obtained from oxidized must were distinctly higher than in the reductively produced lot.

Figure 18: Impact of aging and must treatment (with vs. without SO_2 to must) on the evaluation of aroma profile in Riesling.

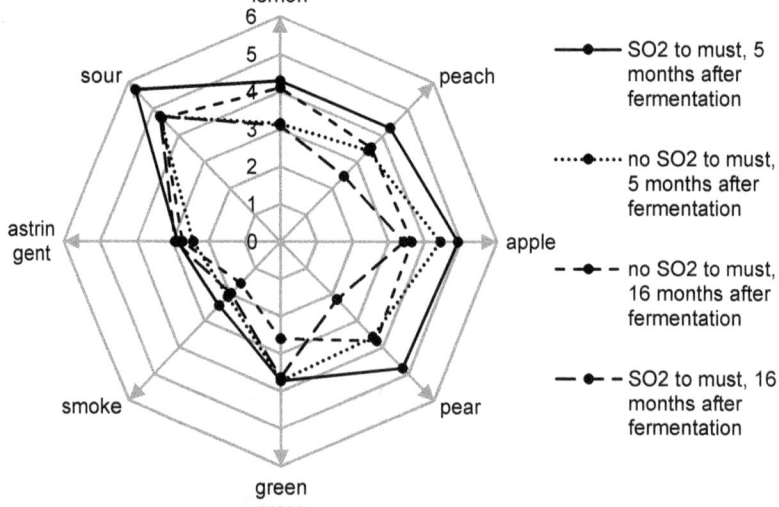

2. Typical and oxidative aging

After must oxidation, fruity aroma attributes are more stable over time, while they are faster masked by increasing attribute intensities of oxidative aging in wines produced reductively. Positive effects of must oxidation are usually not observed in the stage of young wine, but only become evident after some time of storage. Insofar, must oxidation is an investment in the future of wine with the aim of improving its resistance to typical aging. However, comparative sensory evaluations are mostly carried out on young wines without taking into account the aging effect. Spectacular aromas in the young wine are of little use if they are already broken down when the wine is consumed.

Stabilization and storage of very reductively produced wines

Trials with extremely reductive must processing using high additions of SO_2, ascorbic acid and nitrogen blanketing before, during and after pressing are not a phenomenon of modern age, but were already conducted in the 1970's in several European countries. They were quickly abandoned when serious problems with wine shelf life arose. Depending on zeitgeist and dominating doctrine, such trials are repeated periodically. One of the reasons is the global propagation of Sauvignon blanc whose aroma does indeed require rigorous measures of oxidation protection from the moment grapes are crushed.

Very reductive must handling provides fragile wines intended for early consumption, but hardly white wines suitable for longer bottle aging. It requires gentle grape processing and a thorough must clarification to keep flavonoid levels at a minimum. Furthermore, it requires a likewise markedly reductive handling of wines during stabilization and storage, including careful protection against oxygen uptake, in order to take account of their poor oxidation stability. Depending on the flavonoid content of these wines, the use of fining agents to reduce flavonoids can become advisable (Chapter 2.4.1). When such finings are performed, the rules of gentle wine treatment (Chapter 2.6.4) must be respected.

However, under industrial conditions, stabilization treatments post fermentation are not always gentle, but often lead to oxygen uptake which does not at all comply with the oxygen sensitivity of such wines. If the answer to premature oxidative aging is an even more reductive must processing, a vicious circle closes.

A question of the market segment

As noted previously, the matter of reductive or oxidative must processing cannot be cut down to the simplified categories of 'good' or 'bad'. Extremely reductive must handling meets a trend towards producing white wines designed for fast consumption. Though such wines might be highly medaled as long as they are young, aroma quality frequently leaves much to desire one year post bottling. This explains the high demand of very young, sometimes hardly finished white wines of the same year in many growing countries. It's the reaction of the market to a widespread tendency towards attaching more importance to the production of white wine flavor profiles than to their preservation.

Scorings comparable to those of aged premium segment red wines are largely unknown in the white wine area. White wines aged in a positive way, especially those of cult appeal, do exist but are rare exceptions. In the growing regions where they are produced reductive must handling has never been a crucial issue.

The question of shelf life and ageability becomes even more important when bottles are stored several days in a shipping container not air-conditioned and exposed to sun and heat, several weeks on the shelves of food retailing, or even several months in well heated restaurants or consumers' homes (Chapter 2.7). Tasting back his own wines in an unbiased manner after those kinds of storage conditions would be awfully educational to any wine producer. It can provide a unique experience and a reason to question one's own winemaking strategies.

2.5. Effect of reducing agents in wine

Introduction: Whilst oxygen uptake and browning of must is less harmful than most winemakers believe and can even be beneficial for wine quality and shelf life, oxygen pickup post-fermentation is highly detrimental to white wine quality and flavor stability. In order to mitigate or prevent wine oxidation, various exogenous and endogenous antioxidants are employed. Sulfite is the most important of them; its operating mechanism is discussed in detail. The use of ascorbic acid and post-fermentation yeast lees can also be helpful. This chapter presents data on the variable effectiveness of all these antioxidants. None of them is able to completely protect wine against oxidative aging when oxygen is picked up; some of them are almost useless. Therefore, it is essential to prevent uncontrolled oxygen uptake. When one succeeds in doing so in a perfect way, using some technical effort and profound expertise in wine chemistry, it is also possible to produce lasting fruity white wines without added sulfites.

2.5.1. Effect of sulfur dioxide on oxygen-related reactions

The use of sulfur dioxide (SO_2) in winemaking pursues three distinctive objectives:

- inhibition of fault-producing spoilage microorganisms,
- protection against excessive oxidation,
- binding with free acetaldehyde and other carbonyls and converting them into odorless addition products.

For impeding undesirable oxidation of wine, there are two basic approaches available – adding SO_2 or protecting wine from oxygen pickup. The wine industry relies largely on the first, using SO_2 as the traditional and almost universal antioxidant aiming at keeping oxidation under control. This chapter covers the role of SO_2 as a reducing agent and its effectiveness in oxidation control.

In aqueous solutions such as wine, sulfur dioxide exists in forms other than only dissolved SO_2. First, there is a free and a bound form, with the sum of these two representing total SO₂. Bound SO₂ is basically inactive. Its amount is predetermined by wine composition or, more precisely, by the concentration of its binding partners. Enological interest regarding wine shelf live is focused upon free SO_2.

Three different forms of free sulfur dioxide

Free sulfur dioxide dissociates in aqueous solution. As a result, it exists in three states – molecular (SO_2), bisulfite (HSO_3^-), and sulfite (SO_3^{2-}). These forms are in a dynamic equilibrium with one another according to the formula

$$SO_2 + H_2O \rightleftharpoons H^+ + HSO_3^- \rightleftharpoons SO_3^{2-} + H^+$$

Each form has different properties. Molecular SO_2 is dissolved as a volatile gas, has an antimicrobial effect and is sensorially active due to its pungent smell. The bisulfite form binds with many wine components including acetaldehyde, higher aldehydes, keto acids, glucose, phenols, and quinones. These bound products are essentially non-reactive and make up the bound fraction of total SO_2. The sulfite form does not have any enological interest.

The quantities of these different forms of free sulfur dioxide depend on pH. Their relative proportions in the range of wine pH are shown in Figure 19. They explain why pH has also some importance in oxidation control.

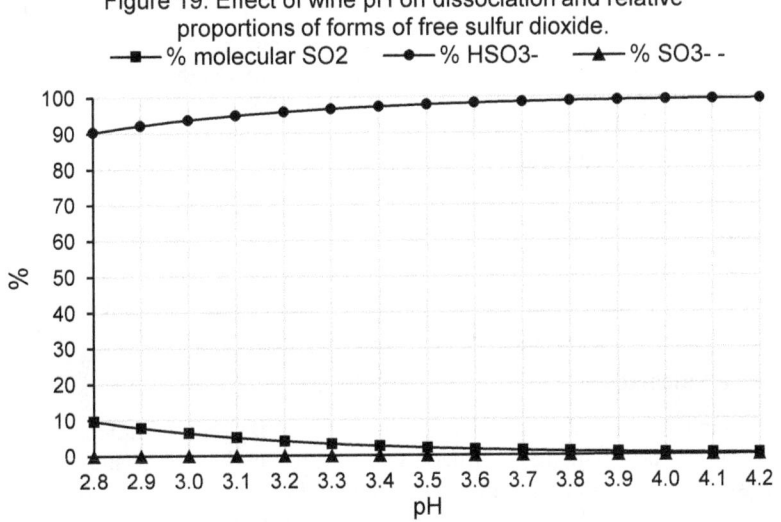

Figure 19: Effect of wine pH on dissociation and relative proportions of forms of free sulfur dioxide.

This commonly known graph makes clear that

- the predominant form of free SO_2 in the pH range of wine is the bisulfite ion (HSO_3^-),
- the sulfite ion (SO_3^{2-}) concentration is very small and can essentially be ignored,
- the molecular form (SO_2), although also small at wine pH values, is of crucial importance and becomes increasingly significant with only a small decrease in pH values.

The sulfite (SO_3^{2-}) is the only form of SO_2 able to react directly with oxygen according to the formula

$$2\ SO_3^{2-} + O_2 \rightarrow 2\ SO_4^{2-}$$

However, at wine pH, the concentration of sulfite is so minute that its reaction with oxygen is infinitely slow. Therefore, sulfite is not an effective antioxidant in wine.

In contrast to sulfite, the molecular form of SO_2 is quite reactive. For example, it traps hydrogen peroxide (H_2O_2) in accordance with the formula

$$H_2O_2 + SO_2 \rightarrow H_2SO_4$$

in a spontaneous way. This reaction is of outstanding importance and will be examined in detail hereafter.

SO_2 reacts with oxidation products rather than with DO

Phenols are the primary oxygen acceptor in wine. Their oxidation induces a sequence of oxidation of other wine compounds (Chapter 2.2.1). It generates two initial oxidation products that can be reduced by SO_2 – the quinones of the original phenols as well as H_2O_2 produced upon phenol oxidation (Figure 2).

It is crucial to understand that sulfur dioxide does not react with oxygen in a direct way, but with quinones and H_2O_2 appearing upon oxygen consumption. Concurrently, it is oxidized to sulfate. When this happens, free and total SO_2 are decreased simultaneously, but not necessarily to the same extent. In contrast, free SO_2 decreases somewhat less than total SO_2. The reason for this is that it is partially replaced by "fresh" SO_2 released from the pool of bound SO_2 when free SO_2 reaches low concentrations (Waterhouse et al. 2016). Hence, when DO is measured after oxygen uptake and to be related to SO_2 losses, it is indispensable to measure total SO_2 instead of free SO_2.

The sulfate produced upon SO_2 oxidation is not any more measured neither as bound nor as total SO_2. In a certain way, this behavior can be considered as a chemical removal of SO_2. It is well known in the wine industry, for example when wine picks up oxygen during barrel aging or at bottling.

Some basic calculations

To understand the quantitative relationships between oxygen, oxidation products, SO_2, and the extent to which SO_2 protects wine against oxidation, it is indispensable to delve somewhat deeper into chemistry. Though this is one of the most fascinating areas of enology, it will also be hard stuff for pure hands-on practitioners! Those not willing to dig into chemical details can skip and move on to chapter 2.5.2. The challenging issue covered in this subsection is to know how much of the primary oxidation products, H_2O_2 and quinones, is actually reduced back.

As a reminder: Scavenging of H_2O_2 and reduction of the quinones back to the phenols they stem from are the primary tasks of free sulfur dioxide, carried out by its molecular form. Under ideal conditions, 2 moles of SO_2 are required to reduce the oxidation products brought about by 1 mole of O_2:

- 1 mole SO_2 for trapping the H_2O_2, and

- 1 mole SO_2 for reducing the quinones back to the phenols.

Thus, the molar ratio of $O_2:SO_2$ is 1:2 (Danilewicz et al. 2008). This is illustrated in figure 20 with the molar weights of O_2 and SO_2 given in brackets. They are 32 grams for 1 mole of O_2 and 2 x 64 = 128 grams for 2 moles of SO_2.

Figure 20: Molar and mass ratios of oxygen consumed for phenol oxidation and SO_2 required for the reduction of the oxidation products.

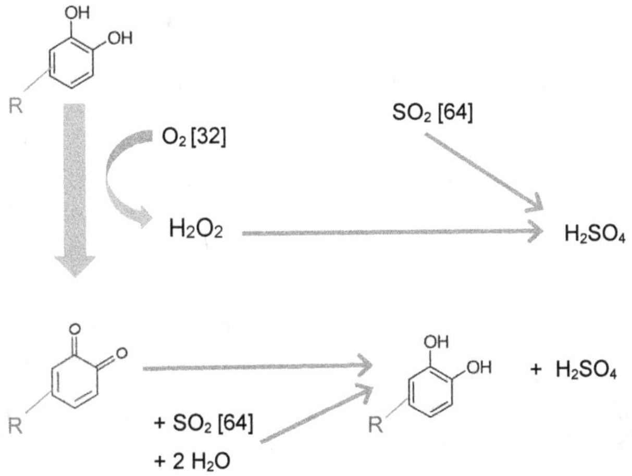

Expressed as the mass ratio, this means that 4 mg SO_2 are oxidized by 1 mg O_2, corresponding to a $SO_2:O_2$ mass ratio of 4:1 (Danilewicz 2016). When this happens, the effect of oxygen consumption is entirely reversed by SO_2, and stoichiometric rules would be fulfilled. However, reality in wine is different, and SO_2 does not fully protect against the effects of oxygen consumption. Otherwise, there would be no oxidative aging.

To understand the difference between ideal and real wine conditions, it is useful to move out from the simpler chemical systems in which wine oxidation principles have traditionally been established and which chemists like to work with, and have a deeper insight into the more complex wine matrix with its additional influences.

Oxidation products are only partially reduced by SO_2

It's time to summarize again: Oxygen does not react with SO_2 directly, but the net result regarding SO_2 consumption is the same. First, all oxygen is converted into H_2O_2 and quinones before it reacts further (Figures 2 and 20). When the loss of both oxygen and SO_2 is measured at a mass ratio of 4 mg SO_2 to 1 mg O_2, the net oxygen consumption exactly matches SO_2 consumption in a stoichiometric relationship. This means that 1 mg/L O_2 would consume 4 mg/L SO_2.

However, under real wine conditions, this mass ratio is lower than 4:1, meaning that some oxygen is remaining irreversibly with other wine compounds and not with SO_2. Hence, the DO measured in the wine at a given moment does not allow for stoichiometrically calculating the decrease of SO_2 to expect.

In an attempt to evaluate where the oxygen actually ends up, a total of 7 mg/L DO was supplied to 20 white wines containing 40 to 60 mg/L free SO_2, no ascorbic acid, and stored in hermetically sealed glass vessels. The DO decrease was monitored using non-invasive DO measurement through the vessel walls by a fiber optic meter based on luminescence quenching. When DO was entirely consumed after two months, losses of total SO_2 were measured and related to the initial amount of DO.

The box-whisker plot in figure 21 shows that 1 mg/L DO oxidizes variable amounts of SO_2, which strongly depend on the individual wine. Instead of 4 mg SO_2 per 1 mg/L DO ($SO_2:O_2$ ratio = 4:1), the median was only 2.86 mg SO_2 per 1 mg DO ($SO_2:O_2$ ratio = 2.86:1) or 71.5 %, respectively. The remaining 28.5 % of oxygen was not intercepted by SO_2, but available for irreversible oxidation of other wine constituents. Interestingly, 50 % of the wines lie within the range of 2.49 to 3.21 mg SO_2 per 1 mg DO, and 95 % in the range of 1.90 to 3.93 mg SO_2 per 1 mg DO. The average was a loss of 2.87 mg/L SO_2 per 1 mg/L DO.

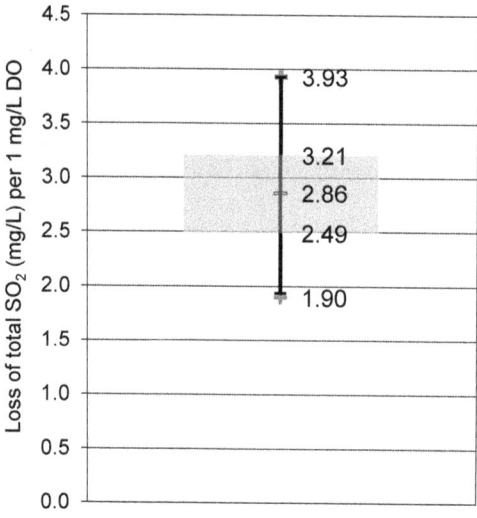

Figure 21: Loss of total SO_2 (mg/L) per 1 mg/L DO in 20 white wines supplemented with 7 mg/L DO. Wines containing 40 to 60 mg/L initial free SO_2 and no ascorbic acid.

This high variability of data suggests a closer look at how they are influenced by wine compositional data. For that purpose, a commercial white wine was adjusted to three different pH levels using NaOH or H_2SO_4. Each of the aliquots thus obtained was adjusted to three levels of free SO_2. The nine samples were supplied with oxygen to make up 7 mg/L DO, hermetically sealed, and stored in the dark until DO was totally consumed after 10 weeks. Then the decrease of total SO_2 was measured in comparison with the non-oxygenated references, and related to the amount of DO consumed. Figure 22 demonstrates that both pH and initial free SO_2 have an impact on the $SO_2:O_2$ ratio.

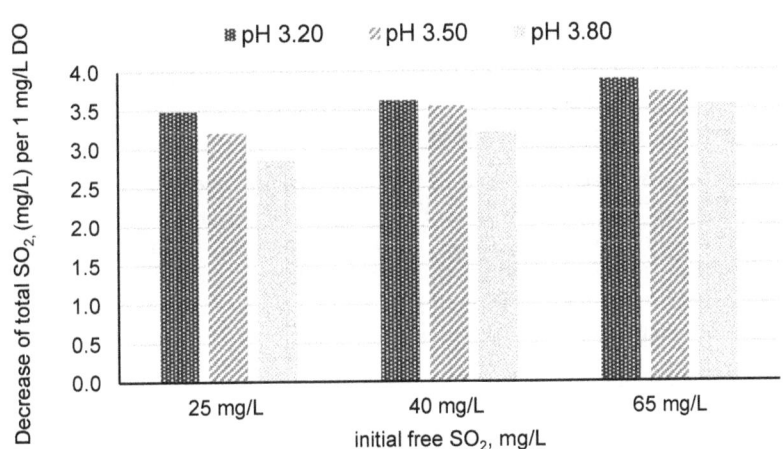

Figure 22: Decrease of total SO_2 (mg/L) per 1 mg/L O_2 as affected by pH and initial free SO_2

Effect of pH

The higher the pH, the less SO_2 is consumed by 1 mg/L DO and the more DO reacts with other wine compounds than SO_2. There are two reasons for that:

- When pH increases, the molecular SO_2 percentage of free sulfur dioxide able to trap H_2O_2 decreases. As a result, more oxygen ends up with intrinsic wine compounds, causing oxidative aging.

- The other reason is phenol chemistry. Phenols are the first oxygen acceptor initiating an oxidation sequence. They are weak acids. Their acid strength expressed as pKa is 9 to 10 indicating poor dissociation into anions at wine pH. Hence, there is only a very small percentage of phenolate anions ready to oxidize to quinones. However, the more the wine pH increases, the more of the phenols dissociate into anions, which oxidize much more easily than the protonated phenols with undissociated hydroxyl groups. At a high pH for wine, for example 4.0, there would be roughly ten times as much phenolate anions as at pH 3.0, and their oxidation rate should be ten times as fast (Singleton 1987). As oxidized phenols tend to undergo regenerative polymerization (Chapter 2.2.1), some of them are lost before they can react with SO_2. As a result, the oxygen consumed by that portion of oxidized phenols is not any more available for interaction with SO_2. Regenerative polymerization of phenols explains the whereabouts of the major part of oxygen not consumed by SO_2. No further wine constituents are able to bind these relatively high amounts of oxygen. Thus, the higher the pH, the more oxygen is irreversibly consumed by phenol oxidation.

On a more practical level, lowering pH by acid additions for the sole purpose of better protecting wine against oxidation is a bad idea since it can considerably change wine style. Protecting wine against oxygen pickup (Chapter 2.6) is the better approach.

Effect of initial free SO_2 level

As expected, the higher the initial free SO_2 level, the higher the SO_2:O_2 ratio, the more DO is consumed by SO_2, and the less DO oxidizes phenols and further wine compounds. The other way round, in wines with low free SO_2 levels, a larger part of the oxygen reacts with intrinsic wine constituents, thus accelerating the appearance of flavor profiles associated with oxidative aging. This behavior appears obvious. Free SO_2 and phenols compete for oxygen as ultimate oxygen acceptors.

The results demonstrate that peroxide and quinones produced upon oxygen uptake are not completely reduced by SO_2. They explain standard observations made on commercial scale winemaking, which show that free SO_2 is not able to totally protect wine against oxidative aging when it picks up oxygen. Several 100 mg/L of free SO_2 would be necessary to withdraw all DO from reactions with wine compounds other than SO_2.

The importance of the SO_2:O_2 ratio

It follows from the above that the SO_2:O_2 ratio has considerable practical importance. Its measurement allows one to identify wines that will become easily oxidized, to assess to what extent free SO_2 protects the wine against oxidation, and to evaluate the percentage of oxygen not scavenged by SO_2 and thus available for oxidative aging (Waterhouse et al. 2016).

This said, another challenging question arises: Where does the oxygen not scavenged by SO_2 exactly end up? As stated previously, the minor amounts of heavy metals present in wine only act as catalysts but cannot bind significant amounts of oxygen. The only group of compounds able to do so are phenols (Singleton 1987, 2001). The side-product generated thereby is hydrogen peroxide, which can convert into oxygen radicals (Figure 2). These aggressive oxidants are able to oxidize any compounds that are not directly oxidizable by molecular oxygen, for example ethanol into acetaldehyde (Chapter 2.2.1).

Contribution of phenols, ethanol, and other compounds to DO consumption

In an attempt to get an insight into the relative importance of further reaction pathways and end products of white wine oxidation, the oxygen consumption of various model wines was monitored under aerial oxygen saturation conditions using Warburg "respirometry". Under these conditions, the model wine is vigorously stirred to equilibrate with the air-containing headspace from which oxygen is consumed, such that the pressure in the constant-volume headspace drops proportionally to oxygen consumption of the solution.

For that purpose, a standard solution consisting of 13 % ethanol, 75 mg/L free SO_2 and tartaric acid (pH 3.5) was supplied with various amounts of ferrous ions (Fe^{++} as $FeSO_4$), grape tannin, or both, according to concentrations found in real wines. Table 2 displays the oxygen consumption of these solutions over 10 days, the decrease of SO_2 and the formation of acetaldehyde resulting therefrom.

2. Typical and oxidative aging

Table. 2: Impact of iron and phenols (grape tannin) on oxygen consumption of model solutions during 10 days under conditions of unlimited oxygen availability.
TP = total phenols

	mg/L O_2 consumed in 10 days	SO$_2$ consumed by oxidation		formation of acetaldehyde from ethanol	
		decrease of SO_2	% O_2 used for SO_2 oxidation	acetaldehyde, mg/L	% O_2 used for ethanol oxidation
standard solution	0	0	0	0	0
+ 200 mg/L TP	3	11	92	0	0
+ 400 mg/L TP	4.5	16	89	0	0
+ 2 mg/l Fe^{++}	14	47	84	2.3	5.9
+ 4 mg/l Fe^{++}	30	75	63	4.8	5.8
+ 200 mg/l TP + 2 mg/l Fe^{++}	21	75	89	3.7	6.3

These data allow for the following statements:

- In the absence of phenols or heavy metal ions as iron, no oxygen is bound. According to expectations, SO_2 does not directly react with oxygen but requires the presence of the aforementioned catalysts to be oxidized.
- At concentrations typically found in white wines, iron and phenols compete for oxygen. In a first step, it reacts preferentially with iron, while its direct reaction with phenols is noticeably slower. In a standard white wine, only a minor amount of 10 to 20 % directly reacts with phenols.
- The major portion of oxygen - 63 to 92 % under these conditions - is used for indirect oxidation of SO_2. This magnitude is in line with results given in figures 21 and 22. Sulfite scavenges intermediate peroxide and reduces both heavy metals and phenols that have become oxidized (Danilewicz et al. 2008).
- Iron as an individual compound as well as in conjunction with phenols catalyzes the oxidation of ethanol to acetaldehyde. This reactions requires approximately 6 % of the oxygen consumed. This suggests that under conditions of realistic storage and oxygen pickup, the non-enzymatic formation of acetaldehyde is measurable but without practical significance. It forms an odorless adduct with SO_2 as long as free SO_2 is present.
- The rest of 2 to 31 % of the oxygen consumed is used for irreversible oxidation of phenols and other wine compounds.

The real existence of intermediate peroxide and oxygen radicals it generates is proven by the oxidation of low amounts of ethanol to acetaldehyde (Wildenradt and Singleton 1974). However, the sensory importance of these strong oxidants is considerably increased by their ability to oxidize a much larger array of molecules comprising also aroma-active compounds.

Exploring intermediate peroxide

Based on an experimental approach derived from enzymatic analysis and using the reaction system of NAD/NADH$_2$-peroxidase, instantaneous concentrations of H$_2$O$_2$ produced in the course of aerial oxygenation at wine pH and ambient temperature were measured. Table 3 shows that at the beginning (day 0) of oxygen consumption by white wines containing free SO$_2$, no H$_2$O$_2$ was detectable.

Table 3: Instantaneous concentration of intermediate peroxide and formation of acetaldehyde in the course of continuous oxygen supply to white wine.

Stoichiometry: 1.0 mg H$_2$O$_2$ produces 1.0 mg acetaldehyde from oxidation of 1.35 mg ethanol.

	hydrogen peroxide (H$_2$O$_2$), mg/L			formation of acetaldehyde, mg/L		
time (days after start)	0	10	50	0	10	50
white wine, untreated	0	0.8	1.3	0	20	26
white wine after fining with 0.8 g/L PVPP	0	0.7	1.2	0	6	20
white wine + 20 mg/L catechin	0	1.0	1.5	0	16	26
white wine + 50 mg/L catechin	0	1.0	1.7	0	12	19
white wine + 100 mg/L grape tannin	0	1.0	2.2	0	9	18

The spontaneous reaction of H$_2$O$_2$ with free SO$_2$ explains why no H$_2$O$_2$ can be measured at the start of the assay. Under these conditions, degradation of H$_2$O$_2$ is faster than its formation. Only when free SO$_2$ is totally depleted by oxidation in the course of further oxygen uptake, H$_2$O$_2$ accumulates to measurable and increasing concentrations. These amounts are net concentrations resulting from the equilibrium between formation and degradation of H$_2$O$_2$. Addition of grape phenols results in a stronger formation of H$_2$O$_2$, decreasing phenol content by PVPP fining in a lower one.

The crucial outcome of that kind of trials is that free SO$_2$ and H$_2$O$_2$ cannot occur simultaneously because they spontaneously react one with another. This outcome will be different when H_2O_2 is generated in the neutral pH range where no molecular SO_2 is present to trap it (Héritier et al. 2016).

Peroxide that is scavenged by SO_2 ends up as sulfate without sensory consequences. Peroxide scavenging is the primary purpose of SO_2 in the oxidation process of wine (Waterhouse and Laurie 2006, Danilewicz 2007). But how complete is this reaction?

Intermediate peroxide is not entirely trapped by SO_2

To answer this question, 15 dry white table wines containing 19 to 99 mg/L free SO_2 were supplied with an amount of H_2O_2 previously set to decrease 40 mg/L SO_2 in water (pH 3.5 with sulfuric acid) by exactly 20 mg/L. After a reaction period of 30 minutes, the decrease of total SO_2 in the wines was measured and related to the decrease in the aqueous solution (100 %). Figure 23 depicts the results.

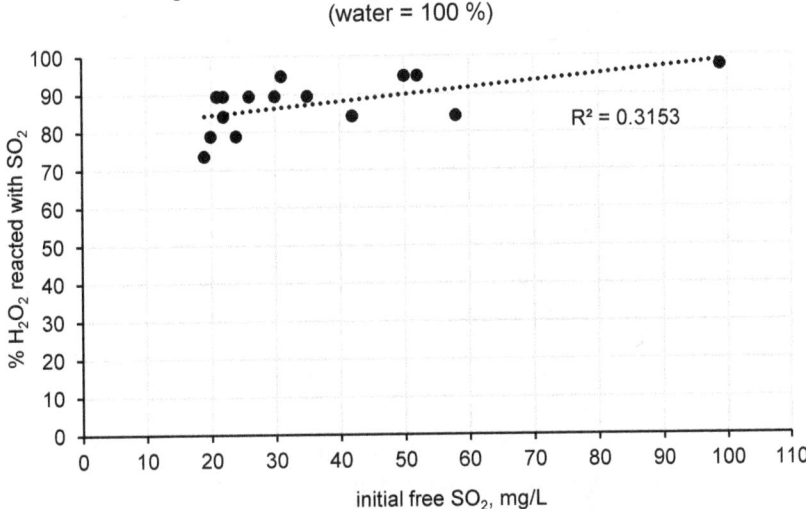

Figure 23: Percent H_2O_2 in wine reacting with SO_2 (water = 100 %)

In the wines, the decrease of SO_2 was only 87.5 % (74 to 97 %) on average of that observed in water. These results clearly demonstrate that in contrast to current doctrine, not all peroxide generated upon oxygen uptake is scavenged by free SO_2. The difference of roughly 13 % must be attributed to reactions of H_2O_2 with other wine compounds than SO_2 and not contained in the aqueous solution. Furthermore and according to expectations, there is a positive correlation ($R^2 = 0.32$) between the percentage of H_2O_2 reacting with SO_2 and the initial level of free SO_2. However, this correlation is a weak one suggesting that within the feasible range of free SO_2 in wine, increasing its level, for example from 30 to 60 mg/L, is not a reliable means to scavenge more H_2O_2 and better protect wine against oxidation.

The additional reactions of H_2O_2 are explained by its behavior in wines without SO_2. These wines were modeled using commercial white grape juice with and without addition of 12 % ethanol, using water (pH 3.5 with tartaric acid) as a control.

After their spiking with 13 mg/L H_2O_2, the decrease of H_2O_2 was monitored by enzymatic analysis. Figure 24 gives the results.

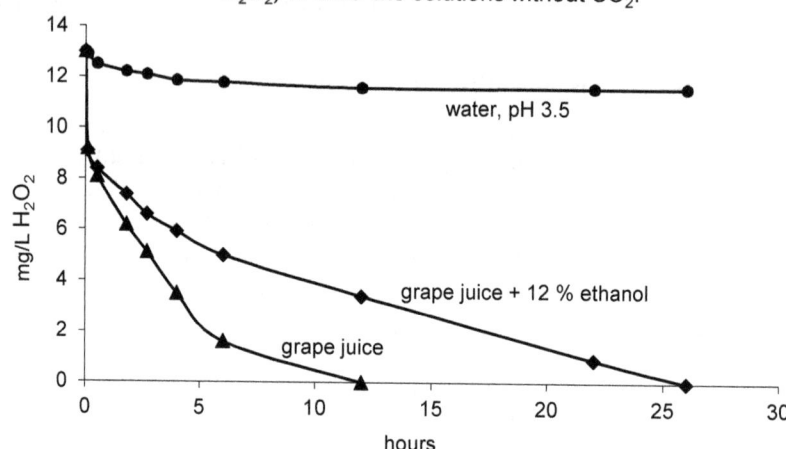

Figure 24: Consumption of hydrogen peroxide (13 mg/L H_2O_2) in wine-like solutions without SO_2.

In both grape juices, H_2O_2 had totally disappeared after 12 or 26 hours, respectively. After that, 8 mg/L of acetaldehyde were measured in the grape juice spiked with ethanol, while it was 0 mg/L in the juice without ethanol as precursor.

Based on the stoichiometric ratio of 1 mg H_2O_2 required to produce 1.3 mg acetaldehyde by ethanol oxidation, the data show that roughly half of the peroxide not scavenged by SO_2 is actually consumed for oxidation of ethanol to acetaldehyde. The remaining part of H_2O_2 is available for other reactions entailing aromatic changes of the wine.

These results are in contrast to those of other studies (Danilewicz 2016) deducing from measured $SO_2 : O_2$ ratios that SO_2 is fully effective in removing H_2O_2. It is likely that direct monitoring of H_2O_2 degradation is more sensitive a means to inform about where it remains.

The existing data can be summarized in an approximate

Peroxide Balance:

In filtered wines, dissolved oxygen (DO) does not directly react with sulfites, but first oxidizes phenols whereby it is converted into hydrogen peroxide. In the white wine scenario with presence of free SO_2 and traces of transition metals, the peroxide produced in this process reacts in different ways:

- ***H_2O_2 consumption by SO_2***: Depending on the wine matrix, 74 to 95 % of the peroxide is spontaneously scavenged by SO_2 (Figure 23 and Table 2). Inherently, that portion will depend on wine pH and the initial level of free SO_2. Its magnitude is in accordance with the data concerning the whereabouts of initial DO presented in Figures 20 and 21.

- ***H_2O_2 consumption by ethanol***: From the remaining 5 to 26 % of peroxide, approximately the half is consumed in the course of an oxygen radical chain reaction (Fenton reaction) leading to the oxidation of ethanol to acetaldehyde (Figure 24). This half equates to approximately 6 % of the total DO initially supplied (Table 2). Stoichiometrically, 1 mg/L DO oxidizing ethanol yields 2.75 mg/L acetaldehyde. Hence, an oxygen uptake of 10 mg/L DO as it commonly occurs in the course of stabilization, bottling, and storage of white wines would result in the production of 10 x 0.06 x 2.75 = 1.65 mg/L acetaldehyde. This magnitude is in line with data obtained from bottled wines sealed with closures of various oxygen ingress rates (Waterhouse et al. 2016).

  The sensory outcome of this acetaldehyde increase is irrelevant in wines containing free SO_2. As a quick reminder: 1 mg acetaldehyde combines with 1.45 mg SO_2 to form an odorless addition product. As long as free SO_2 is present, there is no free acetaldehyde with its typical smell reminding bruised apples; one excludes another. Elevated acetaldehyde contents requiring high SO_2 additions are rather caused by yeast metabolism than by chemical oxidation.

- ***H_2O_2 consumption by further compounds***: The other half of the 5 to 26 % of peroxide not consumed by SO_2, hence 2.5 to 13 %, leads via oxygen radical chain reaction to an irreversible and broad-spectrum oxidation of other wine compounds (Waterhouse and Laurie 2006). This reaction is responsible for the formation of various oxidation products, primarily higher aldehydes and ketones, which are characteristic for the aroma profile of wines affected by oxidative aging. If peroxide was fully scavenged by SO_2 and ethanol, these aroma alterations would not take place.

Quinones are not entirely reduced by SO_2

As has been shown and contrary to general expectations, a minor portion of intermediate peroxide is not reduced by SO_2. Thus, the legitimate question arises as to what extent quinones are reduced by SO_2.

In oxygenated model solutions containing SO_2, quinones were recycled to the original phenols to an extent of 79 % for epicatechin and 96 % for catechin (Danilewicz and Wallbridge 2010). These data give little information about the degree of quinone reduction by SO_2 in real wine, but they confirm that other substances compete with SO_2 for reacting with quinones.

Indeed, quinones are able to react with a large array of other compounds such as thiol groups contained in amino acids (Chapter 2.5.5), in volatile sulfur compounds causing reduction flavor (Chapter 3.1), and in aromatic thiols of cultivars like Sauvignon blanc (Chapter 2.2.1). In red wines they also react with aldehydes. However, it is doubtful whether all these compounds in the concentration range they occur in white wines are able to bind with an appreciable amount of quinones.

Another feature of quinones is their ability to bind with phenols. This is the reaction referred to as regenerative polymerization. In the resulting polymers, the original phenolic hydroxyl groups are regenerated so that the quinones do not exist anymore (Chapter 2.2.1). In this way, they are diverted from reduction by SO_2. The oxygen used for their generation from phenols has become irreversibly bound and does not consume any SO_2. This is another reason why the SO_2 consumption by DO is less than 4 mg SO_2 per 1 mg O_2 as required by stoichiometry.

Phenol polymerization induced by oxidation can be the cause of far-reaching changes on the palate. When flavonoid phenols are involved in the polymerization process, browning occurs and astringency increases (Chapter 2.2.2). Color deepening of white wines with free SO_2 demonstrates most impressively that quinones partially polymerize and that SO_2 is not able to entirely reduce them back to the original phenols.

In conclusion, it can be stated that in the course of oxidative aging, common levels of free SO_2 neither prevent olfactory alterations caused by hydrogen peroxide nor gustative alterations induced by quinone polymerization.

Limited protection against oxidative aging by elevated free SO_2 levels

The fate of oxygen consumed as described before differs considerably from that of high-phenol red wines or turbid young white wines still containing suspended yeast lees (Chapter 2.5.6). In filtered white wines, free SO_2 is usually the most important, although not the only ultimate DO acceptor. Therefore, adjustment, control and preservation of an appropriate level of free SO_2 are important instruments to optimize shelf life of standard white wines. But as seen before, they do not suffice.

After storage of white wines containing 35 vs. 55 mg/L free SO_2 over seven months at 20° C, they displayed identical concentrations of acetate esters, ethyl esters, and terpenols (Roussis et al. 2007). Therefore, bottling with excessively elevated levels of free SO_2 is not a suitable way to resolve problems with premature oxidative aging. To protect fruity white wines against the adverse effects of oxygen uptake only by means of SO_2, their storage and bottling would require free SO_2 levels that would be extremely disturbing in sensory terms. In other words, due to the olfactory impact of free SO_2, sensory requirements do not allow for conserving wine with as much free SO_2 as needed to reach a $SO_2:O_2$ ratio = 4:1 that is required for complete oxidation protection.

Only the gaseous, molecular form of free sulfur dioxide is sensorially active with its distractingly pungent smell. As shown in figure 19, the molecular SO_2 percentage of free SO_2 strongly depends on pH. Its absolute concentration can be calculated according to the formula

$$SO_2 \text{ molecular (mg/L)} = \text{free } SO_2 : [1 + 10^{(pH - 1.81)}],$$

in which the subtrahend 1.81 comprised in the power is the pKa value or the acid constant of sulfurous acid.

As a consequence of this logarithmic dependence of molecular SO_2 on pH, a common level of 40 mg/l free SO_2 smells twice as much in a wine with pH 3.1 than in a wine with pH 3.4. For most wines, sensorially acceptable upper limits of free SO_2 range from 30 to 60 mg/L, depending also on wine temperature and taster sensitivity.

More important than the level of free or molecular SO_2 is its stability over time, which strongly depends on oxygen uptake. A significant speed-up of oxidative aging of bottled white wines is observed when free SO_2 levels fall below 10 mg/L (Godden et al. 2001). The typical smell of free acetaldehyde reminiscent of bruised apples or Sherry only arises when free SO_2 falls to 0 mg/L (Chapter 2.1).

2.5.2. Wines without added sulfites

The use of SO_2 in winemaking is a hotly debated subject in the wine writer and consumer community. Thus, consumer health concerns are one of the reasons why wines without added sulfites are produced here and there. However, conventional wines only contain a small fraction of the amounts of SO_2 contained in many other foods, while less than 1 % of the population is reported to be affected by a sulfite allergy. It is debatable whether such an allergy can exist at all since the human body produces and metabolizes more than a gram of sulfite per day, which corresponds to approximately ten times the amount of sulfite contained in a bottle of wine. Ethical considerations might play a greater role. Thus, dispensing with SO_2 additions is frequently associated with organic and biodynamic winegrowing. This explains why there is a small market for non-sulfited wines. Such wines require preservation by other means.

Wines without any SO_2 do not exist. During primary fermentation, yeasts produce commonly some 20 mg/L SO_2 with deviations upward and downward. A level of 10 mg/L total SO_2 is the upper limit below which the warning "contains sulfites" must not be mentioned on the label. There are only a very few selected yeast strains producing SO_2 below this limit under optimal nutritional conditions. Indigenous yeasts carrying out spontaneous fermentation usually exceed it.

In principle, winemaking without added SO_2 is feasible and from some viewpoints it is even easier with the oxygen-sensitive white wines than with red wines. In this context, feasibility means that such wines should not display oxidation flaws or the smell of free acetaldehyde. However, to achieve this objective and prevent oxidation, much more knowledge and technical input are required than for conventional winemaking with SO_2. Winemaking without added SO_2, while maintaining quality and hygiene standards, requires control of virtually every facet of production from the crush pad to the bottled wine.

It is important to emphasize that the basic issue in producing wines without added SO_2 is not so much the microbial stability SO_2 additions would provide. Microbial safety can easily be obtained by physical means such as sterile filtration and cooling. After all, the technical facilities for that purpose are almost universally available in the world of modern enology. Conversely, the issue is first and foremost about oxidation rather than microbial stability.

White wines without free SO_2 require consistent protection from oxygen uptake by systematic and thorough use of inert gas (argon or nitrogen) as soon as primary fermentation comes to an end. This is a common and indispensable procedure in the brewing industry as beer is extremely sensitive to oxidation, even more than white wine, but it still needs getting used to in the wine industry (Chapter 2.6). At bottling, headspace inertization and the use of bottle closures with a low oxygen ingress are an essential element in this approach. Working with a DO meter is highly recommended to check the amounts of DO picked up and understand where it comes from.

Prior to fermentation, deliberate must oxidation and thorough clarification (Chapter 2.4) are recommended to lower the phenolic fractions that would otherwise substantially contribute to the sensory consequences of oxidative aging of that kind of wine.

Primary fermentation must run smoothly under conditions of satisfactory nutrient supply. Otherwise, total acetaldehyde levels in the wine would exceed 5 mg/L. As long as they are lower, they are bound by the SO_2 produced by yeast. As a reminder: 1.0 mg/L acetaldehyde requires 1.45 g/L SO_2 to get bound as an odorless adduct. When there is less SO_2 than required to bind acetaldehyde, free acetaldehyde would strongly affect aroma quality (Chapter 2.1). In conventional winemaking, the usual step to overcome this problem is adding more SO_2.

Another approach to minimize elevated acetaldehyde contents is malolactic fermentation. It is suitable to lower total acetaldehyde to less than 5 mg/L. When it is completed and malic acid less than 0.3 g/L, wines are stored in the cold at not more than 5° C (41° F), perfectly topped without any liquid surface or treatments until they are sterile filtered. Under commercial winemaking conditions, headspace blanketing with inert gas is not a means reliable enough to protect against oxygen uptake to the extent required for such wines. Post-fermentation yeast lees provide further protection against oxidation (Chapter 2.5.6) and also absorb some acetaldehyde as long as they are not settled.

2.5.3. Effect of ascorbic acid

Ascorbic acid (AA) can be found in appreciable amounts in many fruits and juices produced therefrom. In grapes, it occurs at much lower levels that quickly vanish upon oxygen exposure during grape processing. Hence, wines usually do not contain ascorbic acid naturally.

AA is reputed as a strong antioxidant and reducing agent. Therefore, it is sometimes added to wines in order to complement the antioxidant effect of SO_2. Its addition to must and wine is legal in most wine growing countries, though limited to 250 mg/L in some of them. However, its impact on oxidative wine aging is controversial and debatable (Barril et al. 2016).

Direct reaction with oxygen

The reaction rate of the various reducing agents is variable. AA reacts fast, SO_2 much more slowly, and phenols even more slowly. This is because AA has a lower redox potential than the common phenolics (0.55 vs. 0.78 to 1.07 mV) (Danilewicz 2003). As a consequence, it can partially replace phenolic compounds as the primary oxygen acceptors and hence protect them from oxidation.

2. Typical and oxidative aging

In contrast to SO_2, AA is able to efficiently scavenge DO. This feature provides a direct removal of DO that is not ascribed to SO_2, which is instead known to act indirectly by reversing phenol oxidation processes.

When AA binds with oxygen, it is oxidized to dehydroascorbic acid (DAA). In stoichiometric terms, 11 mg AA bind with 1 mg DO according to the formula

$$AA + O_2 \rightarrow DAA + H_2O_2$$

The most striking outcome of this reaction is the production of H_2O_2, which is trapped by SO_2 as long as free SO_2 is present. Thus, SO_2 oxidation is coupled with AA autoxidation. A simplified reaction schema is given in figure 25.

Figure.25: Reaction of ascorbic acid with oxygen and subsequent reactions.

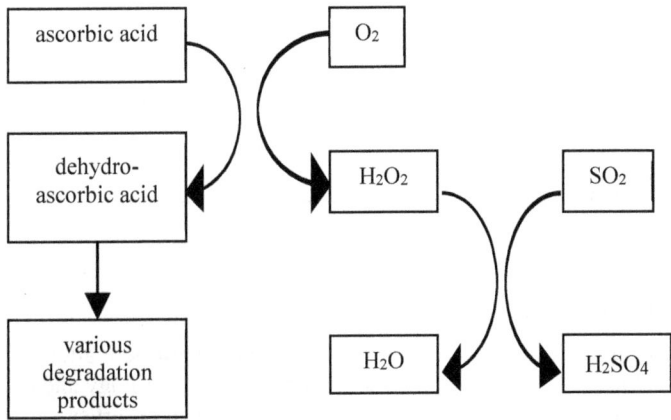

Stoichiometric relationships only apply on condition that oxygen does not concurrently react with other wine compounds. Thus, in the simultaneous presence of free SO_2, the amount of AA consumed by DO is lower than 11 mg AA per 1 mg DO, with the exact ratio depending on the initial molar ratio of SO_2 : AA.

On the other hand, AA also lowers SO_2 losses when oxygen is consumed under conditions of low oxygen ingress as they occur in most bottled wines. This is because AA is able to recycle quinones back to the original phenols. Thus, no SO_2 is required for the reduction of quinones in the oxidation process (Figure 20), but only for trapping H_2O_2. Hence, AA reduces the SO_2 : O_2 ratio by some 50 % (Danilewicz 2016). This means in practical terms that after addition of AA, SO_2 losses per 1 mg /L DO should only be half of those occurring in the absence of AA. This was basically confirmed during bottle storage trials over several years, in which slightly less SO_2 was consumed in white wines supplied with AA before bottling (Skouroumounis et al. 2013).

Ascorbic acid accelerates oxygen consumption

In contrast to claims in older textbooks, the reaction of AA with oxygen is not spontaneous, though it leads to a many times faster consumption of DO in wine when compared to the same wine containing only SO_2 (Figure 26). Heavy metals acting as catalysts accelerate this reaction. However, the extent of the reaction, measured as losses of AA, is solely determined by the amount of available oxygen.

Figure 26: Impact of ascorbic acid on the DO consumption rate in a white wine (40 mg/L initial free SO_2).
▲ without ascorbic acid ● with 150 mg/L ascorbic acid

$y = 4.704e^{-0.104x}$

$y = 4.9524e^{-1.961x}$

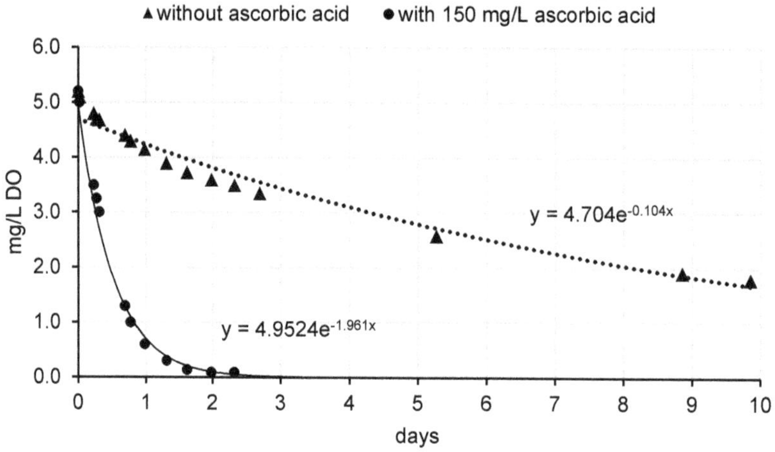

Comparing DO consumption rates

On a closer look at figure 26, it is noticeable that a comparison of both aliquots is more complicated than it seems. Since this issue is a basic one in enology and concerning all wines regardless of the presence or absence of AA, it deserves a more detailed examination at this point.

Indeed, the rate of DO consumption is not the same in all wines over the whole DO concentration range. In contrast, in most wines it depends on the instantaneous DO concentration and is proportional to it. This means that when DO halves, the reaction rate also halves. It slows down when the DO level approaches zero, flatting off asymptotically until no further DO can be measured. This is what is called a first-order reaction kinetics. Hence, it is not admissible to attribute a characteristic DO consumption rate to each wine without considering its momentary DO level. In all wines, the change of DO over time is best fitted with an exponential function, though this might not always be visible on superficial examination.

In order to make calculations easier, the reaction rate can also be presented as the half-life of the reactant, in this case DO. The half-life is the period of time in which the concentration of DO is decreased by half of its value. It is characteristic of every wine and the only valid way to compare DO consumption rates between wines. In five white wines, the average DO half-life measured was 175 hours in the absence of ascorbic acid and 7 hours after ascorbic acid addition. It is noteworthy that such data are highly variable, depending on the chemical make-up of each wine.

Ascorbic acid does not make DO disappear without leaving a trace

As shown in figure 25, hydrogen peroxide is generated when AA consumes oxygen. This is exactly the same byproduct which appears when phenols undergo coupled oxidation (Chapters 2.2.1 and 2.5.1). Hence, it is likely that it is not completely trapped by SO_2, just as it occurs in the absence of AA. More research is needed in this field.

In wine, AA can only act as a reducing agent in conjunction with sufficiently high levels of free SO_2. When no free SO_2 is available, the intermediate peroxide is entirely consumed by remaining AA and by the Fenton reaction (Chapter 2.2.1), which leads to an unspecific oxidation of all organic wine compounds. As a consequence, oxidative aging is even accelerated as long as oxygen is available. Therefore, AA is not a substitute for SO_2, nor is it a means for getting along with lower levels of free SO_2.

Ultimately, AA does not make DO disappear without leaving any traces, but just transfers it in the form of H_2O_2 onto other wine compounds. Thus, DO ends up where it would also get to without ascorbic acid. Just the reaction pathway is different. The widely alleged antioxidant action of AA is based on its ability to reduce quinones back to phenols, as it can easily be observed when its addition impedes or removes browning of oxidized grape musts.

Ascorbic acid may promote oxidation under certain conditions

Time and again, the awareness of the strong oxidation power of intermediate peroxide has arisen doubts about the long-term effectiveness of AA as a reducing agent in wine. These doubts have been supported by the demonstration that an initial antioxidant activity of AA would turn into a pro-oxidant effect in the long term (Marks and Morris 1993, Bradshaw et al. 2003), and that the action of AA depends on age and redox status of the wine (Peng et al. 1998). Eventually it could be shown that the crossover point from antioxidant to pro-oxidant activity only occurs when both AA and free SO_2 are entirely consumed as a result of oxygen ingress (Bradshaw et al. 2003, 2004).

Practical hints

Under practical operating conditions, it is important that wines contain a satisfactory level of at least 30 mg/L free SO_2 when AA is added, and that they are carefully protected from uncontrolled oxygen ingress during further storage. Without free SO_2 available to bind the H_2O_2 generated under conditions of oxygen uptake, AA alone will cause more oxidation than without it. Therefore, the use of AA during barrel aging is not recommended. In standard white wines, its use should be restricted to additions at bottling as long as no earlier addition is required to prevent atypical aging (Chapter 4) in wines prone to develop it.

It is also worth noting that AA does not show any antimicrobial activity, nor does it bind major byproducts of wine oxidation as does SO_2. Furthermore, it interacts with iodine, thus interfering with SO_2 determination by the Ripper titration and leading to falsely high results. When this method is used for SO_2 measurements, 100 mg/L AA simulate 37 mg/L SO_2 more than the wine actually contains.

Moderate benefits with regard to oxidative aging

There are only a few conclusive studies on the benefits of AA for protecting wine aroma from the effects of oxidative aging during bottle storage. Direct comparisons between lots of the kind "only SO_2" and "SO_2 plus AA" are considerably compromised by variable levels of free SO_2 at bottling as well as by differing oxygen uptake in the course of the bottling process, from the bottle headspace, and through the bottle closure.

In storage trials with sparkling wine, addition of ascorbic acid at disgorging did not produce less browning than adding only SO_2. It gave no additional benefits to additions of SO_2 alone. However, there was no extra loss of SO_2 in the 11-months trial in the wines to which AA was added (Marks and Morris 1993).

Extensive storage trials with Riesling and Chardonnay still wines have shown that the addition of 90 mg/L AA at bottling had no impact on aroma during the first six months post bottling. Sensory differences only appeared after three and five years of bottle storage when fruity aroma was rated higher in the lot with ascorbic acid for one wine, but not for the other wine. SO_2 levels were also quite similar regardless of AA additions, or slightly higher in the wines to which AA had been added. In this study, the addition of AA thus complemented the use of SO_2, rather than manifesting a pro-oxidative effect, which might only occur once free SO_2 has been entirely depleted (Skouroumounis et al. 2005 a).

In another trial on Riesling, bottling after addition of 250 mg/L AA resulted in higher intensity ratings of fruity aroma and less intensity of oxidized aroma attributes. With regard to the preservation of fruity aroma, raising free SO_2 from 45 mg/L to 68 mg/L at bottling was less effective than the addition of ascorbic acid. However, beneficial effects of AA addition were canceled after six months of bottle storage when an elevated oxygen ingress at bottling and from the bottle headspace took place (Morozova et al. 2015). Further studies (Godden et al. 2001, Skouroumounis et al. 2005 a, Lopes et al. 2009) indicate that oxygen uptake from the bottle headspace and through the bottle closure has a comparable or even larger impact on oxidative aging than the presence or absence of AA.

According to the current state of knowledge, addition of AA reduces oxidative aging during bottle storage only in some wines, under certain conditions, and to a moderate extent. Benefits may only result from the fact that AA decreases SO_2 losses caused by oxidation since it saves SO_2 otherwise consumed for quinone reduction, thus preserving more free SO_2. However, prerequisite for this is keeping oxygen ingress under control. When free SO_2 is entirely consumed after a high oxygen uptake before, during, and after bottling, the effect of AA will clearly be pro-oxidant. Oxygen supply through the bottle closure is decisive.

Specific applications of ascorbic acid

In some wine growing areas, the assumption is held that AA slows down white wine aging in general. However, this assertion only applies to a very specific kind of aging, which is known as atypical aging (Chapter 4). Inadequate sensory distinction between typical and atypical aging may account for the contradictory statements about the anti-aging effect of AA.

When AA is added to wine, the equilibrium between insoluble trivalent iron (Fe^{3+}) and soluble bivalent iron (Fe^{2+}) is shifted towards soluble Fe^{2+}. As a practical result, slightly higher iron levels can be tolerated. Thus, fining procedures aiming at lowering iron content can sometimes be avoided in borderline cases.

Malodorous thiols, also referred to as mercaptans, play a crucial role in wines affected by reduction flavor. They can be oxidized into disulfides during wine storage. Disulfides are responsible for a kind of reduction flavor difficult to remedy as they do not directly react neither with copper salts nor with oxygen. After addition of ascorbic acid, they start being gradually reduced to the thiols they stem from, which in turn can be removed with copper fining. Thus, the combined addition of AA plus copper ions can allow for removing a kind of reduction flavor, which cannot be removed by simple copper salt additions alone (Chapter 3.3).

AA is also effective in preventing the rare phenomenon of pinking (Lamuela-Raventós et al 2001). Pinking means the appearance of a troublesome salmon-red blush color that occasionally appears in white wines exclusively produced from white grape varieties (Chapter 2.2.2)

In some cases, the addition of AA is associated with an improvement of taste as perceived on the palate, which is based on the slight increase of acidity it entails. This effect is not related to the antioxidant activity of AA but exclusively to its acid properties. It can also be obtained by adding any other acid commonly used for wine acidity management.

Sensory risks and drawbacks

Under conditions of low oxygen ingress through the bottle closure, AA in bottled wines increases the intensity of post-bottling reductive off-flavor in the case the wine is prone to develop it (Godden et al. 2001, Skouroumounis 2005 a, Lopes et al. 2009). This applies in particular to wines sealed with very gas-tight screw caps. The predominant cause is the formation of thiols, partially via reduction of disulfides (Chapter 3.2). Traces of copper may mitigate this effect (Chapter 3.5.2).

On the other hand, AA reduces highly soluble Cu^{2+} to less soluble Cu^+ ions, thus increasing the propensity of wine to develop cloudiness by copper precipitation. Therefore, wines containing AA should not be bottled with more than 0.3 mg/L total copper. Precise copper measurements before bottling are recommended when copper fining for the removal of reduction flavor has become necessary.

Dehydroascorbic acid produced by AA oxidation is not stable but degrades into a variety of products. They comprise furfural, 3-hydroxy-2-pyrone with a caramel-like aroma, xylosone that ultimately contribute to the production of yellow xanthylium pigments, and further unidentified compounds leading to an increase of the yellow-brown color component (Barril et al 2016). This color deepening is moderate, commonly accepted by consumers, not accompanied by oxidized aromas and flavors, and not related to the kind of browning caused by flavonoid phenols upon oxidative aging (Peng et al. 1998).

2.5.4. Effect of ellagitannins

Along with gallotannins, ellagitannins belong to the group of hydrolyzable tannins (Chapter 2.2.2), which are not naturally present in grapes but constitute the most sold commercial tannins legally authorized as wine additives. In colloquial terminology, hydrolyzable tannins are frequently referred to as ellagitannins without further specification but always in contrast to grape tannins. For that reason, this vernacular term is maintained.

Ellagitannins are extracted from suitable wood species like oak, chestnut and quebracho as well as from gall nuts. They are also picked up from wood during barrel aging and upon wine treatment with oak alternatives. Their origin affects their composition and characteristics. The real ellagitannins are complex polymers of ellagic acid, while gallotannins are polymers of gallic acid. Their common feature is their astringency and easy oxidizability. They are odorless when they are properly cleaned as legally required.

Ellagitannins have several hydroxyl (OH) functions in the *ortho* position that are easily oxidized. While there are only two hydroxyl groups for one mole of catechin, there are 15 for one mole of ellagitannin. As a result, they consume oxygen much faster than flavonoid phenols from grapes (Pascual et al. 2017).

Their easy oxidizability yields high amounts of hydrogen peroxide that produce an important increase in acetaldehyde, which favors the condensation between flavonoid tannins and anthocyanins in red wines, their color stabilization, and their softening on the palate. Under conditions of moderate oxygen uptake during red wine barrel aging, they regulate oxidation mechanism by limiting oxidative degradation processes of red wine phenols (Vivas and Glories 1996).

As a result of these findings, the addition of ellagitannins has been intensively promoted by the supply industry and become one of the most important tools in red winemaking. In the meantime, efforts have also been made to extend their use to white winemaking, invoking their action as a natural antioxidant preventing premature aging. However, in contrast to the bulk of research literature covering their effect on red wines, very few studies have been published about their impact on white wines.

Ellagitannins are able to strongly complex transition metals like bivalent iron, thus limiting oxidative damage mediated by the Fenton reaction (Chapter 2.2.1), while gallotannins display the highest radical scavenging capacity (Magalhães et al. 2014).

In model white wine solution containing catechin and stored under oxidative conditions, the effect of three antioxidants on catechin decay was studied: SO_2 protected against browning for a longer time than ascorbic acid, while gallotannins helped to consume oxygen but did not influence the oxidation of the solutions

(Chinnici et al. 2013). In white sparkling wine after disgorging, different polyphenols-based commercial formulas containing ellagitannins, gallotannins and flavan-3-ols were all less effective than SO_2 for preventing oxidative aging over seven months at 15 and 25° C (Fracassetti et al. 2016). Similarly, addition of ellagitannins to white still wines did not extent their shelf life (Panero et al. 2014).

The central feature of ellagitannins, their ability to consume oxygen faster than grape-derived phenols, does not seem to have any impact on the outcome of the Fenton reaction leading to oxidative aging perceived by smell in white wines (Chapter 2.2.1). The oxygen consumption of any kind of phenols generates hydrogen peroxide causing that reaction. Its extent will essentially depend on the amount of dissolved oxygen in the wine. The ability to cause an increase in the rate of oxygen consumption cannot be used as an indicator of the effectiveness of an antioxidant molecule. Furthermore and in contrast to SO_2 (Chapter 2.5.1), ellagitannins do not interact with primary and secondary oxidation products.

Thus far, there are no indications that the addition of ellagitannins protects white wines against oxidative aging. Even if they were able to do so, their use could face serious difficulties on the palate since they contribute to astringency as does any tannin. The astringency they provide is highly variable and depends on the commercial product used and the wine matrix.

Astringency is the primary sensory expression of tannins but a rather unpopular one in fruity white wines. However, research results on gustative thresholds of ellagitannins are scarce and conflicting. This might be explained by variable wine matrices and the compositional variability of ellagitannins. In general, additions of 30 mg/L are perceptible as an increase of astringency in most white wines. This increase becomes significant when 100 mg/L are added.

On the other hand, standard procedures of gentle grape processing (Chapter 2.3.2), must clarification (2.4.2), and phenol removal by fining agents (2.4.1) aim at minimizing astringency. Adding ellagitannins to white wines would invalidate all these efforts. This holds true despite impressive sensory euphemisms such as roundness, structure, palate weight, and length of finish used for their commercial promotion.

Ellagitannins vs. oak alternatives

Using oak barrels for aging of white wine results in specific wine styles that can be highly attractive but stylistically far away from fruity white wines. The supplementation of white wines with oak alternatives such as chips, staves, etc. allows the winemaker to move at the boundary between both styles, depending primarily on the amount and quality of oak added.

Oak alternatives inevitably provide ellagitannins, which are largely bound to yeast lees when they are added before or soon after fermentation. In doing so, excessive astringency can be avoided. This is an essential aspect since in contrast to red wines, ellagitannins hardly integrate into white wines over time.

However, the fundamental difference between commercial ellagitannins and oak alternatives lies in the aroma potential the letter impart into the wine. With increasing oak additions, fruity aroma attributes are progressively complemented or replaced by oak-derived attributes reminiscent of vanilla, cinnamon, cloves, tobacco, coffee, etc. The extent to which oak flavor is desired is a very personal decision depending on marketing considerations.

Minor amounts of oak additions around 0.5 to 1 g/L might add complexity to fruity white wines without impacting their varietal character and shelf life. Larger amounts tend to impart a distinct oak flavor masking varietal character, but they are also able to disguise premature aging. The transition is a seamless one.

2.5.5. Effect of sulfur-containing amino acids

Wine contains sulfur-containing amino acids and peptides like cysteine and glutathione that are able to exert an anti-oxidative effect. They are naturally occurring in grape juice but also released by yeast lees after primary fermentation. They are deemed able to reduce oxidized wine compounds and thus protect wine aroma against oxidative degradation to a certain extent.

Apart from their targeted extraction from post-fermentation yeast lees, they can also be added to wine in the form of commercially available inactive yeast preparations (Pozo-Bayon et al 2009, Aguera et al. 2012, Andújar-Ortiz et al. 2012, Kritzinger et al. 2013, Rodriguez-Bencomo et al. 2014). These preparations are yeast autolysates, which are obtained by thermal and/or enzymatic procedures. Originally they have been developed as yeast nutrients and fermentation aids. In the meantime, they have been largely legalized as wine additives and reducing agents. Their effectiveness is essentially evaluated by their content of reduced glutathione.

Glutathione is a peptide consisting of three amino acids – glutamic acid, cysteine, and glycine. The central cysteine moiety of the molecule is a sulfur-containing amino acid displaying a free thiol or sulfhydryl group (-SH), which is responsible for the reductive properties of glutathione (GSH).

GSH does not directly react with dissolved oxygen, but protects phenols against oxidation by reacting with quinones and reducing them back to phenols just as SO_2 does (Makhotkina and Kilmartin 2009). In doing so, GSH is oxidized and converted from its monomeric form via formation of a disulfide bridge into glutathione disulfide (GS-SG), which is not any more active (Figure 27). These reducing properties are responsible for its global interest in enology.

In contrast to SO_2, GSH does not react with oxygen radicals involved in the formation of hydrogen peroxide (H_2O_2) (Panero et al. 2015). Thus, it cannot prevent H_2O_2-dependent reactions like oxidation of SO_2, alcohols etc. when oxygen is picked up. Furthermore, it is inactivated by copper (Cu^+) ions at a ratio of 4.84 mg GSH per 1 mg Cu^+.

Figure 27: Glutathione and its oxidation to glutathione disulfide

glutathione (GSH)

glutathione disulfide (GS-SG)

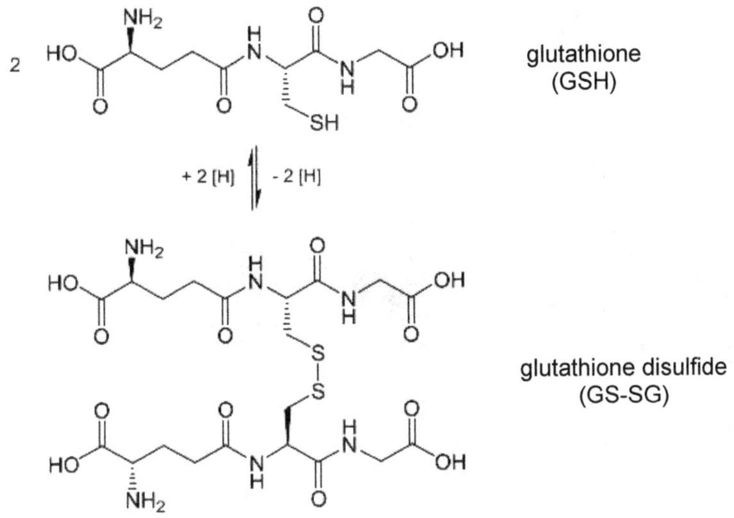

GSH occurs in almost all cells of living nature. Its natural concentration in wine heavily depends on vinification practices, thus varying from 0 to 70 mg/L (Fracassetti et al. 2011). As it is not (yet) legalized as an additive for winemaking, GSH-enriched enological products such as selected active dry yeast strains and inactive yeasts have been developed with the aim of remedying naturally occurring GSH deficiencies. These developments invoke analytical data proving an improved stability of 3-mercaptohexanol, terpenols, volatile esters, and other compounds responsible for fruity varietal aroma in GSH-enriched wines (Fragasso et al. 2010, Papadopoulou and Roussis 2001, 2008, Roussis et al. 2007, 2009, Ugliano et al. 2011).

However, more important than analytical data and the absolute GSH concentrations is the question of the sensory advantage of elevated concentrations. Using white wines of different cultivars, it was investigated whether an increase of their GSH contents would generate sensory benefits with regard to shelf life and aroma stability. For that purpose, six bottled white wines (2 to 4 mg/L GSH, 35 to 50 mg/L free SO_2, no ascorbic acid) were supplemented with 0, 25, and 50 mg/L GSH, respectively. To each of the lots thus obtained, 0, 10, and 20 mg/L O_2 were provided by varying the bottle headspace volume consisting of air. Subsequently, bottles were sealed with screw caps and the oxygen consumption monitored using a non-invasive optical oxygen measurement principle. When all headspace and dissolved oxygen was consumed after two months of bottle storage at ambient temperature, oxidative aging as perceived by smell was scored using a scale ranging from 0 to 5 points. At the time of sensory evaluation, all lots still displayed free SO_2, thus excluding any olfactory interference by the presence of free acetaldehyde (Chapter 2.1). Figure 28 gives the results.

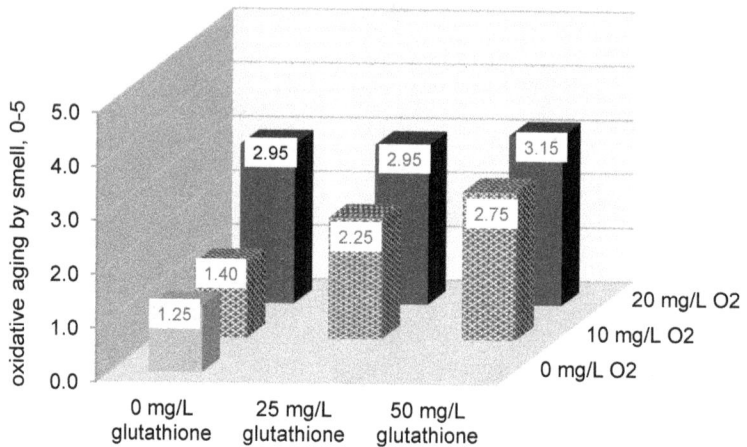

Figure 28: Impact of glutathione added to wine on the intensity (0-5) of oxidative aging as perceived by smell at different oxygen exposure levels. Means of six white wines (Riesling I and II, Chardonnay I and II, Pinot gris, and Pinot blanc).

According to expectations and regardless of glutathione content, the olfactory perception of oxidative aging increased significantly with increasing oxygen exposure. Contrary to expectations, however, was the effect of increasing GSH concentrations. Additions of 25 and 50 mg/L remained largely ineffective after consumption of 20 mg/L O_2. They even enhanced the olfactory perception of oxidative aging in the wines exposed to 10 mg/L O_2. In a nutshell, increasing GSH levels did not result in any sensory benefits with regard to protecting fruity aroma against oxidation in any of these wines, quite the contrary. Similar results were obtained for other varieties from different countries (Wegmann-Herr 2015, Panero et al. 2014, Antoce and Cojocaru 2017).

The olfactory effects produced were not accompanied by any measurable color changes. The mean SO_2 losses were 1.95 mg/L per 1 mg/L O_2 consumed regardless of the initial GSH level and, hence, only 49 % of the stoichiometric amount (Chapter 2.5.1). GSH does not affect SO_2 consumption when oxygen is picked up (Panero et al. 2015).

These results are in contrast to those obtained by other studies (du Toit 2007, Ugliano et al. 2011, Pons et al. 2015) focusing upon the effect of glutathione and inactive yeasts additions to Sauvignon blanc wines. These wines, when obtained from ripe fruit, are known for their exceptionally high and sensorially relevant concentrations of oxidation-sensitive varietal thiols comprising 4-methyl-4-mercaptopentan-2-one, 4-mercapto-4-methylpentan-2-ol, 3-mercaptohexan-1-ol, and 3-mercaptohexylacetate (Coetzee and du Toit 2012).

In an attempt to get to the bottom of these contradictions, the behavior of a Sauvignon blanc wine was compared to a standard white wine obtained from a blend of the four varieties referred to in figure 28. Beyond GSH (25 and 50 mg/L), cysteine and an inactivated dry yeast preparation (Optiwhite™) were also included into the assay. Cysteine is the reducing constituent of GSH. In order to allow for a direct comparison, both were added in equimolar proportions, in which 25 mg GSH equate to 9.85 mg cysteine. Lastly, the addition of 250 and 500 mg/L inactivated dry yeast allowed to provide the wine with 1.5 and 3.0 mg/L GSH, respectively, as well as cysteine and a broad range of other amino acids. All lots were supplied with 0 and 10 mg/L O_2 and stored two months for complete oxygen consumption before sensory evaluation.

Figure 29 shows the results for glutathione. Increasing GSH levels enhance the olfactory perception of oxidative aging in the standard white wine after consumption of 10 mg/L of oxygen. Previous results were confirmed. Sauvignon blanc behaved in the opposite way. The higher its GSH level, the less it developed oxidative aging after consumption of 10 mg/L O_2, and the more it preserved its original varietal aroma.

These results indicate that GSH can actually have a positive effect on the preservation of fruity varietal aroma, but that this effect cannot be generalized. It appears limited to Sauvignon blanc and similar cultivars, in which thiols play an important and sensorially significant role in varietal aroma.

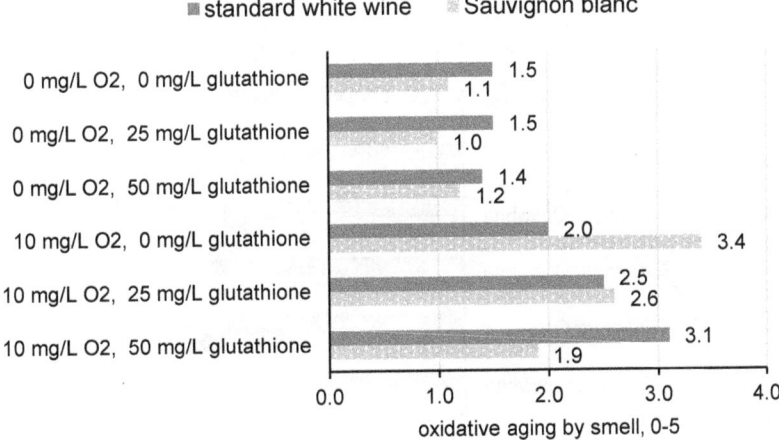

Figure 29: Impact of glutathione added to wine on the intensity (0-5) of oxidative aging as perceived by smell. Comparison of a standard white wine and Sauvignon blanc.

Figure 30 depicts the impact of cysteine additions on oxidative aging. By analogy with GSH and added in an equimolar proportion, increasing cysteine contents protect Sauvignon blanc aroma against oxidation. However, in contrast to the effect of GSH, this effect can also be observed in the standard white wine blend.

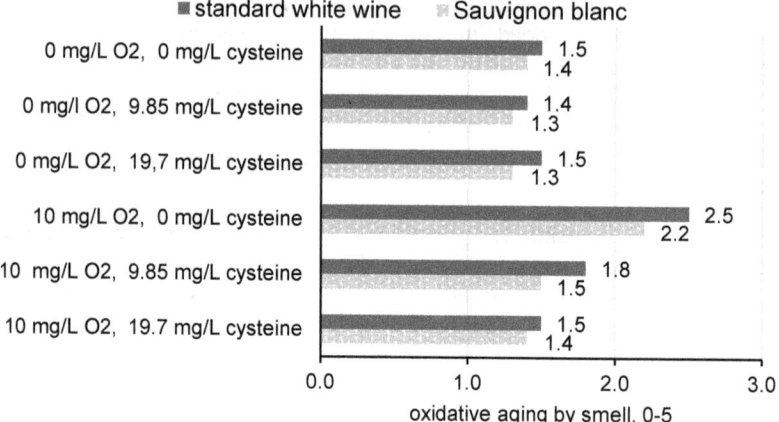

Figure 30: Impact of cysteine added to white wine on the intensity (0-5) of oxidative aging as perceived by smell.

Sensory results obtained after addition of inactivated dry yeast are highlighted in figure 31. They are similar to those obtained from cysteine-enriched wines; increasing additions of inactive yeast better preserve fruity aroma in both wines after consumption of 10 mg/L O_2. The changes in color and final SO_2 content they caused were not significant.

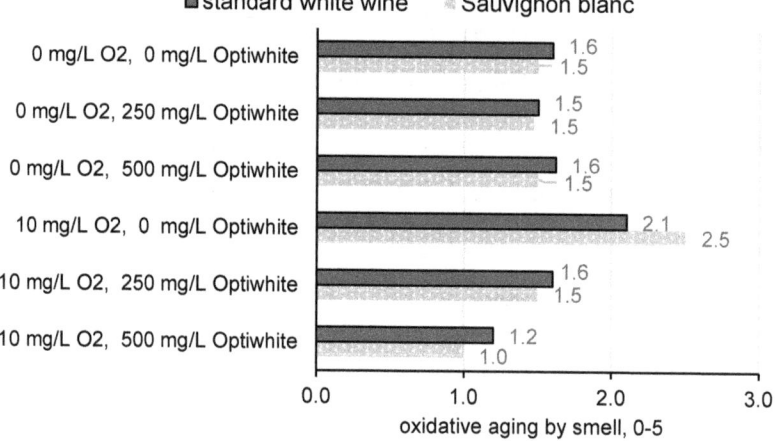

Figure 31: Impact of inactive yeast (Optiwhite ™) added to white wine on the intensity (0-5) of oxidative aging as perceived by smell.

Dry inactivated yeast preparations also increased varietal aroma attributes of ripe tropical fruit in Sauvignon blanc wine when added to the must, while this effect was not always observed after glutathione additions (Gabrielli et al. 2017).

2. Typical and oxidative aging

Only wines characterized by aromatic thiols can benefit from glutathione

The results summarized above confirm that reducing amino acids protect fruity varietal aroma from oxidative aging, provided that they consist of cysteine or a mix of reducing amino acids extracted from inactivate yeast. Under industrial conditions, the content of these compounds can be increased by adding commercially available preparations of inactivated dry yeast or by lengthy contact of the wine with the yeast lees before racking and filtration. However, GSH enriched by this procedure is not directly related to a better protection of terpenols against oxidation (Rodrigues-Bencomo et al. 2014). Sensory benefits of enhancing merely GSH levels have been proven for wines of Sauvignon blanc (du Toit 2007, Ugliano et al. 2011, Aguera et al. 2012, Pons et al. 2015, Gabrielli et al. 2017) and similar varieties (Burkert et al. 2018) with elevated concentrations of thiols participating in varietal aroma, but do not occur in all cultivars. They seem to depend on the intrinsic capacity of the wine matrices to resist against oxidation (Nikolantonaki et al. 2018)

The mystery of off-flavor generated by glutathione additions

Wines obtained from common cultivars as those referred to in figure 28 do not contain appreciable amounts of oxygen-sensitive thiols relevant for varietal aroma. Since GSH does not impede H_2O_2 production upon oxygen uptake (Panero et al. 2015), it is understandable that it cannot prevent the subsequent oxidation of alcohols to higher aldehydes responsible for the off-smell of oxidative aging (Chapters 2.1 and 2.2.1) in these wines. However, it is less understandable why elevated GSH levels not only fail in protecting wine aroma, but even tend to increase the sensory perception of oxidative aging under comparable conditions of oxygen exposure. Since both GSH and the GS-SG produced upon oxygen uptake are odorless compounds, the cause of this behavior is not yet definitely explained and is open to speculations.

A non-oxidative breakdown of GSH has been proven (Desmukh et al. 2009). Similarly to the Maillard reaction and in the presence of glucose, this breakdown gives rise to various volatile compounds whose olfactory properties are reminiscent of the smell of wines having undergone oxidative aging (Shedid 2010). Other data support the thesis that the initial reducing effect of GSH can turn into the opposite after its total breakdown (Sonni et al. 2011). Under these conditions, the glutathionyl radical produced upon GSH oxidation could exert a pro-oxidative effect (Schöneich and Asmus 1990, Wegmann-Herr 2015). However, if these reactions are sensorially relevant, they must be expected to occur in any wine. Masking effects that are well known in sensory analysis could explain the divergent behavior of Sauvignon blanc and similar varieties.

An increased propensity to produce reduction flavor (Chapter 3) after addition of GSH to both must (Wegmann-Herr et al. 2016) and wine (Burkert et al. 2018) has been reported. This suggests that GSH is able to undergo non-oxidative degradation reactions releasing its sulfide group, which is incorporated into the pool of S-containing compounds responsible for the appearance of reduction flavor. The production of hydrogen sulfide as a reaction product has been shown in this context (Bekker et al. 2017).

2.5.6. Oxygen consumption by post-fermentation yeast lees

The release of reducing amino acids is one of the features of postfermentation yeast lees (Chapter 2.5.5). Furthermore, yeast lees are also able to absorb oxygen dissolved in the wine (DO) and use it for chemical reactions within the yeast cells. The DO consumed by that way is not any more available for oxidation of wine compounds. This is one of the reasons why aging on the lees has become an enological concept for pursuing specific stylistic goals. This concept is based on the assumption that after primary fermentation lees consist predominantly of yeast cells. A distinction is made between light lees that remain in suspension for a long time and heavy lees that settle at the bottom of the container.

During the first couple of weeks after primary fermentation, DO absorbed by yeast lees can be consumed by the respiration metabolism of yeast cells still alive. After cell death and throughout the subsequent months and years, it is used for oxidation of lipids and ergosterol localized in the cell membrane (Fornairon et al. 1999, Salmon et al. 2000, Rosenfeld et al. 2002, Fornairon-Bonnefond and Salmon 2003). This reaction grinds to a halt upon pasteurization, though no enzymatic activity has yet been proven to be involved in it (Schneider 2005 c).

In an attempt to quantify the rate and extent to which DO present in wine is consumed by variable amounts of suspended yeast cells as compared to filtered wines, the effect of technological parameters on the rate of this reaction, and its significance under practical winemaking conditions, a specific approach has been developed (Schneider et al. 2016). Using the example of six commercially available selected yeast strains (A to F), it provided the following results:

Impact of yeast concentration

Oxygen consumption rate (OCR) and yeast cell concentration measured as nephelometric turbidity units (NTU) are the pivotal variables in this context. The OCR informs about how fast light yeast lees suspended after primary fermentation consume DO. Suspended yeast cell concentrations expressed as NTU closely correlate ($r = 0.99$) with the cell number, 1 NTU equating to $6.3 \cdot 10^6$ cells/mL. Interference of other suspended solids is less than 2 % when white wines are obtained from properly clarified musts.

In a first step, the effect of yeast concentration on OCR was evaluated in model solution (13 % alcohol, pH 3.5) at 20° C, thus circumventing any interfering DO consumption by other wine constituents than yeast. Table 5 depicts the results.

Although all yeasts were harvested and trialed within a narrow time frame after fermentation, there were remarkable differences in the OCR among yeast strains at given concentrations. According to logical expectations, OCR increases with increasing yeast concentrations, but not always in a linear way. OCR deemed useful for enological purposes requires a minimum concentration of 50 NTU suspended yeast lees. Above that minimum level, OCR ranged from 0.27 to 2.09 mg/L/h O_2.

Table. 5: Oxygen consumption rate (mg/L/h O_2) of six yeast strains in model solution as affected by yeast concentration.

Yeasts were harvested and trialed one to four weeks after the end of alcoholic fermentation. Free SO_2 = 0 mg/l; temperature = 20° C, NTU = nephelometric turbidity units.

yeast strain	yeast lees concentration						
	5 NTU	25 NTU	50 NTU	100 NTU	200 NTU	300 NTU	400 NTU
	OCR, mg/L/h						
A	0.00	0.04	0.39	0.58	0.80	1.15	1.75
B	0.00	0.04	0.44	0.64	0.80	1.04	1.21
C	0.00	0.03	0.34	0.77	1.07	1.55	2.09
D	0.00	0.04	0.51	0.57	0.60	0.68	0.74
E	0.00	0.04	0.68	0.72	0.85	0.96	1.13
F	0.00	0.03	0.27	0.38	0.53	0.61	0.67
mean	0.00	0.04	0.44	0.61	0.77	1.00	1.27

In this context, it is important to correctly interpret turbidity units caused by suspended yeast lees: Young white wines display 500-1000 NTU right after primary fermentation. In the course of settling over several months, turbidity decreases to 50-500 NTU, depending on the type and height of the storage vessel. After diatomaceous earth filtration, wines usually display only 5-20 NTU. A turbidity of 50 NTU equates to a clearly visible opalescence.

Impact of storage and yeast lees aging

Storage duration of the unfiltered wine and aging of the yeast lees have a minor impact on the OCR of yeast. Figure 32 illustrates that there is a slow and irregular decrease of the OCR during the first three months post fermentation.

A residual activity of 11 to 100 % of the initial OCR right after fermentation has been reported (Fornairon et al. 1999), while there was even some oxygen consumption by yeast lees after three years of storage (Salmon 2006). However, this might not be the case in any wine.

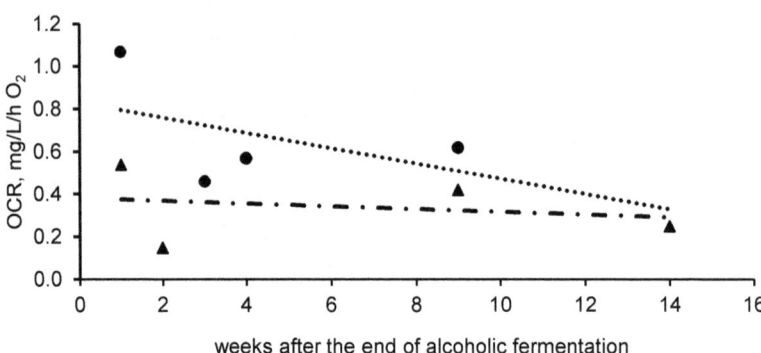

Figure 32: Impact of yeast lees age on their oxygen consumption rate (OCR).

Impact of SO_2

Since wines are stored with variable concentrations of free SO_2 after fermentation, its impact on the OCR of postfermentation yeast cells was also investigated using six yeast strains suspended at 200 NTU in model solution (13 % alcohol, pH 3.5) spiked with increasing amounts of SO_2. Figure 33 demonstrates that the OCR strongly decreases when free SO_2 increases. At an average wine pH of 3.5, there is a critical limit around 20 mg/L free SO_2 above which the OCR of yeast becomes drastically reduced.

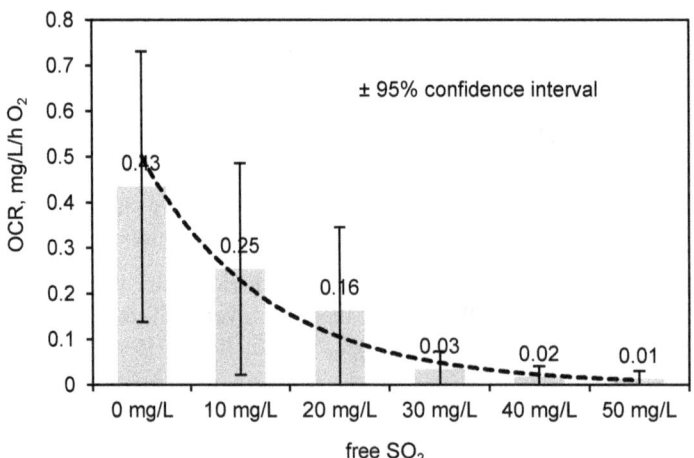

Figure 33: Impact of free SO_2 on the oxygen consumption rate (OCR) of yeast lees in model solution (13 % alcohol, pH 3.5) at 20° C. Means of six yeast strains harvested two weeks after fermentation and adjusted to 200 NTU.

2. Typical and oxidative aging

Impact of temperature

The effect of temperature on the OCR of postfermentation yeast lees was studied in model solution and shown to be significant for all yeast strains (Table 6). Under the conditions of cool wine storage, the OCR decreases markedly. At 5° C, it is only 68.5 % of that at 20° C.

Table 6: Impact of temperature on the oxygen consumption rate (OCR, mg/L/h O_2) by different yeast strains in model solution (13 % alcohol, pH 3.5) at different temperatures.

Yeasts were harvested two weeks after fermentation and adjusted to 200 NTU. Free SO_2 = 0 mg/L.

yeast strain	temperature		
	5° C	15° C	20° C
	OCR (mg/L/h O_2)		
A	0.32	0.47	0.51
B	0.03	0.04	0.05
C	0.14	0.19	0.24
D	0.02	0.05	0.10
E	0.57	0.61	0.71
F	0.59	0.78	0.83
mean	0.28	0.36	0.41

On the other hand, the oxygen consumption rate in filtered wines, caused by chemical oxidation of wine compounds, also proceeds at a lower rate when the temperature is decreased (Figure 41). Therefore, when yeast lees and oxidizable wine compounds compete for DO in real wines, the yeast percentage contribution to total oxygen consumption is not necessarily affected by temperature.

Total oxygen consumption capacity of yeast lees

After the rate of oxygen consumption by yeast lees and its dependence on enological variables has become known, another pertinent question relates to the total amount of DO a typical concentration of suspended yeast lees in young wines is able to consume. The total oxygen consumption capacity of yeast suspensions was measured in model solution under conditions of unlimited oxygen supply in a manometric device (Schneider et al. 2016). Three yeast strains were assayed at a concentration of 300 NTU.

As shown in figure 34, oxygen consumption of yeast lees follows an almost linear pattern at the beginning, followed by a transition to a steady state indicating depletion of the yeast's oxygen uptake resources after 40 to 60 mg/L of consumed DO. These results indicate that even minor concentrations of suspended yeast cells corresponding to approximately 50 NTU visible turbidity as occurring in slightly turbid wines would suffice to consume one saturation concentration (8 mg/L) of DO. Under industrial winemaking conditions, total oxygen consumption capacity of yeast lees is not a limiting factor to protect wine against oxidation.

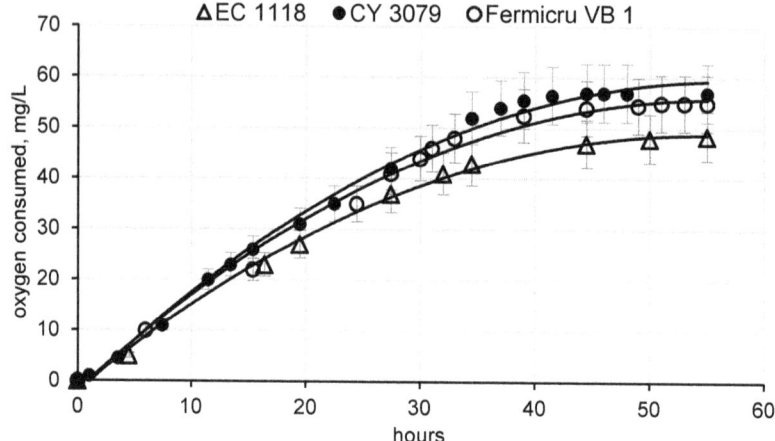

Figure 34: Total oxygen consumption capacity and consumption kinetics shown through DO consumed by suspended yeast cells in model solution of 300 NTU one month after fermentation.
Temperature = 20° C; error bars indicate the standard deviation.

However, the ability of yeast lees to consume appreciable amounts of DO should not hide the fact that they need a certain period of time for doing so. During that time, DO is also partially available for oxidation of the wine. Yeast lees and oxidizable wine components compete for DO. Hence, yeast lees can never protect wine against oxidation to 100 %, though they can act as a very effective anti-oxidant likewise sulfur dioxide. This is one of the reasons why cloudy young white wines devoid of free SO_2 can take so much time to brown.

Combined effects of lees concentration, age, and free SO_2

Real wines have variable amounts of suspended yeast lees of variable age, and different levels of free SO_2. The interactions resulting therefrom complicate the assessment of the oxygen consumption by yeast lees.

In a large-scale field trial, samples were taken at different time points from 25 unfiltered young white wines that had been fermented with different commercial selected yeast strains. The samples were split into two aliquots, one of them containing the original yeast and the other one being filtered to serve as a blank. After oxygen supply by aeration, the DO decrease in both aliquots at 20° C was plotted against time. Yeast concentration in the wines ranged from 8 to 310 NTU, initial free SO_2 from 0 to 57 mg/L, and the age of the wines from 2 to 26 weeks after alcoholic fermentation.

In most of the samples regardless of filtered or unfiltered, the plots took the form of a more or less convex curve fitting a negative exponential function. They correspond to a first-order reaction kinetics indicating the change of the OCR over time (Chapter 2.5.3). Figure 35 gives an example.

2. Typical and oxidative aging

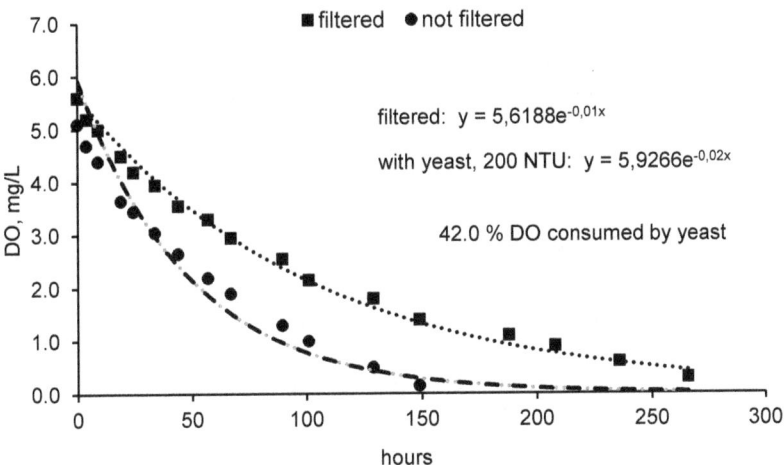

Figure 35: Exponential DO consumption in white wine (43 mg/L free SO_2) with suspended yeast at 50 NTU and after filtration, 8 weeks postfermentation.

In the unfiltered wines containing yeast lees, both DO consumption by the yeast and DO consumption due to chemical binding by intrinsic wine compounds accumulated to a total, the amount of which changes throughout the test period according to the instantaneous DO concentration. Under these conditions, only mathematical treatment (Schneider et al. 2016) of the equations of both curves provides the percentage and the absolute amount of DO consumed by yeast, with the remaining part corresponding to the DO consumed by chemical oxidation of the wine matrix.

In this field trial, DO consumed by yeast ranged from 0 to 47 %. Trends of the large impact of yeast strain, yeast concentration, free SO_2, and age could be observed and confirmed results obtained on model solutions. However, statistical significance tests failed for easily comprehensible reasons: The combination and interaction of the various enological parameters do not allow for a reliable prediction of yeast reactivity towards DO in a given wine. That is to say that it is hard to forecast how much of the DO is consumed by yeast lees and how much by chemical oxidation of the wine matrix, respectively.

DO consumption by yeast lees does not increase acetaldehyde

Acetaldehyde is the key binding partner of SO_2, and any increase of its level would require higher SO_2 additions to bind it. In the worst case, total SO_2 content can ultimately exceed legal levels. Hence, any acetaldehyde increase as a result of DO consumption by yeast lees would be of crucial importance.

Total acetaldehyde was measured after complete depletion of DO in the 25 wines referred to above. Differences in acetaldehyde concentration between the filtered and the unfiltered aliquots of each wine were not significant and did not exceed ±3 mg/L in any case. These results indicate that the consumption of up to 7.5 mg/L DO by postfermentation yeast lees of Saccharomyces cerevisiae strains does not elicit any increase of acetaldehyde content. They are in contrast to what happens during oxygenation of film-forming yeast cultures such as those used in the production of Sherry, and also in in contrast to the chemical oxidation of ethanol to acetaldehyde by the Fenton reaction (Chapters 2.2.1 and 2.5.1). Furthermore, they confirm the absence of any respiratory metabolism, thus supporting the assumption that DO is mainly used for cell lipid oxidation (Salmon et al. 2000, Fornairon-Bonnefond et al. 2003).

In conclusion, making use of the DO consumption and reducing properties of post-fermentation yeast lees does not increase acetaldehyde levels and SO_2 requirements.

Enological use of DO consumption by yeast lees

In the course of standard winery operations like racking, fining, filtration, blending etc., wines pick up variable amounts of oxygen ranging from 0.5 to 4.0 mg/L DO upon each treatment. Furthermore, an uncontrolled oxygen uptake occurs through the liquid surface when containers are not thoroughly topped or through oxygen-permeable container materials (Chapter 2.6).

In unfiltered wines, common amounts of suspended yeast lees are able to consume several saturation concentrations of oxygen at a rate of 0.5 to 1.0 mg/L DO per hour. However, the yeast lees are not able to entirely consume the DO since a part of it is concurrently bound to oxidizable wine compounds. Both reactions of DO decrease are mutually competitive. A similar competitive behavior is known from SO_2 as a reducing agent. SO_2 only consumes a portion of DO, while the remaining part undergoes irreversible reactions with intrinsic wine compounds (Chapter 2.5.1).

The faster DO is consumed by yeast lees, the less DO is available for wine oxidation. The rate yeast lees consume DO can become practically useless when free SO_2 exceeds some 20 mg/L. Therefore, the reducing effects of both SO_2 and yeast lees cannot always be used simultaneously for the purpose of protecting wine against oxidation.

Figure 36 illustrates that when a wine displays 40 mg/L free SO_2, the presence of yeast lees does not affect the DO consumption kinetics in a meaningful way as compared to the sterile filtered lot. Only when no free SO_2 is present, the yeast lees consume DO much faster.

Since DO consumption by yeast lees is strongest at low levels of free SO_2 or in its complete absence, it is a valuable enological tool during elaboration and aging of wines without added SO_2. Furthermore, it explains why barrel aging of white wines is traditionally associated with low SO_2 levels and periodical stirring of yeast lees. Wood is a gas-permeable container material allowing for an oxygen uptake to an extent (Chapter 2.6.1) that would otherwise cause premature oxidative aging in filtered white wines.

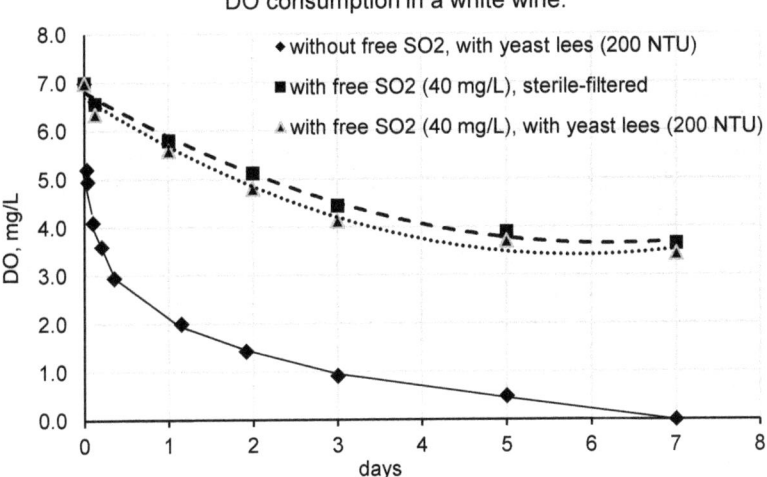

Figure 36: Effect of suspended yeast lees and free SO_2 on DO consumption in a white wine.

2.5.7. Working with yeast lees in practice

In summary, the reducing effect of postfermentation yeast lees is based on their ability to release reducing amino acids (Chapter 2.5.5) and to directly consume oxygen, which is withdrawn from wine oxidation and used for the oxidation of yeast cell compounds (Chapter 2.5.6). These properties are much more pronounced in suspended yeast cells than in settled yeast bottoms.

Moreover, when yeast lees autolyze, they release colloidal polysaccharides like mannoproteins that add beneficial texture, palate weight, and creaminess to the wine. They provide a sense of sweetness as a result of bridging the sensations among phenolic compounds, acidity and alcohol, aiding in wine harmony and integration. They also interact with volatile aroma compounds, whose concentration and volatility diminishes while the persistence of aromatic sensations increases (Voilley et al. 1990).

Autolysis is the self-destruction of yeast cells by their own enzymes. However, when yeast autolysis proceeds too far, leesy aromas reminding toasted bread, hazelnuts, and almonds will develop. Although these aromas are an intrinsic flavor characteristic of some white still and sparkling wine styles, they are usually not desired when one is trying to create a very delicate, fresh wine just highlighting the gossamer essence of the grape. At latest when they start to develop, clarification and filtration of this kind of wine becomes advisable. As long as wines are stored cool (< 15° C / 59° F), this rarely happens before the first half year post-fermentation.

Other than oxygen, yeast lees also absorb further undesirable compounds of wine. These include some ellagitannins originating from the wood of oak chips or barrels. Ellagitannins also bind with mannoproteins released from yeast cells. This feature is of outstanding importance when white wines are aged in barrels since it decreases astringency and causes a noticeable tannin softening.

The question of racking

Racking means the transfer of the wine above its solid sediments into another container. This operation does by no means imply that the transferred wine would undergo any clarification making it less turbid than it was before, though this assumption is still widely upheld. In contrast to filtration or fining, racking does not remove turbidity inducing elements.

In former times, wines were racked off several times post-fermentation. Since careful must clarification has become more widespread, this approach has changed and the number of rackings diminished. Clean yeast lees absolve the winemaker from superfluous rackings. Indeed, one way of working with yeast lees is postponing or simply skipping racking after fermentation. This approach requires some explanations.

Winemakers use to differentiate between light or secondary lees and heavy or primary lees. Heavy lees can be defined as those that settle within the first week post-fermentation, and are composed of large particles consisting of bitartrate crystals and grape solids that have not been removed by must clarification. Light lees can be defined as all those that require several weeks or months to settle more or less; they comprise essentially yeast cells.

Traditionally, there has been seen little advantage in storing wines on heavy lees. Such storage can result in off-aroma and flavors. Grape solids in no way contribute to the quality of fruity white wines. Therefore, wines have been racked off the heavy lees before storing on the fine lees has started.

In the meantime and in conjunction with technical progress towards the production of highly fruity wines, this point of view has changed. The reason for this lies in the vigorous clarification most musts are subject to. As a result, heavy lees considered detrimental to wine quality do not exist anymore in wines obtained from those musts. Their solids, be settled or suspended, consist essentially of yeast cells. Furthermore, the total of these yeast cells is considerably less, often only a mere fraction, than in wines obtained from less clarified musts since yeast reproduction is reduced in the absence of grape solids.

As a result of the presence of 'clean' yeast bottoms, the need of racking is more and more questionable. At least, its time point can be delayed when it is considered essential. The key question in that kind of decision making is the effectiveness of must clarification, evaluated as residual turbidity (Chapter 2.4.2). The less turbid the must before inoculation, the more post-fermentation racking can be delayed or abandoned.

Dispensing with traditional racking after primary fermentation means less mechanical strain with all its sensory effects on sensitive white wines (Chapter 2.6.4). However, there is one exception calling for immediate racking: When heavy amounts of lees are left undisturbed at the bottom of the aging vessel for too long, they can start to produce reduction flavor. When this is perceived as strong, time has come to rack off the lees and take further steps to deal with this kind of off-flavor (Chapter 3.3).

Delayed filtration protects against oxidative aging

Another way of working with yeast lees is postponing filtration. This approach requires specification of the conditions allowing for doing so, for how much time, and the advantages that might result therefrom.

After filtration, oxygen inevitably picked up upon treatments like acidity corrections, finings, blendings, or crystal stabilization impacts the wine at full strength. Hence, it is counterproductive to first filter the wine and realize afterwards that it requires fining for stabilization and being filtered again. Premature filtration within the first one or two months post-fermentation conflicts with the goal of producing fruity white wines. It is only justified for microbiologically unstable wines like those stored at high temperatures (> 15° C / 59° F), with residual sugar, high pH, or deleterious bacteria populations under development.

On the other hand, filtered white wines stored in stainless steel tanks already displaying oxidative aging within the first year after harvest are far from unknown. Delayed filtration helps to mitigate or prevent this kind of aroma defect.

It might be attempting to make use of the widespread availability of modern filtration equipments just to get clear wines, but polishing a young wine only for aesthetic reasons does not contribute to quality. Filtration rarely creates a rounding effect that softens the wine's edges. Moreover, compelling very cloudy white wines to pass through tight filter media might stress and cause the wine to fall apart in a way that is not always temporary.

Wines that are filtered late pass through the filter much easier, causing less pressure difference between filter inlet and outlet. Thus, they suffer less mechanical strain, turbulences in the outlet pipe and filtrate tank, oxygen uptake, and stripping out of fermentation aromatics by CO_2 escaping from the filtrate (Chapter 2.6.4). These details are often neglected. Although they do not necessarily affect a barrel aged Chardonnay, producers of the most highly rated Riesling wines in the world are well aware of the quality losses they might cause (Schneider 2005 a). It is all about gentle self-clarification vs. wearing mechanical clarification of sensitive white wines characterized by fruitiness and freshness.

The appearance of reduction flavor is no reason to panic and hasten filtration. Most wines with reduction off-flavor are treated with copper salts when no other means are available. Suspended yeast cells causing the typical turbidity of a young wine are able to absorb large amounts of copper ions. This behavior is of considerable enological interest since it allows for removing residual copper left after copper fining to a large extent (Chapter 3.3.3).

Taking into account the benefits of an adequate amount of suspended yeast lees, the question arises why they are removed by early filtration without any need in so many cases.

Delayed filtration and aging on the lees: Differences and effects

Delayed filtration does not mean storage on the lees, but differences between both are gradual and require careful consideration:

As shown previously and further developed in chapter 2.6.4, reducing superfluous treatments to an absolute minimum is an important measure to preserve quality and flavor of fruity white wines. Under commercial conditions, skipping racking, delaying filtration, and combining racking with the first filtration in one single step several months post-fermentation are useful approaches to achieve this goal, though they are not always applicable to any wine. Microbial or reduction issues can become a concern. Each wine is different, and different wines require different approaches and appropriate monitoring.

In contrast to barrel-aged wines, most fruity white wines are bottled within the first year post-fermentation. Within this timeframe and as long as no stirring takes place, prolonged contact with suspended yeast lees slightly enhances texture, palate weight, and creaminess to an extent that is compatible with the sensory features looked for in fruity white wines without masking varietal flavor by yeast-derived aromatics. It is in no way comparable with a focused aging on the lees (Köhler et al. 2007). To understand the difference and find an intermediate way of working with lees, it is fundamental to be aware of the practical handling and sensory outcomes of methodical

Aging on the lees

Aging on the lees is a means to deliberately promote yeast autolysis and sensorially impact the wine with autolysis products. For that purpose, yeast strain, the volume of yeast lees, yeast stirring and its frequency, and the duration of lees contact are the most important variables, both as practical and stylistic considerations.

Settled yeast lees are not very helpful, while periodic stirring of the lees (bâtonnage) increases the content of polysaccharides and yeast-derived amino acids. Polysaccharides, especially mannoproteins released from yeast, lower the sensory perception of astringency, sourness, fruit, and oak, while they increase the wine's body, volume, and protein stability. Amino acids can act as aroma precursors and possibly enhance wine complexity. Reducing amino acids protect the wine against oxidation to some degree (Chapter 2.5.5).

Stirring causes an oxygen uptake able to change the sensory balance between fruit, yeast, and wood. Although stirring is thought to be an oxidative process, it is debatable to what extent oxidation reactions take place since post-fermentation yeast lees and reducing amino acids substantially contribute to oxygen consumption, thus protecting wine against oxidation (Chapter 2.5.5 and 2.5.6). It can be assumed that the redox regime is highly variable between wines and individual barrels, depending on the oxygen uptake controlled by the intensity and frequency of stirring, and the oxygen consumption by variable amounts of yeast lees.

This picture is further complicated by rackings and SO_2 additions. Early additions tend to keep the amount of components that bind to subsequent SO_2 additions at a higher level. Acetaldehyde is a typical example of these compounds. On the other hand, early SO_2 additions also hamper the onset of malolactic fermentation frequently sought for that kind of wine. It is quite possible to run aging on the lees over more than half a year without any SO_2 and without any signs of oxidation, relying only on the reducing capacity of suspended yeast lees. At the latest, SO_2 should be added upon aerobic racking or when the wine starts browning from the surface downwards. This usually happens when stirring is ceased to prepare the wine for filtration, blending, or bottling. Browning indicates the beginning of irreversible oxidation reactions and should be prevented in any kind of table wine.

In the broadest sense, aging on the lees in barrels favors oxygen uptake. During aging, wines have a higher oxidation-reduction potential in barrels than in tanks. This is the main reason why wines stored in large volume tanks are often not stored on lees for a longer period, though this is not totally impossible. However, one must be aware that such storage can cause the production of "reductive" or sulfur-derived off-flavors (Chapter 3.1). Stirring can help to mitigate the occurrence of reduction flavor if it allows for an oxygen uptake high enough to raise the oxidation-reduction potential.

Generally, stirring frequency depends on the time span suspended yeast needs to settle. The faster it settles, the more often it should be stirred in order to prevent oxidation of the topmost liquid layer. Thus, stirring frequency varies between once per day until once per month. Instead of stirring with a mixer, pumping around from the bottom to the top can also be used.

The settling rate strongly depends on the individual wine and its oxidation-reduction regime. Figure 37 illustrates how both SO_2 (60 mg/L) additions and oxygen uptake under conditions of aerial oxygenation increase the yeast lees settling rate and accelerate clarification. It explains why yeast lees settling is much slower in stainless steel tanks than in wooden barrels allowing for oxygen uptake.

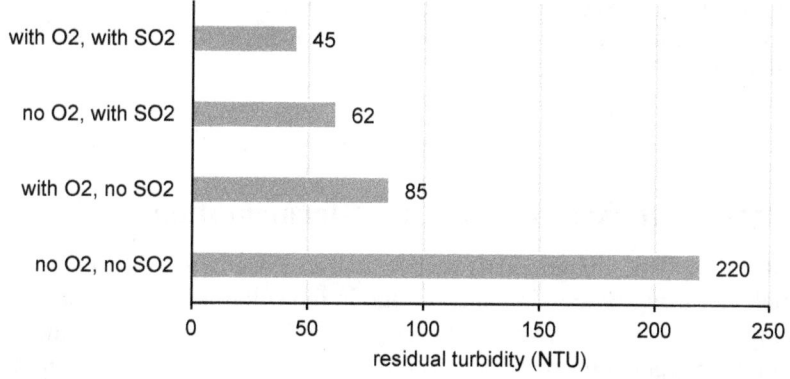

Figure 37: Impact of oxygen uptake and SO_2 (60 mg/L) additions on settling of post-fermentation yeast lees, measured as residual turbidity (NTU) after 24 hours in standardized containers.

Clearly, there cannot be any fixed rules for stirring frequency. Sensory goals play a further role in scheduling stirrings.

Also depending on stylistic goals, the duration of lees contact is highly variable. Half a year is a very general rule when it is carried out in barrels in the traditional way. During that time, it is often associated with the occurrence of malolactic fermentation.

Addition of an exogenous ß-glucanase enzyme considerably enhances yeast autolysis, the release of mannoproteins, and the sensory consequences resulting therefrom. However, it cannot perform miracles when there are not enough yeast lees available or when fermentation was run with a yeast strain which releases low levels of polysaccharides. Differences between yeast strains are considerable, and some commercial strains are marketed specifically for the purpose of enhancing polysaccharide levels during fermentation and subsequent lees contact.

Proper aging on the lees requires carefully clarified must to obtain "neat" yeast with the least grape solids as possible. On the other hand, thoroughly clarified musts lower yeast proliferation during fermentation and the amount of yeast biomass available for systematic aging on the lees. To overcome this conflicting behavior, some winemakers add supplementary yeast bottoms obtained from other containers. When there is a deficiency of yeast biomass, sensory drawbacks of oxygen uptake during stirring easily outweigh the benefits of yeast autolysis. Clearly, stirring in the case of shortage of yeast does not make any sense.

In the meantime, commercial proprietary products based on lysated (broken) yeasts or yeast-derived mannoproteins are available. Their addition can complement and partially replace traditional aging on the less, but must not do so. Addition of purified mannoproteins can enhance weight and volume on the palate in some wines immediately. However, the sensory impact of these preparations is highly variable. Hence, they should not be used without previous bench trials.

Furthermore, selected dry yeast strains have become commercially available and recommended for the sole purpose of adding them post-fermentation. Results have been rather modest since standard additions of these products do not provide enough biomass for proper aging on the lees. In contrast, they cause aroma losses via absorption by these dry yeasts that have never become saturated with aroma during fermentation. Such aroma losses are extremely harmful for fruity white wines. Going through a fermentation cycle seems indispensable to resolve both kinds of problems.

2.6. Impact of oxygen uptake post-fermentation

Introduction: This chapter deals with the various sources of oxygen a wine can pick up during processing and storage in the cellar and the variable oxygen ingress through bottle closures. Methods of best cellar practice aiming at limiting oxygen uptake under commercial winemaking conditions including bottling are discussed in detail. They lead to the enological principle of gentle wine treatment. Data on the sensory effects of precisely measured amounts of oxygen and the impact of bottle closures are presented.

2.6.1. Oxygen uptake through container materials

Inadvertent oxygen pickup, oxidation and oxidative aging of white wines are serious concerns in the wine industry. Otherwise, the use of antioxidants would not be such an important topic. But the problem can also be seen from a different perspective, trying to tackle the causes instead of relying only on the effectiveness of antioxidants. This approach would make lots of things easier. It is more a technical than a chemical issue.

In enology, none of the natural or added antioxidants used – SO_2, ascorbic acid, sulfur containing amino acids and peptides, and post-fermentation yeast lees – is able to totally protect wine against oxidation when oxygen uptake occurs. In particular after filtration, when there is no more oxygen consumption by yeast lees, white wines are extremely sensitive to oxidation. Hence, it is obvious that there is a need to limit or exclude oxygen uptake by the wines. Technical measures taken for that purpose are current practice in the brewing industry but much less common in winemaking. Therefore, it is vital to get an idea of the potential sources for oxygen uptake, the amounts of oxygen picked up from each of these sources, and the sensory changes caused by them.

Wineries use storage containers made of different materials displaying variable gas permeability rates. On one hand, they allow to meet the different oxygen requirements of white and red wines when they are used consciously. Red wines benefit from some oxygen uptake, and vessels suitable for that purpose are not necessarily appropriate for the storage of fruity white wines. On the other hand, however, storage containers are often used quite carelessly without taking into account their real oxygen permeability.

Wooden containers of the size of a standard barrel provide the wine with considerable amounts of 10 to 30 mg/L oxygen per year (Vivas 1999). Materials such as stainless steel and glass are the other extreme and absolutely impermeable to oxygen. This qualifies them for long-term storage under exclusion of oxygen on condition that the containers are really topped to the brim. The various plastic materials display large differences with regard to oxygen diffusion. The diverse polyethylenes (PE) are highly permeable to atmospheric oxygen with permeability rates depending on the PE specification, while the oxygen diffusion rate through the so-called barrier polymers is lower by a factor of approximately 1,000.

However, the oxygen diffusion rate through the container material is not the only criterion. It is also crucial to consider the wine volume that absorbs the oxygen provided by a given container wall surface area. This leads to the surface-area-to-volume ratio. It increases with decreasing volume. Storing wine in a small container with a high oxygen permeability easily causes over-oxidation.

2.6.2. Oxygen uptake through wine surface and headspace inertization

Uncontrolled oxygen uptake frequently takes place through the wine surface, which can be undisturbed or agitated. An undisturbed, static surface occurs when wine is stored in containers that are not completely topped. Upon stirring of such a wine, the surface becomes agitated. Agitated surfaces can also be observed when wine flows through hoses, filters, and pumps containing air pockets because they have not been carefully vented.

Gases dissolve in liquids to a certain degree. When a liquid becomes saturated, no more gas can be dissolved in the liquid. At normal pressure, wine can absorb up to 8 mg/L O_2 at 20° C (68° F) and even 11 mg/L O_2 at 10° C (50° F). Table 7 shows how oxygen solubility increases when temperature decreases. These data represent the saturation concentration of dissolved oxygen (DO) at different temperatures. They give the average since they slightly depend on alcohol content.

Table 7: Solubility of oxygen in wine as affected by temperature.

Temperature	Solubility, mg/L O_2
0° C / 32° F	14.5
10° C / 50° F	11
20° C / 68° F	8
30° C / 86° F	7

Although a cold wine can hold more oxygen in solution than a warm one, this general rule does not provide any information about the speed at which wine takes up oxygen from the atmosphere. Only rough estimates of this essential value are available in the standard literature. The reason is that oxygen dissolved in wine is gradually consumed by chemical binding. After its disappearance, it cannot be measured any more.

The importance of liquid movement

For precise measurement of the oxygen uptake through the surface, a wine-like model solution (13 % ethanol, pH 3.5 with tartaric acid, 2 mg/L Cu^{2+}) was sparged with nitrogen to remove all DO, supplemented with 200 mg/L ascorbic acid, and stored at different temperatures in open wide-necked bottles of 1,000 mL with a defined surface area. Under these conditions, oxygen picked up is consumed by ascorbic acid in a stoichiometric relationship (Chapter 2.5.3). The decrease of ascorbic acid over time allows to directly calculate the amount of oxygen (in mg $O_2/m^2/h$) through the liquid surface. Figure 38 reports some of the results.

The undisturbed liquid stored at 20° C picks up 20.2 mg $O_2/m^2/h$ or 484.8 mg O_2/m^2/day. This value increases 16-fold when the same solution at 20° C undergoes constant stirring to generate an agitated surface. The latter value depends on the intensity of stirring and surface movement, obviously.

The impact of temperature is also crucial. The better oxygen solubility at low temperatures might lead to the careless assumption that oxygen diffusion from the atmosphere into the liquid also increases under these conditions. However, direct comparison of the diffusion rates of the undisturbed aliquots at 7 and 20° C proves the opposite (Figure 38): Decreasing temperature from 20° C to 7° C lowers the diffusion rate 2.8 times from 20.2 to 7.2 mg $O_2/m^2/h$. This result might appear surprising at the first glance but has a simple physical explanation.

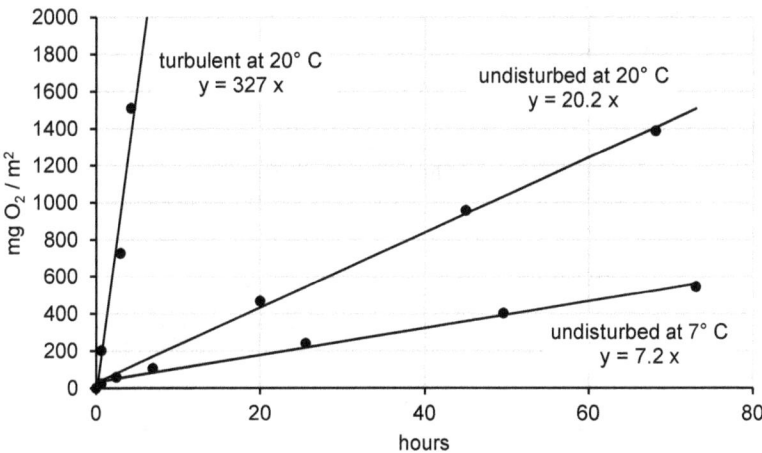

Figure 38: Diffusion of atmospheric oxygen through the surface of a wine-like model solution at normal pressure. Effect of surface agitation and temperature.

The uptake of a gas by a liquid proceeds in two steps (Vivas 1999):

1. Passive diffusion of the gas from the atmosphere through the liquid surface into the upper boundary layer of the liquid. This process is almost spontaneous and only active over a small distance. At a given pressure, its rate depends on temperature, the surface tension of the liquid, and the saturation degree of the gas in the liquid. It is described by Henry's law. Dissolved carbon dioxide lowers the oxygen diffusion rate through the liquid surface (Devatine et al. 2011).

2. Transportation of the gas into the liquid's interior. This process follows Fick's law. Its driving force is the continuous renewal of the boundary layer. This can be caused by thermal convection or by mechanically induced turbulence. In both cases, low-oxygen liquid is transported from below towards the surface, where is absorbs more oxygen. This step becomes more and more rate-determining with increasing distance from the surface.

As a basic principle, the diffusion of a gas within the liquid decreases when the temperature decreases. Although the solubility of oxygen in wine is higher in the cold, low temperature slows down its distribution in the undisturbed wine and, consequently, all downstream reactions of oxidation. However, when coldness and turbulences interact one with another, oxygen uptake reaches extreme values. This is in particular the case when bitartrate crystal stabilization is carried out using the contact process without previously purging the container with an inert gas.

Conversely, oxygen uptake in the cold is reduced when the liquid surface is undisturbed as oxygen diffusion within the liquid slows down. In this way, the effect of a higher oxygen solubility at low temperature is cancelled out. Hence, wines not completely topped and stored in the cold oxidize more slowly, though oxygen solubility is higher.

Time has come to rethink traditional thoughts telling that wine stored in the cold picks up more oxygen and oxidizes faster. It is a kind of doctrine only valid when wine is kept moving in a manner allowing to evenly disperse dissolved oxygen in the whole liquid volume.

The data set used to obtain figure 38 allowed to calculate the oxygen transfer coefficients through the liquid surface in mg $O_2/m^2/h$. For a better overview, some of them are summarized in table 8.

Table 8: Oxygen transfer coefficients (in mg $O_2/m^2/h$) through the liquid surface of wine-like model solution.

~ : depending on the agitation intensity

	20° C / 68° F	7 °C / 45° F
stagnant surface	20.2	7.2
agitated surface	~ 327	~ 950

Surface area is more important than headspace volume

In practical cellar work, it is vital to be aware of high and barely controllable amounts of oxygen a wine can pick up from the headspace when the container is not completely topped and its headspace not purged with inert gas. This oxygen uptake is a diffusion process controlled by temperature and the wine surface area. The headspace height or the missing wine volume are not decisive.

Expressed as mg/L O_2, wine stored or processed under an air-containing headspace in small containers has to withstand a many times higher oxygen load than wine in large containers. In the same line of thinking, tall slender tanks are preferred to short, wide tanks because taller tanks have less exposed wine surface area.

The considerations above take us to the notion of what is called "specific surface area", expressed in cm^2/L or $inch^2/gal$. Its meaning becomes understandable by a simple example: A surface area of 1 m^2 above 1,000 liters imparts ten times more oxygen (in mg/L) to the wine than above 10,000 liters.

Headspace blanketing with inert gases

In the hope of minimizing wine-air contact, headspace inertization with an inert gas attempts to drive out headspace oxygen and maintain an inert gas layer above the wine surface. In order to prevent the growth of aerobic microorganisms on the wine surface, the oxygen concentration must be reduced from 20.9 % O_2 found in air to 0.5 % or less at the wine surface. A similar level is required to prevent wine oxidation. This is not an easy task. Even when one succeeds in doing so, evaporation of volatile wine aromatics is not prevented; the reasons are explained in chapter 2.6.4.

2. Typical and oxidative aging

Effective blanketing requires more than just shooting some inert gas into the headspace until it feels well. High turbulent gas flow rates create a churning effect causing the gas to mix with the air. Thus most of the gas is lost to the outside of the vessel, while the purity of the gas inside becomes diluted. Therefore, effective headspace inertization requires an appreciable amount of inert gas corresponding to 3-5 times the headspace volume, depending on the gas and the way of working. There are some practical details to optimize the process:

The flow rate of the gas as it exits the tubing determines the make-up of the final headspace gas. The maximum flow rate while maintaining a low-turbulent flow depends on the diameter of the gas delivery tubing. It should be a laminar one comparable to a gentle bleed. Generally it is provided by the lowest setting the regulator can be set and still flow. However, the regulator might be adjusted to create a flow that will be as high as one can go while still maintaining a soft low-pressure bleed.

In order to check whether oxygen has been driven out, the flame of a lighter can be used. It must be held just below the rim of the container. If it stays lit, there is still much headspace oxygen left. When it eventually goes out, oxygen has been removed to a large extent, but not necessarily to the desired 0.5 % level. Oxygen meters for assessing atmospheric oxygen are available and useful.

For headspace inertization, several gases are used: Nitrogen, argon, carbon dioxide (CO_2), or mixtures of them.

CO_2 is heavier than air and nitrogen. Thus, it can temporarily form a layer on the wine surface, but it tends to dissolve in the wine creating a vacuum that sucks air from the outside, pulls the lids inward, or makes the tank contract in the worst case. Thus its protection is short-lived to a couple of weeks or requires continuous replenishment.

Nitrogen has a very low solubility (14 mg/L) in wine and a slightly higher density than air. Thus, it disperses easily in the headspace but does not act as a protective layer on the wine surface.

Argon is also quite insoluble. Similar to CO_2, it is denser than air and therefore often supposed to stratify as a protective layer above the liquid. However, that stratification does not occur on the long term because molecular diffusion of gases breaks down any stratifying effect.

None of all these solutions is able to create an absolutely inert headspace quickly and easily. A perfect inertization can only be obtained when the container is pre-evacuated. For this purpose, it is first completely filled up with water before the water is pressed out with inert gas so that the entire volume is filled with that gas. Taking into account all shortcomings and difficulties of headspace inertization, it is generally accepted that there is no better substitute for the protection from oxygen than storage in completely full containers.

Historical solutions

In historical times, a layer of olive oil or paraffin was sometimes dispensed on top of the wine stored in half full vessels. This was considered to prevent wine from oxygen pickup, but created other problems. The use of more recent antimicrobial agents such as allyl isothiocyanate disks floating on the wine is prohibited in most countries, does not impede oxygen pickup, and would impart unpleasant off-odors. Thus, the development of tanks with a lid floating on the wine was a logical step.

Variable capacity tanks

Stainless-steel variable capacity tanks with a floating lid are generally constructed to store smaller wine volumes of up to 2,000 liters (529 gallons). Their lid is simply inserted into the tank and then allowed to float on the wine surface. The lid is equipped with an inflatable bladder around its circumference. This bladder is inflated using a PE tube connected to a hand air pump, thus supposed to create an airtight seal on the inner circumference of the tank to protect the wine from air. A pressure gauge indicates the bladder pressure, which can be adjusted at any time to maintain the seal tight. The pump has a release valve to deflate the bladder when the lid is to be removed.

This apparently perfect storage solution for small wineries would be used much more if the bladders and air pumps had a more solid design. Indeed, the commonly employed vinyl bladders and the air pump gasket can have trouble forming a good seal, which can allow oxygen to flow into the wine. Therefore, in practice these tanks are not useful for extended storage. More robust materials would be welcome to allow them to fulfill their potential.

2.6.3. Oxygen uptake upon wine treatments

Apart from container headspace, wines also pick up oxygen when they are treated in the winery by racking, fining, filtration etc. because there are variable amounts of air in the machinery and pipes. Table 9 shows the large range of oxygen uptake measured during different treatments and storage conditions (Vidal et al. 2001, 2003, 2004 a, Schneider 2005 d, Valade et al. 2006, 2007, Castellari et al. 2004, Calderón et al. 2014).

The large variance of oxygen uptake for each treatment rules out the specification of more precise data or average values. It can be explained by two phenomena:

1. Oxygen pickup strongly depends on carbon dioxide dissolved in the wine when the treatment takes place (Devatine et al. 2011). When a container is filled from the top, more oxygen is picked up when the wine has already lost the largest portion of its carbon dioxide resulting from fermentation. In contrast, less oxygen is picked up by young wines because they release CO_2 upon entering the receiving tank, which purges its headspace and removes a part of the oxygen it contains. When young wines with much CO_2 are transferred by filling the container from the bottom, there is almost no measurable oxygen uptake because oxygen is largely stripped by CO_2 or rapidly consumed by post-fermentation yeast lees.

2. The wine volume treated plays a crucial role: The dissolution of oxygen occurs preferentially at the beginning of a transfer or treatment when the pipes are still

filled with air, and at the end of the process when the pipes are drained. At these stages, highest oxygen uptake takes places when a wine is filtered due to a larger liquid surface, turbulent wine flow, and filter pressure. In this way, small wine volumes are exposed to a higher oxygen uptake, expressed in mg/L O_2, than large wine volumes. Small-scale winery operations are clearly disadvantaged.

Table 9: Oxygen uptake caused by various wine treatments in small and medium-sized wineries.

Treatment	O_2 uptake, mg/L
transfer / racking into top-filled tanks	2 - 4
transfer / racking into bottom-filled tanks	0.1 - 1
transfer with loose suction hose	5 - 7
centrifugation	0.3 - 2
kieselguhr filtration	0.1 - 2
pad filtration	0.1 - 1
cross-flow filtration	0.2 – 1.5
membrane filtration	0.1 – 1.5
electrodialysis	0.3 – 1.3
stirring for fining or blending	1 - 2
cold stabilization using the contact process	1 - 3
transportation in containers not topped	3 - 5
storage in large wooden casks, per year	5 - 10
storage in barrels (225 L), per year	20 - 40
bottling	0.5 – 0.0

Oxygen pickup upon one single treatment might be negligible. However, the question is to what total amount the oxygen pickup at many consecutive treatments will add up. In this context, practical experience, the cellar staff's craftsmanship, and guidelines for good cellar practice are essential.

Monitoring process-related oxygen uptake

Measuring the process-related oxygen uptake at each treatment can provide valuable information on technical weak spots in a winery, provided that it is executed on a stage-by-stage basis. Stage-by-stage control means that values are determined at consecutive places within a process chain, for example in the starting container, at the filter inlet, at the filter outlet, and in the receiving tank. This kind of measurement has to be performed on the spot in the winery and in a timely manner. Modern portable DO-meters with a precision of better than 0.1 mg/L O_2 provide valuable support for inline-measurements. Sampling, transportation, and storage of samples frequently distort DO readings. Storing or shipping samples to an external lab is even less suitable as DO decreases over time by chemical binding.

The time factor plays a crucial role when process-related oxygen pickup is assessed. Two different situations can arise in practice:

- The dissolution of oxygen in the wine proceeds faster than its binding by wine compounds. Thus, an increase of DO is observed.
- The dissolution of oxygen in the wine proceeds at a slower rate than its binding. In this case, no DO can be measured.

The DO concentration measured by analytical means corresponds to the instantaneous net difference between oxygen uptake and oxygen binding.

The measurement of DO at a given moment provides useful information about how carefully a wine has been handled, and about potential improvements. However, it does not provide any historic information on the total amount of oxygen the wine has picked up.

2.6.4. Importance and measures of gentle white wine treatment

Oxygen uptake during cellar operations is associated with CO_2 and aroma losses by evaporation. Both processes occur simultaneously and require a liquid surface under air-containing headspace. Their sensory effects add up. Their extent depends to a large degree on the cellar staff's craftsmanship. Their understanding requires a closer look at details of the real-world way of working in a winery.

Aromatics are perceived by smell because their relatively low boiling point and high vapor pressure make them volatile. This volatility enables them to make their way up to the olfactory epithelium located in the nose. It also causes aroma losses by volatilization as soon as there is a surface. For that reason, oxygen uptake through the liquid surface is always associated with a decrease of volatile aromatics. The banal escaping of these molecules into the atmosphere adds to aroma losses by chemical oxidation. In some wineries these effects can be dramatic and explain why some wines are bottled when they are already exhausted.

Inert blanketing does not prevent aroma losses through evaporation

When there is a headspace, an inert gas blanket to drive off the oxygen can prevent oxidation when it is properly done, but it can never impede aroma losses by evaporation into the headspace. Evaporation is a mass transfer from the liquid phase into the gas phase. It requires a concentration gradient of the evaporating compound, which tends to balance out. Concentration balance is reached when the partial pressure of the compound in the gas phase corresponds to its partial pressure in the liquid phase. Only when that state of equilibrium is achieved, aroma evaporation comes to a halt.

From the above it is understandable that a headspace filled with inert gas can take up as much aroma as a headspace filled with air. The sole fact that oxygen is driven out and air replaced by an inert gas does not have any impact on the evaporation of volatile wine compounds through the liquid surface into an atmosphere whatever it is composed of. Therefore, headspace blanketing is not a full-fledged substitute for perfect topping of white wines.

Aroma losses resulting from evaporation inevitably go along with CO_2 losses. To the extent one succeeds in preserving some fermentation-derived CO_2 until bottling, this is also a substantial contribution to preserving white wine aroma and overall quality. In many fruity white wines low levels (< 1.5 g/L) of CO_2 are accepted and sometimes even expected as long as there is no distinct perlage. Early and heavy CO_2 losses post-fermentation are a clear indication of too weary a wine processing. It is useful to identify the point in the production sequence where this happens.

When working on very small wine volumes at is frequently happens in micro-vinification trials, adding glass beads to make up the missing volume can be a good solution.

Operating pumps

Since each pumping cycle is considered one too many, the use of gravity flow grows in importance worldwide when new wineries are designed. However, moving wine by gravity flow is not automatically a perfect solution. When the downward pipes are not filled with wine across their entire cross section, a turbulent flow with air pockets will be produced. This results in dissolution of oxygen and evaporation of aroma compounds. Moving wine by slightly pressurizing the headspace of the source tank with nitrogen can be a good alternative to strenuous pumping operations. This approach is in some way comparable to what happens in the well-known Cornelius kegs at much higher headspace gas pressure.

In a more realistic scenario, moving wines by pumping and choosing the appropriate pump is one of the main concerns in any winery. Pumps should be self-priming, have deadhead capabilities, and generate enough pressure to force the wine through a filter. In the particular context of sensitive white wines, they should avoid aeration and minimize agitation and shearing. Centrifugal pumps do not fulfill these requirements. Due to the absence of self-priming capabilities, they must be placed below the level of the tank outlet. When there is an air pocket in the sucking pipe, they tend to homogenize air in wine.

Screw pumps, also referred to as progressive cavity or mohno pumps, minimize shearing and agitation. They are also highly tolerant to sediments and solids. Flexible rubber impeller pumps strike a good balance of feature for most wineries, though they can be a little physically rough on the wine when they are run at full speed. Therefore, many of them feature a bypass or are driven by variable frequency drivers to adjust the flow rate. Both screw pumps and rubber impeller pumps cannot run dry. When they do so, rubber shavings can penetrate the wine flow and impact wine flavor. Furthermore, they continue working against a closed valve. To ensure the safety of the pump and pressure hose, they frequently feature dry-run and deadhead capabilities able to automatically stop them.

Diaphragm and eccentric disc pumps are further options that provide shear-sensitivity and gentle wine transfer, but at least as important as the kind of pump is what happens in the hoses on the suction and the pressure side. Chapter 2.6.2 deals with the quality losses related to an agitated wine surface. Such a surface associated with a turbulent liquid flow can also occur in a transfer line. When this happens, there is even more turbulence produced in the receiving tank. As a consequence, degassing of CO_2 and volatile aroma compounds occur altogether with oxygen uptake. Laminar flow in the transfer lines prevents or minimizes turbulences.

The flow is laminar when the wine moves slowly in parallel layers without disruption of the layers, transverse flow, or mixing. To keep a flow laminar, flow velocity must not exceed 1.5 meter (~5 feet) per second, corresponding to the speed of a walker. This can only be achieved when the pump delivery rate does not exceed 3,000 L/h (~ 800 gal/h) for 25 mm (~ 1 in), 7,000 L/h (~ 1,850 gal/h) for 40 mm (~1.6 in), and 11,000 L/h (~ 2,900 gal/h) for 50 mm (~ 2.0 in) nominal tube diameter, respectively. The narrowest point of the whole tubing system is decisive.

Since the default tubing diameter can hardly be ever changed in a winery, variable frequency drivers allowing adjustable pump capacity are of great benefit.

Operating filters

The question of the gentlest filtration technique – kieselguhr, pad, membrane, or cross-flow filtration – is reevaluated at periodic intervals of little more than every ten years. When this happens, one or another technique is regularly discredited. However, systematic investigations on quality losses caused by filtration of white wine are scarce and barely applicable to all wineries. Nevertheless, personal experience made under specific operating conditions is frequently generalized. On the basis of case studies, it is easy to understand that the way a technical device is used by humans exerts often more sensory impact on the wine than the device itself. Some examples may help to clarify the reasons.

Centrifuges are reputed to strain white wines. During operation they are filled to the rim and hermetically closed. No gas exchange with the surrounding atmosphere takes place. Shearing forces acting upon the wine are less than in any filter. The wine withstands the centrifugal forces without any problems as it behaves in the centrifuge just as in a full bottle rotating around its own axis. The problem starts when the internal pressure of some 5 bar exerted on the wine in the centrifuge is relieved to normal pressure at the outlet. There appears the well-known effect one can observe upon pressure relief of any liquid containing volatile compounds, for example when a bottle of sparkling wine is opened: Spontaneous degassing occurs, even more increased by the wine turbulence.

The same phenomenon occurs at the outlet of a filter. It can in no way be solved by restricting the filter outlet flow or applying counter pressure in the outlet pipe. At some point pressure relief must take place, at the latest when the wine flows into the receiving tank. At this point, degassing occurs, facilitated by the wine surface that is more or less agitated. Figure 39 illustrates this effect.

Figure 39: Pressure curve in the course of wine transfer; pressure release and CO_2 losses.

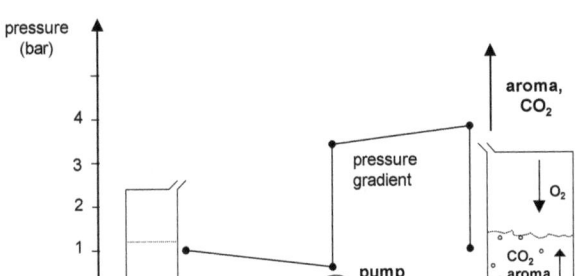

Considerable splashing and bubbling occur at the beginning of any wine transfer. Much agitation is produced on the wine surface where turbulence and bubbles can magnify the exposed wine surface area several times. Under these conditions, the surface area of the receiving tank is crucial for aroma and CO_2 losses as well as oxygen uptake. Tall slender tanks are preferred to wide tanks because taller tanks have much less specific surface area (Chapter 2.6.2) causing mass exchange. Further improvement can be achieved dispensing with filtering in the high pressure range.

When the outlet hose of a filter or any other tubing runs downwards, a suction is produced creating a negative pressure as a function of the height difference. If the pipe is not filled with wine over its entire cross section, there will be an agitated wine surface in the pipe causing aroma losses, which will be reinforced furthermore by the negative pressure above the wine. The aroma compounds accumulate in the pipe's gas phase and are stripped out altogether with CO_2 in the receiving tank where considerable splashing and bubbling occur each time a turbulent wine flows into it. In the worst case, the effect is comparable with sample degassing before measuring TA in the lab. Each time a pipe is not completely filled with wine and contains gas pockets, venting is urgent to create a laminar flow without gas bubbles.

When a filter starts fouling, throughput becomes reduced and the wine surface in the filtrate tank, related to a given wine volume, remains agitated for more time. There will probably be no quality losses on red or barrel aged white wines. However, when a sensitive white wine is split into two fractions during filtration, a first one provided by fast filtration and a second one resulting from slow filtration at high pressure difference, quality losses are likely to be observed in the second fraction pressed though the filter. As a general rule, it can be assumed that the lower the filter pressure difference and the higher the filter throughput, the less will be aroma losses and oxygen uptake during filtration. Moreover, low temperatures help to reduce aroma evaporation through an agitated wine surface.

In summary, good cellar craftsmanship suggests the following guidelines for

Gentle white wine handling in practice

- **Complete topping:** Careful and complete topping of all containers until they spill over is recommended. The quality of topping depends on the remaining wine surface area (in m^2 or square feet) in contact with the headspace atmosphere. It does not depend on the missing wine volume or the height of the headspace. The mass exchange is exclusively controlled by the wine surface area. An increase of cellar temperature can cause some overflow, but many winemakers prefer losing a bucket of wine to any ullage.

- **Early topping:** It is useful to top containers already by the end of primary fermentation when foaming over is not any more possible, and thus remove any liquid surface. In most cases this is possible when two thirds of the initial sugar have disappeared. A small bleed pipe or a pressure release is helpful. Under these conditions, yeasts continue producing fruity fermentation-derived aroma compounds, which cannot escape any more through the liquid surface. The outcome is an aroma accumulation. Although oxygen supply from the headspace or by other means is reputed to improve yeast fermentation activity, it is not any more effective in the very final stage of fermentation.

- **Considering blending:** When wines are racked, it is useful to consider in advance which wine can be used to completely fill the container. When distinct varietal wines are to be produced, addition of a few percent of another variety can be less detrimental to varietal style than leaving a headspace. However, not all varieties are compatible.

- **Headspace inertization:** It is the next best solution when no adequate wine is available for complete topping. When doing so, it is vital to take into account that one needs an inert gas volume corresponding to three to five times the headspace volume to reduce headspace oxygen satisfactorily. CO_2 is less useful for that purpose as it dissolves in the wine within two to three weeks, thus creating a negative pressure sucking in atmospheric oxygen. Both nitrogen and argon are suitable for headspace blanketing. See chapter 2.6.2 for details.

- **Appropriate storage vessels:** Tall slender tanks are preferable to wide tanks as they allow for less wine surface area in proportion to the wine volume.

- **Short tubings:** When wine is racked, blended, filtered etc., the length of hoses and hose couplings should be limited to what is necessary.

- **Hose connections:** Loose suction hose connections must be avoided; they would suck atmospheric oxygen into the wine flow.

- **Pump seals:** Leaky pump seals must be secured; they would act just as loose hose connections.

- **Purging hoses with water:** Purging transfer lines with an inert gas to displace oxygen has limited effects. Before transfers and filtrations, it is appropriate and easy to first pump water throughout the whole system in order to remove any air pockets in tubings and filter, draining the water on the floor. When the system is vented, connect the inlet hose to the wine without sucking air. Taste on the fly using a three-way valve fixed to the receiving tank. When the switch from waste to the receiving tank is ready to be made, switch the valve to connect to the receiving tank. When finished, repeat the operation pushing through with water to displace the wine in the system. Simultaneous cleaning is a pleasant side effect.

- **Purging hoses with inert gas**: Purging treatment circuits with an inert gas is possible and frequently done, particularly at the end of the process to displace the wine in the hose into the receiving tank. However, filter pads are easily damaged by high gas pressure. Running water through the whole system for venting is faster and easier provided one is able to distinguish wine from water when tasting on the fly.

- **Adjusting pump capacity:** Pump output should be adjusted to tubing diameters in order to avoid turbulences in hoses and in the receiving tank. Wine flow should be laminar.

- **Tubing diameter for kieselguhr filtration:** When wines are filtered with kieselguhr, it is particularly important to adjust filter performance and tube diameter one to another. Kieselguhr filters require a flow rate of at least 1,500 L/h (~400 gal/h) per 1 m^2 (~10.8 sq. ft.). Otherwise the kieselguhr would be unevenly distributed on the filter plates, causing a breakthrough of solids or early fouling of the filter. Thus, hose diameter becomes the limiting factor for laminar flow in gentle filtration when high-performance filters are used. Frequently, hoses are too small in diameter or filters too large. A filter area of 5 m^2 (~54 sq. ft.) requires a minimum flow rate of 7,500 L/h (~2,000 gal/h), which in turn require 40 mm (~1.6 in) diameter in the feeding hose and outlet hose. On the other hand, when nominal hose diameter is only some 30 mm (~1.2 in), filter area should be limited to roughly 3.5 m^2 (~38 sq. ft.). Both components must be carefully adjusted for gentle filtration.

- **Filling tanks from the bottom:** For racking, filtration, or any other transfer, it is good practice to fill the receiving tanks from the bottom. Splashing wine through air causes an enormous and agitated wine surface enhancing oxygen uptake and aroma evaporation. Splashing a white wine conceived to be fruity only once in its history is the best way to transform it into a simple wine for easy drinking.

- **Purging the receiving tank:** When white wines are filtered or subject to further transfers after filtration, it is useful to purge the receiving vessel, especially when working on small wine volumes. Purging is best accomplished by introducing the inert gas at the tank's bottom port. This ensures a more complete displacement of oxygen out of the top.

- **Mixing using appropriate mixers:** The use of compressed air, inert gas, or pumping over should be avoided for mixing wine. Too much aroma would be stripped or oxygen dissolved. Tank mounted propeller mixers screwed onto a tank fitting, e.g. a shut-off valve near the bottom of the tank, provide the most efficient and gentle mixing with minimized oxygen uptake. Variable speed mixers provide additional benefits as they allow for adjusting stirring intensity to match the wine volume.

- **Preserving some dissolved CO_2:** Oxygen pickup during wine treatments correlates with losses of CO_2 and volatile aroma compounds by evaporation. The longer natural CO_2 is preserved, the less burdensome cellar operations are for the wine. Moreover, CO_2 provides a tactile sensation, magnifies the sense of acidity, enhances the fruit character, and enlivens the palate. Thus, it is becoming something of a stylistic tool in most white wine production today. Some wineries add CO_2 before or during bottling, but sensory and legal limits must be respected. CO_2 is perceptible in wine at about 0.4 g/L. Fruity white wines with lower levels taste flat, while levels greater than 1.2 g/L can cause undesired bubble formation.

- **Controlling residual CO_2 prior to bottling:** In view of the key role of residual CO_2 in the sensory perception of fruit-driven white wines, the use and monitoring of CO_2 in the wine prior to bottling by Carbodoseur™ or similar devices is beneficial in adjusting concentrations up or down according to style. These simple gadgets involve a glass-tube measuring the amount of CO_2 out-gassed from a fixed wine volume by shaking. Comparing results with a calibration curve provides the concentration of CO_2 in mg/L or g/L of wine.

- **Avoiding sparging:** Nitrogen sparging is sometimes used to strip DO or volatile sulfur compounds causing reduction flavor. The procedure may be effective but it is even more effective in stripping positive aroma compounds from fruity white wines. Treating reductive notes with copper salts is more specific (Chapter 3.3.3).

- **Making use of low storage temperatures:** Low cellar temperatures reduce evaporation of CO_2 and aromatics. However, they require carefully avoiding of turbulences and air pockets in pipes to keep oxygen uptake under control. Remind that low temperature increases the solubility of oxygen, while the liquid movement facilitates its fast distribution in the whole liquid volume, thus allowing more oxygen uptake (Chapter 2.6.2).

- **Reconsidering cold stabilization:** It is a very strenuous intervention on sensitive white wines, especially when it is used in conjunction with additional filtration steps, crystal seeding, and stirring. Apart from oxygen uptake and aroma losses during the process, the removal of unstable potassium bitartrate causes noticeable losses of volume on the palate due to potassium loss. As an alternative, the addition of metatartaric acid for short-term bitartrate stabilization up to one and a half years or carboxymethylcellulose (CMC) for long-term stabilization preserves quality.

- **Minimizing wine movements:** Each white wine movement is one treatment too much. Hence, it is vital to limit such movements as much as possible. This approach leads to the enological concept of minimal treatment (Schneider 2005 a). It critically reviews traditional treatment steps, scrutinizing for example to what extent traditional racking is still necessary under conditions of drastic must clarification (Chapter 2.4.2). When wine does not display reduction flavor, it can often be combined with coarse filtration, thus dispensing with one wine movement. In wines considered microbiologically stable, the concept of minimal treatment gives preference to self-clarification through sedimentation over early forced clarification by filtration. After thorough must clarification, the solids of young white wines devoid of malolactic fermentation consist of more than 98 % of yeast cells (Schneider et al. 2016).

Under real-world conditions, a number of the above recommendations cannot be taken into account because of operational constraints. However, when all of them are neglected, it will be a challenging journey to produce a serious white wine able to withstand premature aging. When only a few of them are respected, new ways to improve white wine quality will present themselves.

Minimal treatment by doing nothing

Bad fruit, inadequate grape and must processing, and the neglect of microbial concerns are the primary reasons for quality deficiencies that can be mitigated by cellar repair strategies, albeit not totally rectified. Anyone who needs too many wine treatments after fermentation makes mistakes during harvest time and is far away from creating great wines. Since treatments use to have unwanted side effects to a greater or lesser extent, they always impose a burden on sensitive wines intended to be fruity. Therefore, movement of wine should be limited as much as possible. The optimal way of white wine handling is achieved when finings and comparable treatments become superfluous post-fermentation. Above a certain quality standard, winemaking proceeds necessarily in a near-natural manner almost compatible with the demands on organic products.

Great white wines with long shelf life require the best fruit, delicate grape processing, and stringent implementation of juice clarification. Post-fermentation cellar technology must be used cautiously if one intends to make individual wines full of character standing out from the crowd. These wines are the result of controlled idleness, whereby emphasis in on 'controlled'. Controlling comprises a close sensory monitoring and making use of analytical tests whenever doubts arise. At best, after post-fermentation topping and SO_2 addition, human interventions in the natural development of wine only take place depending on the needs of the individual wine. Then the principle of minimal treatment is fulfilled.

Pushed to the extreme, this approach has given birth to many great white wines, which have been moved only once between the end of fermentation and bottling. A fundamental prerequisite for such an approach is the willingness to question familiar habits and query cherished routines deemed indispensable. Above all, it requires logical thinking and sound knowledge in natural sciences.

In any case, evidence-based or hypothetical quality losses caused by interventions such as filtration do not justify a retreat into myths. In an attempt to contrast crafted wines with so-called industrial ones, some winemakers try to rely on fining for wine clarification. The use of such finings goes back several centuries. Indeed, they might be a rather fascinating operation to witness in romantic old wine cellars.

Some of them actually contribute to clarification of red wines, where they accelerate the settling of mucous or solid grape residues as they do in musts (Chapter 2.4.2). However, contemporary white wines mostly originating from carefully clarified juices no longer contain such residues but only yeast cells causing turbidity (Chapters 2.5.6 and 2.5.7). Yeasts are not able to chemically interact with any fining agents. Hence, any attempt to clarify these wines by fining must fail. Different white winemaking conditions and a growing body of scientific knowledge justify a rationale that is different from conventional wisdom employed decades ago.

2.6.5. Sensory assessment of oxygen uptake in filtered wines

When wine picks up oxygen, two consecutive processes take place:

1. The transfer of oxygen from the atmosphere into the liquid and its dissolution therein. This is a purely physical process. At normal pressure and 20° C, wine can dissolve up to 8 mg/L O_2, which is the oxygen saturation point. The oxygen dissolved as a gas (DO) can be measured by analytical means. It does not have any taste or odor properties. Hence, there are not yet any sensory consequences.

2. The gradual chemical bonding of DO on oxidizable wine compounds. This reaction causes sensory changes. Bonding consumes oxygen so that it cannot be measured any more, at least not in a direct way.

The chemical bonding of DO roughly follows first-order kinetics. This means that its consumption rate is proportional to its instantaneous concentration. High DO levels decrease faster than low DO levels. This behavior can be expressed as a negative exponential function for most wines (Chapter 2.5.1). Figure 40 gives examples for two white wines.

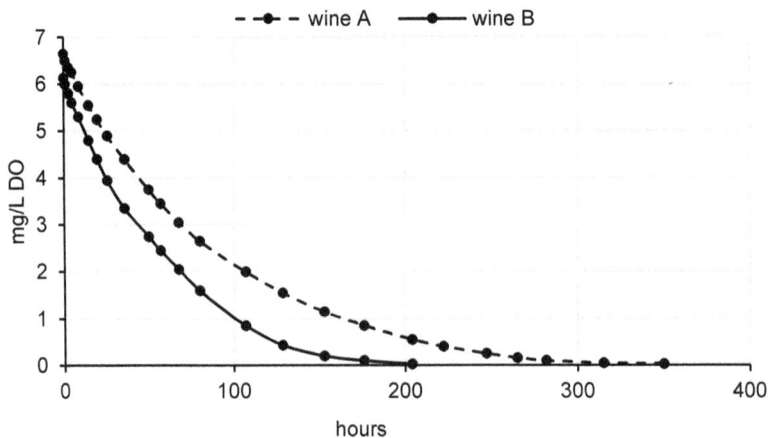

Figure 40: DO consumption in two different sterile-filtered, unoaked white wines at 20° C.
No ascorbic acid, initial free SO_2 = 40 mg/L.

2. Typical and oxidative aging

DO consumption rates are remarkably different between wines and difficult to predict. They depend on wine composition and temperature. The strong effect of temperature is shown in Figure 41. DO consumption increases exponentially with temperature. The extent of oxidation, however, is not controlled by temperature but dependent on the amount of oxygen picked up.

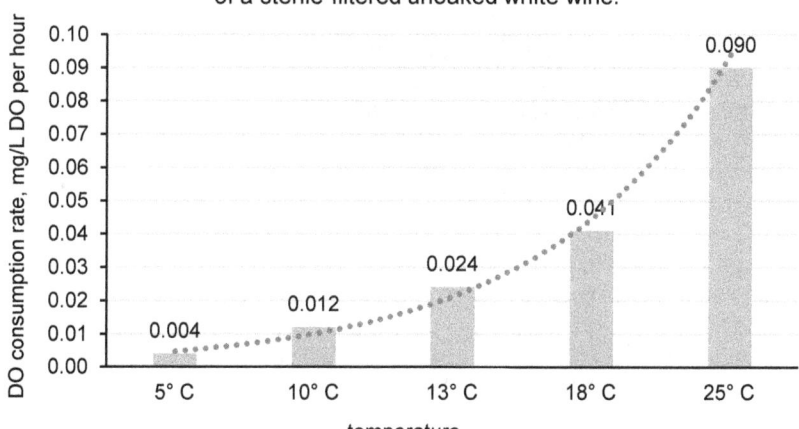

Figure 41: Effect of temperature on the DO consumption rate of a sterile-filtered unoaked white wine.

Oxygen requires response time. Or: What happens in the tasting glass?

In summary, wines need variable time spans to bind the dissolved oxygen they contain. Starting at a high concentration level, DO decreases relatively fast at the beginning and reacts more slowly when it reaches low concentrations. Since the DO consumption curves approach the zero value asymptotically, low DO concentrations can require several weeks until they completely disappear. This behavior explains why full sensory effects of oxygen pickup can only be observed after a time delay of up to several weeks or months. What this means in concrete terms is better explained by a practical example:

After a wine is poured into a glass, it is frequently swirled in a circular motion without being spilt. One of the reasons of this action is to aerate the wine. Aeration is deemed to 'open' the bouquet of the wine or, at least, to alter or improve it. Indeed, it does, but the question is how much time this process requires.

The measurements described in chapter 2.6.2 (Table 8) demonstrate that wine picks up approximately 20 mg O_2 per hour and m^2 (~11 sq. ft.) when its surface is stagnant. After some conversions, one obtains an oxygen pickup of 5 mg/L O_2 within 15 minutes for an average tasting glass filled with 50 mL wine displaying a typical 50 cm^2 surface area. If the wine is swirled in the glass, it becomes almost oxygen saturated in even less time.

On the other hand, figures 35, 36 and 40 clearly show that a typical wine cannot bind more than 0.5 to 1.0 mg/L DO per day. As a result, the wine in the aforementioned glass will need several days to consume the DO it contains. Only after that there will be sensory changes on the palate owing to oxidation and polymerization of phenolic compounds (Chapter 2.2.2). In white wines, phenols are present in a concentration range of some 200 mg/L, which require their reaction with a considerable amount of 2 to 5 mg/L DO to alter their gustatory properties if such a change occurs at all. Sensory effects owing to CO_2 losses are not considered in this context.

Under realistic wine tasting conditions, the observation period after wine aeration extends over a few hours at best. During that period, wine consumes only a minor fraction of 0.1 to 1.0 mg/L of the DO it contains. This amount suffices to cause significant oxidation reactions with aromatic compounds and modify their olfactory expression. They can also suffice to make disappear evident or subliminal hints of reduction flavor caused by volatile sulfur compounds (Chapter 3.2). The decisive point is that odor-active aroma compounds are present in a very low concentration range quantified in µg/L, which is about four orders of magnitude less than the concentration of phenols binding oxygen. Accordingly, short-term aeration of any kind of wine is quite able to modify aroma as perceived by smell, but there will be no sensorially perceptible aging effects on the palate within the short time span of a couple of hours apart from CO_2 losses.

How much oxygen does a fruity white wine tolerate without quality losses?

While there are extensive data on oxygen pickup under commercial winery conditions (Table 9), there is much less knowledge about the medium and long term impact of defined amounts of oxygen on the aroma profile of fruity white wines. Sensory studies of this kind are complicated by the variable oxygen consumption of post-fermentation yeast cells (Chapter 2.5.6) and by the rapid aroma improvement upon DO consumption when wines display subliminal 'reducing notes'.

In an early investigation (Schneider 2003) on this subject, 50,000 L of Riesling wine were completely topped, supplied with 40 mg/L free SO_2, and filtered immediately after primary fermentation. Subsequent storage over three months took place under absolutely anaerobic conditions in a hermetically sealed stainless steel vessel. Then portions of the wine were sterile-filtered directly into bottles. Filter, tubings, and bottles had been previously evacuated by completely filling them with water subsequently pressed out with nitrogen (Chapter 2.6.2), thus ruling out any post-fermentation oxygen pickup common in commercial winery conditions. A portion of the bottles was immediately sealed with tin-Saran lined screw caps and without any oxygen in the bottle headspace (Chapters 2.6.6 and 3.4.2), while another portion was previously supplied with 6 mg/L O_2 into the bottles.

After five months of bottle storage, sensory evaluation yielded higher intensities of fruity aroma attributes in the aliquot treated with 6 mg/L O_2 upon bottling. This effect was reversed when additional oxygen was taken up in bottles closed with natural corks. These results corroborate anecdotal evidence that a very low oxygen uptake after removal of oxygen-consuming yeast lees by filtration (Chapter 2.5.6) can promote the development of fruity aroma attributes. This effect can be partially

2. Typical and oxidative aging

explained by increasing levels of ß-damascenone after limited oxygen uptake. ß-damascenone is a grape-derived cyclic monoterpene ketone that reinforces the olfactory intensity of fruity aroma attributes (Ugliano et. al 2015).

A further trial on Riesling (Morozova 2013) demonstrated a significant decrease of fruity aroma attributes three months after bottling with 11.5 mg/L O_2 picked up from the air-containing headspace.

Under comparable experimental conditions (Schneider 2015 a), six unoaked white wines with 27-46 mg/L free SO_2 obtained from various cultivars were supplied with 0, 10, and 20 mg/L O_2 through varying air-containing headspace. After two months of bottle storage under screw caps and complete consumption of headspace and dissolved oxygen, the intensity of "oxidative aging by smell" was rated. Figure 42 reports the results.

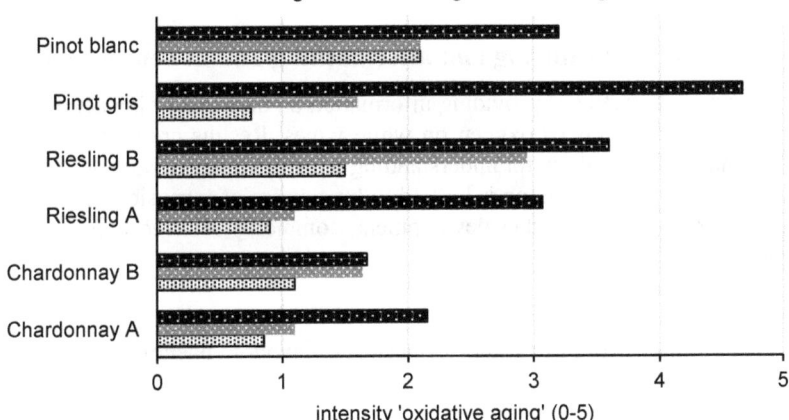

Figure 42: Intensity ratings (0-5) of oxidative aging perceived by smell as affected by oxygen uptake post filtration.

Depending on the individual wine, 10 or 20 mg/L O_2 were necessary to obtain a significant increase of oxidative aging without olfactory bias caused by the appearance of free acetaldehyde. Other authors reported strong losses of fruity varietal aroma after consumption of only 2.5 mg/L O_2 (Morozova and Schmidt 2011).

The available knowledge can be summarized as follows:

- Absolute exclusion of oxygen from the end of primary fermentation through stabilization, storage, and bottling until consumption generates white wines with diminished varietal aroma when this aroma is defined as fruity-floral. Therefore, complete protection against oxygen uptake does not make sense in most cases, particularly when wine still contains suspended yeast lees (Müller-Späth 1977, 1990, Müller-Späth et al. 1977, 1978, Pfeifer 2000, Schneider et al. 2016).

- The amount of oxygen beneficial to the intensity of fruity-floral varietal aroma does not exceed approximately 5 mg/L O_2 picked up after filtration. In commercial wineries and under conditions of gentle or minimal white wine treatment (Chapter 2.6.4), this amount is almost always picked up until bottling.
- Amounts of oxygen exceeding this limit are detrimental to quality of filtered fruity white wines. Free SO_2 and ascorbic acid are not able to rectify the quality losses they cause (Chapter 2.5.1 and 2.5.3).
- The sensory impact of a given amount of oxygen picked up at a given point of time depends on the composition and prehistory of the wine.
- For that reason, control, quantitative compilation, and limitation of oxygen uptake are of primary importance for preserving quality of fruity white wines.
- From this perspective, it is desirable that the wine industry attaches the same importance to DO control as it does to controlling free SO_2. The brewing industry sets an example by showing how rigorous DO control can work.

2.6.6. Oxygen uptake during and after bottling and its sensory impact

There are only a few studies providing information on the sensory impact of accurately measured amounts of oxygen on white wines. Results are outlined in the previous chapter. They allow for understanding the importance of post-bottling oxygen uptake. As soon as a wine is bottled, a long series of intrinsic and extrinsic variables decide upon its further development, commonly referred to as aging or maturation:

- the history of the wine,

- its content of free SO_2, further antioxidants, and flavonoid phenols,

- the amount of DO at bottling,

- the volume and gas composition of the bottle headspace,

- the bottle closure and its oxygen permeability,

- the storage temperature.

The impact of oxygen is so far-reaching that a white wine exposed to different oxygen levels during and after bottling can result in completely different wines. This is particularly true for wines undergoing a long bottle storage of more than one year.

Post-bottling SO_2 losses are a rough measure to estimate the amount of oxygen a wine is exposed to in the bottle since they weakly correlate with oxygen consumption (Chapter 2.5.1). However, it is impossible to directly measure the oxygen ingress in wine-filled bottles as the oxygen incorporated and entering the bottles disappears through reaction with wine constituents.

2. Typical and oxidative aging

Relatively low oxygen pickup in the filling process

In many small and medium-sized wineries wines are still bottled without any protection by inert gas. Under these conditions, wines take up 0.5 to 3.0 mg/L O_2 in the filler bowl and when they flow from the bowl into the bottle (Table 9). The length of the fill spouts and the type and force of the liquid jet play a role. Oxygen uptake tends to be only 0.5 to 1.0 mg/L O_2 when modern bottling lines are used and when the bottling process runs smoothly without interruptions. As a comparison of what is technically and commercially possible, it is worth mentioning that average bottling lines in the beer industry operate with 0.2 to 0.4 mg/L O_2 pickup (Crochiere 2007).

Thus, oxygen pickup when the wine goes through bottling must not be overestimated when a modern filler is used. Technical options are discussed below. These options are interrelated with headspace oxygen, which must be distinguished from oxygen pickup at filling.

Much more oxygen than that due to bottling can be taken up during the preceding steps preparing wine for bottling by blending, mixing, filtration, etc. (Chapter 2.6.3). The oxygen pickup occurring in these upstream processes is frequently underestimated and its consequence erroneously attributed to the bottling system. When this happens, investments in a new filling system will not resolve problems with premature oxidative aging.

It is vital to understand that DO measurements on the freshly bottled wine represent the combination of the DO at the base of the filler, i.e. before bottling, and the oxygen pickup during the filling process. Subtracting DO at the base of the filler from DO in the bottle gives the DO pickup occurring as the wine goes through filling. Since most fillers run up to 50 % deviation in DO pickup, it is useful to run DO measurements on several bottles and calculate the mean.

At the end, all these measurements inform us about the oxygen that is in the liquid. Any oxygen left in the headspace is left uncounted. This is another critical issue.

Potentially high oxygen uptake from the bottle headspace

After sealing the bottle, there is a variable headspace. It may contain plain air causing more oxygen uptake, or it may have undergone a headspace treatment using vacuum or inert gas to remove its oxygen to a greater or lesser extent. The oxygen trapped in the headspace has a higher partial pressure than the oxygen dissolved in the wine. Hence, it gradually dissolves in the wine and reacts with wine constituents. In that way, the headspace acts as an oxygen reserve (Vidal and Moutounet 2006).

Some simple calculations are useful to illustrate the importance of headspace oxygen: In standard bottles, 1 cm (0.39 in) headspace height equates to 2.9 mL gas volume. When this gas consists of air, it includes 0.86 mg O_2. Calculation basis is the fact that air contains 20.8 % oxygen, which has a density of 1.43 mg/mL. When this amount of oxygen is trapped in a standard bottle of 750 mL, the wine will be exposed to 0.86 : 0.75 = 1.15 mg/L O_2.

When wines are sealed with screw caps, a typical headspace height is 5 cm (1.97 in). In the absence of any headspace treatment with inert gas, it contains approximately 15 mL of air, which in turn contains 3.12 mL or 4.48 mg O_2. Depending on the bottle size, this amount of headspace oxygen acts upon the wine to a variable extent, for example with 4.48 mg/L O_2 for a bottle with 1,000 mL filling volume or with 5.97 mg/L O_2 for a standard bottle with 750 mL filling volume.

For an identical headspace volume, the relative impact of headspace oxygen on the total amount of oxygen (TPO) decreases to the extent that the bottle size increases. This means that expressed as mg/L O_2, oxygen exposure is higher in smaller bottles than in larger ones.

Total pack oxygen

Total pack oxygen (TPO) is a calculated value that combines the dissolved and the headspace oxygen, i.e., the mass of the oxygen in the liquid plus the oxygen in the headspace divided by the volume of liquid in the bottle. It is the total amount of oxygen that is trapped in the bottle at the moment of filling and available to react with the wine volume in that bottle. These relationships and their calculation basis are illustrated by an example given in Table 10.

Table 10: Calculation of total pack oxygen (TPO) in bottles with different nominal volume and identical headspace (15 mL) containing air and 3 mg/L O_2 dissolved (DO) in the wine.				
nominal volume of the bottle (mL)	375	750	1000	1500
oxygen (mg O_2) in the headspace containing 15 mL air	4.48	4.48	4.48	4.48
+ amount of oxygen dissolved in the wine volume having 3 mg/L DO	1.13	2.25	3.00	4.50
= total amount (mg O_2) of oxygen in the bottle (TPO)	5.61	6.73	7.48	8.98
total amount of oxygen converted into mg/L O_2	14.96	8.97	7.48	5.99

For clarification, the TPO data given in table 10 represent high but quite realistic values. A TPO below 3 mg/L can be considered optimum in the wine industry. However, if not managed well, the TPO at bottling can be more significant than the oxygen ingress through the bottle closure over the life of the wine.

Under typical winery conditions, more than 50 % of the oxygen in the bottle is present in the headspace. However, current industry practice focusses upon measuring only DO, thus overlooking the majority of oxygen that is getting into the wine at bottling. In contrast, TPO also takes into account headspace oxygen and is the only calculation that gives a complete picture of the oxygen in the bottled wine. It directly correlates with post-bottling SO$_2$ losses, while DO does not do so. Therefore, TPO is a key parameter in the beverage industry.

Based on an average SO$_2$ loss of 3 mg/L per 1 mg/L DO (Chapter 2.5.1), bottling a wine with 25 mg/L free SO$_2$ and 10 mg/L TPO is likely to result in an oxidized wine without any free SO$_2$ within a few weeks. A high TPO level can cause a shelf life reduction equivalent to many years of oxygen ingress through a well-performing bottle closure.

TPO can be measured by several techniques:

- Oxyluminescence is the reference method, which has only been possible for a few years. It is based on non-destructive oxygen measurements through the bottle wall without opening the bottle. It uses a fiber optic oxygen meter coupled with luminescent oxygen sensor spots glued onto the inner wall of the bottles before they are filled. One sensor spot is positioned at a center position of the inner wall allowing to be in contact with the liquid to provide data for DO. Another sensor spot is positioned in the headspace to provide data for headspace oxygen. Both dissolved and headspace oxygen are added up to TPO.

- Using standard technologies to measure DO such as polarographic probes, also called DO meters, along with appropriate bottle shaking protocols. When bottles are properly shaken during five minutes, the O$_2$ in the liquid and in the headspace will equilibrate to the same partial pressure, also referred to as percent concentration. Shaking and DO measurements must be performed at the same temperature in as short a time frame as possible. Once the oxygen is at equilibrium, DO is measured in the liquid. In a further step, this value is used to calculate TPO, taking into account wine volume, headspace volume or fill height, and temperature (Vidal et al. 2004 b). Calculations of TPO are facilitated by the use of appropriate formula available on online spreadsheets or provided by the DO meter supplier.

Measuring DO without shaking only determines the oxygen content of the liquid, that is to say true DO. The headspace oxygen of a bottle is the TPO minus DO:

$$\text{headspace oxygen} = \text{TPO} - \text{unshaken DO}$$

Similarly to DO, TPO is a snapshot measure immediately after the bottle has been closed. Two to three months after bottling, almost all oxygen trapped in the bottle will be consumed by the wine. From this point forward closure permeability becomes the important factor controlling post-bottling oxygen ingress into the wine.

Minimizing headspace oxygen

When bottles are sealed with screw caps, the headspace is many times larger than when natural, technical, or synthetic corks are used for sealing. Under these conditions, the relatively low oxygen permeability of many screw caps (Chapter 3.3.2) is not fully benefited from when there is too much oxygen in the headspace. Therefore, oxygen management in the headspace is of paramount importance.

Possible procedures for lowering headspace oxygen include

- flushing bottles with nitrogen before filling,
- flushing the bottle headspace with nitrogen after filling,
- injection of liquid nitrogen (nitrogen dropping) before or/and after filling,
- addition of solid CO_2 (dry ice) before or/and after filling,
- vacuum evacuation of bottles before or/and after filling.

For using corks as bottle seals, corking machines are available that supply a vacuum in the headspace prior to cork insertion. When using such a vacuum corker, it is extremely critical to optimize the vacuum level and headspace volume in order to minimize oxygen ingress during cork recovery, i.e. cork expansion after insertion.

A better headspace inertization can be achieved by flushing the headspace with a small amount of CO_2 or nitrogen, or by a controlled dosage of liquid nitrogen into the wine after filling. Best results are obtained when bottles are inertized before filling using liquid or gaseous nitrogen. This applies for all kinds of bottle closures. The use of CO_2 for that purpose would strongly increase CO_2 levels in still wines.

Regardless of whether applying a vacuum, inert gas flushing, liquid nitrogen dosing, or a combination of these procedures, the time and distance from the filler to the closing machine must be kept as short as possible. Moreover, if there is an interruption in the bottling process, bottles already purged or dosed with liquid nitrogen are left on the conveyor, allowing the inert gas to escape and oxygen to enter the bottle. These bottles are then sealed with additional oxygen. Therefore, if a bottling line stoppage has occurred, it is advisable to remove all bottles in question and dose them again.

In conclusion, there are sophisticated filling and closing devices on the market, which allow for an effective lowering of oxygen pickup during the filling process as well as from the bottle headspace.

Post-bottling decline of SO_2 and DO

Oxygen dissolved in the wine gradually decreases when no further oxygen is picked up. Thus, when the bottle closure does not allow for any oxygen permeation, both headspace and dissolved oxygen are completely consumed after a certain spell of time, and the bottle will be free of oxygen. From this point forward, SO_2-losses caused by oxidation come to an end. Screw caps fitted with tin-Saran layer, properly fixed, constitute an almost absolute barrier against atmospheric oxygen (Vidal et al. 2011).

Figure 43 gives an example of the oxygen decrease in a commercial standard white wine stored at 20° C after filling in bottles of 750 mL with air-containing headspace and sealed with screw caps using tin-Saran liner. In this wine, the initial DO was almost entirely (< 0.1 mg/L DO) consumed after 10 days, while the headspace oxygen took 45 days to disappear. After expiration of that time, all oxygen contained in the bottle had reached the zero value and SO_2-losses came to a standstill.

The behavior shown in figure 43 will change when closures with higher oxygen permeability supply the wine with high amounts of oxygen throughout its bottle storage. In this case, neither dissolved nor headspace oxygen drop to zero because atmospheric oxygen is taken up approximately as fast as it is consumed by the wine (Waterhouse et al. 2016). As a result, TPO stabilizes at an equilibrium value, which is the result of oxygen ingress through the closure and oxygen consumption by the wine.

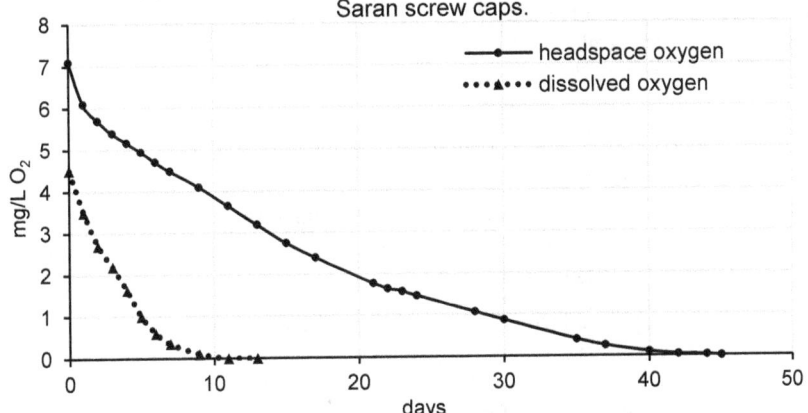

Figure 43: Decrease of headspace oxygen and dissolved oxygen after bottling of a standard white wine sealed with tin-Saran screw caps.

The headspace functions as an oxygen reserve for the wine as long as the wine consumes oxygen. The partial pressure of oxygen in the gas phase is always higher than that of the liquid phase. Thus, there is a diffusion of oxygen from the headspace into the wine, which is driven by the pressure gradient. This purely physical process is limited by the small liquid surface area. Finally, the oxygen exchange kinetics between headspace and liquid in the bottle outweigh the kinetics of oxygen penetration from the external atmosphere through the closure into the bottle. During the first weeks and months post-bottling, the oxygen trapped in the headspace has a stronger impact on the decrease of TPO and SO_2 than the oxygen diffusion through the bottle closure (Vidal and Moutounet 2006).

Within a certain range of variation, more than 95 % of the oxygen trapped in the bottle is consumed after two to three months of bottle storage. Accordingly, highest losses of SO_2 ranging from 20 to 25 mg/L are commonly observed during the first three to six months post-bottling and regardless of the bottle closure as long as the bottle headspace is not inertized (Scrimgeour and Wilkes 2014, Jung and Schüssler 2016). Only after the oxygen trapped in the bottle at filling has been entirely consumed by chemical bonding, the SO_2 decrease will be considerably slowed down, depending from now on exclusively on the oxygen permeation through the bottle closure.

The time required to deplete TPO is approximately in line with the duration of what is frequently perceived as bottle sickness if it is possible to perceive it at all. It is a tempting speculation to associate bottle sickness with chemical reactions related to oxygen consumption when TPO is depleted.

Variable oxygen uptake through bottle closures: OTR

Different closure types display variable permeability regarding the diffusion of atmospheric oxygen. This permeability is measured as "oxygen transmission rate" or "OTR" and expressed as mg O_2/year or µg O_2/day.

Most screw caps and technical corks are at the lower end of the variation range with OTR data ranging from 0.0 to 1.5 mg O_2/year. Synthetic corks have been found at the upper end for a long time, with OTR values between 3 and >10 mg O_2/year (Karbowiak et al. 2010, Diéval et al. 2011). OTR data of screw caps as affected by the liner type they are fitted with are presented in detail in chapter 3.4.2.

In more recent times, there has been a continuous development towards synthetic corks and screw caps with defined OTR rates tailored to match particular types of wine. Concurrently, the initial tendency of synthetic corks towards high OTR rates has started to diminish. As an example, one manufacturer of synthetic corks has added a premium version with OTR = 9.3 mg O_2/year to his standard version with OTR = 17.5 mg O_2/year (Diéval et al. 2011).

Natural corks occupy an intermediate position between screw caps/technical stoppers and synthetic stoppers, with OTR values reported to range from 1 to 4.8 mg O_2/year during the first twelve months post-bottling (Lopes et al 2006, 2007, Silva et al. 2011, Oliveira et al. 2013). From the specific viewpoint of oxygen sensitivity of fruit-driven white wines, they perform more poorly than tightly sealing screw caps. Figure 44 gives an example of the sensory differences resulting therefrom during bottle storage of unoaked white wines obtained from two cultivars. However, taking into account the considerable variation of OTR between individual corks, there can be exceptions from this general trend.

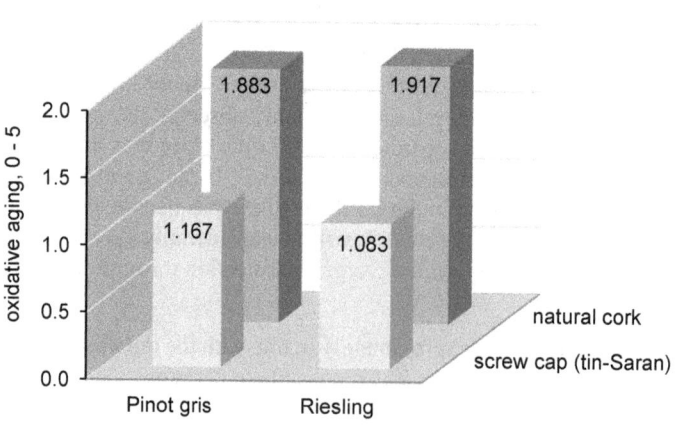

Figure 44: Impact of bottle closure (natural cork vs. screw cap) on oxidative aging as perceived by smell in two white wines after 10 months of bottle storage.

2. Typical and oxidative aging

Oxygen uptake through the cork is understood as a diffusion of atmospheric oxygen through the cork tissue and/or along the interface between cork and glass (Casey 1989, Lopes et al. 2007, Oliveira et al. 2013). However, throughout the first year of bottle storage, natural corks provide additional amounts of oxygen, which is initially entrapped in the cork lenticels and is gradually forced into the bottle after the cork is compressed upon insertion (Waters et al. 1996).

Cork is a natural product. Therefore, its properties are subject to substantial fluctuations. This also applies to OTR. There are large differences in OTR between cork lots as well as between individual corks within a lot (Caloghiris et al. 1997, Oliveira et al. 2013). Examples of cork-to-cork differences within the same lot are given in figure 45. Thus, outliers upwards can cause problems with over-oxidation of individual bottles of the same wine (Waters and Williams 1997). This phenomenon is called 'random oxidation'. Even without distinctive oxidation defects, bottle-to-bottle differences in wine development and aging can thus be explained. They can be further exacerbated by sporadic malfunctions of the sealing process.

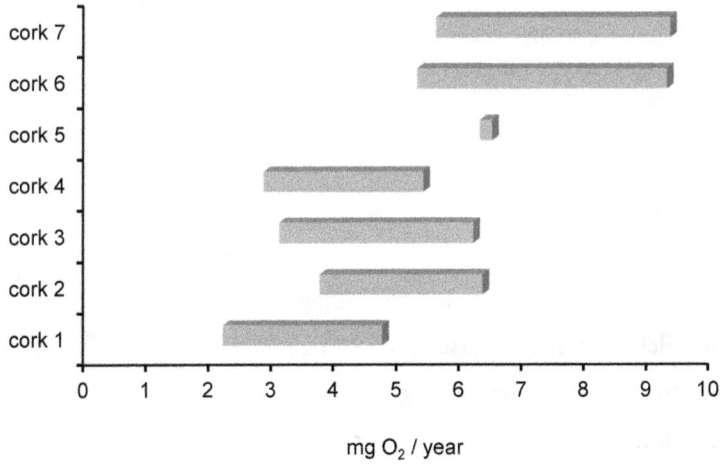

Figure 45: Oxygen ingress (mg O_2/year) through natural corks from different lots during upright storage at 10-15° C. Bars represent variation between three individual corks per lot.

As a summary, it can be concluded that natural corks can provide highly variable amounts of oxygen to the wine. These amounts are significantly larger during the first year post-bottling than in subsequent years due to oxygen release from the cork tissue. This phenomenon is not related to headspace oxygen. As a consequence, post-bottling SO_2-losses caused by natural corks are particularly high during the first year after bottling. They vary from one lot to another and even between corks within the same lot. This behavior complicates tailoring SO_2 additions pre-bottling. Figure 46 depicts an example.

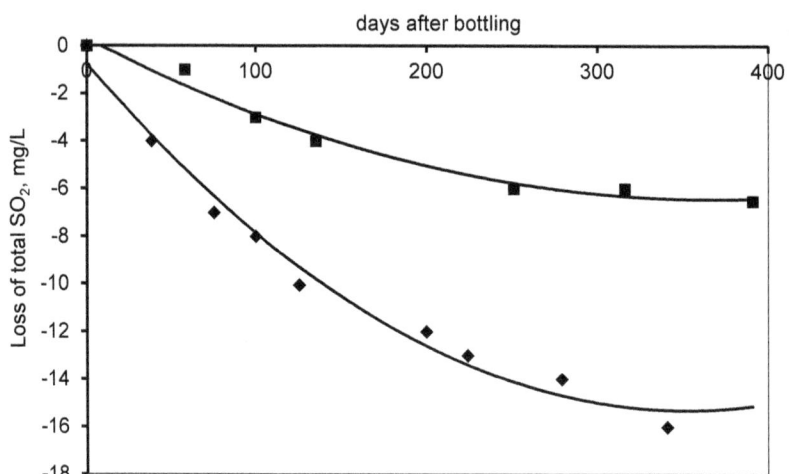

Figure 46: Decrease of total SO_2 by oxidation during bottle storage of a white wine sealed with two different natural corks.

Due to their highly variable OTR, natural corks are not suitable as a reference in bottle closure trials. In contrast, screw caps fitted with tin-Saran liner are preferred as a standard in most studies upon closure behavior. They are considered to seal hermetically against oxygen ingress (Vidal et al. 2011), to not contain any oxygen trapped in the sealing material, and to display no differences between individual specimens. However, from a more practical perspective, the high uniformity of screw caps is more important than the oxygen barrier they provide.

Oxygen exposure determines the level to which free SO_2 is to be adjusted

Ultimately, the oxygen uptake of bottled wine results from five potential sources:

- the oxygen dissolved in the wine before bottling,

- the oxygen picked up in the course of the filling process,

- the oxygen trapped in the bottle headspace,

- the oxygen diffusing through the bottle closure,

- the oxygen trapped in the cork tissue when natural corks are used.

Thus, the total pack oxygen (TPO) calculated according to table 10 is increased by the oxygen provided by the bottle closure. This leads to an extended notion of TPO. Figure 47 illustrates how extended TPO is made up.

Figure 47: Oxygen in bottled wine: The extended notion of "total pack oxygen" (TPO)

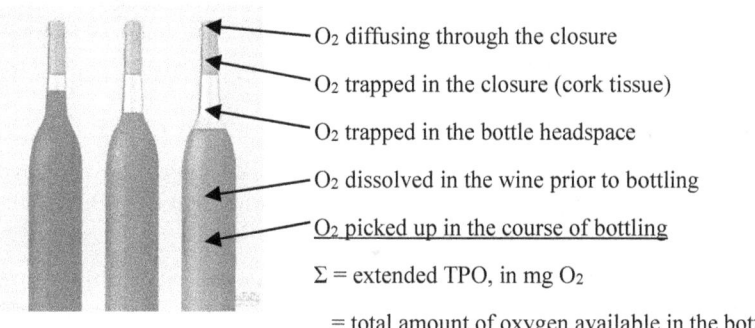

- O_2 diffusing through the closure
- O_2 trapped in the closure (cork tissue)
- O_2 trapped in the bottle headspace
- O_2 dissolved in the wine prior to bottling
- O_2 picked up in the course of bottling

Σ = extended TPO, in mg O_2

= total amount of oxygen available in the bottle

When SO_2 is adjusted prior to bottling, all five sources of oxygen must be taken into account. Their sum value determines losses of SO_2 post-bottling. Hence, the specific knowledge of the free SO_2 level before bottling is only valuable in association with the amount of oxygen expected to be available in the bottle. The DO in wine just before filling starts is not the only but an important element in the whole picture. It provides information on what is called SO_2 stability. Therefore, many wineries tend to combine both SO_2 and DO measurements when a wine is going to be bottled.

In chapter 2.5.1 and more particularly in figures 21 and 22, it is outlined that the oxygen available is not entirely consumed by SO_2 in the stoichiometric ratio of 1:4, but only up to an average amount of 75 %. Therefore, each mg/L O_2 must be compensated by an additional 3 mg/L free SO_2.

The concentration of molecular free SO_2 is important in the control of wine microorganisms. Levels of 0.5 to 0.8 mg/L molecular SO_2 are considered as safe. In the pH range of 3.2 to 3.5, this corresponds to 20 to 40 mg/L free SO_2 (Figure 19). When wines are sterile-bottled according to standard industry practice, molecular SO_2 loses its importance as there are no microorganisms left to be controlled. Under these conditions, it is more logical to base SO_2 additions before bottling on expected TPO rather than on pH.

TPO values in the wine industry are generally higher than those that are technically and economically feasible. On the other hand, since wines containing free SO_2 are more resilient to oxygen than other beverages like beer, it is more valuable for wineries to focus initially on striving for consistent TPO rather than for the absolute lowest possible TPO (Crochiere 2007).

Sensory effects

It is not a surprising insight that a wine bottled with different closures develops divergent sensory and chemical profiles. The sensory differences are not necessarily significant in the first year post-bottling (Jung and Schüssler 2016), but become more evident during longer bottle storage.

Fruity white wines require bottle closures with a consistently low OTR to minimize oxidative aging. On the other hand, these closures facilitate the occurrence of post-bottling reduction flavor (Godden et al. 2001, 2005, Skouroumounis et al. 2005 b, Schneider 2006 c, Lopes et al. 2009, Ugliano 2013) when a wine is prone to develop it. The issue of post-bottling reductive taints in the context of bottle closures with low OTR is discussed in chapters 3.4 and 3.5.

As outlined before, the OTR of a bottle closure is not the only factor impacting post-bottling oxygen uptake. The effect of a closure displaying a low OTR can be relativized and canceled out when wines are bottled with high DO (Dimkou et al. 2013) or high headspace oxygen levels (Dimkou et al. 2011).

In Sauvignon blanc wine, a high DO level at bottling and the additional use of bottle seals highly permeable to oxygen caused strong oxidative aging according to sensory and analytical criteria after two years of bottle storage. Conversely, the same wine sealed under more airtight conditions as with screw caps featuring a tin-Saran liner displayed highest levels of varietal aromatic thiols, SO_2, and hydrogen sulfide (H_2S), the latter eliciting a reduced dominating character of the wine. Further aliquots sealed with natural corks and screw caps featuring a Saranex liner presented negligible reduced and oxidized characters (Lopes et al. 2009). Screw caps with tin-Saran liner have an OTR of approximately 0.0 mg O_2/year, screw caps with a Saranex liner show a slightly higher OTR of 1.0 to 1.5 mgO_2/year (Vidal et al. 2011) provided that they are appropriately rolled on to the bottle. It is obvious that even minor differences in the OTR of bottle closures have a noticeable effect on the post-bottling development of white wine.

Screw caps have found broad acceptance in many wine growing countries since 2005 and considerably improved white wines' stability against oxidative aging. However, these improvements are not always evident after the first year of bottle storage. The essential question is to which other bottle closures screw caps are compared.

As shown in chapter 2.6.5, oxygen uptake of 10 mg/L O_2 after filtration is able to cause distinctive oxidative aging, while only 2.5 mg/L O_2 might suffice to affect the wine in more general terms. There are strong indications that a minor oxygen uptake of less than 5 mg/L O_2 post-filtration can enhance fruity varietal aroma. The annual oxygen permeation rate of various bottle closure types is of this order of magnitude. Additional oxygen uptake prior to bottling, in the filler, and from the bottle headspace is another issue that must not be mixed up with oxygen diffusion through the bottle closure, but is frequently the proverbial straw that breaks the camel's back.

On the other hand, when white wine is consistently protected against oxygen uptake throughout storage, stabilization, and bottling, fruit aroma intensity can benefit from a minor oxygen ingress through the bottle closure during the first one or two years of bottle storage. Clearly, oxygen uptake before and after bottling must be seen in context. Bottle closures with the lowest possible OTR are not always the best solution, but they are advisable for wineries facing difficulties in limiting oxygen pickup before and upon bottling.

2.7. Effect of storage temperature

Introduction: Post-bottling storage temperature is a widely underestimated factor affecting white wines' shelf life. Undesirably high temperatures accelerate typical aging even in the absence of oxygen. The respective effects of heat, oxygen uptake through the bottle closure, and unfavorable wine composition are difficult to distinguish in sensory terms. Sensory data are presented on how such undesirable high temperatures in conjunction with storage duration potentiate the adverse effect of unfavorable wine compositional data on its shelf life. Finally, practical guidelines for bottle storage are given.

Simply put, the well-known Arrhenius equation stipulates that the rate of chemical reactions increases exponentially with the increase of temperature. A long time ago, it was also shown that the relative rates of oxygen uptake, browning, and SO_2 losses in bottled wines increase when the temperature rises (Ough 1985). And yet, the impact of temperature on wine aging during bottle storage is one of the most neglected topics in enology if indeed ever discussed at all.

In many wineries the problem takes absurd dimensions: Strong and impressive fruit aroma in white wines boosted by high enological input and extremely low fermentation temperatures are systematically destroyed by uncontrolled high storage temperature in the first summer post-bottling. In quite many cases, efforts and energy required for cooling would be better invested in the bottle storage area than during primary fermentation.

Everybody knows that elevated temperature shortens the shelf life of food. Therefore, meat, sausage, cheese, and eggs are stored in the refrigerator. In contrast, wide sectors of the wine business are not yet aware of how sensitive white wines are to heat, in any case more sensitive than red wines (Scrimgeour et al. 2015). Experience and research have shown that improper storage conditions during distribution through the entire supply chain – from winery to restaurant or consumer – is the most common cause of losses in white wines' quality and value.

Results from heat exposure in accelerated aging tests

Chardonnay with and without oak aging displayed significant sensory differences in aroma after only five to nine days of storage at 40° C as compared to 5° C. There was a decrease of fruity-floral aroma attributes and a simultaneous increase of attributes associated with aging such as honey, tea, tobacco, and rubber, after 15 days of warm storage. Prolonging warm storage up to 45 days only caused minor additional aroma changes (de la Presa-Owens and Noble 1997).

A similar study imitated shipping conditions. White wines from four varieties (Riesling, Sauvignon blanc, Chardonnay, and Gewürztraminer) were stored at 40° C over three weeks and compared with the references stored at 20° C. Both analytical and sensory results showed significant differences. Samples stored at 40° C displayed higher concentrations of vitispirane, p-cymene, and TDN, and reductions in several esters and acetates that are characteristic of aged wines (Robinson et al. 2010).

In a study upon Semillon and Chardonnay, a three weeks' storage at 45° C in the absence of air produced a decrease of floral aroma and an increase of aroma attributes as oak, tobacco, and smoke. In contrast, heat treatment over several minutes caused no significant aroma changes as compared with the controls (Francis et al. 1994). These results indicate that a short-term heat exposure under controlled conditions as it occurs upon pasteurization is less harmful to wine quality than a long-term storage in too hot a bottle storage area. In real life, however, most producers are more afraid of pasteurizing their wines than of uncontrolled long-term heat exposure in their bottle storehouse.

It is important to differentiate between the effect of heat exposure as such under anoxic conditions and the coupled effect of heat plus oxygen. Elevated storage temperatures in conjunction with oxygen exert a synergistic impact on the decrease of terpenols, norisoprenoids, and esters that are responsible for the fruity-floral aroma of young white wines. Concurrently, they accelerate the appearance of off-flavors reminiscent of honey, boiled potatoes, and farm-feed caused by elevated concentrations of phenylacetaldehyde and methional (Ferreira et al. 2002).

Results from real-world trials on bottled wines

The rate constants of chemical reactions are all different functions of temperature. It logically follows that during wine aging, each of the underlying reactions is affected differently by temperature changes. Thus, short-term storage at elevated temperatures ranging from 40 to 45° C does not necessarily reflect the effect of heat exposure at more realistic storage conditions.

The interaction between temperature and exposure time requires further clarification. There is strong evidence that short-term exposure to elevated temperatures as it occurs upon professional wine flash pasteurization at 90° C over a couple of minutes, followed by immediate recooling, causes no sensory damage in white wines. In contrast, long-term exposure to 45° C for three weeks as it occurs in many bottle storage areas of the wine production and distribution chain produces strong aging effects (Francis et al. 1994). Similar but less pronounced results can be expected after several hours of bottle storage at the same temperature in a car's trunk.

The combined effects of heat and oxygen were confirmed by storage of a Chardonnay packed in bag-in-box and bottles sealed with four different bottle closures. The wine was stored in these five different packaging configurations for three months at three different temperatures. Under these conditions, increased storage temperature induced the largest changes in the wine. The aliquot stored in bag-and-box at the highest temperature level showed the strongest increase of oxidation-related aroma and color. In contrast, bottle storage with various closures produced less aging, depending on the closure OTR (Hopfer et al. 2012).

Storage of bottled Italian white wines at 4, 15, and 25° C showed in an impressive way that shelf life was longer than two years at 4° C, approximately 20 months at 15° C, and only 7-9 months at 25° C (Barbanti et al. 1997).

2. Typical and oxidative aging

Storage of bottled German white varietal wines over a 10 months' period at 22° C produced considerably greater losses of fruity varietal aroma and correspondingly stronger intensity scorings for oxidative aging than at 12° C. In the realistic temperature range, a temperature difference of 5° C exerts a significant impact on aroma stability (Schneider 2000). Figure 48 gives an example.

Wine obtained from the Grüner Veltliner cultivar in Austria showed almost no aroma changes after one year of bottle storage at 2 and 10° C. In contrast, a four months' storage at 20° C caused significant losses of fruity varietal aroma that were noticeable for consumers (Stöckl 2013).

When Sauvignon blanc wine from New Zealand was stored at 5, 10, 18° C and room temperature for 12 months, storage at 18° C and room temperature caused lower concentrations of acetate esters, including the prominent varietal thiol 3-mercaptohexanol acetate, and ethyl esters of fatty acids, than the lots stored at lower temperatures. Sensorially, the lots stored at cooler temperatures were characterized by higher fruity and fresh vegetal aromas, whereas the wines stored at warmer temperatures exhibited more woody, flinty, buttery, and canned asparagus notes Makhotkina et al. 2012).

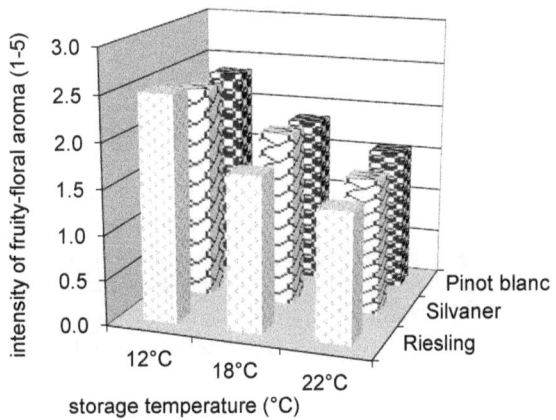

Figure 48: Impact of storage temperature on fruity-floral varietal aroma ratings of three white wines after 10 months' bottle storage.

In order to get a deeper insight into the real heat exposure upon shipping of bottled wines through the national distribution chain across the USA, bottles equipped with temperature loggers were stored at various points in regular non-refrigerated containers with different types of insulation. The accumulated heat exposure (time x temperature) was calculated using ethyl carbamate formation as a wine quality indicator, and different kinetic models for wine aging were applied to make a comparison with wine storage under ideal cellar conditions. These calculations suggested that some wines were exposed to heat during transport that corresponded to an added bottle age between 1 and 18 months when compared with conventional cellar storage ((Butzke et al. 2012).

During bulk shipment of Chardonnay from Australia to Europe over 8 to 9 weeks, temperature inside containers ranged from 4 to 47° C, with peak temperatures reached during daytimes in ports depending on season and location of the containers on the vessel. When shipping scheduling and logistic conditions were associated with high temperatures, sensory ratings increased for honey and decreased for freshness, with the loss of freshness most pronounced when wine temperature reached >25° C (Walther et al. 2018).

Oxidation and thermal stress produce similar aroma profiles

As outlined in chapter 2.1, a large array of compounds eliciting the aroma profile of typical aging is produced even under anoxic storage conditions when the temperature is high enough. Hence, wines can also develop this kind of aging after bottling with extremely air-tight screw caps. It is fairly difficult to differentiate by sensory means between typical aging caused by too much oxygen, or only by heat exposure under oxygen-free storage conditions. Only very trained tasters are able to identify under certain circumstances aroma attributes described as smoky, pungent, and flinty produced after heat exposure under anoxic storage conditions, and to distinguish them from more oxidation-related terms such as cooked vegetables, boiled potatoes, farm-feed, and black tea.

The whole of the sensory results obtained by studies upon storage temperature allows us to draft the following

Guidelines for bottle storage

The potential for wine aging during transportation results primarily from heat exposure, temperature fluctuations or, more precisely, a complex metric of peak and average temperatures experienced. For long-term storage of wines, the ideal storage temperature rage is considered to be 13° C to 15° C (55° F to 60° F). This is conventional wisdom and advice given by collectors and experts. Within this range, wines can age gracefully if any aging is desired in fruit-driven white wines. It makes historical sense since wine storage in the Old World has been typically carried out in caves where the natural underground temperature is in that range. Thus, the 'ideal' seems to have been the result of regional custom and practice rather than scientific study.

In times when freshness and elegance are considered prominent quality characteristics of most fruity white wines, there is nothing to prevent the storage of such wines at even lower temperatures. At an average refrigerator temperature of 5° C (41° F) or below, chemical reactions causing aging are largely inhibited. This is particularly true for the oxidation process occurring in opened bottles, which should always be stored in the refrigerator. Under these conditions, the chemical reactions leading to oxidative spoilage will be slowed down by a factor of approximately 10 times compared with storage at room temperature. At worst the risk of harmless protein hazes and bitartrate precipitations increases when wines have

2. Typical and oxidative aging

been poorly stabilized against these aesthetic flaws. The freezing point of most wines is -5 to -6° C (21 to 23° F).

Exposure to temperatures between 20 and 25° C (68 to 77° F) should not exceed one month. Temperatures above 30° C (86° F) should be avoided in any case during storage and the entire distribution chain from winery to consumer even for a short time. They are fatal to aroma quality of fruit-driven white wines, while the resulting headspace pressure may cause the closure to leak and bottles of sparkling wine to burst. Unfortunately, these temperatures occur when wines are shipped in non-refrigerated containers in the warm season. When no refrigeration is available, wrapping bottles or pallets with insulating thermal blankets helps restrict temperature peaks during transportation (Butzke et al. 2012). It can be argued that wine should be shipped and stored under conditions that are at least equal to much less precious commodities as milk, meat, cheese,

Bottles sealed with cork require some additional care. When corks dry out, they lose their elasticity, which might cause air to seep into the bottle. Therefore, the old rule recommending horizontal storage of such bottles remains still valid.

More harmful, however, are extreme or frequent fluctuations in temperature. The volume of the wine expands when the temperature rises, decreasing the headspace volume and placing pressure on the closure. When the temperature falls, the wine contracts, decreasing the headspace volume and causing a negative pressure able to suck air through the interface between the closure and the inside of the bottle neck. In some way, this change of ullage volume is comparable to what happens in a piston pump. Bottles sealed with screw caps, which provide a tighter seal than most corks, are expected to be less susceptible to oxygen transfer caused by these pressure changes than corks that have lost their elasticity as a result of aging or upright storage.

White Wine Enology

3. Reductive aging and post-bottling reduction flavor

3.1. Volatile sulfur compounds eliciting aging off-flavor

Introduction: Reductive aging means the formation of a stinking reduction taint in filtered wines, particularly post-bottling. It is due to a chemical conversion of odorless or little odor-active sulfur-containing precursors, which are produced by yeast metabolism, into other more odor-active compounds detracting from flavor quality. However, two such compounds are an exception, highly appreciated in some wines and known to contribute to what is called minerality, which must be distinguished from reduction flavor. This chapter clarifies chemical terms and sensory characteristics of the most important of these compounds.

3.1.1. Definitions, causes, and important key compounds

Wines affected by reduction flavor remind in some way the smell of putrefaction. It might appear strange at first glance defining this flaw as a specific kind of wine aging since it is commonly considered to occur during fermentation and in young wines. At this early stage, wines are carefully screened for its appearance and when it is detected, it is universally rejected and removed. In contrast, it is much more tolerated when it appears many months post-bottling, in many cases even in highly awarded wines. There is a certain irony of enology in that reductive taints are systematically rejected by some tasters, while they are benevolently accepted or even euphemistically elevated to an expression of terroir by other tasters in a different context. This chapter focusses upon their appearance in bottled wines, giving rise to what is called reductive aging.

Reduction flavor is caused by elevated contents of volatile sulfur(S)-containing compounds (VSCs). When their concentration exceeds the olfactory threshold, they elicit a smell reminiscent of burnt rubber, rotten cabbage, rotten onions, rotten eggs, rancid meat, garlic, sewage, or boiled corn. However, there are other VSCs that are not involved in what is described as reduction flavor. Besides SO_2, they comprise volatile aromatic thiols viewed as positive and reminding passion fruit, grapefruit, and black currents. They significantly contribute to the varietal aroma of some cultivars, in particular Sauvignon blanc. There are also other ones eliciting a smell of flintstone involved in an aroma designated as mineral (Chapter 3.3.2).

Reduction flavors are perceived in a very subjective way. Furthermore, they are variable in their chemical and sensory characteristics. Hence, there have been numerous attempts to define them in sensory terms. The most broadly accepted definition is that they disappear upon addition of minor amounts of copper ions in a relatively short spell of time. However, there are many exceptions to that rule. Another definition claims that they only appear in wines displaying a low redox potential in the absence of dissolved oxygen. Albeit there is a connection, this is not a compelling necessity as they sometimes can also occur in part-oxidized wines.

Very origin in primary fermentation

It is standard knowledge in enology that reductive off-odors are the ultimate result of nutrient deficiencies in the fermenting must, particularly in musts displaying low levels of yeast assimilable nitrogen (YAN). However, this primary cause is not always evident because it is superimposed upon and differentiated by a large number of additional winemaking variables. Chemical reduction as opposed to oxidation is just one of these variables, albeit an important one impacting the occurrence of reductive sulfurous off-odors as a specific kind of aging. The chemistry underlying the post-bottling formation of reductive taints is highly elusive. It starts with primary fermentation and ends with the choice of the bottle closure.

When grape must is deficient in YAN, yeast is stimulated to produce elevated amounts of malodorous VSCs during primary fermentation. There are two main precursor groups and pathways of VSCs formation during fermentation (Rauhut 1996, Ferrari 2002):

- Inorganic sources as sulfate (SO_4), sulfite (SO_2), and elementary sulfur (S_8) contained in the must and used by yeast through its sulfate assimilation pathway to produce hydrogen sulfide (H_2S). This is the way used by yeast to incorporate sulfur into amino acids for the synthesis of the essential S-containing amino acids methionine, cysteine, and glutathione. When there is a lack of precursors of these amino acids, the surplus of H_2S is released into the must and able to chemically or enzymatically react with other must or wine compounds, thus yielding more complex VSCs with variable odor intensity.

- Organic sources as the same S-containing amino acids referred to above and vulnerable to enzymatic or chemical degradation. Under conditions of YAN-deficiency, yeast is forced to turn to them as a nitrogen source and partially metabolize them, splitting off H_2S able to produce additional VSCs by enzymatic pathways in must or merely chemical pathways in wine.

Thus, the amount of VSCs produced during primary fermentation depends basically on must nitrogen supplementation and the specific YAN demand of yeast strains. As a result, the choice of the yeast strain and adequate YAN supply is considered a first but insufficient step to mitigate problems with reductive taints appearing pre- and post-bottling.

Due to its reactivity, H_2S is an essential precursor compound of a large array of other VSCs (Kinzurik et al. 2016). Therefore, its amount produced by yeast during fermentation gives us a rough though insufficient clue to the proneness of the resulting wine to develop reductive taints. Figure 49 shows the high variability of H_2S production of various yeast strains during primary fermentation and the impact of YAN supplementation by common diammonium phosphate (DAP) additions. H_2S produced throughout fermentation was quantified by specific gas detection tubes used as fermentation locks (Park 2008).

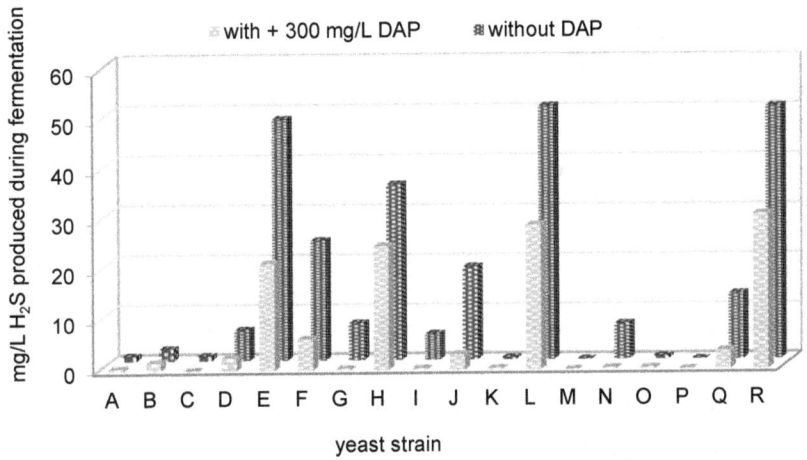

Figure 49: Impact of yeast strain and DAP supplementation on H_2S production during primary fermentation. H_2S released measured using gas detection tubes. Must data: 21 Brix, 35 NTU, 175 mg/L YAN.

Working with yeast strains with an unknown sulfur metabolism entails the risk of aggravating problems with post-bottling reductive aging. This holds especially true for spontaneous fermentations. On the other hand, yeast strains with a favorable sulfur metabolism do not guarantee that it will not occur at the present state of knowledge.

As the very origin of VSCs lies in primary fermentation, reductive off-odors are typically considered a flaw of young wines. When they are identified in those wines, they are commonly removed by addition of copper salts (copper sulfate or copper citrate), aerated yeast lees, or silver chloride. Another, more traditional procedure relies on wine oxygenation as it is achieved by micro-oxygenation, pumping over and splashing. In doing so, the oxygen picked up is able to temporarily oxidize some of the off-flavor causing VSCs to other ones of lower odor intensity or, as in the case of H_2S, to entirely eliminate them.

Once a wine shows a tendency to develop reduction off-odors in the first months after fermentation, it often suffers this problem again during further storage in bottles with a low permeability to oxygen, even if the off-odor has been successfully removed. On the other hand, wines remaining 'clean' until bottling are able to form the off-odor for the first time post-bottling. The appearance of reduction flavor is difficult to predict at any stage of winemaking and storage.

Post-bottling reduction flavor has become more topical in recent times

In contrast to the attention paid to reduction flavor in young wines pre-bottling, its appearance in bottled wines has been neglected by the wine industry for a long time. This attitude has changed since natural corks as the traditional bottle closure have been partially replaced by other closures with lower oxygen permeability. Although historical numbers are lacking, it is likely that post-bottling reduction flavor has become more common in recent years with the increased popularity and use of bottle closures displaying a low oxygen transmission rate (OTR), especially screw caps. Thus, increasing awareness of this kind of malodor fault has first started rising after the widespread dissemination of screw caps in New Zealand and Australia since the turn of the millennium. Numerous research reports dealing with this matter within the last decade reflect the importance of the problem.

The formation of post-bottling reductive taints is closely related to the redox chemistry of the bottled wine. Redox chemistry means the reversible equilibrium between oxidation and reduction processes. This equilibrium is associated with the OTR of the bottle closure and the TPO (*total pack oxygen*) of the bottled wine (Chapter 2.6.6). Nevertheless, the primary cause of reductive taints formed during wine bottle aging are compounds produced by yeast metabolism, which are easily subject to abiotic transformations in the filtered wine during aging.

All wines contain volatile sulfur compounds

VSCs are normal by-products of any alcoholic fermentation. As stated above, their concentration and chemical make-up depend on yeast strain and YAN supply. Many of them are easily purged out by the stream of CO_2 produced during fermentation, and only small subthreshold levels remain not posing any sensory problem in most young wines. The purging effect depends on the boiling-point of individual VSCs because some of them, frequently those with a low odor intensity and a high boiling point, are not affected and remain in the wine.

As a result, primary fermentation leaves a kind of fingerprint of such compounds, which is strongly dependent on the interaction between must composition and the individual yeast strain. Ultimately, no wine can be bottled free from any VSCs even if they are not detectable by smell at the moment of bottling. The best that can be done to limit their formation at this very early stage of winemaking is a perfect must clarification (Chapter 2.4.2), inoculation with a yeast strain known for its low VSC production, and supplying the must with yeast nutrients whenever necessary to achieve a YAN concentration of 250 mg/L at least.

The most important and easily identifiable VSC produced during primary fermentation is H_2S. It readily reacts with ethanol and acetaldehyde, thus forming simple thiols (mercaptans, sulfides). This reaction is only the first step in a more complex plethora of reactions leading eventually to post-bottling reductive taints. Indeed, VSCs are fairly reactive, which explains why a large variety of them can be found in any wine. The most important of them contributing to the formation of reduced off-flavor during aging, their synonyms and molecular formulas are listed in table 11. This list represents traditional knowledge, is not exhaustive, and subject to continuous expansion.

3. Reductive aging and post-bottling reduction flavor

Table 11: Volatile sulfur compounds involved in reduction flavor, their synonyms, molecular formulas, odor thresholds, and olfactory profiles.

compound (synonym) formula	odor threshold, µg/L		odor description
	wine	ethanol 12 %	
hydrogen sulfide H_2S	1 - 15	1	rotten eggs, rotten seaweed
methanethiol (methyl mercaptan) $CH_3\text{-}SH$	1.5	0.3	burnt rubber, rotten cabbage
ethanethiol (ethyl mercaptan) $CH_3\text{-}CH_2\text{-}SH$	1.1	0.1	burnt rubber, rotten onions, garlic, striking match
dimethyl sulfide (methyl thiomethane) $CH_3\text{-}S\text{-}CH_3$	10 – 160	5 - 10	asparagus, truffles, boiled corn, olives, molasses
dimethyl disulfide $CH_3\text{-}S\text{-}S\text{-}CH_3$	10 - 45	2.5	cooked cabagge
diethyl disulfide $CH_3\text{-}CH_2\text{-}S\text{-}S\text{-}CH_2\text{-}CH_3$	4 – 40	20	rotten onions, burnt rubber, garlic
methyl thioacetate (S-methyl acetothioate, thioacetic acid methyl ester) $CH_3\text{-}C(O)\text{-}S\text{-}CH_3$	40 – 50		cheese, eggs, rotten onions, sulfurous
ethyl thioacetate (S-ethyl acetothioate, thioacetic acid methyl ester) $CH_3\text{-}C(O)\text{-}S\text{-}CH_2\text{-}CH_3$	10 - 70		garlic, eggs, rotten onions, old meat, sulfurous

The odor thresholds and odor attributes reported in table 11 have been taken from the literature (Goniak and Noble 1987, Mestres et al. 2000, Ferrari 2002). However, odor thresholds must be interpreted with caution. Their fluctuation margins indicate that they strongly depend on wine matrix and experimental design used for their determination. Professional expert tasters as well as consumers respond with highly variable sensibility to the more or less stinky properties of VSCs. Based on identical concentrations in the same solvent, differences in sensory response of an order of magnitude are not uncommon. This explains conflicting threshold concentrations reported in the literature.

In quantitative terms, dimethyl sulfide is the most important of these compounds in bottled wines, but its contribution to the odor profile is not necessarily detrimental. At low concentrations, it even enhances the fruity aroma notes. When it reaches higher concentration in the course of aging, it provides additional truffle and black olive notes (Segurel et al. 2004).

The most important species involved in post-bottling reductive taints are methanethiol and H_2S at suprathreshold concentrations (Scrimgeour and Wilkes 2014, Ugliano et al. 2015, Ferreira et al. 2018).

Clarifying chemical terms

Of special importance in this context is the clarification of a semantic problem. Terms such as mercaptans, sulfides, sulfhydryls, and thiols are frequently used as synonyms and arbitrarily interchanged in the literature. In accordance with more recent scientific standards, preference is given to the terms "thiols" or "sulfhydryls" hereinafter.

By definition, thiols are organosulfur compounds that contain a carbon-bonded sulfhydryl (-SH) group as in methanethiol (CH_3-SH). When the functional sulfhydryl group is bound to a hydrogen, the compound is hydrogen sulfide (H-SH or H_2S). The sulfhydryl group is able to easily react with oxygen, copper, and other metals. Hence, thiols and H_2S react in a similar manner and are often collectively referred to as "sulfhydryls".

Addition of copper salts, particularly copper sulfate, is the most common way to remove reductive off-odors and has considerable enological importance (Chapter 3.3).

3.1.2. The difference between reductive taints and minerality

Reductive taints are often confounded with minerality. This is a term that is widely used in wine description and promotion, albeit it is a kind of buzzword without any clear meaning. Its inflationary use tends to summarize a broad range of olfactory, retronasal, and gustative perceptions without duly distinguishing between all these sensations. Sometimes it is also misused to euphemistically qualify reduction taints. Hence, it is an ill-defined term calling for a linguistic adjustment and exact definition.

There is a wide consensus that the perception of minerality on the palate is enhanced by a high titratable acidity (Deneulin et al. 2014, Heymann et al. 2014). In contrast to popular belief, it is not related to the taste of minerals transported through the vine from the vineyard rocks and soils because these minerals represent complex crystalline structures of high molecular size that cannot be taken up and transported by the roots. Although attempts to explain the perception of minerality involve allusions to geological materials, these are irrelevant to its origin from a geological perspective (Maltman 2013). The minerals contained in wine such as potassium, sodium, calcium etc. are alkali or alkaline metallic cations not related to geological minerals and without any flavor properties. In particular, they are not involved in the taste sensation of what is described as salty.

So far we have considered the purely gustatory dimension. By smell, minerality is most often associated with attributes like wet stones, wet sand, conglomerate pebbles, chalk, iodine, oyster shells, flint stones struck against themselves, struck matches, smoke, high levels of free SO_2, low intensity levels of fruit aroma, and reductive taints (Deneulin et al. 2014, Heymann et al. 2014, Parr et al. 2016). All studies underline the role of the tasters' cultural background in the definition of perceived minerality and the underlying wine composition, thus explaining divergent results. Studies on chemical substances eliciting specific aroma attributes described as mineral are scarce and limited to two compounds:

Benzene methanethiol

Benzene methanethiol, also known as benzyl mercaptan or benzyl thiol, has been identified as a VSC that contributes to the empyreumatic smell of flintstone and struck matches. Its odor threshold is 0.3 ng/L in aqueous-alcoholic solution. It was found at 30 to 100-fold higher concentrations in some French white wines. Addition of 4 ng/L to a Chardonnay containing 7 ng/L caused a noticeable aroma of combustion (Tominaga et al. 2003).

Benzene methanethiol is a small molecule with a thiol group displaying the chemical structure C_6H_5-CH_2-SH and a boiling point of 195° C. There is little knowledge about its response to copper ions and oxygen (Chapter 3.2). It can only be stated that the aroma attribute described as flintstone is enhanced when bottled wine is sealed with screw caps with low oxygen permeability (Godden et al. 2001, 2005) and when it additionally contains ascorbic acid and high levels of free SO_2 (Skouroumounis et al. 2005 a). This behavior indicates that its occurrence is favored under reductive storage conditions as it also applies to most other VSCs. On the other hand, addition of copper ions in amounts frequently used to remove reductive taints does not have a noticeable impact on the perception of flintstone and struck matches in young or barrel-aged wines.

Since benzene methanethiol does not occur in the soil, it must be produced by yeast in a direct or indirect way. Soil is expected to play an indirect role in that it impacts must composition, nitrogen status, and yeast metabolism, thus explaining why yeasts are able to produce higher levels of these compounds in musts originating from certain soils.

Hydrogen disulfane

In a study on natural flint stones and dark pebbles scraped together, the odor produced was described as reminiscent of gun powder, struck matches, burnt hairs, cold firework, etc. Immediate rinsing of the struck stones yielded hydrogen disulfane (H-S-S-H), hydrogen trisulfane (H-S-S-S-H) and further S-containing compounds in the solvent. Gas chromatography coupled to an olfaction port was used to generate aroma descriptors for disulfane contained in the solvent. They were denominated as flint, matches, firework, and cold ashes. Odor intensity of disulfane was estimated to be 5 to 10 times higher than H_2S.

Within a series of 80 wines, the occurrence of disulfane was confirmed for the two wines described as the most mineral ones by smell. After addition of iron ions, the concentration of disulfane increased by a factor of 10, albeit with a short half-life. It was concluded that polysulfanes could be the compounds responsible for the flintstone odor associated with minerality (Starkenmann et al. 2016).

Sensory and chemical differences

Both hydrogen disulfane and benzene methanethiol do not occur in soil in an ionic form able to be taken up and stored by vines. They trace back to yeast metabolism. Their formation pathways remain unknown, taking into account the complex chemistry of generation and interconversions of VSCs.

The odor profile these compounds elicit is predominantly observed in wines stored under reductive conditions as in stainless steel or glass bottles, though it can also occur in barrel-aged wines. Since barrel aging goes along with a relatively high oxygen uptake, their occurrence in these wines indicates that their formation and preservation are not necessarily linked to reductive wine storage. Rather they seem to be the response of yeast metabolism to must composition as affected by soil and climate. This would explain why their olfactory impact is limited to wines obtained from a few varieties cultivated in strictly defined growing areas having stony soils, but not necessarily flint containing soils. Due to the lack of firm scientific data, all further hypotheses belong to the realm of pure speculation at this point of time.

As VSCs, both compounds can easily be associated with reduction flavor in mere chemical terms. However, this kind of analogy is difficult to justify in sensory terms since neither of these compounds elicits the typical stinky smell of reductive taints reminiscent of rotten eggs, old meat, burnt rubber, and garlic caused by the VSCs listed in table 11. They just smell as scraped flintstone, gun powder, smoke, and struck matches. Their odor in wine is hardly ever experienced as unpleasant but rather as an aroma characteristic of an outstanding wine. The French term "fumé" (smoky) in Sauvignon blanc fumé from the Sancerre area alludes to that aroma.

The fact that a mineral aroma profile is quite distinct from a reductive off-odor in sensory terms does not exclude a chemical interconnection between these two sensory concepts. The well-known ability of VSCs to undergo chemical interconversion (Kreitman et al. 2018) even suggests such an interconnection. Mineral aroma attributes generally appear only after one or two years of aging. Therefore, their appearance can surely be classified as a kind of aging, though there is no sound basis allowing for characterizing that aging as reductive or oxidative.

Furthermore, it is unknown whether the underlying molecules are only formed during the aging period or already present since the end of primary fermentation and temporarily masked by more short-lived, predominantly fruity fermentation-derived aromatics. Interestingly, the mineral odor they impart to wine is not affected by copper salt additions (~ 0.3 mg/L Cu^{++}) or intentional oxygen exposure (~5 mg/L O_2) in amounts commonly used for removal of reductive off-odors.

3.2. Reactions and evolution of volatile sulfur compounds

Introduction: After we have seen the compounds involved in reductive aging, the following section specifies the various precursors responsible for their generation, the diverse chemical reactions involved in that process, and the conditions promoting it. It is a complex chemistry which is not yet understood in all details, although some fundamentals are evident.

3.2.1. The importance of precursors

How can it be explained that some wines produce a reductive off-flavor some months after they have been bottled under sterile conditions without any flaws? The most obvious answer is that there is simply a lack of knowledge of what is transferred upon filling into bottles after fermentation and stabilization procedures. Yeasts can certainly not be responsible for the formation of VSCs in a sterile-filtered wine. For a deeper understanding, it is indispensable to go into some details of the formation, reactions, and treatment procedures of reduction flavors in bulk wines before bottling.

Besides the strongly odor-active S-compounds such as H_2S and simple thiols (mercaptans), fermenting yeasts also produce other ones displaying lower odor intensity, i.e. a higher odor threshold, or no odor activity at all. The most important of these compounds comprise

- dialkyl disulfides, more precisely dimethyl disulfide and diethyl disulfide,
- thioacetates, in this case methyl thioacetate and ethyl acetate,
- methionine and cysteine, both sulfur-containing amino acids.

In low concentrations, these compounds are not necessarily perceived as causing a sulfidic off-odor. However, they are able to act as precursors of VSCs with higher odor intensity, which are eventually responsible for the appearance of post-bottling reductive taints. There are a wide array of pathways responsible for that phenomenon (Kreitman et al. 2018), but four of them are of particular importance:

- Hydrolysis of thioacetates:

Thioacetates represent the methyl and ethyl esters of acetic acid. Comparable with many other esters in wine, they tend to undergo acidic hydrolysis. In this process, methanethiol (methyl mercaptan) and ethanethiol (ethyl mercaptan) are formed. They display approximately 50-fold higher odor intensities than their parent molecules. The reaction is promoted by low pH values, high storage temperature, and a high initial concentration of thioacetates (Bekker et al. 2018). However, it proceeds regardless of the absence or presence of oxygen. Thus, when there are high initial levels of thioacetates, thiols can be produced within a few weeks and at concentrations that exceed their thresholds (Rauhut and Kürbel 1994, Rauhut et al. 1994 b).

- Reduction of disulfides

Disulfides can be produced by yeasts under difficult fermentation conditions, but also arise during wine storage and treatments as oxidation products of thiols. When a wine showing reduction flavor is supplied with oxygen by micro-oxygenation, simple splashing or any other form of aeration, the stinky smell can disappear. The explanation lies in the fact that highly odor-intensive thiols easily oxidize to disulfides with lower odor intensity according to the reaction scheme

$$2 \text{ R-SH} \rightarrow \text{R-S-S-R}$$
$$2 \text{ thiols} \rightarrow 1 \text{ disulfide}$$

A further observation frequently made under commercial winemaking conditions is that after aeration, the stinky smell can revert within a couple of months or emerge for the first time. When this happens, the reason is the reduction of disulfides back to thiols. In this case, the aeration must be repeated (Limmer 2005 a, 2005 b).

It is crucial to understand that these reactions do not follow stoichiometric rules. Thus, though oxidation of wine containing thiols results in their decrease, the increase of disulfides is not an equivalent one because thiols also couple with quinones resulting from phenol oxidation (Chapter 2.2.1). After addition of dimethyl disulfide to wine, it produced maximum yields of only 72 % of methanethiol under reductive conditions, but still enough to show the importance of disulfides as precursors of key 'reductive' compounds in wines post-bottling (Bekker et al. 2018). Generally, disulfides occur at subthreshold concentrations, but there are exceptions.

- Photochemical degradation of methionine

The S-containing amino acid methionine can be oxidized via a reaction route that is induced by light exposure and catalyzed by riboflavin, resulting in the formation of methanethiol and dimethyl disulfide (Grant-Preece et al. 2013). This reaction requires a photochemically triggered drop in redox potential to less than 130 mV (Maujean et al. 1978). Its sensory significance is controversial:

When white wine was bottled in clear glass, a significant increase of reduced aroma attributes could be observed after one hour of exposure to sunlight (La Folette et al. 1993) or three hours of storage under fluorescent light comparable with sunlight (Dozon and Noble 1989). This effect has become known as light-struck flavor. It is much less pronounced in wines bottled in green or brown glass. In another study, photochemically induced sensory changes of that kind only occurred after an unrealistically long light exposure time (Jung et al. 2007).

- Metal-catalyzed degradation of sulfur (S)-containing amino acids

This reaction refers to a desulfhydration of the S-containing amino acids methionine, glutathione, and cysteine leading to the formation of methanethiol and H_2S.

It is catalyzed primarily by copper ions and more important in white and rosé than in red wines (Franco-Luesma et al. 2016 a). However, cysteine and glutathione additions were only associated with small H_2S increases after bottle aging (Bekker et al. 2018).

A more comprehensive survey of putative but less investigated or less important precursors of post-bottling reduction flavor is given in Kreitman et al. 2018. It is a dynamic research area in continuous development.

It is crucial to keep in mind that none of these precursors can be removed with the common copper salt additions because there is no sulfhydryl group in their molecules (thioacetates, disulfides) or their reaction products with copper are soluble (S-containing amino acids). This explains the major drawback of copper fining in that it does not directly affect their concentrations. For that reason, reduction flavor can reappear when a tainted wine has been successfully treated with an appropriate amount of copper salt.

3.2.2. Variability and reactivity of volatile sulfur compounds

As has been shown, reduced taints are not a clearly defined wine fault but composed of an amazing variety of different VSCs displaying variable chemical and sensory properties. They are not a static appearance but subject to chemical dynamics and some kind of aging. In this process, interconversions and de-novo synthesis of VSCs occur.

The manner the trajectory of VSCs proceeds is not a linear one. Rather, the levels of sensorially important VSCs such as H_2S and methanethiol in bottled wines show fluctuations up and down over time. This dynamic process is affected by the oxygen ingress through the bottle closure (Scrimgeour and Wilkes 2014) and heavy metal (Cu, Fe, Mn, Zn, and Al) concentrations (Viviers et al. 2013). Therefore, reduced off-odors can grow, diminish, or recur in the course of time, depending on the storage conditions. Under anoxic conditions, the accumulation of methanethiol and H_2S is favored.

For a first quick overview, figure 50 outlines schematically the formation of relevant compounds involved in reduced off-odors in the course of fermentation and aging of wines. It is important to note that although this schematic diagram only displays basic reaction pathways which have been considerably complemented by more recent research, it is still valid as an introduction to a highly elusive field of wine chemistry. However, it does not explain why some wines are more prone to develop reductive aging than others.

In the following, abiotic reactions of VSCs leading ultimately to the appearance of reductive aging, the equilibrium between their various forms, and the enological parameters affecting this equilibrium are outlined in more detail.

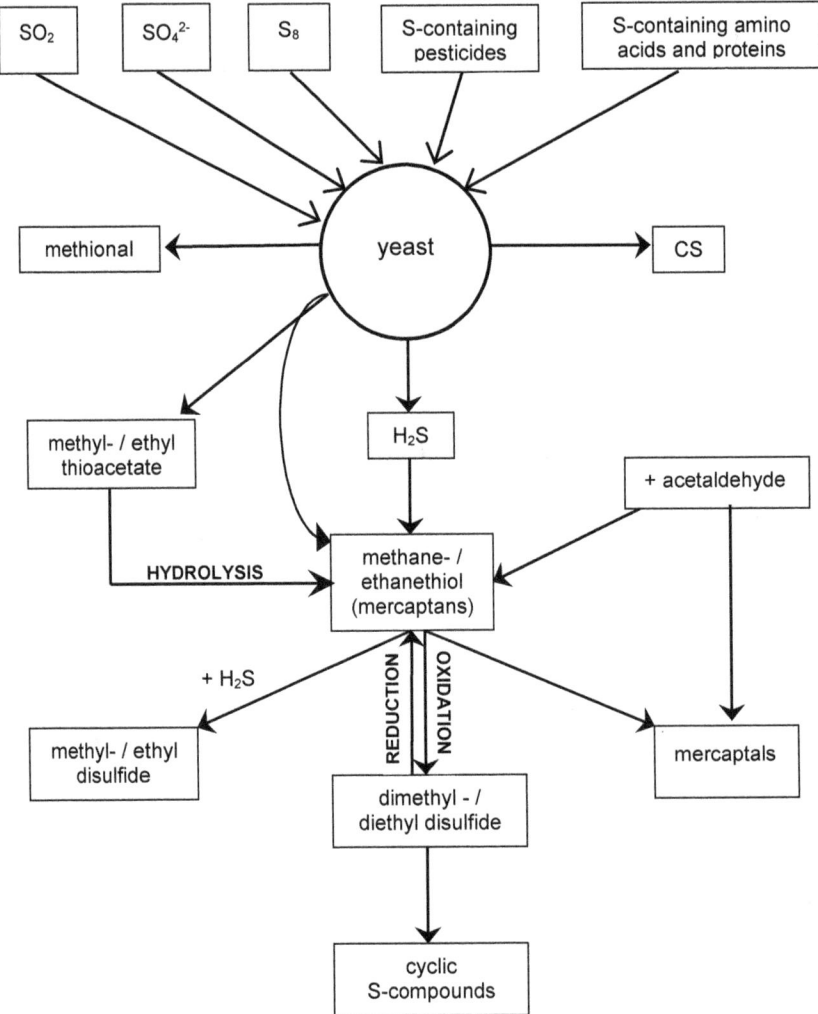

Figure 50: Formation of important volatile sulfur compounds involved in reduction flavor.

The thiol-disulfide equilibrium

The reduction of disulfides to more odor-active thiols outlined in the previous chapter is only one of the possible reactions, albeit an important one. It explains why reduction flavor caused by thiols can reappear after it has been removed by oxidation via aeration. The reason for this is the reversibility of the reaction: In the absence of oxygen and under conditions of a low enough redox potential, disulfides can be entirely reduced back to the thiols they originated from. Disulfides are in redox equilibrium with their corresponding thiols (Vela et al. 2018). Amongst other things, this equilibrium depends on the availability of oxygen (Limmer 2005 a, Limmer 2005 b, Scrimgeour and Wilkes 2014).

During bottle storage, wines can pick up small amounts of oxygen whose levels depend on the OTR of the closure used (Chapter 2.6.6). Under these conditions, wines reach an equilibrium point at which the rate of formation of disulfides equates the rate of their spontaneous reduction to thiols. This equilibrium will be manifested by a specific redox potential and by a corresponding thiol : disulfide ratio. It is possible that there are only disulfides above a certain redox potential >50 mV, and only thiols when the redox potential is low enough (Ferreira et al 2018). By that means, the closure OTR influences the intensity of post-bottling reductive off-odors.

For the reaction couple 'diethyl disulfide – ethanethiol', it has been shown that the reduction of disulfide to thiol follows the kinetics of a first order reaction with regard to the concentrations of disulfide and sulfite (SO_3^{2-}) (Bobet et al. 1990). This means that the accumulation of thiols increases when the concentrations of disulfide and sulfite increase. It slows down at low levels of free SO_2. However, as it is dependent on two variables, it is difficult to specify a SO_2 level low enough to alleviate this problem of thiol accumulation. In practice it is important to understand that high levels of free SO_2 and low pH values promote the reduction of disulfides to highly odor-active thiols.

Due to the interconversion of disulfides and thiols, aeration of white wines displaying reduced off-odors is not necessarily a lasting solution (Vela et al. 2018). This applies in particular to white wines processed and stored under reductive conditions. When they display reduction flavor, it is largely attributable to thiols. In these cases, aeration as a treatment is frequently of short-term success as it just shifts the equilibrium from thiols to disulfides for a limited period of time. In any case, it lacks specificity as it heavily affects fruity aroma compounds (Chapter 2.6.5). Therefore, fining with copper salts continues to be of great importance in commercial winemaking, albeit the long-term effect of copper ions (Cu^+ / Cu^{++}) has also been questioned (Chapter 3.5.2).

The role of metal-complexed volatile sulfur compounds

When copper fining is carried out, Cu^{++} ions supplied react essentially with sulfhydryls, i.e. H_2S and thiols. On reaction of Cu^{++} with H_2S, no simple precipitation of insoluble copper sulfide (CuS) takes place but rather the production of various compounds including Cu_2S and CuS_2. On reaction of Cu^{++} with thiols, copper (I) thiolates with the general structure R-S-Cu are produced. When these compounds are formed, there is a transfer of charge between the Cu and S atoms.

The reason why fining with copper (II) salts removes or reduces S-containing off-odor compounds has traditionally been based on the assumption that the copper-complexed sulfhydryls produced would completely precipitate due to their very low solubility in aqueous solution, thus allowing for their physical removal from the wine by racking or filtration. However, such a precipitation has never been observed in practical winemaking. More recent research (Clark et al. 2015, Ferreira et al. 2018, Kreitman et al. 2018) has shown that these copper precipitates remain in the wine dispersed as complex aggregates or nanoparticles. This finding also applies to other metal-complexed forms of sulfhydryls as with iron, zinc, and manganese.

As a result of this behavior, metal-complexed sulfhydryls will be available to cleave and release free thiols and H_2S under anoxic conditions of low redox potential at a later point of time. In doing so, they act as latent precursors in the abiotic appearance of reduction flavor post-bottling. For that reason, appropriate filtration as discussed in chapter 3.3.3 is vital to partially remove them when copper fining is carried out before bottling.

Release of odor-active sulfhydryls from copper complexes

The reason why the cleavage of metal-complexed sulfhydryls is promoted by a low redox potential is not yet completely investigated. There are two possible explanations (Kreitman et al. 2018):

— The accumulation of glutathione and cysteine formed by reduction of their corresponding disulfide forms like GSSG (Chapter 2.5.5). These reducing amino acids are the major nonvolatile thiols in wine, accompanying H_2S and volatile thiols by a large molar excess. Thus, their sulfhydryl groups compete for copper ions, which are released from the copper-complexed sulfhydryls, thus freeing their odor-active sulfhydryl moiety.

This competitive behavior suggests that wines containing surplus copper, which is the wine metal with the highest bonding constants with sulfhydryls, will release a smaller fraction of volatile sulfhydryls for an equivalent production of competing nonvolatile thiols (Ferreira et al. 2018). It confirms observations from commercial winemaking that the presence or addition of copper upon bottling makes more difficult or retards the release of free VSCs during anoxic storage, but does not totally impede it.

— The copper-sulfide complexes are not clearly identified but supposed to contain both oxidized (Cu^{++}) and reduced (Cu^+) copper. During reductive storage, Cu^{++} can be reduced to Cu^+ which forms complexes with a higher copper-sulfur molar ratio, i.e. containing less sulfhydryls. This conversion would result in a release of free sulfhydryls.

A more complex equilibrium

The existence of metal-complexed sulfhydryls, essentially H_2S and methanethiol, intervenes in the thiol-disulfide equilibrium and makes it part of a more complex reaction equilibrium which can be written for thiols as

$$\text{R-S-Me} \quad \rightleftharpoons \quad \text{R-S-H} \quad \rightleftharpoons \quad \text{½ R-S-S-R}$$
$$\text{metal-thiol complex} \qquad \text{thiol} \qquad \text{disulfide}$$

Conclusively, each wine contains a total amount of H_2S and thiols distributed into free, oxidized (disulfides), and metal-complexed forms interconnected through reversible redox equilibria. The metal-complexed forms can make up more than 97 % of total H_2S and 75 % of total methanethiol (Franco-Luesma and Ferreira 2014).

They are able to partially disrupt and release free thiols and H_2S when equilibrium displacements occur, thus acting as an additional precursor in the appearance of post-bottling reduction flavor.

The role of redox potential

Wine redox potential plays an essential role in determining the relationship between free and metal-complexed sulfhydryls and their oxidized precursors. Under strict anoxic conditions, it is known to spontaneously decrease and become reductive. This process requires a source of electrons. It has been hypothesized that spontaneous phenol polymerization taking place in anoxia could be that source of electrons, which would first reduce Fe(III) to Fe(II) and subsequently all disulfides and polysulfides to thiols and H_2S (Ferreira et al. 2018). When anoxia is interrupted by oxygen pickup, redox potential increases again, and the process can be completely reversed.

Redox potential measurements are not accessible to quality control in commercial winemaking. Moreover, they yield results which strongly depend on wine pH, DO concentration, and alcohol level. Therefore, they can neither be used to compare between wines nor to make a statement about the proneness of wine to develop post-bottling reduction flavor via generation of free sulfhydryls from metal-bound or oxidized forms. Instead, an accelerated reductive aging test as will be proposed in chapter 3.5.1 is a more workable hands-on test to obtain this information in commercial winery settings.

3.3. Identification and removal of reduction flavor pre-bottling

Introduction: Reduction flavor can be identified and removed by addition of copper salts, most frequently copper sulfate, and in rarer cases by aeration or fining with silver chloride. Copper requirements must be exactly determined in previous bench trials using sensory evaluation. After copper fining, residual copper must be controlled and excessive copper has to be removed by specific fining agents, residual yeast lees, and filtration. This chapter describes how to proceed in a hands-on situation pre-bottling and gives numerous practical hints. It also emphasizes that there is no treatment able to efficiently remove potential precursors of reduction flavor, which under certain conditions can recur at a later stage after it has once been successfully removed.

3.3.1. Practical identification of reduction flavor

As outlined before, VSCs are involved in the aroma expression of any wine even at concentrations below their identification threshold, which is the minimum concentration causing them to be sensorially perceived as reduction flavor. Therefore, reductive taints are not always reliably recognized by smell. The borderline between a clean and a faulty wine can be fluid. Hence, it is obvious that a slight reduction taint can be considered as positively contributing to overall aroma in sensory border-line situations, while the same wine is unequivocally rejected as faulty by other tasters. Due to the ubiquitous occurrence of malodorous VSCs and their typical smell, it can be assumed that quite a few flavors euphemistically described as "terroir" or "minerality" (Chapter 3.1.2) must be traced back to reduction flavor at the lower end of the perception threshold.

Many of the misjudged, slight, or subliminal reduction taints remain unnoticed as long as one does not purposefully search for them by adding a minor amount of copper ions into the tasting glass. When a bottled wine displays a fruitier and cleaner aroma a couple of minutes after addition of some drops of copper sulfate solution (0.01 %), evidence is provided that the wine is tainted by reduction flavor (Limmer 2005 a, Schneider 2008). However, when the smell does not change upon copper addition, this does not necessarily mean that the wine is clean as there might be VSCs that do not respond to copper.

The more casual "penny test" also works from time to time. Although pennies consist predominantly of zinc instead of copper in modern times, they are at least copper-plated and can release enough copper to clean up a glass of tainted wine. Care must be taken that the penny surface is darkened, indicating that there is enough oxidized copper (Cu^{++}) available to dissolve and react in the wine within a reasonable spell of time. Time requirements are highly variable and depend on the conditions of the penny that is used.

Aeration is clearly the less appropriate means to clearly identify reductive taints. Albeit many of them may disappear upon aeration of very young wines, there are other ones which are not responsive to oxygen.

3.3.2. Determination of copper requirements for treatment

Copper fining by addition of copper ions is the most common way to remove reduction flavor. The amounts of copper required are usually determined by a preliminary bench sensory trial. In the vast majority of cases, they are much less than the copper stability limit of 0.5 mg/L Cu^{++} (Cowey 2008, Schneider 2008), above which copper haze can occur. The implementation of such a preliminary test, also called "copper test", is fairly simple and described in table 12.

Wines displaying reduction flavor caused by thiols and H_2S respond to copper additions within a few minutes, but there will be a subsequent creep reaction leading to a further decrease of reduced off-odor over the following 24 hours. At the end of that period, copper requirements for taint removal are usually assessed lower than immediately after test preparation.

This simple test can and should be implemented as a standard tool in any winery. It substantially contributes to improve sensory skills. Were it systematically applied on a broader basis, reduction flavors would be less an issue of passionate discussions and more readily removed. Concurrently, the debate about the use of copper fining in wine would be freed from its emotionality since the amounts of copper required for treatment rarely become relevant as compared with copper contents of other food items and the human body (Chapter 3.5.3).

Table 12: Determination of copper requirements for removal of reduction flavor.
- Dissolve 100 mg copper sulfate ($CuSO_4 \cdot 5\ H_2O$) in water and make up the volume to 1 liter. The use of this stable solution is based on the following calculations:
- 1 mL / 100 mL wine (tasting glass) = 1.0 mg/L copper sulfate = 0.25 mg/L Cu^{++} (pure copper).
- Prepare samples with increasing additions of 0.05, 0.10, 0.15, 0.20, 0.25.... mg/L Cu^{++}, ideally using a graduated pipette of 1.0 mL total volume and 0.01 mL scaling.
- Evaluate the samples after 3 to 5 minutes at ambient temperature. Repeat the evaluation the next day.

From a chemical point of view, it is vital to understand that a high molar excess of copper is required to remove VSCs than would be calculated according to stoichiometry. This results from the fact that wine contains additional copper complexing compounds as S-containing amino acids, other organic acids, pectines, polysaccharides and proteins, which compete for copper with VSCs. Complexed copper is not any more available to react with sulfhydryls, but it can explain the coexistence of copper and sulfhydryls in the same wine (Clark et al. 2015).

Since no mathematical approach is possible, the only way to determine copper sulfate requirements is an empirical one using preliminary bench tests based on sensory evaluation. By analogy, these tests can also be performed by using copper citrate. For that purpose, some basic conversions are required:

Copper citrate vs. copper sulfate

Copper sulfate ($CuSO_4 \cdot 5\ H_2O$) contains 25.5 % pure copper (Cu^{++}). Therefore, a typical addition of 1.0 mg/L copper sulfate increases the wine copper level only by 0.25 g/L Cu^{++}. Legal limits for residual copper are 0.5 mg/L Cu^{++} in the USA and 1.0 mg/L Cu^{++} in the EU and most other countries. Up to 0.5 mg/L Cu^{++} can remain as soluble in the wine without posing the risk of a post-bottling appearance of copper haze, provided that the wine does not contain any ascorbic acid. In the presence of ascorbic acid, the soluble maximum content decreases to 0.3 mg/L Cu^{++}.

Copper citrate ($Cu_2C_6H_6O_7 \cdot 2.5\ H_2O$) contains 33.5 % pure copper, i.e. 31 % more than copper sulfate. Therefore, treatment of a given reduction flavor in a given wine with copper citrate requires only 69 % of the application rate that would be necessary when copper sulfate was used.

Copper citrate is not very soluble in wine. In order to facilitate its handling and dosage as a fining agent, it is commercialized as a cover layer coated onto bentonite and commercialized as a 2 % concentration in granule form branded Kupzit™. These proportions must be taken into account in bench sensory trials and practical application. The maximum dosage of this preparation is 0.5 g/L, which is the equivalent of 10 mg/L copper citrate or 3.35 mg/L pure copper (Cu^{++}). It is dissolved in water likewise bentonite, whereafter it is added to the wine which is mixed thoroughly to ensure even distribution. As the bentonite solids have to be removed by filtration, it cannot be added immediately before bottling.

According to manufacturer claims and as compared with copper sulfate, the copper contained in the copper citrate preparation would not totally go into the ionic form since citric acid is an organic complexing agent. Thus, it should not leave as much residual copper in the wine as does copper sulfate, allowing for higher additions. Furthermore, less pure copper should be required for treatment.

It is questionable whether there is a measurable complexing effect exerted by the relatively small amounts of added citrate against the background of the citric and all other acids wines naturally contain. Especially tartaric acid (Clark et al. 2015), but also S-containing amino acids, proteins and polysaccharides have been shown to strongly complex copper, thus making it unavailable to react with odor-active sulfhydryls. It is also highly questionable why copper added to the wine as copper citrate should be more effective than the same amount of copper added in the sulfate form. At best, there are a few measurements indicating slightly less residual copper for the same amount of added copper when copper sulfate is replaced by copper citrate. This phenomenon might be explained by the presence of bentonite in the commercial copper citrate preparation.

In the absence of serious scientific research on these issues, only some scarce technical reports on the use of copper citrate are available (Renner and Pour Nikfardjam 2016, 2017). Their conclusions are not very explicit, but on average not indicating a significant advantage of copper citrate over copper sulfate.

Copper citrate is the only copper salt legalized for treatment of organic wines to the disadvantage of copper sulfate. It is highly debatable whether this legal requirement makes any sense. Both anions - citrate and sulfate - naturally occur in wines at comparable concentrations of approximately 200 mg/L. Insofar, none of these anions is closer to the nature of wine than the other. The active ingredient of both copper salts is the pure copper cation. However, it must be acknowledged that citrate sounds much nicer than sulfate to laypersons in basic chemistry.

Inactivated yeast products with immobilized copper

More recently, a mixture of copper-infused inactivated yeast and bentonite has become commercially available as Reduless™. Its goal is to minimize copper uptake by wine. Amounts of 0.1 to 0.3 g/L are required over 3 to 5 days of contact time before they are removed by filtration. The procedure is only useful in young wines with slight reductive taints. Under these conditions, only minimal residual copper is observed, but effects on reduction flavor are also limited. It has not yet been investigated whether it has an advantage over copper salt additions, based on the same levels of residual copper.

3. Reductive aging and post-bottling reduction flavor

No removal of precursors

In general, the remedial action of copper fining has an immediate impact decreasing the intensity of reductive off-odors or completely removing them. Copper ions quickly react with free, odor-active thiols and H_2S, which are responsible for the reductive off-odor in the majority of wines affected by that kind of flaw due to their high odor intensity.

Some wines, however, cannot be readily cleaned up with simple copper salt additions regardless of the added amount. In these wines, elevated levels of VSCs such as disulfides or thioacetates are at least partially responsible for the sulfidic off-odor. Since they do not display a sulfhydryl group able to react with copper, they remain behind, able to be converted into even more odor-active sulfhydryls at a later point of time. In some of these wines, the addition of ascorbic acid can help (Chapter 3.3.3).

For the same reason, reductive taints can reappear some time after they had been successfully removed by copper fining. It is known by experience that once a wine shows a tendency to develop reductive off-flavor, it is more susceptible to develop it again during aging. When this happens after bottling, reductive aging appears as a specific kind of wine aging. However, it can also appear in wines which have never shown any reductive off-flavor pre-bottling. In any case, the causes can be found in precursors and reaction pathways outlined in chapter 3.2.2.

For practical reasons, it is important to understand that copper fining of a young wine does not give a guarantee against the reappearance of reduction flavor at a later point of time, and even after bottling.

Copper salts vs. silver chloride

The usability of silver chloride (AgCl) for removal of reduction flavor has been known for a long time, but its legal approval and practical application in some countries is more recent. Since it is almost insoluble over the whole pH range of wine, it is coated as a layer on a carrier material such as silica dioxide, bentonite, cellulose, or diatomaceous earth in order to facilitate its incorporation and even distribution in the wine. These preparations usually contain 2 % AgCl. The use of up to 10 mg/L pure AgCl (500 mg/L preparation) has been authorized by OIV.

Scientific reports about the action of silver chloride do not yet exist. Basically, silver cations (Ag^+) must be expected to react with thiols and H_2S similarly to copper cations but producing silver sulfide and silver thiolates instead of the copper complexes. However, there must be some minor differences not yet investigated. Practical experience has shown that silver chloride is able to clean up some wines that cannot be efficiently treated with copper salts, and vice-versa.

A decrease of ethyl thioacetate and dimethyl disulfide by 20 % each has been shown after additions of 100 mg/L of the silver preparation (1.5 mg/L Ag^+), while the levels of these compounds remained unchanged after addition of 1.0 mg/L Cu^{++} (Renner and Pour Nikfardjam 2016, 2017). However, it is not clear whether this decrease is to be explained by direct reaction of silver with these compounds, or rather by their conversion into other S-compounds reacting with silver when an equilibrium displacement occurs upon silver addition. In any case, the spectrum of activity of silver ions in wine seems to be slightly different from that of copper ions. This empirical evidence calls for more research.

The S-containing reaction products generated upon silver chloride addition produce an insoluble dispersion or deposit, which has to be removed by pad filtration. In doing so, the legal limit of residual silver (0.1 mg/L Ag^+) is met without need for removal of excess silver by fining as it might be required for removal of excessive copper levels. There is no knowledge about the long-term effect of residual silver after bottling.

3.3.3. Removal of reduction flavor in practice

Reductive off-odors appear more frequently in fruity white wines than in red wines since the former are more carefully protected against oxygen uptake. As a consequence, there is often a need to clean them up by copper fining before bottling. Understanding the basics of this practice provides further insight into the mechanisms of the formation of post-bottling reductive aging and its mitigation. Therefore, this very specific kind of wine treatment is also covered in the context of wine aging.

Treatment of reduction flavor in aged wines can be more complicated than right after primary fermentation. When young wines start displaying reduction flavor during or shortly after fermentation, H_2S is usually the most predominant one of the VSCs involved. Due to its low boiling point, it tends to evaporate and can easily be stripped by purging with any inert gas if it is not stripped by CO_2 evolving in the course of fermentation. This is a purely physical process.

H_2S also reacts with SO_2, resulting in the formation of elemental sulfur (S) according to the formula

$$2\ H_2S\ +\ SO_2\ \rightarrow\ 2\ H_2O\ +\ 3\ S$$

For that reason, reduction flavor sometimes disappears upon the first SO_2 addition post-fermentation.

H_2S can also vanish through direct oxidation according to the schema

$$2\ H_2S\ +\ O_2\ \rightarrow\ 2\ H_2O\ +\ 2\ S$$

when young wines pick up oxygen upon the first racking post-fermentation.

Aeration can help, but with collateral damages in most white wines

The easy oxidizability of H_2S explains why aeration by pumping-over is the most traditional way to remove sulfidic off-odors in young wines. It is also the reason why red wines processed under conditions of higher oxygen uptake are less prone to develop them. However, intentional aeration of white wines designed to be fresh and fruity should be performed with extreme caution. Whilst it might be effective in removing a stinky smell in the short-term, it also removes a large portion of volatile aroma compounds by volatilization and oxidation (Chapters 2.6.3). It is opposed to the precepts of gentle white wine treatment (Chapter 2.6.4) and is rather a way of ill-treatment of that kind of wine.

Oxygenation only removes H_2S without trace. When thiols are already present, they are oxidized to less odor-active disulfides susceptible to be reduced back to thiols during further storage. Moreover, reductive taints may also occur in part-oxidized wines. Giving more oxygen to those wines would not be a good idea and result in more oxidation rather than in removing the stinky smell. All these collateral damages outweigh the short-term effects of aeration on reductive taints in white wines.

Copper salts instead of aeration

Ultimately, H_2S easily reacts with copper and silver salts as discussed in the previous chapter:

$H_2S + CuSO_4 \rightarrow H_2SO_4 + CuS$ (and other dispersed Cu-S nanoparticles)

$H_2S + 2\,AgCl \rightarrow 2\,HCl + Ag_2S$

In view of the restricted effect of aeration, the use of copper salts, in particular copper sulfate, is the most common way to remove reduction flavor. Copper fining is the most effective when it is performed on the young wine as soon as primary fermentation is accomplished. Under these conditions, thiols are also removed before they are oxidized to disulfides.

The benefits of suspended yeast lees

As an additional advantage of treating young wine, there are still plentiful suspended yeast lees available to absorb large amounts of residual copper (Chapter 2.5.7). While unfermented musts can contain up to 5 mg/L Cu^{++}, only 0.1 mg/L Cu^{++} or less can be found in wines, provided that no copper uptake from brass-containing metal fittings or other winery metal material takes place. The difference is removed with the yeast lees upon racking or filtration. The same applies after copper fining of turbid young wines. Additionally, heterogeneous precipitates during subsequent storage and cold stabilization can result in co-precipitation of copper.

This removal of excessive copper by lees is of great practical importance as more than 0.5 mg/L residual Cu^{++} (0.3 mg/L Cu^{++} in the presence of ascorbic acid) is susceptible to cause post-bottling copper haze.

Copper in must is counterproductive

On the other hand, copper additions before or during fermentation are absolutely counterproductive as they increase the amounts of H_2S produced by yeast (Dittrich and Staudenmayer 1972, Eschenbruch and Kleynhans 1974). Figure 51 shows that this effect strongly depends on the yeast strain. H_2S released throughout fermentation was quantified by colorimetric gas detection tubes mounted onto the fermentation vessels (Park 2008).

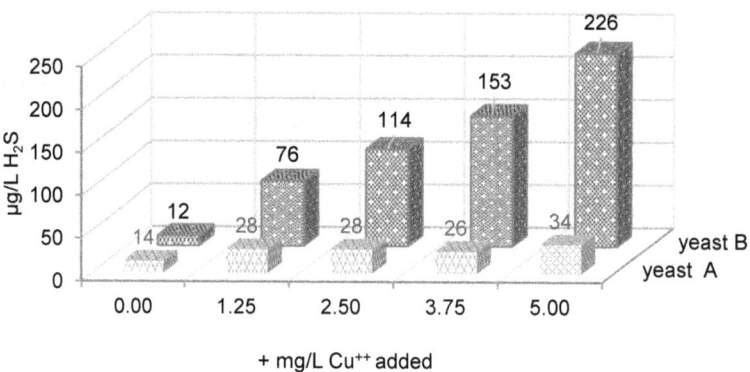

Figure 51: Production of H$_2$S during fermentation with two yeast strains as affected by pre-fermentation copper additions to an identical must..

The reason why copper within the yeast cells triggers H$_2$S production is not well understood. Obviously, it affects some enzymatic pathways involved in fermentation and nitrogen assimilation. From a practical point of view, this behavior leads to three important conclusions:

- Reduction flavor occurring in the course of alcoholic fermentation must be tackled with the addition of nitrogen-containing yeast nutrients (DAP) as often and as much necessary to remove it.
- Reduction flavor appearing post-fermentation is removed with copper salt additions.
- Elevated must copper levels resulting from the use of copper pesticides in crop protection cannot be expected to mitigate the appearance of reductive taints, but rather the opposite.

As shown previously, not all off-odor causing VSCs react with copper, and even less of them are responsive to oxidation. This applies in particular to wines having undergone some time of aging allowing for the formation of less reactive VSCs.

Complementary use of ascorbic acid

When the reductive off-odor is caused mainly by disulfides formed during primary fermentation or, more frequently, subsequent oxidation during storage, simple addition of copper salts does not remove it. The reason has been explained in chapters 3.2.2 and 3.3.2: Disulfides do not carry a sulfhydryl group able to react with copper ions or oxygen. The only way to remove them is their previous reduction to the corresponding thiols by addition of ascorbic acid (~150 mg/L) followed by anoxic storage. As a side effect of that addition, some H$_2$S is also released from its copper complexes (Chen et al. 2017).

3. Reductive aging and post-bottling reduction flavor

The action of ascorbic acid can take several weeks or months to come into effect. When it is accomplished, the thiols can be removed with copper additions. Unfortunately, this treatment is not always successful, in particular when more complex VSCs are present. In these cases, trials with silver chloride additions or sparging with an inert gas can be helpful.

Table 13 summarizes which kind of off-odor causing VSCs can be removed by treatments currently in use for that purpose. It provides a practical framework for the technical implementation of the results obtained by the bench trials described in table 12.

Table 13: Wine treatments for removal of off-odor causing S-compounds: Operating principle and effect as affected by individual VSCs.

S-compound	treatment
H_2S	- volatilization (wine surface, splashing) - oxidation (wine surface, splashing, micro-oxygenation) - complexation with copper salts or silver chloride and subsequent filtration
thiols (mercaptans)	- complexation with copper salts or silver chloride and subsequent filtration - reversible oxidation to disulfides (wine surface, splashing, micro-oxygenation)
disulfides	- reduction to thiols by ascorbic acid addition, complexation of thiols with copper salts or silver chloride, and subsequent filtration - purging with nitrogen or argon over several hours
all other VSCs	- purging with nitrogen or argon over several hours

Luckily, reduction taints not susceptible to successful treatment are relatively scarce. Most of reductive faults can easily be remedied by addition of less than 0.25 mg/L Cu^{++}, which equates to 1.0 mg/L copper sulfate. These additions provide copper in amounts below the copper stability and legal limits. They do not require subsequent finings to remove surplus copper. However, care must be taken that the wine does not already contain traces of copper taken up by previous treatments or from copper-containing alloys in winery equipment.

After any addition of copper salts, copper measurements should be performed on a filtered sample. They provide information about copper stability and further measures to be taken.

Practical hints: Sampling for copper measurements

Precise copper measurements are easy to perform by AAS (atomic absorption spectroscopy) and should be a standard procedure whenever copper salts are used in winemaking. Older colorimetric methods do not meet the precision required in modern times.

Care must be taken upon sampling: Without propeller mixers, even copper distribution and representative samples are difficult to obtain. Furthermore, sampling valves, side glass valves, racking and training ports mounted on stainless steel tanks, despite being considered stainless, are less inert than expected and tend to release copper accumulating in the small wine volume they contain. Therefore, the first 1,000 mL of sample volume taken from these valves should be discarded to avoid falsely high results. Otherwise, sampling from the top using a PE or rubber hose is more reliable.

Removal of excessive copper by blue fining with potassium ferrocyanide

In the worst case, excessive copper has to be decreased by fining procedures. Blue fining by addition of potassium ferrocyanide is a traditional and very efficient means to lower copper and iron levels without detracting from wine quality. However, it risks to leave toxic cyanide residues when it is not appropriately performed by trained staff. Therefore, it is not authorized in some countries such as the USA. As a substitute, the proprietary compound Cufex™ has been legalized in the USA but is apparently not marketed any more. It is a mixture of bentonite, ferrous sulfate and potassium ferrocyanide, with the latter acting as the active component. Thus, its use equates essentially to blue fining, albeit it is claimed to reduce the likelihood of over-fining and cyanide residues.

Potassium ferrocyanide (PFC) primarily reacts with iron, which with it forms a colloidal complex displaying a blue color. From a practical point of view, the reaction with copper and other metals is a side-effect. Without the presence of several mg/L of iron, blue fining is not possible. This applies to most wines produced in contemporary wineries equipped with stainless steel.

Iron occurs in wine in the reduced ferrous, divalent (Fe^{2+}) form and the oxidized ferric, trivalent (Fe^{3+}) form. PFC reacts with both reduced (Fe^{2+}) and oxidized (Fe^{3+}) iron ions, producing several insoluble salts. If all the iron was Fe^{3+}, then 5.65 mg of PFC would be required to eliminate 1.0 mg of iron. The reaction involving Fe^{2+} is more complex and produces various salts. Between 3.78 mg and 7.56 mg of PFC are theoretically needed to remove 1.0 mg of iron, depending on the Fe^{2+} : Fe^{3+} ratio of the wine. In practice, it is considered that 6 to 8 mg of PFC are required to remove 1 mg of iron from wine.

The reaction of PFC with Fe^{3+} can be time consuming, since most of the Fe^{3+} is combined in soluble complexes with organic acids. On addition of PFC, these complexes start breaking down to reestablish the initial equilibrium and generate more Fe^{3+} ions. This process can take several hours or days. It takes more time at high pH, as larger amounts of complexed Fe^{3+} are present. Hence, there is a risk that unreacted PFC may decompose forming hydrocyanic acid (cyanide) when the reaction is strongly delayed.

In contrast, the reaction of PVC with Fe^{2+} is much faster because less Fe^{2+} is combined in complexed forms than Fe^{3+}. Therefore, wines should be in a reducing state and contain free SO_2 before blue fining takes place. Addition of ascorbic acid further facilitates the reaction.

Taking into account the above considerations, it is clear that standard additions of PFC are not feasible, nor can any addition be based on the wine's iron content. Instead, preliminary bench trials are necessary on every container of wine to be fined in that way. These tests work with increasing additions (0.01 g/L, 0.02 g/L, 0.03 g/L, etc.) of PFC and an amount of gelatin or caseinate corresponding to 0.03 g/L. After sample filtration half an hour or so later, the filtrates are tested for excess PFC by addition of a few drops of saturated ammonium iron (III) sulfate solution. The solution turns blue if excess PFC is present. It is thus possible to determine the highest amount of PFC that is completely precipitated under these conditions.

At least 1 mg/L residual iron should be retained in the wine. PFC addition rates that achieve maximum removal of copper and iron increase the possibility of over-fining and the retention of excess ferrocyanide which, in time, liberates cyanide, thus rendering the wine unsalable and possibly toxic.

Preliminary trials and final treatment must be performed under the supervision of a trained enologist or chemist. The samples used in these trials should be in the same redox-state as the wine to be treated. Therefore, the wine must not be handled between sampling and fining. As a precautionary measure, 0.01 g/L less PFC is used in treatment than the maximum amount identified in the preliminary test. Residual cyanide is limited to contents of 20 to 100 µg/L total hydrogen cyanide, depending on the country. More than 20 µg/L indicates that blue fining has taken place.

For the removal of excessive copper as a side reaction, the amounts of PFC are as unpredictable as for the removal of iron. In general, 0.03 to 0.05 g/L PFC are needed. These amounts require the presence of sufficiently high levels of iron in the range of 4 to 7 mg/L.

To make blue fining absolutely safe and avoid cyanide residues, careful lab work must be complemented by additional safety measures when the fining is implemented in the cellar. These measures comprise

- the use of efficient propeller mixers instead of archaic pumping-over to ensure the immediate and even distribution of the compound in the tank,

- the addition of small amounts of 'gelatin + silica gel' or 'gelatin + isinglass' to facilitate the flocculation of the colloidal blue fining reaction product,

- filtration within one week after blue fining to remove insoluble ferrocyanide complexes before they start disintegrating into soluble cyanide.

The final filtration must not be confounded with a previous one required after any copper salt addition to remove the dispersed copper-sulfhydryl complexes produced upon that addition. Otherwise, PFC would immediately remove the copper moiety from the copper-sulfhydryl complexes and release free sulfhydryls, thus cancelling the effect of the copper addition.

Removal of excessive copper by fining with PVI/PVP

More recently, a synthetic polyvinylimidazole-polyvinylpyrrolidon copolymer (PVI/PVP) has been introduced to overcome the disadvantageous use of potassium ferrocyanide for copper and iron removal. Compared with other fining agents based on yeast, proteins, and bentonite, it has been shown to be the most effective one, removing up to 94 % of copper in 72 hours. Thus, it is an effective alternative to blue-fining. Typical additions are 0.25 to 0.50 g/L. The higher the dose, the greater the percentage decrease of heavy metals (Nicolini et al. 2004, Mira H. et al. 2007, Friedenberg et al. 2018).

PVI-PVP is not absolutely selective to heavy metals but also shows some side reactions, for example a slight decrease of titratable acidity and the adsorption of some phenolic material. The latter effect may be desired in some white wines displaying high levels of flavonoid phenols (Chapter 2.4.1), but can also produce thin and stripped wines when there are no critical phenols to be removed. Bench trials including copper measurements are recommended.

Importance of filtration to remove reversible copper-sulfhydryl complexes

Most wines requiring copper fining can be successfully treated with 0.5 mg/L Cu^{++} or less. These amounts are within the legal limits and do not cause copper haze. Thus, there is no need to lower them by fining with PCF or PVI/PVP and, hence, no need to remove these fining agents by filtration. In contrast, filtration is required after any copper salt addition, even with the copper allowed to remain in the wine, with the purpose to better protect the wine from the reappearance of the reduction flavor.

As outlined in chapter 3.2.2, the copper-sulfhydryl complexes formed with H_2S and thiols upon copper salt addition are not as insoluble in wine as they have been supposed to be for decades, but rather produce a kind of invisible nanoparticles dispersed in solution. In this physical state, they are susceptible to undergoing chemical reactions with S-containing amino acids and release their odor-active sulfhydryl moiety (Clark et al. 2015, Ferreira et al. 2018). The instability of these complexes is one of the reasons why reductive taints can reappear after they have been successfully treated by copper fining. Hence, there is enormous interest in removing them to ensure long-term flavor stability. Since they cannot be diminished by finings, the practical approach of doing so is focused upon filtration.

The particle size of these nanoparticles is around 0.2 μm and below, thus calling for a rather tight filtration. Polyethersulfone and nylon membranes of 0.20 and 0.45 μm have been shown to remove up to 40-90 % of sulfhydryl-bound copper particles. Taking into account the particle size, this removal is due to absorption rather than to particle size discrimination (Kontoudakis et al. 2019). As an adsorption phenomenon, it can be expected to even better perform on depth filtration media like filter pads offering a larger adsorption surface area, but no reliable data are available at this point of time.

In commercial winemaking, tight filtration commonly takes place at bottling or earlier. In contrast, many laboratory studies on copper fining dispense with that step, leaving the dispersed copper-sulfhydryl complexes behind and able to compromise the long-term effect of the treatment. For that reason, copper fining to prevent or remove sulfidic off-odors in the long-term works out much better under industrial conditions than suggested by some research papers (Viviers et al. 2013, Bekker et al. 2016, Vela et al. 2017).

3.4. The role of bottle closure and oxygen in reductive aging

Introduction: One of the conditions for the formation of reductive aging is a low or nil oxygen transmission rate of the bottle closure. Such closures do not systematically cause this off-flavor, but they facilitate its appearance in wines which are prone to develop it. Screw caps fitted with tin-Saran liner rank among these closures, but there are other screw caps featuring waddings allowing for more oxygen ingress post-bottling. Ultimately, the choice of a bottle closure with a given oxygen transmission rate decides upon whether wine aging tends to be more oxidative or more reductive under sensory aspects.

3.4.1. Importance of the gas tightness (OTR) of bottle closures

In the context of wine aging as affected by bottle closures, gas tightness refers to their tightness with respect to atmospheric oxygen, also denominated as oxygen barrier. It is inversely related to the oxygen transmission rate (OTR) of closures. It has a tremendous impact on flavor stability during wine bottle storage (Chapter 2.6.6).

Since screw caps have found increasing use as wine bottle closures, the frequency of post-bottling reduction flavor has increased. Numerous storage trials have shown that compared with natural or synthetic corks, wines sealed with very gas-tight screw caps lose less SO_2 and develop less browning, but also produce higher odor intensities of reduction-like aroma attributes (burnt rubber, flintstone) and higher concentrations of H_2S and methanethiol. Concurrently, screw-capped wines also displayed a better preservation of varietal aroma compounds, particularly of varietal thiols such as 3-mercaptohexanol in Sauvignon blanc (Godden et al. 2001, Skouroumounis et al. 2005 b, Godden et al. 2005, Lopes et al. 2009, Dimkou et al. 2011, Silva et al. 2011, Ugliano et al. 2011, 2015, Ugliano 2013, Scrimgeour and Wilkes 2014).

Accelerated aging of 24 wines under anoxic conditions at 50° C showed that the accumulation of methanethiol and H_2S was not only the result of reductive cleavage of disulfides and hydrolysis of thioacetates, but primarily due to a release from dissolved metal-complexed sulfhydryl complexes. Furthermore, there was a de-novo synthesis of H_2S and methanethiol not explained by the aforementioned pathways but basically related to the desulfhydration of cysteine and methionine. This release of sulfhydryls from these S-containing amino acids accounted for the major portion of the sulfhydryls accumulated in that set of white and rosé wines aged under the conditions described, but less so in red wines (Franco-Luesma and Ferreira 2016 a, Ferreira et al. 2018).

These observations also provide further evidence about the fate of the copper-sulfhydryl complexes formed upon copper salt additions: Since they remain largely in solution as nanoparticles instead of precipitating, they tend to partially release their sulfhydryl moiety. As a result, they contribute to the accumulation of methanethiol and H_2S during anoxic storage as long as their levels are not substantially decreased by tight filtration (Chapter 3.3.3).

Closure OTR controls accumulation of odor-active sulfhydryls

Differences in the frequency and intensity of reductive off-odors post-bottling are attributed in particular to different OTR-values of bottle closures (Chapter 2.6.6). Oxygen ingress through most natural or synthetic corks helps to mitigate the release of odor-active sulfhydryls from their metal-complexed forms and shift the thiol-disulfide equilibrium towards the less odor-intensive disulfides. In contrast, many screw caps with their traditionally low OTR cause a low redox potential in the bottle, which acts in the opposite way (Chapter 3.2.2). This is the most essential cause of reductive aging. Based on the same chemical rationale, it can also occur when filtered wines are stored under strict anaerobic conditions in stainless steel tanks.

Interestingly, the redox status of wines pre-bottling does not affect their proneness to generate odor-active sulfhydryls post-bottling. In other terms, it is irrelevant whether the wine has been stored under more oxidative or more reductive conditions before bottling. Thiols are produced in all bottled wines regardless of their history and bottle closure. The way the bottle closure OTR intervenes is in that it decides upon their accumulation in the long-term and the reductive off-odor associated therewith. Thiols are either preserved under anoxic conditions, or they are oxidized to their corresponding disulfides when oxygen ingress is possible (Limmer 2005 b, Limmer 2006, Vela et al. 2018).

Proneness to post-bottling reduction flavor is wine-dependent

To make it even more complicated, there is no clear-cut link between the use of bottle closures of low OTR and the appearance of post-bottling reduction flavor because some wines are more prone to develop it than other wines. More precisely, gas-tight screw caps are not directly responsible for the formation of reductive taints in the bottle, but they increase the likelihood of their appearance and their odor intensity on conditions where the wine is prone to develop them. Moreover, post-bottling reductive taints are not limited to wines sealed with screw caps but can also be observed when other closures are used, particularly those with a low OTR. Neither the type or visual appearance of the closure decides upon the chemistry taking place in the bottle but rather its OTR.

3. Reductive aging and post-bottling reduction flavor

The impact of oxygen available in the bottle (Chapter 2.6.6) on the formation of reductive off-odors has only begun to be understood since precise techniques of non-invasive oxygen measurements have become available (Lopes et al. 2006, 2007, Diéval et al. 2010, Roget et al. 2010). These measurements allow for a reliable quantification of oxygen transmission through the various bottle closures. Without that analytical innovation, opening the bottles for measurement would be necessary and distort data.

One of the most essential results of OTR measurements showed that screw caps fitted with a tin-Saran liner displayed an OTR of 0 mg O_2/year and those fitted with a Saranex liner an OTR of 1.0 to 1.5 mg O_2/year (Vidal et al. 2011). In contrast, OTR of natural corks ranged from 1 to 5 mg O_2/year (Lopes et al. 2006, 2007, Silva et al. 2011, Oliveira et al. 2013).

The question of the optimal OTR

The most obvious approach to mitigating the problem with post-bottling reductive taints would be the use of bottle closures with higher OTR. A slight oxygen ingress through closures with slightly increased OTR would inhibit the accumulation of thiols in a natural way. That is precisely what has happened when natural corks have been used over the last centuries.

Under commercial winemaking conditions, it is impossible to predict for each wine an optimal closure OTR, above which it would not produce noticeable reduction flavor post-bottling. That OTR must be at least high enough to prevent the accumulation of thiols and H_2S, based on sensory experience, but not too high as to trigger excessive oxidative aging. The only possibility to identify such an optimal OTR would be bottling the same wine with closures displaying variable OTR rates and periodically submitting it to sensory evaluation. This is a kind of approach building up valuable experience. For that reason, bottling trials with different bottle closures are of greatest practical importance.

Bottle closure is part of an active packaging strategy

Different packaging strategies lead to different effects on the wine during subsequent bottle storage. Some absorption of VSCs by natural and synthetic corks (Silva et al. 2012) has been proven as well as the absorption of TDN causing petrol flavor (Chapter 5.3) and methoxypyrazines eliciting green-vegetative aroma attributes (Pickering et al. 2010). These effects are not directly related to the variable oxygen ingress through the bottle closures, which represents a distinct aspect focused upon in this context.

Ultimately, the choice of the bottle closure is an important element of an active packaging strategy. From the moment wine is bottled with different bottle closures, different wines start being produced from the same base wine. In this process, the storage period and temperature play an essential role.

During the first six to nine months post-bottling, the oxygen exposure of wine is largely determined by the oxygen already dissolved in the wine before bottling plus the oxygen trapped in the bottle headspace. In contrast, the oxygen uptake through the bottle closure is of secondary importance in this initial period. Only after complete consumption of headspace and dissolved oxygen, these conditions start changing, and the importance of the oxygen permeation through the closure gains in importance for the evolution of the wine. Therefore, significant sensory differences caused by the closure OTR are frequently observed only one year post-bottling (Jung and Schüssler 2016). As a consequence, the choice of the closure OTR is an essential factor affecting the evolution and aging of wines which are bottle-stored more than one year. It is less important for wines designed for early consumption.

Headspace oxygen and closure OTR are variables whose impact on wine quality can be much larger than the impact of viticultural and enological factors. In terms of wine style and shelf life, white wines respond to oxygen uptake in a much more sensitive way after bottling than red wines. High oxygen uptake of white wines promotes oxidative aging through the formation of higher aldehydes (Chapter 2.1) and strongly limits shelf life (Chapter 2.6.6). In contrast, low oxygen uptake better preserves fruity varietal aroma but, simultaneously, increases the risk of accumulating reductive aroma attributes, thiols and H_2S (Godden et al 2001, Skouroumounis et al 2005 b, Scimgeour and Wilkes 2014, Ugliano et al. 2009, 2015).

Figure 52 provides a schematic view of how the choice of the bottle closure OTR drives the evolution of wine more in one or the other direction, more towards oxidative or more towards reductive aging. This effect increases as bottle storage proceeds. It explains a basic dilemma in packaging strategy: Low oxygen ingress helps in protecting varietal and fruity aroma, but may increase the wines' tendency to develop reductive aging.

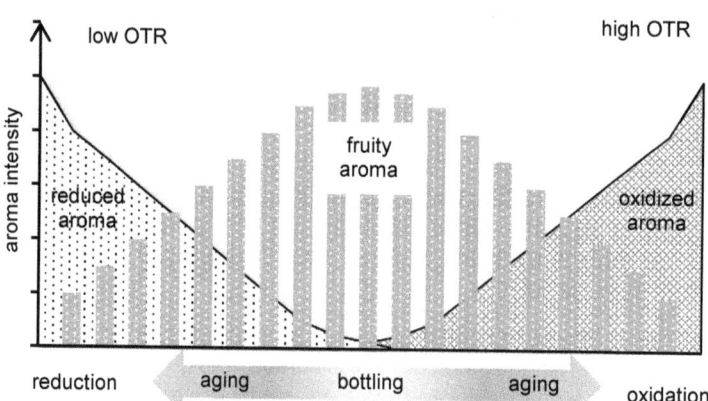

Figure 52: Impact of bottle closure OTR on the evolution of white wine post-bottling (adapted from Ugliano et al. 2009)

Closure trials are performed to find out the sound balance between reductive and oxidative aging for a given type of wine. However, whenever they are run, one must take into account that natural corks display much more variability in their

OTR than any other bottle closures (2.6.6). Hence, a sufficient number of replicates is required to obtain a reliable average.

Industrially manufactured closures such as screw caps and synthetic corks are standardized products guaranteeing a fairly high consistency between single pieces. In the meantime, they are produced with different OTR values, thus enabling winemakers to meet the oxygen needs of individual types of wine. Their uniformity facilitates closure trials aiming at better matching the closure OTR with a given kind of wine.

3.4.2. Screw caps using liners with variable OTR

All screw caps consist of an outer aluminum cylinder fitted with a neutral sealing insert on the inside wadding that makes a seal with the bottle mouth. The outer cylinder holds the sealing insert in the correct position on the bottle mouth, pressing it with the required pressure when it is rolled onto the bottle thread. Its length is variable, depending essentially on marketing strategies, and in no way related to the tightness of the closure. For wine bottles, the dimension measuring 30 x 60 mm (diameter x length) is a widely used international standard, also known as BVS. It provides a customer-friendly appearance.

The sealing insert is the working end of the screw cap because it is the actual bottle seal. It separates the wine from the aluminum skirt and provides protection against the diffusion of liquid from the inside and oxygen from the outside. It is responsible for the tightness of screw caps and determines their OTR.

Although screw caps are considered by some wine producers as an undifferentiated type of closure, they differ in the kind of their sealing insert. Compared with a vast number of screw cap manufacturers, there are considerably less manufacturers of sealing inserts. Usually the screw cap producers and distributors focus on manufacturing the aluminum shirt and purchase the sealing inserts.

The crucial role played by the sealing inserts requires a more detailed description of their composition and the consequences for their OTR resulting therefrom. At the very beginning, screw caps were only fitted with a single one-layer material serving as insert. This insert, frequently referred to as 'compound mass', completely met the requirements of mineral water and soft drinks. In the meantime, these plain inserts have been further developed. Thus, there are still inserts made up exclusively of a single compound mass consisting of PVC (polyvinyl chloride) or LDPE (low density polyethylene) and displaying an OTR of 1.4 mg O_2/year (Müller and Weisser 2002). Other ones containing no PVC even display lower OTR values and a behavior more similar to that of the very well sealing BVS screw caps fitted with so-called liners (Jung and Schüssler 2016). In more recent times, sealing inserts consisting of compound mass are used predominantly in screw caps designated for bottles with MCA mouth.

In the wine industry, compound mass as a sealing insert has largely been replaced by liners. Traditionally, there have been two different kinds of liner widely spread:

1. Saranex™ liners: They consist of expanded polyethylene coated on both sides by a PVDC (polyvinylidene chloride) layer. Their OTR is 1.0 to 1.5 mg O_2/year (Vidal et al. 2011).

2. Tin-saran liners according to the following makeup, from top to bottom:
   - Expanded polyethylene of 1.8 mm thickness whose elasticity ensures the tight fit of the entire liner on the bottle rim. It is almost air-tight, tolerates pressure and temperature fluctuations to a reasonable extent, and prevents leakage. In the meantime, its resistance and durability has been proved over 30 years at least.
   - Paper layer.
   - Tin foil of 0.02 mm thickness providing the actual seal against diffusion of gases such as oxygen.
   - PVDC, also known by its trade name "Saran"®, with 0.019 mm thickness. It is the only component of the tin-Saran liner whose surface is in direct contact with both the wine and the bottle rim.

Tin-saran liners display an OTR of 0.0 mg O_2/year. Thus, they can be considered an absolute oxygen barrier.

Figure 53 depicts the designs of the popular Saranex and tin-Saran liners.

Figure 53: Design of Saranex and tin-Saran liners for screw caps.
(Courtesy Meyer-Seals Incorp., Alfeld, Germany)

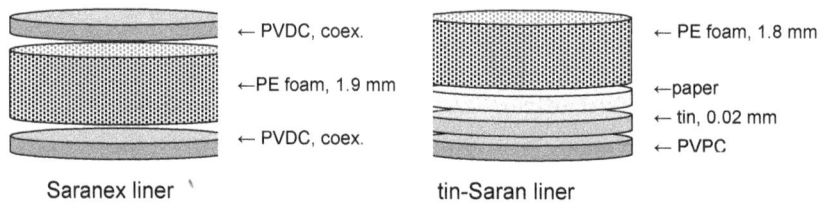

Tin-Saran and Saranex liners are primarily applied to BVS screw caps. They are in a state of continuous development. Thus, the tin foil they contain can be replaced by an aluminum foil.

Screw caps fitted with a liner containing a metal foil are preferentially used for white wines. Owing to their absolute oxygen barrier, they also serve as a reference in comparative bottle closure trials. Hence, they are in the focus of the intensive global debates upon wine bottle closures. Nevertheless, screw caps must never be regarded as a uniform type of closure since their OTR strongly depends on the sealing insert they are fitted with.

Practical hints: Requirements for correctly processing screw caps

For successful sealing of the bottles and guaranteeing the well performing oxygen barrier provided by screw caps, there are much more stringent demands on adjustment and management of the bottling hardware than when stoppers are used. This applies in particular to bottle geometry and its fluctuations. The bottle thread necks tolerate less fluctuations than band necks. The reason is as follows:

As cork stoppers are an internally sealing closure requiring a band neck, it is obvious that the inner surface of the neck is decisive for the tightness of that type of closure. The evenness of the neck rim surface is of minor importance. In contrast, when bottles with thread are processed, the effectiveness of the closure strongly depends on the evenness of the upper rim surface, onto which the liner of the screw cap is pressed before the rollers mold the sleeve of the cap to fit over the ridges on the outside of the neck. Liners adapt less well to irregularities of the rim surface than the more elastic corks adapt to tolerances of the inner surface of the neck. As a result, damaged bottle threads caused during manufacturing, storage, or rinsing can seriously compromise the quality of the sealing.

In some cases, uncontrolled oxygen ingress can also result from the screw caps when application requirements (top load force, side roller force, alignment, thread formation) are not fulfilled or when the liner material reveals microscopic creases where it seals against the glass rim. Temperature of the caps during capping should not be below 10° C (50° F). Otherwise the liner can become brittle, causing problems during application.

Ultimately, OTR data provided for screw caps are only valid if liner and bottle are in perfect condition. Closures, bottles, and the sealing machine interact and must be adjusted one to another, particularly when high-performance bottling lines are operated.

Screw cap liners decide about oxidative or reductive aging

In a storage trial with Chardonnay and Pinot noir over three years, the screw caps fitted with compound mass (LDPE) led to wines with highest values for DO and lowest levels of SO_2. Conversely, screw caps fitted with tin-Saran liner resulted in lowest DO levels and highest SO_2 concentrations. Both wines showed a decrease of H_2S and methanethiol, which was strongest under screw caps with a compound insert and under synthetic corks. Wines sealed with LDPE-compound in the screw caps displayed highest levels of acetaldehyde and ß-damascenone and lowest levels of linalool after three years, whereas the wines sealed with Saranex-lined screw caps occupied an intermediate position (He et al. 2013).

In a similar trial with Sauvignon blanc over two years, the lot sealed with a synthetic cork, highly permeable to oxygen, was relatively oxidized in aroma, high in sotolon content, brown in color, low in SO_2, ascorbic acid, and varietal thiols compared to the lots sealed with other closures. Conversely, wines sealed under more air-tight conditions as with screw caps fitted with tin-Saran liner had the lowest rate of browning, and displayed the greatest contents of antioxidants and varietal thiols, but also high levels of H_2S, which were responsible for the dominating reduced aroma character in these wines. The oxygen ingress through natural corks and screw caps fitted with Saranex liner proved to be optimal for the preservation of fruity aroma compounds because they occupied an intermediate position, presenting negligible reduced or oxidized aroma characters. The OTR rate of closures was shown to be an important tool for predicting the shelf life of wine (Lopes et al. 2009).

These results clearly demonstrate that apparently small differences in the OTR between different screw caps liners, in this case 0.0 vs. 1.5 mg O_2/year, are of great sensory importance over a two years' bottle storage. They control the accumulation of sulfhydryls and the appearance of reductive taints during bottle aging. Hence, screw caps require a differentiated consideration with regard to their OTR and the liner they are fitted with. This holds true in particular when one has to expect a prolonged bottle storage in the distribution chain and after purchase.

Furthermore, these results raise the question of whether the widespread use of the tightly sealing tin-Saran lined screw caps makes sense under all conditions. It is widely ignored that the very first large-scale use of screw caps started as early as in the 1970's in Switzerland. Since then, these screw caps are predominantly Saranex-lined and have never caused acute problems with reductive aging.

3.5. Measures to prevent post-bottling reductive aging

Introduction: The analytical determination of potential precursors of compounds responsible for reductive aging does not give any information about the extent to which these compounds are released post-bottling. An accelerated heating text under reductive conditions provides results closer to reality. In sensory terms, traces of copper are able to scavenge the odor-active compounds in statu nascendi to a large extent and significantly lower the proneness of wine to develop reductive aging, albeit analytical data are somewhat contradictory. When wine is bottled with traces of copper, legal and stability limits must be observed. From a toxicological and ethical point of view, the amounts required for that purpose in a bottle of wine are much lower than the recommended copper daily requirements or the copper levels per pound human mass body. As an alternative to copper additions, a functionalized screw cap containing immobilized copper capable of irreversibly binding stinky sulfur-containing compounds has been developed. It relocates the interaction between these compounds and copper as they are known to occur in wine from the bottle into the liner without copper getting in contact with the wine.

3.5.1. Assessing wines' proneness to post-bottling reduction flavor

The relative importance of individual precursors of VSCs involved in the appearance of post-bottling reduction taints remains largely unknown, but it can be reasonably assumed that it depends on the individual wine. It can further be assumed that metal-complexed sulfhydryls, disulfides, and thioacetates rank about the most important precursors (Bekker et al. 2018, Kreitman et al. 2018). Their quantitative measurement is beyond the scope of routine quality control and provides data that

3. Reductive aging and post-bottling reduction flavor

is difficult to interpret. Furthermore, it would only provide a snapshot of a large array of molecules but not give any information about the risk of a wine actually becoming reductive post-bottling. Instead, there is an experimental approach aiming at assessing the proneness of wine to develop post-bottling reduction flavor by means of an informal sniff test.

Limited information by reagent additions

In analytical chemistry, additions of neocuproine, tris(2-carboxyethyl)phosphine (TCEP), ethylenediaminetetraacetic acid (EDTA), or sodium chloride are used to disrupt the copper-sulfhydryl complexes and quantify the sulfhydryls released by that way. These reagents fulfill their purpose to a variable degree (Chen et al. 2017). Their addition to wine in a tasting glass is also able to generate a distinctive reductive off-odor in most wines within a couple of minutes. This behavior confirms the importance of copper-complexed sulfhydryls as putative precursors of post-bottling reduction flavor. Theoretically, evaluating the sulfhydryls released by analytical or sensory means could be used as a diagnostic tool to predict the wines' proneness to develop post-bottling reduction flavor.

On the other hand, this approach does not take into account the presence of additional, known or unknown precursors. Furthermore, it does not give any information about the extent to which they would release odor-active compounds under real-world aging conditions. Thus, it fails in giving a holistic picture of the wines' proneness to actually undergo reductive aging.

More information by heat tests

An accelerated reductive aging (ARA) test performed under anoxic conditions would anticipate results of reductive aging and potential post-bottling reduction taints. Such a test was developed and carried out over 12.5 days at 50° C under strictly anoxic conditions with the purpose of quantitatively releasing and measure H_2S and methanethiol in whatever form they were bound, complexed, oxidized, or de-novo generated. The concentrations released correlated satisfactorily with those obtained after one year of storage at 25° C (Franco-Luesma and Ferreira 2016 a, 2016 b).

A 12.5 day ARA test is still rather slow as compared to other winery bench tests such as checking potassium bitartrate or protein stability, which can be completed within a couple of hours. On the other hand, the sulfhydryl release is strongly temperature-dependent. Increasing the temperature by 25° C resulted in a 30-fold increase in the sulfhydryl release rate (Franco-Luesma and Ferreira 2016 a). Thus, this assay was adapted to commercial winery and laboratory settings, leading to the following test protocol:

Implementation of the accelerated reductive aging test

A sample of the 'clean' smelling, filtered wine is adjusted to 30-50 mg/L free SO_2 and supplied with 200 mg/L ascorbic acid. Subsequently, it is poured into a bottle filled to the rim, sealed with a screw cap, and stored in an oven or water bath at 60° C during one week. At the end of the incubation period, this sample is compared by smell with the untreated reference at ambient temperature. When the test sample displays a reductive taint, the wine can be considered prone to develop post-bottling reduction flavor. Countermeasures are described in the next section. They can be implemented on a trial basis on the test samples displaying reduction flavor after removal from the oven.

Interpreting results

This ARA test is analogous to shelf life studies of other foods and beverages that rely on elevated temperatures and short times to approximate long-term storage. It is a modification of another assay used to assess the proneness of wine to develop atypical aging (Chapter 4.6), but works with a longer incubation period. Increasing the temperature with the purpose of further reducing the incubation period would be counterproductive. Under these conditions, the excessive formation through Maillard reaction of pungent/burnt smelling flavoring compounds not related to VSCs would disturb sensory evaluation of reductive off-odors. Lastly, the addition of ascorbic acid ensures the disappearance of DO picked up upon sample handling in less than one day, thus creating reductive conditions.

In figure 54, the left column shows results of the ARA test carried out on 22 young white wines with varying initial copper concentrations ranging from 0.02 to 0.48 mg/L Cu^{++}. The intensity of reduction flavor by smell generated under the test conditions is expressed as the amount of Cu^{++} required to remove it. Copper requirements were determined according to the procedure outlined in table 12. A panel of trained tasters sourced from the wine industry was used for that purpose on several days. Maximum copper additions required were 0.125 mg/L Cu^{++}, corresponding to a relatively strong reduction flavor produced in the ARA test. Approximately one third of the wine samples remained 'clean' and did not respond to copper additions.

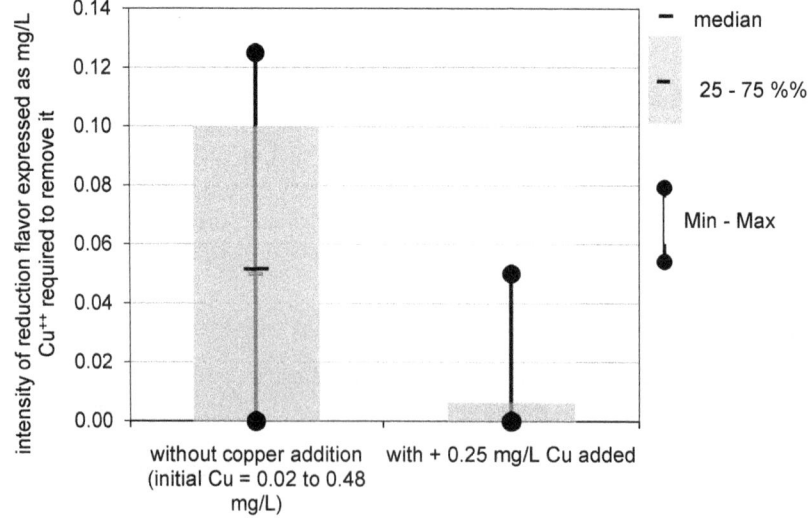

Figure 54: Reduction flavor by smell, expressed as mg/L Cu^{++} required to remove it after ARA test of 22 young white wines with variable copper levels.

3. Reductive aging and post-bottling reduction flavor

The right column in figure 54 gives the results obtained on the same wines after addition of 0.25 mg/L Cu^{++} prior to the ARA test. The enhanced copper levels led to less reduction flavor perceived by smell and, consequently, 85 % less copper additions on average required to remove it. Moreover, 77 % of the wines remained 'clean'. These results strongly indicate that in merely sensory terms, wines with enhanced copper levels better withstand reductive aging.

This test displays in time lapse what would be happening in practice during storage under conditions of low or nil oxygen ingress. Its results correlate satisfactorily with long-term aging effects under commercial conditions. Judicious copper additions to wines revealing potential reduction flavor under test conditions can be one of the means to improve their resistance to post-bottling reductive aging.

3.5.2. Copper management pre-bottling

Chapter 3.3.3 outlines that the addition of copper rapidly removes the off-odor caused by elevated contents of thiols and H_2S, converting them into dispersed copper-complexes which can be removed by filtration to a certain extent. Unfortunately, the concentration of their precursors is not significantly affected by copper fining, thus remaining in the wine and able to release off-odor causing sulfhydryls at a later point of time.

Indeed, there is no suitable way to remove thioacetates. In contrast, removal of disulfides can be feasible through the tedious process of their previous reduction to the corresponding thiols after addition of ascorbic acid (Chapter 3.3.3). Since this procedure is laborious and unreliable, it is currently only applied pre-bottling when elevated levels of disulfides are supposed to be responsible for reduction flavor. Furthermore, it has been shown that ascorbic acid also releases some H_2S from its copper complexes (Chen et al. 2017). This is one of the reasons why ascorbic acid additions upon bottling tend to slightly enhance the proneness of wine to develop post-bottling reduction flavor (Skouroumounis et al. 2005 a).

Despite its shortcomings, the most widespread option for preventing the appearance of post-bottling reductive taints is the simple addition of copper sulfate before bottling. It is based on the assumption that a lack of naturally occurring copper in modern wines is one of the reasons for the increasing occurrence of these faults after bottling. As outlined previously, yeast absorbs the largest proportion of must copper in a way that contemporary wines rarely display more than 0.1 mg/L Cu^{++}. This level will not change as long as there is no copper contamination by copper-containing brass fittings as it commonly happened until a few decades ago.

Copper traces scavenge reduction flavor in *statu nascendi*

Addition of copper ions remedies the lack of natural copper and supplies wine with a slight surplus of reactive copper (Cowey 2008, Schneider 2008). This surplus must be larger than the amount of copper required to bind all thiols and H_2S present, plus the amount of copper tightly bound to S-containing amino acids, proteins and other macromolecules and thus becoming ineffective. Under these conditions and when there is sufficient free surplus copper left, it will trap odor-active sulfhydryls generated after bottling (Limmer 2005 c).

Under commercial winemaking conditions, the amounts of precursors able to release sulfhydryls are unknown. This also applies when an accelerated reductive aging test reveals their existence. There is even less knowledge about the rate and extent at which they will release sulfhydryls under conditions of bottle aging. Hence, the optimal copper level must be adjusted on an empirical basis.

Many years of industrial experience have shown that pre-bottling copper additions of only 0.25 mg/L Cu^{++} (1.0 mg/L copper sulfate), making up a total copper content of approximately 0.3 mg/L Cu^{++} at bottling, suffice to remedy the natural lack of copper and prevent the appearance of post-bottling reductive odors in most wines sealed with tin-Saran screw caps over at least two years. This holds true for more than 90 % of the wines developing post-bottling reduction flavor without copper addition (Schneider 2008). However, in some wines, the effect is limited in time.

The underlying idea of pre-bottling copper additions is to scavenge free sulfhydryls in *statu nascendi*, i.e. to the extent and at the moment they are released from their precursors during bottle storage. Thus, they can be relatively effective in mitigating the development of post-bottling sulfidic off-odors in most wines.

Sensory results contradict analytical data obtained under lab conditions

More recently, the valuable long-term industry experience referred to above has been called into question by some research results causing uncertainty and confusion in the wine industry. The reason lies in the latent instability of the copper-sulfhydryl complexes. Thus, they can act themselves as a precursor of reduction flavor when they release their sulfhydryl group under certain conditions (Chapter 3.2.2).

Indeed, under anoxic storage conditions, an increase of H_2S levels was observed after DO had been entirely consumed some months after bottling when copper additions took place in conjunction with a glutathione addition (Ugliano et al. 2011), when copper was added in unrealistically high amounts to adjust a final content of 3.0 mg/L Cu^{++} (Viviers et al. 2013), and when no filtration after curative copper additions was performed (Vela et al. 2017 b). The cause of this is a certain reversibility of the H_2S binding to copper or its copper-catalyzed release from S-containing amino acids.

It is obvious that these conditions creating a fatal concatenation of unfortunate circumstances have little in common with what happens in commercial winemaking. Furthermore, it is questionable whether measuring two impact compounds, H_2S and methanethiol, tells the whole story. The known diversity of off-odor causing VSCs makes sensory expertise become extremely important.

The sensory approach was used in the trials reported in figure 54. It clearly shows that wines supplied with 0.25 mg/L Cu^{++} developed less or no reductive taint in the ARA test. The general tendency is that wines with more copper produce significantly less reduction flavor perceived by smell. In contrast to increases of H_2S and methanethiol reported in the analytical studies referred to above, the copper additions increased reductive off-odor perceived by smell in no case. This is a typical example of contradiction between analytical and sensory data which sometimes occurs in enology.

Although pre-bottling copper additions are not the most perfect solution, it can be stated that the presence of copper (< 0.5 mg/L Cu^{++}) makes more difficult and retards the appearance of post-bottling reductive off-odor when the wine is prone to develop it.

Drawbacks of pre-bottling copper additions

- In the worst case, pre-bottling copper additions cannot completely impede the formation of a reduced off-aroma when wines are stored under strictly anoxic conditions.

- Copper levels in the wine must be carefully controlled to avoid copper haze and not exceed legal limits. Take into account that 1.0 mg Cu^{++} equals 4 mg copper sulfate in the powder form!

- Copper acts as a transition metal able to catalyze the transfer of oxygen onto phenolic compounds (Chapters 2.2.1 and 2.4.1), thus accelerating oxidative aging. This is a feature it shares with some other metal ions occurring in wine at low concentrations (Cacho et al. 1995). However, this property only takes effect if oxygen can actually be taken up as it happens during barrel aging or when tanks are not thoroughly topped (Chapter 2.6.2). It will be without any effect in wines stored in bottles sealed with tight screw caps or in totally topped stainless steel tanks. Oxygen availability is the limiting factor controlling the rate and extent of oxidation in the long-term. In the absence of oxygen, no oxidation will take place.

- Copper does not react as specifically with VSCs as it would be desirable. Rather it also lowers the levels of varietal aroma thiols of wines obtained from some cultivars. These polyfunctional thiols comprise essentially 4-mercapto-4-methylpentan-2-one (4-MMP), 3-mercaptohexan-1-ol (3-MH), and 3-mercaptohexyl acetate (3-MHA), all of them carrying a sulfhydryl (-SH) group. They elicit flavors reminding passion fruit, grapefruit, and black currents. They are particularly important for the distinct varietal aroma of Sauvignon blanc wines obtained from ripe fruit (Coetzee and du Toit 2012). In such wines, problems can sometimes arise in the sensory differentiation between varietal aroma and reductive taints. This is especially true when bench trials with increasing copper additions (Table 12) are run to remove reduction flavor. The transition of reductive taints to varietal aroma can be flowing in these wines and rise a sensory challenge.

3.5.3. Stability and toxicity of copper

Legal limits of copper in wine are 1.0 mg/L Cu^{++} in most countries but only 0.5 mg/L Cu^{++} in the USA. In general they are higher than the stability limit of 0.5

mg/L Cu^{++} or 0.3 mg/L Cu^{++} in the presence of ascorbic acid, which is the amount of copper able to remain in solution in the long-term without precipitating as a copper haze. The sensory threshold of copper on the palate is around 1.0 mg/L Cu^{++}. At higher concentrations, copper imparts a lingering bitter and metallic aftertaste.

The stability limits referred to above do not represent absolute limits but reflect empirical data obtained on countless wines. This means that when copper concentrations do not exceed these limits, wines can be supposed to not create a copper haze. In some individual cases which are not predictable, wines even remain copper-stable at much higher concentrations. The cause is the strong binding of copper onto other wine compounds as organic acids and colloidal material forming soluble complexes with it. Tartaric acid has been shown to be one of the most important copper complexing compounds in grape wine (Clark et al. 2015).

The formation of these complexes also explain why much higher amounts of copper are required to complex off-odor sulfhydryls than calculated by stoichiometry, and why copper and sulfhydryls can coexist.

In commercial winemaking, it is crucial to check copper levels using reliable up-to-date methods of analysis such as AAS. The result is the concentration of total copper regardless of its speciation, i.e. its distribution among different oxidation states (Cu, Cu^+ and Cu^{++}) and their complexed forms.

After subtraction of complexed copper from total copper, the remaining copper ions occur in their reduced monovalent (Cu^+) or oxidized divalent (Cu^{++}) form. Divalent copper is fairly well soluble, while compounds of monovalent copper display poor solubility. The relative proportions of both forms depend on both redox potential and pH of the wine. The more reductive the wine or the lower its redox potential, the less copper is soluble. This explains why in the presence of ascorbic acid, a strong reducing agent, total copper solubility decreases from 0.5 to 0.3 mg/L, turning the wine more susceptible to producing a copper haze.

The impact of the wine matrix on copper solubility is shown in figure 55. Addition of ascorbic acid lowers copper solubility by approximately 18 %. Addition of gum arabic, a legalized colloidal additive, and lowering pH allow for maintaining remarkably more copper in stable solution.

Addition of citric acid is sometimes recommended to improve the stability of copper and other metal ions. As a commercial consequence, copper citrate has been developed and legalized as an allegedly better substitute for copper sulfate (Chapter 3.3.3). Indeed, citric acid is able to form soluble complexes with copper just as gum arabic, polysaccharides, and pectines, depending on their concentrations. In this capacity, citric acid is not very different from the other organic acids occurring in grape wine (Blum and Schwedt 1998). Compared with typical total acidity levels in current wines, their slight increase by citric acid additions does not significantly impact copper stability.

3. Reductive aging and post-bottling reduction flavor

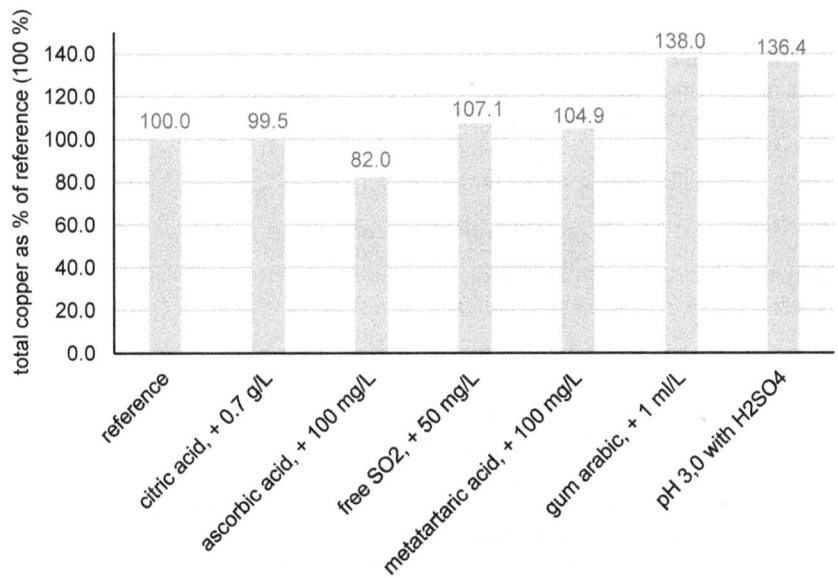

Figure 55: Impact of various wine treatments and additives on the solubility of copper monitored over three months. Means of four white wines. Reference = 100 %.

Furthermore, temperature and light affect the stability of copper. Light reduces its solubility particularly in white wines bottled in clear glass. Certain wave lengths of visible light possibly induce a shift of the wines' redox potential, thus causing a gradual sensitization of a metastable system. Figure 56 displays this effect measured on seven white and seven red wines.

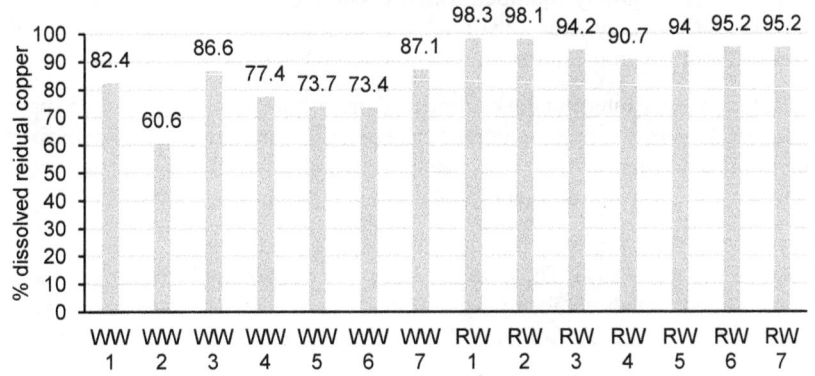

Figure 56: Decrease of copper solubility measured as % residual dissolved copper in 7 white (WW) and 7 red (RW) wines after light exposure during three months' bottle storage at 20° C. Storage in the dark = 100 %.

There are not yet any studies on the precise cause of this behavior. The only certainty is that under conditions of light-induced copper sensitization, red wines retain slightly more copper in solution than white wines because their anthocyanin-based color partially absorbs light.

Proteins in white wines induce additional copper instability since they contain S-containing amino acids able to react with copper. Indeed, copper and proteins frequently precipitate jointly. Proteins destabilize copper, and vice versa. Hence, the appearance of copper hazes is facilitated when wines have not been subject to thorough protein stabilization by bentonite fining (Chapter 2.4.2).

Qualitative, toxicological, and ethical considerations of copper fining

Many winemakers are afraid of adding copper ions to their wines. The fear of quality losses is one of the reasons, ethical or health concerns are another reason.

As outlined in chapter 3.5.2, the aroma of wines obtained from Sauvignon blanc and a few other varieties displaying sensorially significant amounts of varietal thiols is easily affected by copper additions. In contrast, the aroma of the majority of other cultivars is astonishingly little responsive to these additions. This also applies to highly aromatic varieties such as Muscat, Gewürztraminer, Traminette, and Riesling, whose intensive aroma is mainly caused by terpenols at elevated concentrations. This group of aromatics does not react with copper. This can easily be demonstrated by adding 0.5 mg/L Cu^{++} to an absolutely 'clean' wine according to the procedure given in table 13 and comparing it with the untreated standard. When this sensory comparison is conducted as a blind tasting, thus excluding the well-known effects of suggestion in wine evaluation, the irrational fear of aroma losses by standard copper additions (< 0.5 mg/L Cu^{++}) can easily be overcome.

With the come-back of some historical winemaking methods, traditional equipment is sometimes reintroduced by winemakers devoted to antiquities as a means of producing wines supposedly more in harmony with nature. Thus, when wines are stored in concrete eggs not coated with an inner liner, a copper ingress of 0.2 mg/L Cu^{++} per year takes place. When wine is passed through a brass tube or screen to remove reduction flavor in the very traditional Old World way, copper uptake is virtually out of control (Ecchi and Kobler 2008). This also applies to remote times when cellars were regularly equipped with brass hose connections and fittings. Under these conditions, copper uptake of 0.3 to >1.0 mg/L Cu^{++} was quite normal and accepted without any concerns as long as no copper haze appeared.

It is vital to correctly interpret concentration data. A typical addition of 0.25 mg/L Cu^{++} (1.0 mg/L copper sulfate) required to prevent or remove reduction flavor from a wine produced with stainless steel winery equipment results in similar copper levels to those of some decades ago. The absolute concentrations are decisive.

In winemaking, decisions are often driven by a lack of knowledge, emotions, and esoterism in the worst case. Thus, no wonder some people easily accept a passive and uncontrolled copper uptake by using traditional craftsman's procedures, while they strongly reject the controlled additions of precisely measurable amounts of copper salts. But even when enlightened rationalism prevails in enological decision-making, the toxicological issue of copper additions is not yet ruled out.

Table 14: Copper contents of foods. Data extracted from: Lurie et al., 1989.

	mg/kg	
	min.	max.
beef, pork, lamb, veal	0.1	3.9
liver, beef, cooked	34	93
turkey, cooked	0.4	1.9
other poultry	0.1	1.9
breads	1.0	6.0
ready-to-eat cereals	0.2	10.8
milk	0.03	0.16
dairy products	0.02	2,2
chocolate products	0.7	5.1
vegetable oil	0.01	3.2
grain products	0.1	8.7
corn, canned	0.1	0.4
tomatoes, raw	0.5	1.8
beans	1.9	6.7
potatoes	0.7	1.4
walnuts	12.7	14.0
peanuts	6.1	9.5
oysters	7.5	793
crabs	2.7	10.6
bananas	1.0	2.1
grapes	0.35	2.5
peaches	0.3	1.25

As repeatedly pointed out, when one strives for the prevention of post-bottling reduction flavor by copper additions, final copper levels higher than 0.3 to 0.4 mg/L Cu^{++} do not make any sense in the overwhelming majority of wines prone to produce that off-odor. Table 14 shows that these levels are in line with or significantly lower than those found in most other food stuffs.

Copper is an essential trace metal and cofactor for a broad variety of biological functions. The human body contains around 2 mg of copper per kilogram of body mass. Approximately 2 mg dietary copper is needed by humans each day to prevent any symptoms of deficit. Taking into account the totality of these data easily accessible, it is easy to understand that health concerns when drinking a bottle of copper-fined wine do not have any sound scientific basis.

Without any doubt, copper levels in wine are a critical parameter, and the discussion about copper additions easily gets fanned into flames. A more balanced treatment of this issue would be desirable. Aversions and emotions are a bad substitute for factual knowledge on a sound scientific basis.

3.5.4. Screw cap liners scavenging reduction flavor

Since a great deal of decision-making in the wine industry is based on emotions rather than on expertise, many winemakers will continue to be reluctant to willfully add copper to wine for health or ethical reasons. Furthermore, there are some drawbacks to this practice and legal limits for final copper content. Particularly under conditions of low oxygen ingress, the copper complexes initially formed with VSCs may serve as a latent source of free H_2S and thiols in some wines during later storage (Chapter 3.2). Copper can also affect the varietal aroma profile of Sauvignon blanc and some other varieties where aroma thiols play a major role in overall aromatics (Chapter 3.5.2). Hence, there has been no lack of attempts to put wines in contact with copper in an immobilized form so that it cannot accumulate in the wine or even get in touch with it.

One technical solution consisted in immobilizing copper on an inert carrier material and coating the resulting compound with a permeable polymer membrane. VSCs diffuse from the wine through the polymer membrane to the copper, onto which they are bound as far as they are copper-responsive.

This concept has been applied to develop a new screw cap liner inspired by the traditional tin-Saran liner but with the tin layer replaced by an aluminium layer. Furthermore, the new liner contains an additional acceptor layer consisting of immobilized copper, capable of irreversibly binding VSCs after their diffusion through a polyethylene layer in contact with the wine. This polyethylene layer would not allow immobilized copper to migrate into the wine (Schneider et al. 2017).

The objective was to entirely relocate the interactions between VSCs and copper as they are known to occur in wine from the bottle into the liner. At the same time, the absolute oxygen barrier provided by the tin-Saran liner was maintained. The ultimate purpose was the preservation of fruity aroma compounds under strict anoxic conditions excluding any oxidative aging, and simultaneously minimizing the appearance of off-odor causing VSCs without copper or reaction products dissolving or getting in contact with the wine.

In principle, the outcome of this approach has been intended to be a functionalized, active bottle closure providing more than just a sealing. Functionalized packaging materials are not unknown in the food and beverage industry. A typical example of functionalized closures are those containing oxygen scavengers used to remove oxygen from juices and other liquids packed in oxygen-permeable PET bottles.

Decrease of thiols

Figure 57 shows the impact of that kind of active, functionalized liner on a commercial Chardonnay wine displaying VSCs concentrations corresponding to several times the threshold limit. It was bottled with a clearly discernible reduction taint, screw-capped after inertization of the bottle headspace, and stored upright. The same wine bottled and sealed with screw caps containing the traditional tin-Saran liner served as a reference.

Figure 57: Evolution of VSCs and sensorially perceived reduction flavor of a tainted white wine sealed with different screw caps after 8 months' bottle storage (upright, dark, 20° C).

Me-SH = methanethiol, Et-SH = ethanethiol, DMDS = dimethyl disulfide, DMS = dimethyl sulfide

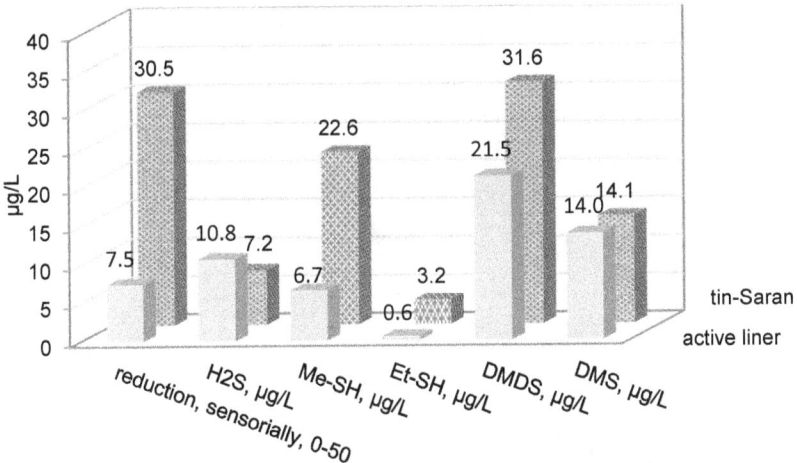

Internally sealing closures such as natural and synthetic corks are able to absorb certain amounts of VSCs regardless of the presence of oxygen (Silva et al. 2012). The functionalized liner for screw caps displays an identical feature but with much higher efficiency. Furthermore, the results confirm the possibility of decreasing Cu-reactive VSCs while maintaining the absolute oxygen barrier of the traditional tin-Saran liner that is essential for preventing oxidative aging. This applies in particular to methanethiol, which is one of the main compounds responsible for the appearance of post-bottling reduction flavor. However, there is a lack of effect on H_2S concentration, which is to be explained by the complex chemistry involved in its formation and fate.

To make this concept work under commercial wine storage conditions, the new liner must also be able to trap sulfhydryls at the rate they are generated in the bottle via the disintegration of their precursors. For verifying this hypothesis, further storage trials were carried out with wines previously spiked with these precursors, bottled under anoxic conditions as described, and sealed with screw caps containing the respective liner before bottle storage was started.

Decrease of thioacetates

Figure 58 demonstrates the results for thioacetates as a precursor. After eight months' bottle storage, their contents in the lot sealed with the active liner were only 47 % of those under the tin-Saran liner. This decrease of thioacetates has to be explained by a displacement of the dynamic equilibrium between thioacetates and the corresponding thiols by hydrolysis (Chapter 3.2.2) in the course of bottle storage. The thiols generated in that way are absorbed by the active liner. This absorption accelerates the hydrolysis of thioacetates and leads eventually to their effective decrease.

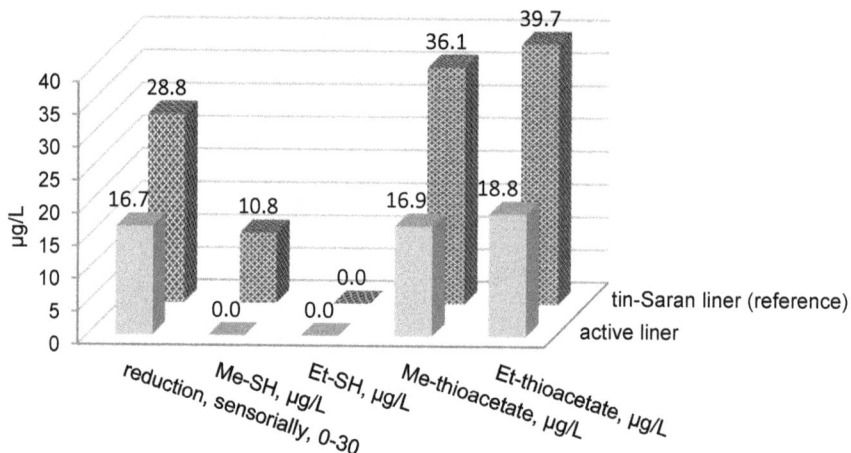

Figure 58: Evolution of VSCs and sensorially perceived reduction flavor of a white wine spiked with 50 µg/L methyl thioacetate and 50 µg/L ethyl thioacetate and sealed with different screw caps after 8 months' bottle storage (upright, dark, 20° C). Me-SH = methanethiol, Et-SH = ethanethiol

In contrast, there can be observed an accumulation of thiols (Me-SH) generated by hydrolysis under the tin-Saran liner, altogether with higher residual amounts of thioacetates. Both effects contribute to the almost two-fold intensity of reduction flavor as perceived by smell after the eight months of bottle aging with tin-Saran.

Decrease of disulfides

A similar trial was conducted after spiking the wine with disulfides. Figure 59 illustrates the outcome after an eight months' bottle storage period. Compared with the tin-Saran liner, the active liner resulted in a decrease of dimethyl disulfide by 75 % and of diethyl disulfide by 100 %. At the same time, there was an accumulation of methanethiol and ethanethiol under the tin-saran liner, which did not occur under the functionalized liner, resulting in a decrease of the sensorially perceived reduction flavor by approximately 50 % caused by the active liner. It is worth pointing out that this effect is persistent since the amount of copper immobilized in the active liner exceeds VSCs concentrations by a multiple molar surplus.

3. Reductive aging and post-bottling reduction flavor

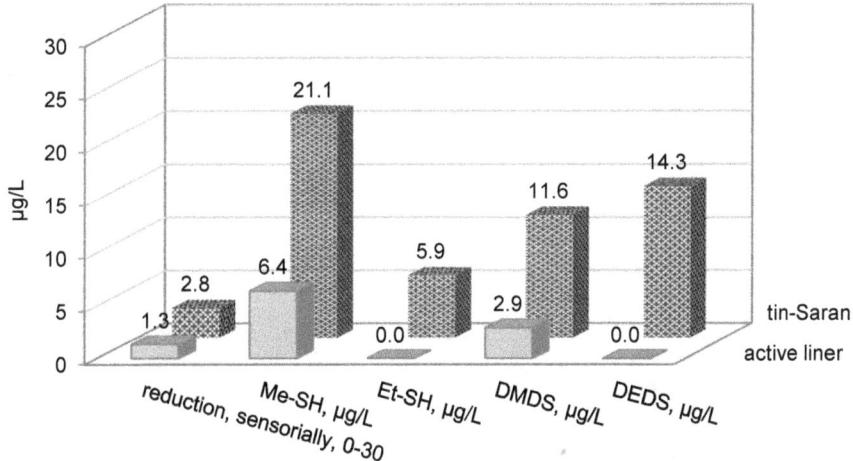

Figure 59: Changes of VSCs and sensorially perceived reduction flavor of a white wine spiked with 33 µg/L dimethyl disulfide and 33 µg/L diethyl disulfide and sealed with different screw caps after months' bottle storage (upright, dark, 20° C).

Me-SH = methanethiol, Et-SH = ethanethiol,
DMDS = dimethyl disulfide, DEDS = diethyl disulfide

However, it cannot be concluded that disulfides have been directly absorbed by the new liner. Since they are not Cu-responsive, it must be assumed that they have first been reduced to the corresponding thiols, which have been bound as such by the functionalized liner.

The entirety of results obtained indicate that in spite of anoxic storage conditions under metal-lined screw caps, the formation of off-odor causing thiols can be prevented or significantly mitigated by the new liner without adding copper to the wine. Thus, the preservation of fruity varietal aromatics under strict exclusion of oxygen is not compromised by the risk of reductive off-odor formation post-bottling.

In the meantime, the new liner has been submitted to long-term field trials. Results obtained on various wines after 18 months of bottle storage indicate substantial progress in the solution of sensory problems associated with the appearance of post-bottling reduction flavor when wines are sealed with screw caps. They can be summarized as follows (Schneider et al. 2017):

- In comparison with the well-known tin-Saran liner, closure-related oxygen uptake and SO_2 decrease resulting therefrom are identical and negligible.

- No measurable release of copper or other metals takes place.

- In comparison with the tin-Saran liner, a significant decrease of thiols, thioacetates, disulfides, and some other VSCs takes place, resulting in a noticeable reduction of aroma attributes described as sulfuric, reductive, and vegetative in wines affected by reductive aging. However, H_2S is not affected.
- No significant decrease of aroma thiols involved in the overall aroma of Sauvignon blanc could be observed by sensory and analytical means. This can be explained by their molecular weights, which are distinctively higher than those of malodorous VSCs. They limit the diffusion rate of aroma thiols through the polyethylene layer in contact with wine. This layer acts as a kind of molecular filter.
- Wines displaying no proneness to develop reduction taints show no sensory differences when compared to the tin-Saran liner after two years of bottle storage.

4. Atypical aging

4.1. Sensory identification and compounds involved

Introduction: Atypical aging refers to a flavor defect which in many cases can appear in rather young white wines obtained from Vitis vinifera grape varieties, in which sensorially perceptible aging effects are not yet expected. It is reminiscent of the smell of mothballs and naphthalene caused by the presence of elevated levels of 2-aminoacetophenone, or of damp towel and urine stone elicited by molecules not yet definitely investigated.

Atypical aging (ATA), sometimes also referred to as untypical aging, is an aroma defect occurring in white wines obtained from Vitis vinifera varieties and first mentioned by anecdotal reports from Germany and Italy at the beginning of the 1990's. In the meantime, it has been observed in most winegrowing countries across the world. However, the attention paid to ATA by producers and consumers is highly variable and not related to the frequency of its actual occurrence in a given winegrowing area. It is not supposed to be a distinctive fault in some countries, often confounded with typical aging, and may even be considered as an intrinsic expression of terroir in other areas. In contrast, many enologists consider it as the most serious challenge in contemporary winemaking and associated with global climate change observed since the 1990's. To distinguish it from typical aging (Chapter 2) which has always been known, it was named "atypical" by that time.

The connection of ATA to some kind of aging process is misleading since it may appear in rather young wines within a few weeks or months after primary fermentation and addition of sulfur dioxide. As a result, its occurrence may not be expected or may simply be ignored due to deficient sensory training. The sensory identification of ATA is complicated by its diverse forms of aromatic expression evoked by variable amounts of underlying odoriferous compounds in a complex flavor matrix. However, deficiencies in sensory discrimination bring about misleading technical advice when it comes to take adequate enological measures against it.

The role of 2-aminoacetophenone

2-aminoacetophenone (AAP) has been described as the chemical marker and sensory impact compound of ATA (Rapp et al. 1993). Its smell is similar to that of acacia blossom and mothballs. The sensory threshold of AAP has been reported to be approximately 1.0 µg/L. In wines obtained from Vitis vinifera not affected by

ATA, AAP levels generally do not exceed 0.3 µg/L. However, things are more complicated and thresholds highly variable.

In spiking trials, increasing amounts of AAP added to sound white wines obviously show a positive correlation with perceived ATA intensity. Figure 60 gives results obtained on 38 wines, in which AAP levels were increased by step-to-step additions of 0.25 µg/L AAP for each step. Tasters were asked to first rate the fruity aroma intensity of the untreated samples and subsequently appoint the amount of added AAP above which a) ATA can be identified, and b) ATA is strong enough to justify rejection of the wine as faulty.

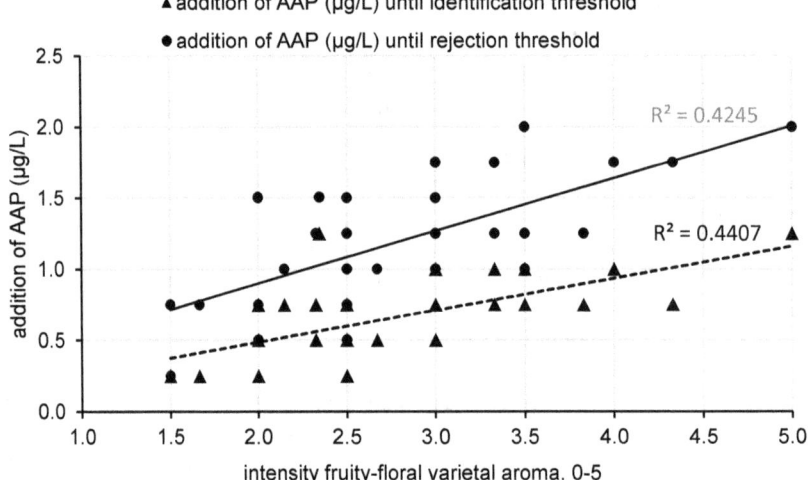

Figure 60: Impact of fruity-floral varietal aroma intensity in 38 white wines on the perception of aminoacetophenone (AAP) by smell.

Both the identification and the rejection threshold depend on the aroma intensity of the original wine with $R^2 = 0.44$ for the identification threshold and $R^2 = 0.42$ for the rejection threshold, respectively. Strongly aromatic wines are able to integrate greater than 1.5 µg/L AAP without being considered faulty, while meager wines might be rejected as tainted by ATA with less than 0.5 µg/L AAP (Schneider 2014). This variability illustrates the difficulty with assessing generally valid threshold data.

The difference threshold is considerably lower with approximately 0.1 µg/L AAP. This is the AAP concentration difference allowing to recognize sensory differences in the wine but not to identify their cause.

In wines obtained under specific New York growing conditions and described as tainted by ATA, AAP was reported to be below the sensory detection threshold. Instead, the perception of ATA was ascribed to a combination of a loss of varietal fruit flavor causing stimulants like terpenols or their psychophysical suppression and the appearance of specific ATA off-flavor attributes (Cheng et al. 2004). Confusing the lack of any smell with ATA is the result of a sensory bias frequently observed when wines are checked for ATA.

In contrast to spiking trials with AAP, when wines actually affected by ATA are submitted to descriptive sensory analysis, they usually show an even poorer correlation between AAP concentration and perceived ATA intensity. In one study, AAP concentration accounted for only 30 % of sensory atypical aging intensity (Linsenmeier et al. 2007 a). Aroma patterns are also different from those elicited by pure AAP. Additions of AAP alone fail to produce the whole sensory spectrum of ATA, although it is clearly involved in the off-flavor of most wines. These results strongly suggest not only masking effects but also the participation of compounds other than only AAP (Christoph et al. 1995, Gessner et al. 1995, 1999 a, Simat et al. 2004).

Sensory bias and confusion with other kinds of aging

On occasion, ATA is mistaken as reduction flavor or post-bottling reductive taints (Chapter 3). More often, however, ATA and reductive taints occur simultaneously (Rauhut et al. 2003). Since the volatile sulfur compounds responsible for reduction flavor are basically traced back to yeast metabolism as a response to nitrogen deficiency (Chapter 3.1.1) in fruit from stressed vineyards, viticultural stress is a common cause for both ATA and reduction flavor. When ATA is suspected to be masked by reductive taints, it can only be detected after copper fining removes the volatile sulfur compounds. A sample treatment with copper ions according to the procedure outlined in table 12 better reveals ATA and helps identify it.

Frequently, ATA is mistaken as typical aging (Chapter 2), which is a more slowly progressing process largely based on oxidation reactions, or even with premature oxidative aging, also known as *premox*. This is not surprising since most of the specialized literature does not make adequate distinction between both kinds of aging and considers oxidative aging as the only type of aging as though there were no other ones. Clearly, sensory bias seems to be responsible to a great extent for conflicting results in research upon wine aging, and more semantic precision is needed to describe ATA and differentiate it from other kinds of aging. There are many ambiguous terms used in wine description that tend to lack meaning.

A more precise sensory picture of ATA

Differences in language use and differences of the sensory expression of ATA at different stages of the wine age make it difficult to compare descriptions of this fault. Just like for typical aging, a plethora of olfactory attributes can be detected in wines affected by atypical aging. With the objective of sensory classification, they can be divided into two groups (Schneider 2014):

Group I: Mothballs, naphthalene, laundry detergent powder, soap, floor polish, furniture polish, antique wax, jasmine acacia blossom, lemon blossom, dry linen, and fusel alcohols. This odor pattern is reinforced by high levels of free sulfur dioxide.

Group II: Damp towel, wet wool, dirty dish rag, washing machine, and urine deposits. This aroma profile marks the sensory transition to reduction flavor and may complicate the sensory identification of ATA.

In affected wines, the attributes of either one or the other group are dominant but can also occur concurrently in some wines. They interact with different aroma compounds present in the normal aroma matrix of wine, resulting in a kind of mixed flavor. In either case, the fruity, floral, or mineral varietal aroma characteristics disappear to a great extent, partially driven by ester hydrolysis and oxidation reactions associated with typical wine aging (Chapter 2.1). Thus, the sensory intensity of ATA will increase over time. On the palate, tainted wines often come out meager and thin, displaying a metallic bitterness and astringency that is not related to the presence of any metals or tannins, and a light color.

Addition of AAP to sound wines evoked only aroma attributes referred to in group I above and described as mothballs and acacia blossoms, whereas the "stinky" descriptors of group II could not yet be generated in any wine. The group II set of descriptors is assumed to be more related to intermediates in the synthesis of AAP such as indole and skatole. Since skatole displays a strong fecal odor, it is able to elicit the olfactory attributes of group II, but reliable sensory data on its role are still lacking (Schneider 2014).

In conclusion, AAP levels greater than 1 µg/L confirm the presence of ATA, but sole AAP measurements are of dubious benefit for the analytical characterization of ATA. Low AAP concentrations do not exclude the presence of what is sensorially described as ATA.

4.2. Limited significance of microbial formation

Introduction: The contribution of yeast metabolism to the formation of ATA is of secondary importance when primary fermentation is carried out by strains of Saccharomyces cerevisiae. ATA cannot be prevented by the selection of the yeast strain used for inoculation.

2-aminoacetophenone (AAP) is partially responsible for the "foxy" smell of non-vinifera varieties, but does not occur in grapes and musts from Vitis vinifera (Acree et al. 1993). In wines obtained from V. vinifera varieties, indole-3-acetic acid (IAA) is considered the primary precursor of AAP.

During alcoholic fermentation under stress conditions in a synthetic medium containing IAA as precursor, yeast metabolism was shown to produce significant amounts of AAP, skatole, and indole-3-acetic acid. Figure 61 shows the molecular structures of these compounds.

4. Atypical aging

Figure 61: Molecular structures of indole-3-acetic acid, skatole, and 2-aminoacetophenone.

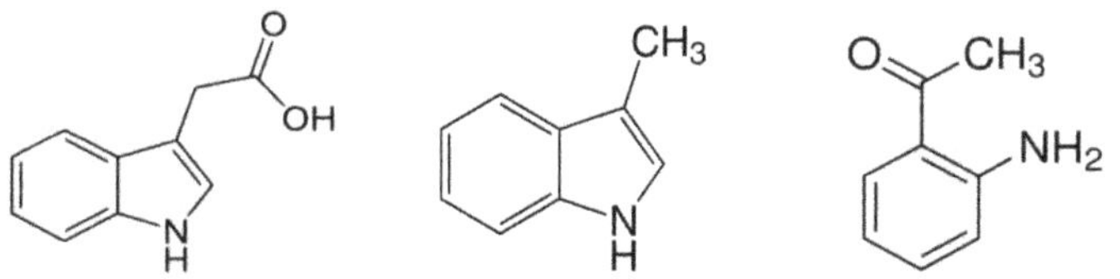

indole-3-acetic acid   skatole   2-aminoacetophenone

The synthesis of these compounds was enhanced by specific nutritional conditions comprising a lack of pantothenate and the concurrent presence of aromatic amino acids such as tryptophan. (Ciolfi et al. 1995). Also in fermentation media as in natural grape musts, IAA was considered the relevant precursor. It was converted into AAP by yeast metabolism with a modest conversion rate of merely 0.06 to 0.08 mol-% (Gessner et al. 1996). However, regarding a natural pool of total IAA in grape musts of approximately 100 µg/L, this conversion rate will yield only 0.07 µg/L AAP. A maximum formation of 0.4 µg/L AAP during fermentation was observed (Gessner et al. 1996). These amounts are clearly below the odor threshold.

The fermentations trial results indicate that the formation of AAP by yeast is not a significant contributor to the amounts of AAP found in real wines as long as fermentations are carried out by S. cerevisiae strains. They corroborate the general finding that under commercial winemaking conditions performing the prompt initiation of fermentation with active dry yeast, the synthesis of odor-active amounts of AAP and the appearance of ATA are not the direct consequence of yeast metabolism. For that reason, they cannot be observed immediately after fermentation without any further interventions on the wine. However, there might be exceptions when juices are submitted to spontaneous fermentation involving non-Saccharomyces yeast strains (Simat et al. 2004).

4.3. Chemical formation of 2-aminoacetophenone

Introduction: ATA is formed when a phytohormone called indole-3-acetic acid undergoes degradation to elevated amounts of 2-aminoacetophenone and other compounds. This complex chemical pathway is triggered by oxygen radicals generated upon the first addition of sulfur dioxide post-fermentation. The amount of oxygen required for that purpose is negligible and for below the levels required for oxidative aging. Its uptake cannot be avoided under commercial winemaking conditions. There is no meaningful correlation between precursors and the final 2-aminoacetophenone concentration. In contrast, its production is inhibited by sufficiently high levels of phenolic compounds acting as oxygen radical scavengers.

IAA is the direct precursor of AAP. It is a phytohormone occurring in grapes and also one of the intermediate products of the tryptophan metabolism of yeast, but the only one able to act as a potential precursor of AAP. In wines spiked with IAA, its conversion rate to AAP was 0.5 to 3.0 mol-% for white and 0 mol-% for red wines, depending on time and temperature.

The presence of free sulfur dioxide is indispensable to induce the conversion of IAA into AAP. As a consequence, for average levels of IAA in white wine of ~100 µg/L at the time point of the first SO_2 addition post-fermentation, the formation of sensorially relevant concentrations of greater than 1 µg/L AAP is possible within a few weeks after SO_2 addition (Christoph et al. 1998, Hoenicke et al. 2002 a). In the worst case, ATA can be perceived within a few days.

The behavior of indole-3-acetic acid as the precursor

IAA occurs in a free and a bound form, both making up total IAA. With free IAA acting as the primary precursor of AAP, it can be assumed that its concentration in young wines must be of importance for the propensity of a wine to produce ATA. In grape musts, however, IAA occurs almost exclusively in the bound form, while its free form that is able to react in the presence of SO_2 is nearly absent. Only during fermentation reasonable amounts of free IAA are produced by hydrolysis of bound IAA and de-novo synthesis by yeast (Christoph et al. 1998, Hoenicke et al. 2001, 2002 b).

Juices from late harvested grapes display more total IAA than those from early harvested grapes. However, after fermentations, wines made from late harvested grapes tend to show lower levels of free IAA than wines obtained from early harvested grapes of the same vineyard. This means that the amount of free IAA at the moment of SO_2 addition post-fermentation is influenced more by yeast metabolism, its nutritional status and fermentation conditions than by the initial IAA content of the must.

Yeast produces more free IAA in musts from stressed fruit, and wild yeasts produce higher amounts of free IAA than strains of S. cerevisiae. Fermentation on the skins, addition of complex yeast nutrients, and lower fermentation rates at cool temperatures reduced the content of free IAA in the wines (Hoenicke et al. 2002 a, Simat et al. 2004).

The significance of IAA levels in wine for AAP formation is not conclusive. In one study, there was a significant but low correlation between free IAA levels prior to the first SO_2 addition post-fermentation and the amount of AAP in the wine, indicating that 30 to 50 % of the AAP produced might be traced back to the amount of the precursor IAA at the time point of the SO_2 addition (Simat et al. 2004). In another study, neither the amount of total IAA in must nor the content of free IAA in young wines at the time of SO_2 addition showed a positive correlation with the formation of AAP and perceived ATA in wine. Thus, the appearance of ATA is

4. Atypical aging

not necessarily linked to a higher amount of IAA in the fruit, must, or wine (Hoenicke et al. 2002 b, Linsenmeier et al. 2007 b).

Clearly, the role of free IAA levels is ambiguous. Although it is the potential precursor of AAP, its amount is not a reliable means to predict the propensity of a wine to produce AAP and ATA. Reasons for this are matrix effects. They are more important than the amount of free IAA since they control its conversion rate into AAP. This is particularly demonstrated in red wines. Although IAA levels in reds are approximately 10 times higher than in white wines (Bonerz et al. 2008), they never display ATA or significant amounts of AAP. Rosé wines take an intermediate position, depending on their skin contact time, total phenol levels, and color. Slightly colored rosés tend to behave like white wines.

As a practical conclusion, it must be stated that IAA measurements do not make any sense to predict the appearance of ATA. Other wine compositional parameters are more important.

Factors affecting the conversion of IAA into AAP

This conversion is based on perplexing complicated chemical reactions, which have been described in a series of articles (Christoph et al. 1998, Hoenicke et al. 2002 a, 2002 b). In a nutshell, there is first a non-enzymatic oxidation of IAA by oxygen radicals formed during the aerobic oxidation of sulfite (SO_2) to sulfate. Then decarboxylation and cleavage of the oxidized IAA occurs, leading to a reaction sequence which can be written as

$$IAA \rightarrow skatole \rightarrow 2\text{-formylaminoacetophenone} \rightarrow AAP$$

The oxygen radicals involved are basically identical with those produced when phenols oxidize, leading subsequently to the oxidation of higher aldehydes to higher alcohols through the Fenton reaction and to oxidative aging (Chapter 2.2.1). However, they convert free IAA into AAP only in the presence of free SO_2, which allows for the indispensable sulfonation of IAA as an intermediate step in the reaction sequence (Hoenicke et al. 2002 a).

In conclusion, it can be noticed that free SO_2 triggers the chemical conversion of IAA into AAP. The potential role of skatole as potentially contributing to ATA is discussed above.

Since oxygen radicals are responsible for the decay of IAA and the formation of AAP and related compounds, antioxidants able to scavenge oxygen radicals can reduce the tendency to ATA formation. Such oxygen radical scavengers acting as antioxidants are phenolic compounds in wine. Their amounts seem to depend on the ripeness of the grapes. Wines obtained from late harvested fruit reveal significantly higher antioxidative capacity and lower sensory ratings for ATA than wines from early harvested grapes. Red wines are reputed to be protected against ATA by their high tannin content (< 1500 mg/L total phenols) acting as a radical scavenger (Hoenicke et al. 2002 b). Conversely, white wines affected by ATA generally display total phenol levels below average and lower than 100 mg/L.

Wine alcohol is also assumed to boost the reaction, while pH was shown to exert no influence (Schneider 2014).

Oxygen required for ATA formation is too low to generate oxidative aging

The formation of oxygen radicals bringing about the conversion of IAA into AAP requires aerobic oxidation, i.e. the temporary availability of dissolved oxygen (DO). However, when SO_2 is added to young white wines, the wines are usually not yet filtered and contain significant amounts of suspended yeast lees known for their ability to consume DO (Chapter 2.5.6), thus raising the question where the oxygen originates.

In adding controlled amounts of oxygen to model solutions containing a typical concentration of 100 µg/L IAA, it was shown that levels as low as 0.15 to 0.50 mg/L DO are sufficient to produce the typical smell of ATA (Schneider 2013). These minute amounts are inevitably taken up even when white wines are carefully protected against oxygen ingress during cellar operations, for example through the wine surface when containers are not completely topped (Chapters 2.6.2 to 2.6.4). However, they are far too low to elicit any sensory effects of oxidative aging, which require the consumption of at least ~10 mg/L DO by filtered white wines (Chapter 2.6.5).

Obviously, these orders of magnitude regarding oxygen requirements are totally different. They explain why, despite the involvement of oxygen, ATA must be unequivocally distinguished from oxidative aging (Chapter 2.1) from a sensory and chemical point of view. As a consequence, post-fermentation oxygen management does not impact the appearance of ATA nor does the variable oxygen transmission rate of bottles.

4.4. Viticultural causes and countermeasures

Introduction: In contrast to typical aging which is caused by enological deficiencies, atypical aging is the multi-causal result of viticultural problems associated with drought, elevated UV radiation, nutrient deficiencies, and overcropping. Frequently these factors are linked one to another. They result in a lack of physiological ripeness that is only weakly correlated with alcoholic ripeness expressed as Brix readings and exacerbated by premature harvest. Global climate change plays a role. This section depicts how to address ATA in the vineyard.

While premature typical aging traces back to enological deficiencies extensively outlined in chapter 2, atypical aging is caused by viticultural problems. It is mainly triggered by a lack of oxygen radical scavengers, i.e. basically phenolic compounds originating from the fruit. Hence, it is indispensable to analyze the viticultural factors responsible for that shortage.

4. Atypical aging

Reports on empirical evidence refer to overcropping, premature harvest, drought, excessive UV radiation, green cover, and reduced fertilization as the main viticultural factors triggering ATA under cool-climate conditions (Köhler et al. 1995, Löhnertz 1996, Schwab et al. 1996, Müller 1999, Cheng et al. 2004). All these factors induce a physiological stress in the vine or impact ripeness adversely with the appearance of ATA as a result. Frequently, they are linked one to another, thus making it difficult to identify one factor as the sole cause of ATA. Sometimes, one or the other is in the foreground. Thus, in dry-hot growing conditions, drought is supposed to be the most important triggering factor.

Vineyard management is crucial. It explains why some wineries are strongly affected by ATA while others are not within a narrowly bounded growing area.

Ripeness

Wines obtained from late harvested fruit tend to be less afflicted by ATA than those produced from early harvested fruit from the same plot (Gessner et al. 1995, Schwab et al. 1999, Hoenicke et al. 2002 b). The combination of premature harvest and high crop load tends to strongly predispose wines to the formation of ATA.

However, Brix readings are an equivocal parameter for evaluating the propensity of a wine to develop ATA. One study showed no relationship between Brix data and the occurrence of ATA (Linsenmeier et al. 2007 a), while other studies reported Brix readings to correlate negatively with perceived ATA intensity Gessner et al. 1995, Köhler et al. 1995). Since ATA may also appear in wines obtained from fruit with high Brix readings grown under hot-climate conditions, traditional Brix figures rather reflect only alcoholic ripeness as opposed to aromatic ripeness, the latter precluding the formation of ATA.

In times of global climate change, the discrepancy between grape sugar content and aromatic ripeness is increasingly accentuated. As a result, aromatic ripeness does not run proportional to alcoholic ripeness, expressed as Brix. In extreme cases, that can cause a wine from 25 Brix or more to remind one of an aroma profile of 17 Brix grapes. Modern winegrowers claim that they do not rely on Brix numbers but if they actually did not, the extent to which ATA affects white wines would not be that apparent. In conclusion, winemakers should pay more attention to the sensory evaluation of aromatic ripeness of fruit.

Yeast assimilable nitrogen (YAN) in juice shows a weak correlation with the propensity of wine to develop ATA. However, this correlation is not a causal one. While low YAN levels indicate a high propensity for ATA formation, high YAN levels do not necessarily exclude it. Considering all these observations, there are not yet any reliable analytical tools to predict ATA by analysis of the fruit.

Nutrient deficiencies

Research on the impact of nitrogen (N) status and fertilization has given inconsistent results. Under cool-climate conditions, increased N fertilization reduced the occurrence and intensity of ATA (Schwab et al. 1996) or was without any effect (Müller 1999). Drought-induced low N status during veraison and early fruit ripening was considered to trigger ATA formation, while both irrigation and foliar N application reduced off-flavors associated with ATA and improved varietal aroma (Cheng et al. 2004).

In a long-term trial, variable N fertilization affected AAP concentration in the wine as much as the growing conditions during the year. Generally, ATA intensity and AAP concentration increased with increasing N fertilization. Antioxidant capacity in the finished wines accounted for 13 to 67 % of the total variance of ATA. However, N fertilization regimes were not sufficient to explain ATA. Despite significant effects of the fertilization regime and the growing conditions accounting for ~20 % of the total variance, a high residual variance accounting for more than 50 % of the total variance of ATA intensity in wine could not be explained. As a conclusion, fertilization with 60 kg/ha (54 lbs/ac) was recommended, while higher amounts increased the propensity of the wines to produce ATA (Linsenmeier et al. 2007 a, 2007 b).

Hydric stress and irrigation

Since ATA occurs primarily in wines from harvests characterized by dry summers, drought stress during ripening has been shown to be one of the most important causes of ATA. While the annual precipitation rate is meaningless, precipitations occurring from June to August seem to be decisive to decrease the ATA potential in the northern hemisphere.

As cover crops compete for water and N, the effect of drought is reinforced under conditions of green cover. Soil treatment (Schwab et al. 1996, 1999), judicious irrigation (Cheng et al. 2004), and application of farmyard manure (Schwab and Peternel 1997) decrease perceived ATA intensity. Especially for vineyard soils with low water-holding capacity, it is recommended to remove green cover by mulching or plowing in alternate rows around bud break.

UV radiation

Under viticultural stress situations, protection from UV-B radiation by repeated spraying of a synthetic UV-B absorption reagent resulted in lower AAP concentrations in the wine. This is explained by the fact that precursors of IAA absorb UV light, inducing a photochemical reaction susceptible to contribute to the formation of compounds involved in ATA. Simultaneously, YAN in the juice was increased. Foliar nitrogen fertilization showed similar effects (Hühn et al. 1999).

Figure 62 illustrates schematically how various viticultural stress factors affect must composition and lead eventually to the formation of AAP upon the first SO_2 addition post-fermentation. It cannot be emphasized enough that these factors are frequently linked one to another, though some wineries affected by atypical aging are able to solve the problem by adjusting just one of them.

Figure 62: Causes of atypical aging and formation of 2-aminoacetophenone.

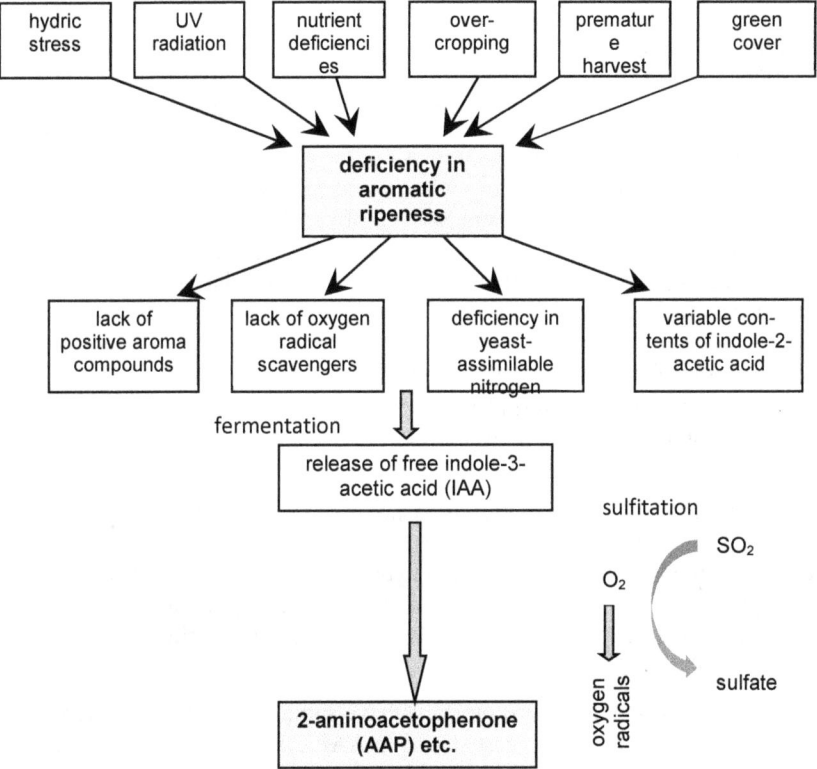

4.5. Enological measures against ATA

Introduction: While yeast nutrient additions have only a minor impact on the formation of ATA, skin contact prior to pressing can help increase grape phenols acting as oxygen radical scavengers and thus mitigate or prevent ATA in less critical cases. However, the only reliable means to safely avoid ATA is the addition of ascorbic acid in a timely manner simultaneously with the first SO_2 addition post-fermentation. Delayed ascorbic acid additions cannot remove ATA already formed, nor are there any other means to remedy affected wines.

There are various pre and post-fermentation strategies aiming at mitigating or preventing the formation of ATA in wines obtained from stressed fruit. However, only one specific measure taken immediately after fermentation is really effective in completely preventing the formation of AAP and the appearance of ATA.

Yeast strain and yeast nutrients

In identical juices, commercially available active dry yeast strains produce different amounts of free IAA, which is the precursor of AAP. Thus, some authors considered IAA metabolism of yeast as decisive for the formation of AAP (Christoph et al. 1999, Hoenicke et al. 2002 b), while other researchers (Linsenmeier et al. 2007) found no correlation between IAA and AAP concentrations.

If AAP were the only causative agent of ATA, then the direct link between yeast strain and AAP level in the resulting wine would be important. After inoculation of an identical juice with two different Saccharomyces cerevisiae strains, AAP levels in the one year old wine were 0.6 and 1.1 µg/L, respectively (Rauhut et al. 2003). Other authors reported active dry yeast strains to produce only low amounts of AAP during fermentation not exceeding 0.4 µg/L and, therefore, below the odor threshold (Gessner et al. 1996). Nevertheless, inoculation with wild yeast strains and spontaneous fermentations were shown to cause higher amounts of AAP (Simat et al. 2004). Yeast strains producing strong fermentation aromatics can delay the perception of ATA by such masking effects, but not prevent it (Köhler et al. 1996).

Likewise, the effect of yeast nutrients is not conclusive. Most research groups (Köhler et al. 1996, Bach 2005, Lorenzini 2009) reported no significant impact of juice supplementation with diammonium hydrogen phosphate (DAP) and inactive yeast preparations on AAP concentration and ATA intensity. However, one investigation (Rauhut et al. 2003) showed that DAP supplementation decreased the amount of AAP.

Obviously, yeast strain and nutrition status have some impact on perceived ATA intensity. Differences between yeast strains in AAP synthesis, release of free IAA and of radical scavengers such as glutathione, and production of masking fruity aromas play a role. However, ATA cannot be considered a by-product of alcoholic fermentation under standard fermentation conditions, but rather the result of stress in the vineyard. Hence, the choice of an active dry yeast strain is not an appropriate tool to mitigate ATA. The crucial parameters of wine composition affecting the conversion of IAA into AAP (Chapter 4.3) are the result of vineyard management.

Pre-fermentation strategies

Skin contact has been shown to decrease AAP concentration by 35 % as well as perceived ATA intensity (Bach 2005). This effect is partially ascribed to an increased extraction of grape phenols able to scavenge oxygen radicals involved in the chemical conversion of IAA into AAP (Gessner et al. 1996, Linsenmeier et al. 2007 a). Accordingly, wines obtained from free-run juice are more prone to produce ATA due to their lower total phenol content than the wine from pressed juice. Higher concentrations of varietal fruit aromatics extracted during skin contact and pressing possibly play an additional role in the sensory perception of ATA by partially masking it. Hence, skin contact and pressing regime can prevent ATA in borderline cases when ATA potential is not too high, but it is not a safe and reliable measure to deliberately impede it.

4. Atypical aging

Although dispensing with SO_2 to must and passive juice oxidation are known to decrease the concentration of phenols by oxidative precipitation (Chapter 2.4.5), the extent of that effect does not increase ATA intensity (Köhler et al. 1996). However, active oxygenation and hyperoxidation should be avoided on juices obtained from stressed fruit, and nitrogen instead of air should be used when they are clarified by flotation. Otherwise the decrease of phenols acting as radical scavengers would be too far-reaching.

Juice clarification is an important step to reduce ATA potential in the resulting wines. In this context, the residual turbidity is far more important than the technical means used to achieve it (Chapter 2.4.2). The fermentation of juice bottoms frequently produces ATA in the resulting wine while the clarified juices do not, suggesting that a large fraction of the precursor is bound to insoluble solids.

Post-fermentation strategies

As might be expected, flavor intensity of ATA increases with wine age (Köhler et al. 1996, Gessner et al. 1999 a, Cheng et al. 2004). Older wines contain higher concentrations of AAP than younger ones. Wine storage at low temperatures can delay the formation of ATA but not prevent it. This temperature effect is valid for all types of aging defect (Chapter 2.7).

Storage on the lees is not a suitable means to decrease AAP concentrations. Even with weekly yeast stirring, no impact on perceived ATA can be observed (Köhler et al. 1996, Lorenzini 2009). Thus, the time point of racking and filtration is not relevant.

Post-fermentation additions of inactivated yeast preparations failed to prevent ATA (Bach 2005). Supplements of commercial tannins (100 mg/L) before and after fermentation do not diminish the formation of AAP, but rather provide bitter and harsh wines with an astringency not desirable in most white wines. Since they do not reach the effective tannin levels found in red wines, the original problem will not be resolved.

Supplements of pure glutathione (20 to 150 mg/L) reduced ATA in some wines, depending on the yeast strain. In these comparative trials, only the addition of ascorbic acid (75 and 150 mg/L) prevented the formation of AAP and ATA systematically (Rauhut et al. 2003). Although yeast nutrients and yeast metabolites might improve the antioxidant capacity of wine, their effect is uncertain and does not equal that of ascorbic acid.

The addition of 100 to 200 mg/L ascorbic acid in a timely manner is the only effective means to protect wines against ATA over a period of at least four years. Since the end of the 1990's, it has been successfully implemented in wines from vineyards with a history of producing wines prone to develop it.

Practical hints: Adding ascorbic acid post-fermentation to prevent ATA

The addition of ascorbic acid (100-200 mg/L) is recommended to take place at or before the first addition of SO_2 after primary fermentation. Additions at a subsequent point of time are possible and sufficient to prevent the intensification of an

ATA off-flavor already existing. However, such additions are definitely not able to remove or mitigate it. Their action is merely preventive since the reactions involved in the formation of ATA are irreversible. For that reason, ascorbic acid additions should occur as soon as possible. During further storage and cellar operations, wines treated in this way must be kept with adequate levels of free SO_2 of at least 30 mg/L and carefully protected from oxygen uptake to avoid the autoxidation of ascorbic acid (Chapter 2.5.3). Vessels must be completely topped and precepts of gentle wine treatment respected (Chapter 2.6.4).

Ascorbic acid added prior to fermentation usually does not protect against the appearance of ATA since it gets largely lost by oxidation before the onset of fermentation. In such cases, a second addition post-fermentation is feasible.

ATA cannot be removed

Any attempts of remedying wines already spoiled by ATA by finings are useless. Their outcome would be an even stronger perception of ATA since all these treatments diminish beneficial aroma compounds which are able to mask it partially. Ascorbic acid addition is the only technical means to prevent this kind of off-flavor in wines prone to develop it. Therefore, its prophylactic addition is recommended to all young white wines suspected to produce ATA.

The long-term perspective

Ascorbic acid additions are quite able to protect wines against the formation of ATA. However, wines treated for that purpose in this way will never become great wines exceeding the quality level of simple wines for easy consumption. Therefore, for wineries suffering from a chronic ATA problem, the addition of ascorbic acid can only be a transitory solution. Since ATA has its ultimate and definitive cause in the vineyard, the long-term solution has to be found in improved viticultural management.

4.6. Assessing the wines' proneness to ATA

Introduction: An accelerated aging test allows to assess a wine's proneness to develop ATA. For that purpose, the clarified wine sample is split into two flasks, one of them containing ascorbic acid, and stored for three days at 45° C (113° F). After the heating period, both samples are compared by smell. When the sample containing no ascorbic acid displays ATA, then the wine is prone to develop it. This test can be carried out in any laboratory.

Viticultural means cannot avoid ATA with certainty, and there are not yet any reliable analytical tools available to predict a wine's propensity for developing ATA. Instead, an accelerated aging test has been proposed and widely introduced into practice (Gessner et al. 1999 b):

A clarified sample of wine containing at least 40 mg/L free SO_2 is poured into two glass flasks, one of them receiving an additional supplementation of 150 mg/L ascorbic acid. Aqueous solutions of 10 mg/mL make the dosage easier. Both flasks are stored at 45 ±3° C for three days. A water bath or an oven set at that temperature can be used for that purpose. After cooling down, both samples are evaluated by smell. When the sample containing no ascorbic acid displays ATA or when the sample with ascorbic acid displays a noticeable better smell, then the wine is prone to develop ATA. A wine spiked with ~2 µg/L AAP is recommended for the purpose of sensory training and as a reference for less trained evaluators. Figure 63 depicts the implementation of this ATA-test.

Figure 63: Implementation of the test to assess ATA potential.

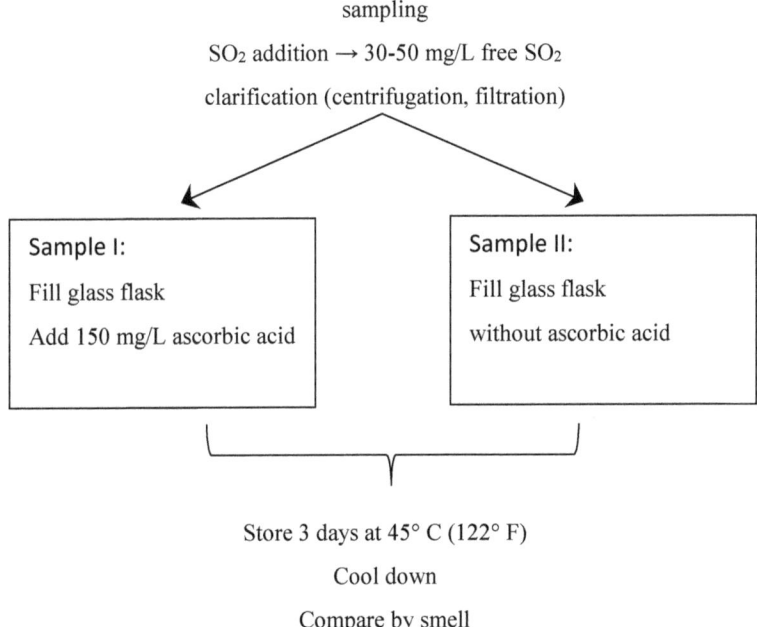

This so-called ATA test is an accelerated aging test more or less comparable to that described in chapter 3.5.1 for evaluating the propensity of wine to develop reduction flavor, but working with a shorter incubation period. Basically, it can also reveal the proneness to development of reductive taints, but with less clarity. When reduction flavor has developed during the incubation period, addition of a drop of copper sulfate solution (0.01 %) removes it and helps identify possible ATA.

When the result of the AATA test is positive suggesting the addition of ascorbic acid, this addition should be performed as soon as possible, be at the moment of adding SO_2 or within a time window of not more than a few days after that. Some wineries add ascorbic acid to any white wine regardless of the outcome of the ATA-test or because they hope to improve the wines' resistance to oxidative aging. This is feasible as long as one takes into account further implications and necessary precautions associated with wines containing ascorbic acid. They are discussed in chapter 2.5.3.

5. Petrol flavor

5.1. Sensory characteristics and causes

Introduction: Petrol flavor is a kind of non-oxidative aging basically limited to Riesling wines obtained from ripe fruit, particularly that grown under hot climate conditions. It is caused by one single compound commonly called TDN and reminiscent of petrol, kerosene, and dried apricots. Depending on its intensity, it is not necessarily rejected as a wine fault.

It is debatable whether petrol flavor, also known as kerosene taint, should be categorized as a specific kind of aging flavor since it is not always associated with an off-flavor. Its appearance is limited to a very few varieties, most notably Riesling followed by Alvariño with some distance behind, which are prone to form the indispensable precursors in grapes in sufficient amounts. However, when petrol flavor appears, its smell can be highly overpowering and one-dimensional in a way that all other kinds of varietal or aging aromas become masked. It is one of the most precisely defined, exquisitely evocative, and easily recognizable terms in the wine tasting vocabulary.

Not an explicit off-flavor but polarizing

Obviously, the acceptance of petrol flavor depends on its intensity, but even more on personal preferences and the consumers' cultural context. There are very few odor impact molecules in wine, which are odor-active and polarizing to that extent.

In Riesling wines grown under cool-climate conditions, petrol flavor can only be perceived after some two years of aging and is generally accepted by consumers. Under these conditions, it is also described as reminiscent of 'dry apricots' when terms like petrol or kerosene flavor are considered too difficult to communicate to novice consumers. However, in hot-climate growing areas, it can arise much earlier and in considerably stronger intensities overwhelming the highly complex, fruity aroma profile of young Riesling wines, thus disturbing the balance and complexity of these wines. In this case, it is considered undesirable and causes the wine to be rejected. Therefore, when Riesling is designed to be released only after one year or more of bottle aging, there is an understandable interest in limiting the intensity of petrol and maximizing the wine's complexity and finesse.

TDN – one single impact compound

1,1,6-trimethyl-1,2-dihydronaphthalene (TDN) has been identified as the impact molecule responsible for petrol flavor in aged Riesling wines. In chemical terms,

TDN is classified as a C_{13}-norisoprenoid that, according to view point and semantic criteria, may be classified as a terpene or not. During aging of Riesling, it is produced in much higher amounts than in most other white varietal wines, where its concentration remains too low to be sensorially detectable (Simpson and Miller 1983). Its odor detection threshold has been reported to be 2 µg/L in both model and neutral white wine, indicating little masking of TDN due to the odorants in real wine (Sacks et al. 2012).

More realistic trials with an untrained consumer panel resulted in an orthonasal detection threshold of 18 to 20 µg/L TDN and a rejection threshold of 80 to 160 µg/L TDN in Riesling, depending on the composition of the wine (Ross et al. 2014). The rejection threshold is the concentration above which the wine is rejected as faulty. There are few aroma compounds in wine that are more distinctive and polarizing than TDN.

Formation of TDN precursors in the grape

TDN is generated from multiple, non-volatile glycoside precursors by acidic hydrolysis (Winterhalter et al. 1990). The research on the nature and relative importance of these precursors in Riesling is far from being completed and reveals a complex picture of reaction pathways. Carotenoids, in particular lutein (Marais 1992), zeaxanthine (Kwasniewski et al. 2010), and a compound designated as Riesling acetal (Daniel et al.2009) range among the precursors investigated up to now.

As early as in the fruit and in particular in the late ripening phase, these precursors start to disintegrate into odorless, glycosidically bound forms of TDN. During wine aging, these TDN-glycosides are gradually split by acidic hydrolysis, thus releasing free, odor-active TDN (Versini et al. 1996, Yuan and Qian 2016).

A concern of hot-climate growing areas

Climate features of the growing area are decisive for wine TDN levels and the sensory impact of petrol flavor. Measuring these levels can be a means to explain whether a given Riesling wine originates from a cool or a hot climate growing region. A comparison of Riesling wines from South Africa, Germany, and Northern Italy showed that wines from South Africa had significantly higher TDN concentrations than those from the cooler European growing areas. The differences were explained by lower average daily temperatures, less daily sunshine hours, and higher average monthly precipitation rates in the European growing regions (Marais et al. 1992 b). This relationship explains why the classic Riesling wines are predominantly obtained in relatively cool growing areas.

In Riesling wines from typical cool-climate regions, petrol flavor is not systematic and requires a certain degree of grape ripeness to develop. Thus, these wines can display an amazingly broad range of aroma features, which vary depending on origin and climate but also as a function of increasing grape maturity. These changes as affected by increasing maturity can be depicted in a simplified form from top down:

5. Petrol flavor

atypical aging (mothballs, naphthalene, damp towel, washing machine)
↓
unripe, green (green apples, green bell pepper, freshly mown grass)
↓
fruity (yellow apples, pears, peaches, pineapple, grapefruit)
↓
mineral (fresh wet concrete, flintstone)
↓
petrol flavor (petrol, dry apricots)
↓
botrytis / noble rot / dessert wine (honey, raisins)

In Riesling wines from hot-climate areas, petrol flavor tends to come to the foreground after approximately one year of aging, while green/unripe or noble rot-based aroma attributes are normally lacking. For producing Riesling with low TDN levels that are sensorially acceptable, such areas require sophisticated viticultural measures to reduce sun and heat exposure of grapes. In the context of global climate change, such measures are going to gain in importance also in cool-climate growing areas.

5.2. Viticultural countermeasures

Introduction: Shading grapes by an appropriate canopy management is the most effective viticultural tool to mitigate TDN formation and the appearance of petrol flavor.

With the purpose of lowering the concentrations of TDN precursors in the fruit and free TDN in the wine, various viticultural experimentations have been carried out. Generally, TDN levels in wine increase when grape ripeness increases. They are higher in wines obtained from sun-exposed fruit than in wines from shaded grapes. Canopy microclimate is of crucial importance (Marais et al. 1992 a).

Going a step further, one study (Kwasniewski et al. 2010) provided a direct comparison of the effects of sun exposure and shading on the levels of TDN and its precursors. A 75 % leaf removal in the fruit zone 33 days past berry set resulted in more than twice as much free and total TDN in Riesling juice than the same leaf removal performed two and 68 days past berry set. These results show that the timing of canopy management and cluster light environment manipulations are an important tool to control TDN levels. In this respect, Riesling may require a kind of canopy management that is different from that used for other varieties. Shading the wines by means of a net can be a useful alternative.

In a long-term field experiment carried out over three years under cool-climate conditions, increasing nitrogen fertilization led to lower TDN concentrations in wines of both young and old vineyard plots. This result was not influenced by storage time (Linsenmeier and Löhnertz 2007 c).

In conclusion, the viticultural causes promoting high TDN levels in Riesling wines are well documented and include:

- low crop yields,
- high temperatures during the growing season,
- high sun exposure of grape clusters,
- drought stress,
- low nitrogen fertilization.

Some of these factors are linked one to another. They are similar to those which might facilitate the production of high-quality white wines other than Riesling under different conditions. However, they do not exclude the possibility of taking specific measures to lower the TDN regime in a given vineyard plot. Among these measures, shading the grapes by appropriate canopy management seems the most promising.

5.3. Enological countermeasures

Introduction: In grapes, TDN susceptible to cause petrol flavor during wine aging occurs glycosidically bound as an odorless precursor, from which it is partially released by yeast glycosidase enzyme activity. The role of the various yeast strains in this process is not yet sufficiently investigated. Additionally, TDN formation is facilitated by low pH and high temperatures. Natural, technical, and synthetic corks absorb TDN to a large extent, while screw caps do not display such an effect. Best measures to mitigate the appearance of petrol flavor post-bottling are dispensing with screw caps and storage at low temperatures.

Studies upon enological means to reduce the sensory intensity of petrol flavor are scarce. In fermentation trials using nine commercial active dry yeast strains, it was shown that only half of the TDN precursors were still present after primary fermentation, while formation of free TDN had already occurred during fermentation. Free TDN levels in the young wines correlated with the specific ß-glycosidase enzyme activity of the yeast strains and the yeast cell number count. Lutein turned out to be the most important precursor of TDN in these wines (Periadnadi 2003).

These results show that TDN precursors are to a large extent bound to glucose, and that these bonds can be cleaved by microbial pathways of yeast and release free odor-active TDN. This finding might open the way to further research on selected yeast strains with low propensity to produce free TDN.

Apart from the microbial release of TDN from glycosidic precursors, it can also be released by acidic hydrolysis. Otherwise TDN and petrol flavor would not increase during aging of sterile-bottled wines. A low pH around 3.2 frequently found in Riesling wines promotes this hydrolysis and fosters the appearance of petrol flavor (Rudy 2015).

In light of historical experience and according to the temperature impact on kinetics of other kinds of wine aging, storage temperature has also a tremendous influence on the appearance of petrol flavor. Storage at 15° C (59° F) was able to keep the intensity of petrol flavor within a sensorially acceptable limit (Marais 1992 c). Figure 64 shows the impact of bottle storage temperature on perceived petrol flavor in a Riesling obtained from a renowned Riesling growing area in Germany. This behavior is in line with the heat effect on typical aging (Chapter 2.7).

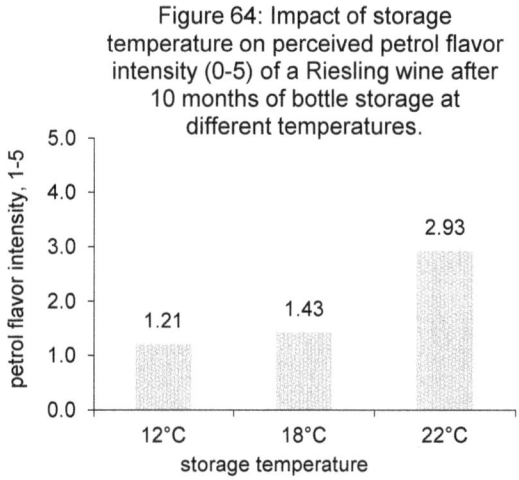

Figure 64: Impact of storage temperature on perceived petrol flavor intensity (0-5) of a Riesling wine after 10 months of bottle storage at different temperatures.

Another effective tool to mitigate petrol flavor makes use of a generally less appreciated feature of bottle closures, which is their variable sorptive capacity leading to the absorption of non-polar volatile wine aroma compounds. After two years of horizontal bottle storage of different wines, natural corks had absorbed approximately 50 %, technical corks 70 %, and synthetic corks 98 % of TDN, respectively. In contrast, screw caps preserved TDN at its initial concentration since they lack appreciable amounts of absorbing material (Capone et al. 2003). Screw caps as bottle closures are a bad choice for sealing Riesling wines prone to develop petrol flavor post-bottling.

This strong influence of the bottle closure relativizes viticultural efforts to control petrol flavor. Attempts to lower TDN concentration in Riesling wine by carrying out particular vineyard practices are pointless if the wine is to be bottled and sealed with synthetic closures. On the other hand, if the wine bottles are sealed with screw caps, then the outcome of viticultural practices intended to modulate the concentration of this compound in the finished wine will be magnified, compared to if the wine is bottled and sealed with natural cork closures.

In conclusion, the use of internally sealing stoppers instead of screw caps and the lowest possible storage temperature throughout the whole supply chain are the most efficient enological means to keep petrol flavor under control.

Prognosticating petrol flavor

There is practical interest in assessing whether a young Riesling wine is prone to develop petrol flavor during aging. This is a kind of information that can impact marketing strategies, the choice of the bottle closure, and storage temperature. As one might expect, an accelerated aging test as described in previous chapters will also work for that purpose. The version used for predicting atypical aging (Chapter 4.6) fully meets this need. No addition of ascorbic acid is required but just an incubation period of three days at 60° C (140° F), after which a simple sniff test will show whether there is any petrol flavor to be expected. With some sensory training it will also be feasible to predict its intensity.

6. Epilog

This book is also a journey through the history of white wine enology and its development over the last decades. One of its first chapters deals with deliberate must oxidation, which continues to be a controversial topic. It dates back to the 1970's when there were serious concerns with typical or oxidative aging of bottled white wines. By that time, first trials had been conducted to answer the question of how much oxygen juices must take up to produce an oxidized wine. As the results were different from expectations, intensive research started, leading eventually to an understanding of the basic differences between must and wine oxidation. However, a detailed breakdown of the compounds eliciting the flavor of oxidative aging was only possible with the advent of more sophisticated analytical tools after the turn of the millennium.

Problems with premature oxidative aging continue to occur as shown by the ongoing topicality of the buzzword *premox*. They are attributable to enological deficiencies and can be solved with more care in the cellar and upon bottling. Just as they had been barely brought under control in some areas of the wine industry, a new challenge emerged in the 1990's when a hitherto unknown kind of aging appeared in relatively young wines. Since it caused a flavor profile that was completely different from typical aging, it was called atypical aging. This was also the time when the effects of global climate change started becoming apparent. Obviously, there is a connection because in contrast to oxidative aging, atypical aging stems from viticultural deficiencies.

With the emergence of more suitable DO meters at the turn of the millennium, uncontrolled post-fermentation oxygen uptake and the harm it causes became better understood. The most obvious solution has been an increased use of very oxygen-tight bottle closures, which contribute to the appearance of the opposite of oxidative aging. Thus, the notion of reductive aging was born. It is simply a reduction flavor developing in bottled wines without the direct intervention of yeast lees.

Finally, there is also petrol flavor, which is another long-known kind of aging, largely limited to Riesling wines, and not unanimously rejected as a flaw. However, it can become unpleasantly strong when this variety is grown under hot-climate conditions. From this point of view, global climate change will probably have an impact on it. Both viticultural and enological tools are available to mitigate it.

Evolution is an essential feature of mankind. New research results can be expected to increase our knowledge and provide hitherto unknown technological options. However, not everything that is technically possible will contribute to improve what we consider as wine quality. As also shown in this book, less intervention and processing in the cellar might be beneficial in many cases. Ultimately, the foundation of quality is laid by the fruit provided from the vineyard. Enology can at best preserve it. This is the actual message of this book.

7. Literature

Acree T.E., Lavin E.H., Shure K., 1993. The aroma of non-vinifera grapes. *In*: Connaissance aromatique des cépages et qualité des vins. Rev. Fr. d'Œnologie (ed.), Actes du Symposium International, Montpellier, France: 51-57.

Aguera E., Samson A., Caille S., Julien-Ortiz, A., Sieczkowski, N., Salmon J. M., 2012. Apport de levures inactivées riches en glutathione en cours de fermentation alcoolique: Un nouvel outil pour la protection des vins blancs et rosés contre l'oxydation. Rev. Fr. d'Œnologie 250: 3-11.

Andrea-Silva J., Cosme F., Ribeiro L.F., Moreira A.S., Malheiro A.C., Coimbra M.A., Domingues M.R., Nunes F.M., 2014. Origin of the pinking phenomenon in white wines. J. Agric. Food Chem. 62 (24): 5651-5659.

Andújar-Ortiz I., Chaya C., Martin-Álvarez P. J., Moreno-Arribas M. V., Pozo-Bayón M. A., 2014. Impact of using new commercial glutathione enriched inactive dry yeast oenological preparations on the aroma and sensory properties of wine. Int. J. Food Prop. 17: 987-1001.

Antoce A.O., Cojocaru G.A., 2017. Sensory profile changes induced by the antioxidant treatments of white wines. The case of glutathione, ascorbic acid and tannin treatments on Feteasca Regala wines produced in normal cellar conditions. AgroLife Scient. J. 6 (1): 19-30.

Arnold R. A., Noble A. C., 1979. Effect of pomace contact on the flavor of Chardonnay wine. Am. J. Enol. Vitic. 30 (3): 179-181.

Arnold R. A., Noble A. C., Singleton V. L., 1980. Bitterness and astringency of phenolic fractions in wine. J. Agric. Food Chem. 28 (3): 675-678.

Artajona J., Bobet R., Marco J., Sabat F., 1990. Expériences d'hyperoxygénation au Penedés. Rev. Fr. d'Œnologie 124: 65-67.

Bach H. P., Hess K. H., 1982. Einfluß des Trubgehaltes auf die Qualität des Weines. Deut. Weinbau 37: 1265-1269.

Bach H.P., 2005. Untypischer Alterungston vermeiden. Winzer-Zeitschrift 9: 32-34.

Bach H. P., Nobis P., 1985. Einfluß der Mostoxidation auf den Wein. Weinwirtschaft-Technik 9: 294-311.

Bailly B., 1990. Essai d'hyperoxygénation des moûts sur cépages locaux en Alsace. Rev. Fr. d'Œnologie 127: 7-14.

Barbanti D., Galassi S., Potentini G., Versari A., 1997. Valutazione della shelf life di un vino bianco in funzione di differenti modalità di confezionamento e di conservazione. Vignevini 24: 21-25.

Baro A. L., Quiros Carrasco J. A., 1977. Les conditions de formation des aldéhydes dans le vin. Bull. de l'OIV 50: 253-267.

Barón R., Mayen M., Merida J., Medina M., 1997. Changes in phenolic compounds and colour in pale sherry wines subjected to fining treatments. Z. Lebensm. Unters. Forsch. 205: 474-478.

Barril C., Rutledge D. N. Scollary G. R., Clark A. G., 2016. Ascorbic acid and white wine production: A review of beneficial vs. detrimental impacts. Aust. J. Grape Wine Res. 22 (2): 169-181.

Bekker M.Z., Smith M.E., Smith P.A., Wilkes E.N., 2016. Formation of hydrogen sulfide in Wine: Interactions between copper and sulfur dioxide. Molecules 21 (9): 1214. https://doi.org/10.3390/molecules21091214

Bekker M.Z., Wilkes E.N., Smith P.A., 2018. Evaluation of putative precursors of key "reductive" compounds in wine post-bottling. Food Chem. 245: 676-686.

Blanck G., 1990. Utilisation de l'hyperoxidation pour la valorisation des moûts de tailles en Champagne. Rev. Fr. d'Œnologie 124: 50-57.

Blouin J., Papet N., Stonestreet E., 2000. Étude de la structure polyphénolique des vins rouges par analyses physico-chimiques et sensorielles. J. Int. Sci. Vigne Vin 34 (1): 33-40.

Blum U., Schwedt G., 1998. Einsatz einer kupferselektiven Kristallmembranelektrode zur Bestimmung der Hauptbindungspartner von Kupfer in Weinen. Vitic. Enol. Sci. 53 (1): 22-26.

Bobet R. A., Noble A. C., Boulton R. B., 1990. Kinetics of the ethanethiol and diethyl disulfide interconversion in wine-like solutions. J. Agric. Food Chem. 38 (2): 449-452.

Bonerz D.P.M., Pour Nikfardjam M.S., Creasy G.I., 2008. A new RP-HPLC method for analysis of polyphenols, anthocyanins, and indole-3-acetic acid in wine. Am. J. Enol. Vitic. 59 (1): 106-109.

Bradshaw M. P., Cheynier V., Scollary G. R., Prenzler P. D., 2003. Defining the ascorbic acid crossover from anti-oxidant to pro-oxidant in a model wine matrix containing (+)-catechin. J. Agric. Food Chem. 51 (14): 4126-4132.

Bradshaw M. P., Scollary G. R., Prenzler P. D., 2004. Examination of the sulfur dioxide-ascorbic acid anti-oxidant system in a model white wine matrix. J. Sci. Food Agric. 84 (4): 318-324.

Braga A., Cosme F., Ricardo-da-Silva J. M., Laureano O., 2007. Gelatine, casein and potassium caseinate as distinct wine fining agents: Different effects on colour, phenolic composition and sensory characters. J. Int. Sci. Vigne Vin 41 (4): 203-214.

Bueno M., Carrascón V., Ferreira V., 2016. Release and formation of oxidation-related aldehydes during wine oxidation. J. Agric. Food Chem. 64 (3): 608-617.

Burkert J., Köhler H.-J., Hartmann M., 2011. Reduktive Trauben- und Mostverarbeitung. Deut. Weinmagazin 18: 35-37.

Burkert J., Müller M.J., Geßner M., Zänglein M., 2018. Wie wirkt Glutathion auf den Wein? Deut. Weinmagazin 01: 26-28.

Burkhardt R., 1976. Analytische Bestimmungen phenolischer Inhaltsstoffe von Mosten und Weinen. Mitt.-Blatt GDCh Fachgruppe Lebensmittelchemie und gerichtl. Chemie 30: 185-189 and 206-213.

Butzke C. E., Vogt E. E., Chacón-Rodriguez L., 2012. Effect of heat exposure on wine quality during transport and storage. J. Wine Res. 23 (1): 15-25.

Cáceres-Mella A., Peña-Neira A., Parraguez J., López-Solís R., Laurie V. F., Canals J. M., 2013. Effect of inert gas and prefermentative treatment with polyvinyl-polypyrrolidone on the phenolic composition of Chilean Sauvignon blanc wines. J. Sci. Food Agric. 93 (8): 1928-1934.

Cacho J., Castells J. E., Esteban A., Laguna B., Sagristá N., 1995. Iron, Copper, and manganese influence on wine oxidation. Am. J. Enol. Vitic. 46 (3): 380-384.

Calderón J. F., Del Alamo-Sanza M., Nevares I., Laurie V. F., 2014. The influence of selected winemaking equipment and operations on the concentration of dissolved oxygen in wines. Cien. Inv. Agr. 41 (2): 273-280.

Caloghiris M., Waters E. J., Williams P. J., 1997. An industry trial provides further evidence for the role of corks in oxidative spoilage of bottled wines. Aust. J. Grape Wine Res. 3 (1): 9-17.

Capone D.L., Skouroumounis G.K., Pretorius I.S., Høj P.B., 2003. Flavor 'scalping' by wine bottle closures. Australian & New Zealand Wine Industry Journal 18 (5): 16-20.

Caputi A., Peterson R. G., 1965. The browning problem in wines. Am. J. Enol. Vitic. 16 (1): 9-13.

Carando S., Teissedre P.L., Pascual-Martinez L., Cabanis J.C., 1999. Levels of flavan-3-ols in French wines. J. Agric. Food Chem. 47 (10): 4161-4166.

Casey J. A., 1989. Closures for wine bottles – a user's viewpoint. Austral. Grapegrower and Winemaker 4: 99-107.

7. Literature

Castellari M., Simonato B., Tornielli G.-B., Spinelli P., Ferrarini R., 2004. Effect of different enological treatments on dissolved oxygen in wine. Ital. J. Food Sci. 16 (3): 387-396.

Cejudo-Bastante M. J., Hermosin-Gutierrez I., Castro-Vazquez L. I., Pérez-Coello M. S., 2011. Hyperoxygenation and bottle storage of chardonnay white wines: Effects on color-related phenols, volatile composition, and sensory characteristics. J. Agric. Food Chem. 59 (8): 4171-4182.

Cejudo-Bastante M. J., Hermosín-Gutiérrez I., Pérez-Coello M. S., 2013. Monitoring of chemical parameters of oxygen-treated musts during alcoholic fermentation and subsequent bottle storage of the resulting wines. Eur. Food Res. Technol. 236 (1): 77-88.

Chen Y., Jastrzembski J.A., Sacks G.L., 2017: Copper-complexed hydrogen sulfide n wine: Measurement by gas detection tubes and comparison of release approaches. Am. J. Enol. Vitic. 68 (1): 91-99.

Cheng L., Lakso A., Henick-Kling T., Martinson T., Acree T., 2004. Conclusions for three years of study on the effect of drought stress and available nitrogen on the formation of atypical aging flavor defect in wine. *In:* Proceedings of the 33rd Annual New York Wine Industry Workshop. T. Henick-Kling (ed.), Cornell University, Geneva, N.Y.: 68-71.

Cheynier V., Rigaud J., Souquet J. M., Barillère J. M., Moutounet M., 1989. Effect of pomace contact and hyperoxidation on the phenolic composition and quality of Grenache and Chardonnay wines. Am. J. Enol. Vitic. 40 (1): 36-42.

Cheynier V., Rigaud A., Souquet J.-M., Duprat F., Moutounet M., 1990 a. Must browning in relation to the behavior of phenolic compounds during oxidation. Am. J. Enol. Vitic. 41 (4): 346-349.

Cheynier V., Rigaud J., Moutounet M., 1990 b. Oxidation kinetics of trans-caffeoyl tartrate and its glutathione derivates in grape and must-like model solutions. Phytochemistry 29 (6): 1751-1753.

Cheynier V., Souquet J.-M., Samson A., Moutounet M., 1991 a. Hyperoxidation: Influence of various oxygen supply levels on oxidation kinetics of phenolic compounds and wine quality. Vitis 30 (2): 107-115.

Cheynier V., Ricardo-da-Silva J. M., 1991 b. Oxidation of grape procyanidins in model solutions containing trans-caffeoyltartaric acid and polyphenol oxidase. J. Agric. Food Chem. 39 (6): 1047-1049.

Cheynier V., Masson G., Rigaud J., Moutounet M., 1993. Estimation of must oxidation during pressing in Champagne. Am. J. Enol. Vitic. 44 (4): 393-399.

Chinnici F., Sonni F., Natali N., Riponi C., 2013. Oxidative evolution of (+)-catechin in model white wine solutions containing sulfur dioxide, ascorbic acid or gallotannins. Food Res. Int. 51 (1): 59-65.

Christoph N., Bauer-Christoph C., Gessner M., Köhler H.J., 1995. Die "Untypische Alterungsnote" in Wein. Teil I: Untersuchungen zum Auftreten und zur sensorischen Charakterisierung der Untypischen Alterungsnote. Rebe und Wein 48: 350-356.

Christoph N., Bauer-Christoph C., Gessner M., Köhler H.J., 1996. Der "Untypische Alterungston" in Wein, Teil VI: Untersuchungen zur Bildung von 2-Aminoacetophenon aus Produkten des Tryptophan-Stoffwechsels vor der alkoholischen Gärung. Rebe und Wein 49: 246-250.

Christoph N., Bauer-Christoph C., Gessner M., Köhler H.J. Simat T.J., Hoenicke K., 1998. Formation of 2-aminoacetophenone and formylaminoacetophenone in wine by reaction of sulfurous acid with indole-3-acetic acid. Vitic. Enol. Sci. 53 (2): 79-86.

Christoph N., Gessner M., Simat T.J., Hoenicke K., 1999. Off-flavor compounds in wine and other food products formed by enzymatical, physical, and chemical degradation of tryptophan and its metabolites. Adv. Exp. Med. Biol. 467: 659-669.

Ciolfi G., Garafolo A., di Stefano R., 1995. Identification of some o-aminophenones as secondary metabolites of Saccharomyces cerevisiae. Vitis 34 (3): 195-196.

Clark A.C., Wilkes E.N., Scollary G.R., 2015. Chemistry of copper in white wines: a review. Aust. J. Grape Wine Res. 21 (3): 339-350.

Coetzee C., du Toit W. J., 2012. A comprehensive review on Sauvignon blanc aroma with a focus on certain positive volatile thiols. Food Res. Int. 45: 287-298.

Coetzee C. et al., 2013. Oxygen and sulfur dioxide additions to Sauvignon blanc must: effect on must and wine composition. Flavor Fragr. J. 28 (3): 155-167.

Cordonnier R. E., Bayonove C. L., 1982. Étude de la phase préfermentaire de la vinification: Extraction et formation de certains composés de l'arôme, cas des terpénols, des aldéhydes et des alcools en C6. Conn. Vigne Vin 15: 269-286.

Cosme F., Ricardo-da-Silva J. M., Laureano O., 2008. Interactions between protein fining agents and proanthocyanidins in white wine. Food Chem. 106: 536-544.

Cosme F., Capão I., Filipe-Ribeiro L., Bennett R. N., Mendes-Faia A., 2012. Evaluating potential alternatives to potassium caseinate for white wine fining: Effects on physicochemical and sensory characteristics. LWT-Food Sci. Technol. 46: 382-387.

Cowey G., 2008. Excessive copper fining of wines sealed under screwcaps – identifying and treating reductive winemaking characters. Australian NZ Winegrower Winemaker 531: 49-56.

Crapisi A. R. et al., 1995. Prefermentative treatments interaction on the white must phenolic composition. *In:* Proceedings of the 4th International Symposium "Innovationen in der Kellerwirtschaft, Stuttgart (Germany) 1995: 79-84.

Crochiere G. K., 2007. Measuring oxygen ingress during bottling/storage. Practical Winery & Vineyard 1: 1-6.

Culleré L., Cacho J., Ferreira V., 2007. An assessment of the role played by some oxidation-related aldehydes in wine aroma. J. Agric. Food Chem. 55 (3): 876-881.

Daniel M.A., Capone D.L., Sefton M.A., Elsey G.M., 2009. Riesling acetal is a precursor to 1,1,6-trimethyl-1,2-dihydronaphthalene (TDN) in wine. Aust. J. Grape Wine Res. 15 (1): 93-96.

Danilewicz J.C., 2003. Review of reaction mechanisms of oxygen and proposed intermediate reduction products in wine: Central role of copper and iron. Am. J. Enol. Vitic. 54 (2): 73-85.

Danilewicz J.C., 2007. Interaction of sulfur dioxide, polyphenols, and oxygen in a wine-model system: Central role of iron and copper. Am. J. Enol. Vitic. 58 (1): 53-60.

Danilewicz J. C, Seccombe J. T., Whelan J., 2008. Mechanism of interaction of polyphenols, oxygen, and sulfur dioxide in model wine and wine. Am. J. Enol. Vitic. 59 (2): 128-136.

Danilewicz J.C., Wallbridge P.J., 2010. Further studies on the mechanism of interaction of polyphenols, oxygen, and sulfite in wine. Am. J. Enol. Vitic. 61 (2): 166-175.

Danilewicz J.C., 2012. Review of oxidative processes in wine and value of reduction potentials in enology. Am. J. Enol. Vitic. 63 (1): 1-9.

Danilewicz J.C., 2015. Folin-Ciocalteu, FRAP, and DPPH* assays for measuring polyphenol concentration in white wine. Am. J. Enol. Vitic. 66 (4): 463-471.

Danilewicz J.C., 2016. Reaction of oxygen and sulfite in wine. Am. J. Enol. Vitic. 67 (1): 13-17.

De la Presa-Owens C., Noble A. C., 1997. Effect of storage temperature at elevated temperatures on aroma of Chardonnay wines. Am. J. Enol. Vitic. 48 (3): 310-316.

Delcour J. A., Vandenberghe M. M., Corten P. F., Dondeyne P., 1984. Flavor thresholds of polyphenolics in water. Am. J. Enol. Vitic. 35 (3): 134-136.

Deneulin P., Le Bras G., Le Fur Y., Gautier L., 2014. Minéralité du vin: Représentations mentales de consommateurs suisses et français. Rev. Suisse Vitic. Arboric. 46 (3): 174-180.

Deshmukh M., Kutscher H., Stein S., Sinko P., 2009: Nonenzymatic self-elimination degradation mechanism of glutathione. Chem. Biodivers. 6 (4), 527-539.

7. Literature

Devatine A., Chiciuc I., Mietton-Peuchot M., 2011. The protective role of dissolved carbon dioxide against wine oxidation: A simple and rational approach. J. Int. Vigne Vin 45 (3): 189-197.

De Villiers J. P., 1961. The control of browning of wines. Am. J. Enol. Vitic. 12 (1): 25-30.

De Villiers A., Majek P., Lynen F., Crouch A., Lauer H., Sandra P., 2005. Classification of South African red and white wines according to grape variety based on the non-coloured phenolic content. Eur. Food Res. Technol. 221: 520-528.

Diéval J.-B., Vidal S., Aagaard O., 2011. Measurement of the oxygen transmission rate of co-extruded wine bottle closures using a luminescence-based technique. Packag. Technol. Sci. 24 (7): 375-385.

Dimkou E., Ugliano M., Diéval J.-B., Vidal S., Aagaard O., Rauhut D., Jung R., 2011. Impact of headspace oxygen and closure on sulfur dioxide, color, and hydrogen sulfide levels in a Riesling wine. Am. J. Enol. Vitic. 62 (3): 261-269.

Dimkou E., Ugliano M., Diéval, J.-B. Vidal S., Jung R., 2013. Impact of dissolved oxygen at bottling on sulfur dioxide and sensory properties of a Riesling wine. Am. J. Enol. Vitic. 64 (3): 325-332.

Dittrich H.H., Staudenmayer T., 1972. Über die Erhöhung der H2S-Bildung während der Gärung durch Kupfer-Ionen. Weinwissenschaft 27 (4): 250-253.

Dozon N. M., Noble A. C., 1989. Sensory study of the effect of fluorescent light on a sparkling wine and its base wine. Am. J. Enol. Vitic. 40 (4): 265-271.

Dubernet M., Ribéreau-Gayon P., 1974. Causes et conséquences de la consommation de l'oxygène par les moûts de raisins. Vitis 13: 233-244.

Dubourdieu D., Lavigne V., 1990. Incidence de l'hyperoxygénation sur la composition chimique et les qualités organoleptiques des vins blancs secs du Bordelais. Rev. Fr. d'Œnologie 124: 58-61.

Du Toit W. J., Marais J., Pretorius I. S., du Toit, M., 2006. Oxygen in must and wine: A review. S. Afr. J. Enol. Vitic. 27 (1): 76-94.

Du Toit W. J., 2007. Effect of different oxygen levels on glutathione levels in South African white must and wines. http://www.wynboer.co.za/recentarticles/200712oxygen.php3

Ecchi E., Kobler A., 2008. Kupfer im Wein. Obstbau & Weinbau 02: 47.

Elias R. J., Waterhouse A. L., 2010. Controlling the Fenton reaction in wine. J. Agric. Food Chem. 58 (3): 1699-1707.

Eschenbruch R., Kleynhans P.H., 1974. The influence of copper-containing fungicides on the copper content of grape juice and hydrogen sulfide formation. Vitis 12: 320-324.

Escudero A., Ferreira V., Hernández P., Cacho J. F., 2000 a. Wine flavor oxidation: Changes in the aroma profiles during oxidation and their potential sensory significance. *In*: Œnologie 99 (A. Lonvaud-Funel, coord.), Éditions Tec & Doc, Paris: 422-424.

Escudero A., Hernández-Orte P., Cacho J., Ferreira V., 2000 b. Clues about the role of methional as character impact compound on some oxidized wines. J. Agric. Food. Chem. 48 (9): 4268-4272.

Escudero A., Asensio E., Cacho J., Ferreira V., 2002. Sensory and chemical changes of young white wines stored under oxygen. An assessment of the role played by aldehydes and some other important odorants. Food Chem. 77: 325-331.

Fernández-Zurbano F., Ferreira V., Peña C., Escudero A., Serrano F., Cacho J., 1995. Prediction of oxidative browning in white wines as a function of their chemical composition. J. Agric. Food Chem. 43 (11): 2813-2817.

Fernández-Zurbano F., Ferreira V., Escudero A., Cacho J., 1998. Role of hydroxycinnamic acids and flavanols in the oxidation and browning of white wines. J. Agric. Food Chem. 46 (12): 4937-4944.

Ferrari G., 2002. Revue bibliographique: Influence de la composition azotée des moûts sur la qualité des vins et eaux-de-vie. Relations avec les arômes et les défauts. J. Int. Sci. Vigne Vin 36 (1): 1-10.

Ferreira A. C. S., Bertrand A., 1996. Évolution de quelques constituants du vin de Porto au cours du vieillissement. Étude particulière des composés carbonylés. *In:* Œnologie 95 (A. Lonvaud-Funel, coord.), Éditions Tec & Doc, Paris: 520-523.

Ferreira V., Escudero A., Fernández P., Cacho J. F., 1997. Changes in the profile of volatile compounds in wines stored under oxygen and their relationship with the browning process. Z. Lebensm. Unters. Forsch. A 205: 392-396.

Ferreira A. C. S., Guedes de Pinho P., Rodrigues P., Hogg T., 2002. Kinetics of oxidative degradation of white wines and how they are affected by selected technological parameters. J. Agric. Food Chem. 50 (21): 5919-5924.

Ferreira A. C. S., Hogg T., Guedes de Pinho P., 2003 a. Identification of key odorants related to the typical aroma of oxidation-spoiled white wines. J. Agric. Food Chem. 51 (5): 1377-1381.

Ferreira A. C. S., Oliveira C., Hogg T., Guedes de Pinho P., 2003 b. Relationship between potentiometric measurements, sensorial analysis, and some substances responsible for aroma degradation of white wines. J. Agric. Food Chem. 51 (16): 4668-4672.

Ferreira A. C. S., 2007. Oxidation management of white wines: Application of chemical sensors to the winemaking process. *In:* Proceedings of the 8th Int. Symposium "Innovationen der Kellerwirtschaft," Intervitis-Interfructa, Stuttgart, Germany: 151-161.

Ferreira V., Bueno M., Franco-Luesma E., 2015. New insights in the chemistry involved in aroma development during wine bottle aging: Slow redox processes and chemical equilibrium shift. *In:* Advances in Wine Research, Am. Chem. Soc. Symposium Series, 1203: 275-285.

Ferreira V., Franco-Luesma E., Vela E. López R., Hernández-Orte P., 2018. Elusive chemistry of hydrogen sulfide and mercaptans in wine. J. Agric. Food Chem. 66 (19): 2237-2246.

Fontoin H., Saucier C., Teissedre P.-L., Glories Y., 2008. Effect of pH, ethanol and acidity on astringency and bitterness of grape seed tannin oligomers in model wine solution. Food Qual. Pref. 19: 286-291.

Fornairon C., Mazauric J. P., Salmon J. M., Moutounet M., 1999. Observations on the oxygen consumption during maturation of wines on lees. J. Int. Sci. Vigne Vin 33 (2): 79-86.

Fornairon-Bonnefond C., Salmon J.-M., 2003. The impact of oxygen consumption by yeast lees on the autolysis phenomenon during simulation of wine aging on lees. J. Agric. Food Chem. 51 (9), 2584-2590.

Fracassetti D., Lawrence N., Tredoux A. G. J., Tirelli A., Nieuwoudt H. H., du Toit W. J., 2011. Quantification of glutathione, catechin, and caffeic acid in grape juice and wine by a novel ultra-performance liquid chromatography method. Food Chem. 128: 1136-1142.

Fracassetti D., Gabrielli M., Costa C., Tomás-Barberán F.A., Tirelli A., 2016. Characterization and suitability of polyphenols-based formulas to replace sulfur dioxide for storage of sparkling white wine. Food Control 60: 606-614.

Fragasso M., Antonacci D., Pati S., Lamacchia F., Balano A., Coletta A., La Notte E., 2010. Influence of glutathione addition on volatile profile of 'Trebbiano' and 'Bombino Bianco' wines. *In:* Proceedings of the 33rd OIV World Congress of Vine and Wine, Tbilisi, Georgia.

Francis I. L., Sefton M. A., Williams P. J., 1994. The sensory effect of pre- or post-fermentation thermal processing on Chardonnay and Semillon wines. Am. J. Enol. Vitic. 45 (2): 243-251.

Franco-Luesma E., Ferreira V., 2016 a. Reductive off-odors in wines: Formation and release of H_2S and methanethiol during the accelerated anoxic storage of wines. Food. Chem. 199: 42-50.

Franco-Luesma E., Ferreira V., 2016 b. Formation and release of H_2S, methanethiol, and dimethylsulfide during the anoxic storage of wines at room temperature. J. Agric. Food Chem. 64 (32): 6317-6326.

Friedenberg D.S., Manns D.C., Perry D.M., Mansfield A.K., 2018. Removal of copper from white wine: Imidazole-based polymers are efficient at copper adsorption. Catalyst 2: 1-6.

7. Literature

Gabrielli M., Aleixandre-Tudo L.L., Kilmartin P.A., Sieczkowski N., du Toit W.J., 2017. Additions of glutathione or specific glutathione-rich dry inactivated yeast preparation (DYP) to Sauvignon blanc must: Effect on wine chemical and sensory composition. S. Afr. J. Enol. Vitic. 38 (1): 18-28.

Garofolo A., Piracci A., 1994. Évolution des esters des acides gras pendant la conservation des vins. Constantes d'équilibre et énergie d'activation. Bull. de l'OIV 67, 757-756: 225-245.

Gawel R., van Sluyter S.C., Smith P.A., Water E.J., 2013. Effect of pH and alcohol on perception of phenolic character in white wine. Am. J. Enol. Vitic. 64 (4): 425-429.

Gawel R., Schulkin A., Smith P. A., Waters E. J., 2014. Taste and textural characters of mixtures of caftaric acid and grape reaction product in model wine. Aust. J. Grape Wine Res. 20 (1): 25-30.

Gessner M., Köhler H.J., Christoph N., Bauer-Christoph C., Miltenberger R., Schmitt A., 1995. Die "Untypische Alterungsnote" in Wein, Teil II: Beschreibende Verkostung von UTA-Weinen, Beziehungen zwischen Sensorik und chemisch-physikalischen Analysenwerten. Rebe und Wein 11: 388-394.

Gessner M., Köhler H.J., Christoph N., Bauer-Christoph C., 1996. Die "Untypische Alterungsnote" in Wein, Teil VII: Untersuchungen zur Bildung von 2-Aminoacetophenon aus Produkten des Tryptophan-Stoffwechsels bei der alkoholischen Gärung. Rebe und Wein 49: 251-255.

Gessner M., Köhler H.J., Christoph N., 1999 a. Die "Untypische Alterungsnote" in Wein, Teil VIII: Auswirkungen von Inhaltsstoffen und Antioxidantien auf die Bildung von o-Aminoacetophenon. Rebe und Wein 51: 264-267.

Gessner M., Köhler H.J., Christoph N., Nagel-Derr A., Krell U., 1999 b. Die "Untypische Alterungsnote" in Wein, Teil IX: Würzburger UTAFIX-Test: Ein einfaches Diagnoseverfahren zur Früherkennung von Weinen mit UTA-Neigung. Rebe und Wein 52: 296-303.

Gessner M., Köhler H.J., Christoph N., Nagel-Derr A, 2000. Erfahrungen zum Weinausbau mit Ascorbinsäure: Durchbruch bei der UTA-Behandlung. Deut. Weinmagazin 19: 34-37.

Gétaz J., Fabre S., 1990. Mesure de l'absorption d'oxygène dans les moûts par la méthode D.B.O. Rev. Fr. d'Œnologie 124: 21-26.

Godden P., Francis L., Field J., Gishen M., Coulter A., Valente P., Hoj P., Robinson E., 2001. Wine bottle closures: physical characteristics and effect on composition and sensory properties of a Semillon wine. I. Performance up to 20 months post-bottling. Aust. J. Grape Wine Res. 7 (1): 64-105.

Godden P., Lattey K., Francis L., Gishen M., Cowey G., Holdstock M., Robinson E., Waters E., Skouroumounis G., Sefton M., Capone D., Kwiatkowski M., Field J., Coulter A., D'Costa N., Bramley B., 2005. Towards offering wine to the consumer in optimal conditions – the wine, the closures and other packaging variables. Wine Industry Journal 20: 20-30.

Goniak O. J., Noble A. C., 1987. Sensory study of selected volatile sulfur compounds in white wine. Am. J. Enol. Vitic. 38 (3): 223-227.

Grant-Preece P., Hongjuan F., Schmidtke L.M., Clark A.C., 2013. Sensorially important aldehyde production from amino acids in model wine systems: Impact of ascorbic acid, erythorbic acid, glutathione and sulphur dioxide. Food Chemistry 141 (1): 304-312.

Guedes de Pinho P., Bertrand A., Guillou I., 1994. Influence de l'hyperoxygénation des moûts sur la composition chimique et sensorielle de vins blancs. Rev. Fr. d'Œnologie 145: 9-17.

Guerzoni M., Zironi E. R., Intrieri C., Magnanini E., 1981. Stabilisation of white wine by early hyperoxidation of white must. Food Technol. Austral. 33: 442-446.

Haigerov V., 1996. Schnelle Methode zur Bestimmung der Bitterstoffe in Weißwein. Vitic. Enol. Sci. 51 (1): 3-5.

Harbertson J.F., Picciotto E.A., Adams D.O., 2003. Measurement of polymeric pigments in grape berry extracts and wines using a protein precipitation assay combined with bisulfite bleaching. Am. J. Enol. Vitic. 54 (4): 301-306.

He J., Zhou Q., Peck J., Soles R., Qian M. C., 2013. The effect of wine closures on volatile sulfur and other compounds during post-bottle ageing. Flavour Frag. J. 28: 118-128.

Héritier J., Bach B., Schönenberger P., Gaillard V., Ducruet J., Segura J.-M., 2016. Quantification of the production of hydrogen peroxide H_2O_2 during accelerated wine oxidation. Food Chem. 211: 957-962.

Heymann H., Hopfer H., Bershaw D., 2014. An exploration of the perception of minerality in white wines by projective mapping and descriptive analysis. J. Sens. Studies 29 (1): 1-13.

Hoenicke K., Simat T.J., Steinhardt H., Köhler H.J., Schwab A., 2001. Determination of free and conjugated indole-3-acetic acid, tryptophan, and tryptophan metabolites in grape must and wine. J. Agric. Food Chen. 49 (11): 5494-5501.

Hoenicke K., Borchert O., Grüning K., Simat T.J., 2002 a. Untypical aging off-flavor in wine: Synthesis of potential degradation compounds of indole-3-acetic acid and kyrurenine and their evaluation of precursors of 2-aminoacetophenone. J. Agric. Food Chem. 50 (15): 4303-4309.

Hoenicke K., Simat T.J., Steinhart H., Christoph N., Gessner M., Köhler H.J., 2002 b. Untypical aging off-flavor in wine: Formation of 2-aminoacetophenone and evaluation of its influencing factors. Anal. Chim. Acta 458 (1): 29-37.

Hopfer H., Ebeler S. E., Heymann H., 2012. The combined effects of storage temperature and packaging on the sensory and chemical properties of Chardonnay. J. Agric. Food Chem. 60 (43): 10743-10754.

Houtman A. C., du Plessis C. S., 1981. The effect of juice clarity and several fermentation conditions promoting yeast growth on fermentation rate, the production of aroma components and wine quality. S. Afr. J. Enol. Vitic. 2 (2): 71-81.

Hühn T., Sponholz W.R., Bernath K., Friedmann A., Hess G., Muno H., Fromm W., 1999. The influence of high-energy short-wave radiation and other environmental factors on the genesis of compounds affecting the wine quality in Vitis vinifera L. cv. Mueller-Thurgau. Vitic. Enol. Sci. 54 (4): 101-104.

Jung R., Hey M., Hoffmann D., Leiner T., Patz C.-D., Beisert B., Rauhut D., Schüssler C., Wirsching M., 2007. Lichteinfluss bei der Lagerung von Wein. *In*: Proceedings of the 8th Internat. Symposium "Innovationen in der Kellerwirtschaft", Stuttgart (Germany) 2007: 45-55.

Jung R., Schüssler C., 2016. Alternative Verschlüsse für Wein. Deut. Weinmagazin 21: 16-19.

Kallithraka S., Bakker J., Clifford M.N., 1997. Evaluation of bitterness and astringency of (+)-catechin and (-)-epicatechin in red wine and in model solution. J. Sens. Studies 12 (1): 25-37.

Karbowiak T., Gougeon R. D., Alinc J.-B., Brachais L., Debeaufort F., Voilley A., Chassagne D., 2010. Wine oxidation and the role of cork. Crit. Rev. Food Sci. Nutr. 50 (1): 20-52.

Kinzurik M.I., Herbst-Johnstone M., Gardner C., Fedrizzi B., 2016. Hydrogen sulfide production during yeast fermentation causes the accumulation of ethanethiol, S-ethyl thioacetate and diethyl disulfide. Food Chem. 209: 341-347.

Koch T., Baumgarten G. F., 1995. Research report on the influence of grape varietals and the oxidation thereof on polyphenols of South African grape juice. *In*: Proceedings of the 4th Internat. Symposium "Innovationen in der Kellerwirtschaft", Stuttgart, Germany, 1995: 60-66.

Kontoudakis N., Mierczynska-Vasilev A., Guo A., Smith P.A., Scollary G.R., Wilkes E.N., Clark A.C., 2019. Removal of sulfide-bound copper from wine by membrane filtration: Filterability of sulfide-bound copper in white wine. Aust. J. Grape Wine Res., 25 (1): 53-61.

Köhler H.J., Christoph N., Gessner M., Bauer-Christoph C., 1995. Die "Untypische Alterungsnote" in Wein, Teil III: Zusammenhänge zwischen dem Auftreten der untypischen Alterungsnote und dem Reifestadium der Trauben (Lesetermin). Rebe und Wein 48: 424-430.

Köhler H.J., Christoph N., Bauer-Christoph C., Gessner N., Curschmann K., 1996. Die "Untypische Alterungsnote", Teil V: Einfluss kellertechnischer Maßnahmen auf die Ausprägung des UTA. Rebe und Wein 7: 213-218.

7. Literature

Köhler H.J., Gessner M., Christoph N., 2001. Vermeidung der Untypischen Alterungsnote: Ascorbinsäure als wichtige Hilfe. Deut. Weinbau-Jahrbuch 52: 219-228.

Köhler H.J., Gessner M., Herrmann J., 2007. Langer Hefekontakt: Vor- oder Nachteil? Deut. Weinmagazin 22: 10-15.

Kramling T.E., Singleton V.L., 1969: An estimate of the nonflavonoid phenols in wines. Am. J. Enol. Vitic. 20 (2): 86-92.

Kreitman G.Y., Elias R.J., Jeffery D.W., Sacks G.L., 2018. Loss and formation of malodourous volatile sulfhydryl compounds during wine storage. Crit. Rev. Food Sci. Nutr. 5: 1-24.

Kritzinger E. C., du Toit W. J., Stander M. A., 2013. Assessment of glutathione levels in model solutions and grape ferments supplemented with glutathione-enriched inactive dry yeast preparations using a novel UPLC-MS/MS method. Food Addit. Contam., Part A, 30 (1), 80-92.

Kwasniewski M.T., Verden-Heuvel J.E., Pan B.S., Sacks G.L., 2010. Timing of cluster light environment manipulation during grape development affects C_{13} norisoprenoid and carotenoid concentrations in Riesling. J. Agric. Food Chem. 58 (11): 6841-6849.

La Folette G., Stambor J., Aiken J., 1993. Chemical and sensory considerations in sur lies production of Chardonnay wines. III. Occurrence of sunstruck flavor. Vitic. Enol. Sci. 48 (3): 208-210.

Lampíř L., 2013. Varietal differences of white wines on the basis of phenolic compounds profile. Czech. J. Food Sci. 31 (2): 172-179.

Lamuela-Raventós R.M., Huix-Blanquera M., Waterhouse A.L., 2001. Treatments for pinking alteration in white wines. Am. J: Enol. Vitic. 52 (2): 156-158.

Lavigne-Cruege V., Cutzach I., Dubourdieu D., 2000. Interprétation chimique du vieillissement aromatique défectueux des vins blancs. Incidence des modalités d'élevage. *In*: Œnologie 99 (A. Lonvaud-Funel, coord.), Éditions Tec & Doc, Paris: 433-438.

Lea A.G.H., 1978. The analysis of cider phenolics. Ann. Nutr. Alim. 32 (5): 1051-1061.

Lea A.G.H., Arnold G. M., 1978. The phenolics of ciders: bitterness and astringency. J. Sci. Food Agric. 29 (5): 478-483.

Lea A.G.H., Bridle P., Timberlake C. F., Singleton V. L., 1979. The procyanidins of white grapes and wines. Am. J. Enol. Vitic. 30 (4): 289-300.

Lee C. Y., Jaworski A. W., 1988. Phenols and browning potential of white grapes grown in New York. Am. J. Enol. Vitic. 39 (4): 337-340.

Limmer A., 2005 a. The chemistry and possible ways of mitigation of post-bottling sulfides. New Zealand Winegrower 1: 34-37.

Limmer A., 2005 b. Do corks breathe? Or the origin of SLO. Australian NZ Grapegrower Winemaker, Annual Technical Issue 497: 89-98.

Limmer A., 2005 c. Suggestions for dealing with post-bottling sulfides. Australian NZ Grapegrower Winemaker, Annual Technical Issue 503: 67-76.

Limmer A., 2006. The 'permeability' of closures. Australian NZ Grapegrower Winemaker, Annual Technical Issue 509: 106-111.

Linsenmeier A.W., Rauhut D., Kürbel H., Löhnertz O., Schubert S., 2007 a. Untypical ageing off-flavor and masking effects due to long-term nitrogen fertilization. Vitis 46 (1): 33-38.

Linsenmeier A.W., Rauhut D., Kürbel H., Schubert S., Löhnertz O., 2007 b. Ambivalence of the influence of nitrogen supply on o-aminoacetophenone in Riesling wine. Vitis 46 (2): 91-97.

Linsenmeier A.W., Löhnertz O, 2007 c. Changes in norisoprenoid levels with long-term nitrogen fertilization in different vintages of Vitis vinifera var. Riesling wines. S. Afr. J. Enol. Vitic. 28 (1): 17-24.

Löhnertz O., 1996. UTA und Rebenernährung. Stress macht alt. Deut. Weinbau 18: 18-23.

Lopes P., Saucier C., Teissedre P.-L., Glories Y., 2006. Impact of storage position on oxygen ingress through different closures into wine bottles. J. Agric. Food Chem. 54 (18): 6741-6746.

Lopes P., Saucier C., Teissedre P.-L., Glories Y., 2007. Main routes of oxygen ingress through different bottle closures into wine bottles. J. Agric. Food Chem. 55 (13): 5167-5170.

Lopes P., Silva M. A., Pons A., Tominaga T., Lavigne V., Saucier C., Darriet P., Teissedre P.-L., Dubourdieu D., 2009. Impact of oxygen dissolved at bottling and transmitted through closures on the composition and sensory properties of a Sauvignon blanc wine during bottle storage. J. Agric. Food Chem. 57 (21) : 10261-10270.

Lorenzini F. 2009. Effet des lies sur le caractère de "stress" des vins. Essais sur Chasselas. Rev. Suisse Vitic. Arboric. 41 (4): 227-230.

Lurie D.G., Holden J.M., Schubert A., Wolf W.R., Miller-Ihli N.J., 1989. The copper content of foods based on a critical evaluation of published data. J. Food Compost. Anal. 2 (4): 298-316.

Magalhães L.M., Ramos I.I., Reis S., Segundo M.A., 2014. Antioxidant profile of commercial oenological tannins determined by multi chemical assays. Aust. J. Grape Wine Res. 20 (1): 72-79.

Makhotkina O., Kilmartin P.A., 2009. Uncovering the influence of antioxidants on polyphenol oxidation in wines using an electrochemical method: Cyclic voltammetry. J. Electroanalytical Chem., 633 (1): 165-174.

Makhotkina O., Pineau B., Kilmartin P. A., 2012. Effect of storage temperature on the chemical composition and sensory profile of Sauvignon blanc wines. Aust. J. Grape Wine Res. 18 (1): 91-99.

Maltman A., 2013. Minerality in wine: a geological perspective. J. Wine Res. 24 (3): 169-181.

Marais J., 1992. 1,1,6-trimethyl-1,2-dihydronaphthalene (TDN): A possible degradation product of lutein and beta-carotene. S. Afr. J. Enol. Vitic. 13 (1): 52-55.

Marais J., Van Wyk C. J., Rapp A., 1992 a. Effect of sunlight and shade on the norisoprenoid levels in maturing Weisser Riesling and Chenin blanc grapes and Weisser Riesling wines. S. Afr. J. Enol. Vitic. 13 (1): 23-32.

Marais J., Versini G., Van Wyk C. J., Rapp A., 1992 b. Effect of region on free and bound monoterpene and C_{13}-noisoprenoid concentration in Weisser Riesling wines. S. Afr. J. Enol. Vitic. 13 (2): 71-77.

Marais J., Van Wyk C. J., Rapp A., 1992 c. Effect of storage time, temperature and region on the levels of 1,1,6-trimethyl-1,2-dihydronaphthalene and other volatiles, and on quality of Weisser Riesling wines. S. Afr. J. Enol. Vitic. 13 (1): 33-44.

Marais J., 1998. Effect of grape temperature, oxidation and skin contact on Sauvignon blanc juice and wine composition and wine quality. S. Afr. J. Enol. Vitic. 19 (1): 10-16.

Marchand S., de Revel G., Bertrand A., 2000. Approaches to wine aroma: release of aroma compounds from reactions between cysteine and carbonyl compounds in wine. J. Agric. Food Chem. 48 (10): 4890-4895.

Marks A. C., Morris J. R., 1993. Ascorbic acid effects on the post-disgorgement oxidative stability of sparkling wine. Am. J. Enol. Vitic. 44 (4): 227-231.

Maujean A., Haye M., Feuillat M., 1978. Contribution à l'étude des "goûts de lumière" dans le vin de Champagne. II. Influence de la lumière sur le potentiel d'oxydoréduction. Correlation avec la teneur en thiols du vin. Conn. Vigne Vin 12 (4): 277-290.

Maury C., Sarni-Manchado P. Levebvre S., Cheynier V., Moutounet M., 2001. Influence of fining with different molecular weight gelatins on proanthocyanidin composition and perception of wines. Am. J. Enol. Vitic. 52 (2): 140-145.

Mayr C.M., Capone D.L., Pardon K.H., Black C.A., Pomeroy D., Leigh I., 2015. Quantitative analysis by GC-MS/MS of 18 aroma compounds related to oxidative off-flavor in wines. J. Agric. Food Chem. 63 (13): 3394-3401.

7. Literature

McMurrough I., McDowell J., 1978. Chromatrographic separation and automated analysis of flavanols. Anal. Biochem. 91: 92-100.

Meistermann E., 1990. Hyperoxygénation des moûts; essais réalisés en Alsace. Rev. Fr. d'Œnologie 142: 62-64.

Mestres M., Busto O., Guash J., 2000. Analysis of organic sulfur compounds in wine aroma. J. Chromatogr. A 881 (1-2): 569-583.

Mira H., Leite P. Catarino S., Ricardo-da-Silva J.M., Curvelo-Garcia A.S., 2007. Metal reduction in wine using PVI-PVP copolymer and its effects on chemical and sensory characteristics. Vitis 46 (3): 138-147.

Moio, L., Ugliano, M., Gambuti, A., Genovese, A., Plombino, P., 2004. Influence of clarification treatments on concentrations of selected free varietal aroma compounds and glycoconjugates in Falanghina (*Vitis vinifera* L.) must and wine. Am. J. Enol. Vitic. 55 (1): 7-12.

Monforte A.R., Martins S.I.F.S., Ferreira A.C.S., 2018. Strecker aldehyde formation in wine: New insights into the role of gallic acid, glucose, and metals in phenylacetaldehyde formation. J. Agric. Food Chem. 66 (10): 2459-2466.

Morozova K., 2013. Impact of oxygen on quality of white wine. Thesis, University of Hohenheim, Germany.

Morozova K., Schmidt O., 2011. Bedeutung von Sauerstoff in der Weinbereitung. Deut. Weinmagazin 04: 18-24.

Morozova K., Schmidt O., Schwack W., 2015. Effect of headspace volume, ascorbic acid and sulphur dioxide on oxidative status and sensory profile of Riesling wine. European Food Research and Technology 240 (1): 205-221.

Moutounet M., 1981. Dosages des polyphénols des moûts de raisin. Conn. Vigne Vin 15 (4): 287-301.

Moutounet M., Cheynier V., Rigaud J., Souquet J.-M., 1989. Les mécanismes d'oxydation mis en jeu lors de la préparation des moûts destinés à l'élaboration de vins blancs. Rev. Fr. d'Œnologie 117: 23-29.

Moutounet M., Rigaud J., Souquet J.-M., Cheynier V., 1990. Influence de quelques paramètres sur l'oxydation des moûts blancs. Rev. Fr. d'Œnologie 124: 32-38.

Muller D. J., Kepner R. E., Webb A. D., 1973. Lactones in wine - a review. Am. J. Enol. Vitic. 24 (1): 5-9.

Müller E., 1999. 15 Jahre Stickstoffdüngungsversuche: Erfahrungen und Konsequenzen. Deut. Weinmagazin 19: 27-31 and 20: 29-32.

Müller K., Weisser H., 2002. Gasdurchlässigkeit von Flaschenverschlüssen. Brauwelt 142: 617-619.

Müller-Späth H., 1977. Neueste Erkenntnisse über den Sauerstoffeinfluß bei der Weinbereitung aus der Sicht der Praxis. Weinwirtschaft 113: 144-157.

Müller-Späth H., 1992. Der POM-Test. Deut. Weinbau 23: 1099-1100.

Müller-Späth H., Löscher T., Schäfer G., 1977. Einfluß des Sauerstoffs bei der Weinbereitung von der Traube bis zur Flaschenfüllung. Deut. Weinbau 32: 384-392.

Müller-Späth H., Moschtert N., Schäfer G., 1978. Beobachtungen bei der Weinbereitung. Eine Bestandsaufnahme. Weinwirtschaft 114: 1084-1089.

Myers T. E., Singleton V. L., 1979. The nonflavonoid phenolic fraction of wine and its analysis. Am. J. Enol. Vitic. 30 (2): 98-102.

Nagel C. W., Graber R., 1988. Effect of must oxidation on quality of white wines. Am. J. Enol. Vitic. 39 (1): 1-4.

Neradt F., 1970. Sauerstoffbindungsgeschwindigkeit bei Traubenmost. Weinberg und Keller 17: 519-526.

Nicolini G., 1992. Variazioni nel profilo sensoriale di vini Sauvignon blanc in relazione all' iperossidazione die mosti. Riv. Vitic. Enol. 4: 35-43.

Nicolini G., Mattivi F., Dalla Serra A., 1991. Iperossigenazione dei mosti: conseguenze analitiche e sensoriali su vini della vendemmia 1989. Riv. Vitic. Enol. 3: 454-56.

Nicolini G., Larcher R., Mattivi F., 2004. Experiments concerning metal depletion in must and wine with Divergan HM™. Vitis 54 (1): 25-32.

Nicolini G., Moser S., Román T., Mazzi E., Larcher R., 2011. Effect of juice turbidity on fermentative volatile compounds in white wines. Vitis 50 (3): 131-135.

Nikolantonaki M., Waterhouse A.L., 2012: A method to quantify quinone reaction rates with wine relevant nucleophiles: A key to understanding of oxidative loss of varietal thiols. J. Agric. Food Chem. 60 (34): 8484-8491.

Nikolantonaki M., Perrine J., Coelho C., Roullier-Gall C., Ballester J., Schmitt-Kopplin P., Gougeon R.D., 2018. Impact of glutathione on wines oxidative stability: A combined sensory and metabolomic study. Front. Chem. 6 (182): 1-9, https://doi.org/10.3389/fchem.2018.00182.

Noble A., 1994. Bitterness in wine. Physiol. Behav. 56: 1251-1255.

Noble A., 1998. Why do wines taste bitter and feel astringent? In: Am. Chem. Soc. Symposium Series, 114: 156-165.

Oliveira C.M., Ferreira A.C.S., de Freitas V., Silva A.M.S., 2011. Oxidation mechanisms occurring in wines. Food Res. Int. 44: 1115-1126.

Oliveira V., Lopes P., Cabral M., Pereira H., 2013. Kinetics of oxygen ingress into wine bottles closed with natural cork stoppers of different qualities. Am. J. Enol. Vitic. 64 (4): 395-399.

Oliveira C.M., Santos S.A., Silvestre A.J., Barros A.S., Ferreira A.C., Silva A.M., 2017. Quinones as Strecker degradation reagents in wine oxidation processes. Food Chem. 228: 618-624.

Ough C. S., Crowell E. A., 1987. Use of sulfur dioxide in winemaking. J. Food Sci. 52 (2): 386-388.

Panero L, Motta S., Petrozziello M., Guaita M., Bosso A., 2014. Effect of SO_2, reduced glutathione and ellagitannins on the shelf life of bottled white wines. Eur. Food Res. Technol. 240 (2): 345-356.

Papadopoulou D., Roussis I. G., 2001. Inhibition of the decline of linalool and γ-terpineol in Muscat wines by glutathione and N-acetyl-cysteine. Ital. J. Food Sci. 13 (4): 413-419.

Papadopoulou D., Roussis I. G., 2008. Inhibition of the decrease of volatile esters and terpenes during storage of a white wine and a model wine medium by glutathione and N-acetyl-cysteine. Int. J. Food Sci. Tech. 43 (6): 1053-1057.

Park S.-K., 2008. Development of a method to measure hydrogen sulfide in wine fermentations. J. Microbiol. Biotechnol. 18 (9): 1550-1554.

Parr W.V., Valentin D., Breitmeyer J., Peyron D., Darriet P., Sherlock R., Robinson B., Grose C., Ballester J., 2016. Perceived minerality in sauvignon blanc wine: Chemical reality or cultural construct? Food Res. Int. 87: 168-179.

Pascual O. et al., 2017. Oxygen consumption rates by different oenological tannins in a model solution. Food Chem. 234: 26-32.

Patrianakou, M., Roussis, I. G., 2013. Decrease of wine volatile aroma esters by oxidation. S. Afr. J. Enol. Vitic. 34 (2): 241-245.

Peng Z., Duncan B., Pocock K. F., Sefton M. A., 1998. The effect of ascorbic acid on oxidative browning of white wines and model wines. Aust. J. Grape Wine Res. 4 (3): 127-135.

Periadnadi N., 2003. Das Vorkommen der die Alterung auslösenden Precursoren und der Einfluss von Mikroorganismen auf die TDN-Bildung in Wein. Thesis, Frankfurt (Germany) University.

7. Literature

Perscheid M., Zürn F., 1977. Der Einfluß von Oxidationsvorgängen auf die Weinqualität. Weinwirtschaft 1/2: 10-12.

Pfeifer W., 2000. Sauerstoffaufnahme bei der Weinbereitung und deren Einfluß auf die Weinqualität: Wieviel Sauerstoff braucht ein Wein? Deut. Weinmagazin 26: 24-27.

Pickering G. J., Blake A. J., Soleas G. J., Inglis D. L., 2010. Remediation of wine with elevated concentrations of 3-alkyl-2-methoxypyrazines using cork and synthetic closures. J. Food Agric. Environ. 08 (2): 97-101.

Pompei C., Peri C., 1971. Determination of catechins in wines. Vitis 9: 312-316.

Pons A., Nikolantonaki M., Lavigne V., Shinoda K., Dubourdieu D., Darriet P., 2015. New insights into intrinsic and extrinsic factors triggering premature aging in white wines. *In:* Advances in Wine Research, Am. Chem. Soc. Symposium Series, 1203: 229-251.

Pozo-Bayón M. A., Andújar-Ortiz I., Moreno-Arribas M. V., 2009: Scientific evidences beyond the application of inactive dry yeast preparations in winemaking. Food Res. Int. 42: 754-761.

Pripis-Nicolau L., de Revel G., Bertrand A., Maujean A., 2000. Formation of flavor components by the reaction of amino acid and carbonyl compounds in mild conditions. J. Agric. Food Chem. 48 (9): 3761-3766.

Puisais J., Guiller A., Lacoste J., Huteau P., 1968. Dosage spectrophotométrique des tanins. Ann. Technol. Agric. 17 (4): 277-285.

Ramey D., Bertrand A., Ough C.S., Singleton V.L., Sanders E., 1986. Effects of skin contact temperature on Chardonnay must and wine composition. Am. J. Enol. Vitic. 37 (2): 99-106.

Rapp A., Mandery H., 1986. Wine aroma. Experientia 42 (8): 873-884.

Rapp A., Versini G., Ullemeyer H., 1993. 2-Aminoacetophenone: Causal component of 'untypical ageing flavor', 'naphthalene note', 'hybrid note' of wine. Vitis 32 (1): 61-62.

Rauhut D., Kürbel H., 1994 a. Die Entstehung von H_2S aus Netzschwefel-Rückständen während der Gärung und deren Einfluss auf die Bildung von böckserverursachenden Metaboliten in Wein. Vitic. Enol. Sci. 49 (1): 27-36.

Rauhut D., Kürbel H., Dittrich H.H., Prior B., Grossmann M., 1994 b. Einfluss von Hefestämmen und deren Ernährung auf die Böckserbildung. *In*: 100 Jahre Hefereinzucht Geisenheim, Forschungsanstalt Geisenheim: 38-55.

Rauhut D., Kürbel H., Dittrich H., Grossmann M., 1996. Properties and differences of commercial yeast strains with respect to their formation of sulfur compounds. Vitic. Enol. Sci. 51: 187-192.

Rauhut D., Shefford P.G., Roll C., Hürbel H., Löhnertz O., 2003. Effect of diverse enological methods to avoid occurrence of atypical aging and related of-flavours in wine. *In:* Œnologie 2003, 7ème Symposium International d'Œnologie, A. Lonvaud-Funel et al. (eds.), Lavoisier Tec & Doc, Paris: 376-379.

Rebelein H., 1965. Beitrag zur Bestimmung des Catechingehaltes in Wein. Deut. Lebensmittel-Rundschau 61: 182-183.

Renner H., Pour Nikfardjam M., 2016: Altbewährtes neu entdeckt. Deut. Weinbau 22: 18-21.

Renner H., Pour Nikfardjam M., 2017. Kupfer- und Silbersalze gegen Böckser. Der Winzer 7: 34-38.

Rigaud J., Cheynier V., Souquet J.-M., Moutounet M., 1990. Mécanismes d'oxydation des polyphénols dans les moûts blancs. Rev. Fr. d'Œnologie 124: 27-31.

Rigaud J., Cheynier V., Souquet J.-M., Moutounet M., 1991. Influence of must composition on phenolic oxidation kinetics. J. Sci. Food Agric. 57 (1): 55-63.

Robichaud J.L., Noble A.C., 1990. Astringency and bitterness of selected phenolics in wine. J. Sci. Food Agric. 53 (3): 343-353.

Robinson A. L., Mueller M., Heymann H., Ebeler S. E., Boss P. K., Solomon P. S., Trengove R. D., 2010. Effect of simulated shipping conditions on sensory attributes and volatile composition of commercial white and red wines. Am. J. Enol. Vitic. 61 (3): 337-347.

Rodriguez-Bencomo J. J., Andújar-Ortiz I., Moreno-Arribas M.V., Simó C., Gonzales J., Chana A., Dávalos J., Pozo-Bayón M. A., 2014. Impact of glutathione-enriched inactive dry yeast preparations on the stability of terpenes during model wine aging. J. Agric. Food Chem. 62 (6), 1373-1383.

Roget W., Macintyre J., O'Brien V., 2010. New innovation for guiding closure selection. Austral. & New Zealand Grapegrower & Winemaker 561: 100-106.

Roland A., Vialaret J., Razungles A., Rigou P., Schneider R., 2010. Evolution of S-cysteinylated and S-glutathionylated thiol precursors during oxidation of Melon B. and Sauvignon blanc musts. J. Agric. Food Chem. 58 (7): 4406-4413.

Rosenfeld E., Beauvoit B., Rigoulet M., Salmon J.-M., 2002. Non-respiratory oxygen consumption pathways in anaerobically-grown Saccharomyces cerevisiae: evidence and partial characterization. Yeast 19 (15), 1299-1321.

Ross C.F., Zwink A.C., Castro L., Harrison R., 2014. Odour detection threshold and consumer rejection of 1,1,6-trimethyl-1,2-dihydronaphthalene in 1-year-old Riesling wines. Aust. J. Grape Wine Research 20 (4): 335-339.

Rossi J. A., Singleton V. L., 1966. Contribution of grape phenols to oxygen absorption and browning of wines. Am. J. Enol. Vitic. 17 (4): 231-239.

Roussis I. G., Lambropoulos I., Tzimas P., 2007. Protection of volatiles in a wine with low sulfur dioxide by caffeic acid or glutathione. Am. J. Enol. Vitic. 58 (4): 274-278.

Roussis I. G., Papadopoulou D., Sakarellos-Daitsiotis M., 2009. Protective effect of thiols on wine aroma volatiles. The Open Food Science Journal 3: 8-102.

Rudy H., 2015. Petrolnote: Entstehung und Reduzierung. Deut. Weinbau 21: 32-35.

Sablayrolles J.-M., Dubois C., Manginot C., Roustan J.-L., Barre P., 1996. Effectiveness of combined ammoniacal nitrogen and oxygen additions for completion of sluggish and stuck fermentations. J. Ferm. Bioengineering 82 (4): 377-381.

Sacks G.L., Gates M.J., Ferry F.X., Lavin E.H., Kurz A.J., Acree T.E., 2012. Sensory threshold of 1,1,6-trimethyl-1,2-dihydohaphthalene (TDN) and concentrations in young Riesling and non-Riesling wines. J. Agric. Food Chem. 60 (12): 2998-3004.

Salmon J.-M., 2006: Interactions between yeast, oxygen and polyphenols during alcoholic fermentations: Practical implications. Food Sci. Technol. 39 (9), 959-965.

Salmon J.-M., Fornairon-Bonnefond C., Mazauric J.-P., Moutounet M., 2000. Oxygen consumption by wine lees: impact on lees integrity during wine ageing. Food Chem. 71: 519-528.

Sarneckis C.J., Dambergs R.G., Jones P., Mercurio M., Herderich M.J., Smith P.A., 2006. Quantification of condensed tannins by precipitation with methyl cellulose: development and validation of an optimised tool for grape and wine analysis. Aust. J. Grape Wine Res. 12 (1): 39-49.

Schmidt O., Weiser K., Amann R., 2003. Sauerstoffmanagement bei der Verarbeitung weißer Rebsorten. Deut. Weinmagazin 13: 28-33.

Schneider V., 1989 a. Weinalterung, Teil III. Weinwirtschaft-Technik 10: 22-27.

Schneider V., 1989 b. Aussagekraft des Catechinwertes. Weinwirtschaft-Technik 2: 17-19.

Schneider V., 1991. Comportement des vins obtenus par oxygénation des moûts blancs. Rev. Fr. d'Œnologie 130: 33-42.

Schneider V., 1992. Entrappen oder nicht entrappen? Weinwirtschaft-Technik 05: 63-65.

Schneider V., 1993. Oxidative Weinalterung. Teil 1: Analytische Ansätze. Deut. Weinmagazin 17: 18-26.

7. Literature

Schneider V., 1994. Neuere Erkenntnisse zur Mostoxidation. Winzer-Zeitschrift 10: 20-23.

Schneider, V., 1995. Evaluation of small amounts of flavonoid phenols in white wines by colorimetric assays. Am. J. Enol. Vitic. 46 (2): 274-277.

Schneider, V., 1996. Einfluss von Maischestandzeit und Mostoxidation auf die Sensorik von Riesling. Winzer-Zeitschrift 7: 22-25.

Schneider V., 1998 a. Must hyperoxidation. A review. Am. J. Enol. Vitic. 49 (1): 65-73.

Schneider V., 2000. Die Aromastabilität von Weißwein. Deut. Weinmagazin 25: 10-14.

Schneider V., 2003: Alterung von Weißwein, IV. Einfluß von Sauerstoff vor und nach der Gärung. Winzer-Zeitschrift 10: 30-32.

Schneider, V., 2005 a. Hochwertige Weißweine: Qualität durch Minimalbehandlung. Der Winzer 10: 6-11.

Schneider V., 2005 b. Mostbehandlung: Einfluss der Vinifikation auf die Haltbarkeit von Weißwein. Der Winzer 9: 6-12.

Schneider V., 2005 c. Postfermentative Phase: Die Hefe nach der Gärung. Der Winzer 11: 13-18.

Schneider V., 2005 d. Aufnahme von Sauerstoff im Keller und bei der Abfüllung. Der Winzer 12: 6-9.

Schneider V., 2006 a. Alterung von Weißwein, II: Die Reaktionen des Sauerstoffs. Der Winzer 1: 8-11.

Schneider V., 2006 b. Gerbstoffe in Weißwein. Der Winzer 3: 6-10.

Schneider V., 2006 c. Alterung von Weißwein, III: Die Stabilität des Aromas abgefüllter Weißweine. Der Winzer 2: 6-9.

Schneider V., 2008. Strategien gegen den Böckser, II. Die Behandlung von Böcksern. Der Winzer 8: 6-9.

Schneider V., 2009. Alterungsverhalten österreichischer Weißweine. Der Winzer 07: 12-16.

Schneider V., 2013. Bedeutung von Sauerstoff für die Bildung von UTA. Winzer-Zeitschrift 11: 32-33.

Schneider V., 2014. Atypical aging defect: Sensory discrimination, viticultural causes, and enological consequences. A Review. Am. J. Enol. Vitic. 65 (3): 277-284.

Schneider V., 2015 a. Aufnahme von Sauerstoff: Konsequenzen für den Wein. Deut. Weinmagazin 2: 28-32.

Schneider V., 2018. Orange Weine: Extraktion von Tannin während der Maischestandzeit. Deut. Weinmagazin 10: 28-31.

Schneider V., Müller J., Schmidt D., 2016. Oxygen consumption by postfermentation yeast lees: Factors affecting its rate and extent under enological conditions. Food Technol. Biotechnol. 54 (4): 395-402.

Schneider V., Schmitt M., Kroeger R., 2017. Wine screw cap closures: The next generation. Grapegrower & Winemaker 638: 50-52.

Scholten G., Kacprowski M., 1992. Zur Analytik von Polyphenolen in Wein. Vitic. Enol. Sci. 48 (1): 33-38.

Schöneich C., Asmus K.-D., 1990. Reaction of thiyl radicals with alcohols, ethers and polyunsaturated fatty acids. A possible role of thiyl free radicals in thiol mutagenesis. Radiation and Environmental Biophysics 29 (4): 263-271.

Schwab A.L., Peternel M., Köhler H.J., Heigel K.P., 1996. Die "Untypische Alterungsnote" in Wein, Teil IV: Beeinflussung durch weinbauliche Maßnahmen. Rebe und Wein 6: 181-187.

Schwab A.L. Peternel M., 1997. Investigation about the influence of a long term green cover on must and wine quality with special consideration of Franconian pedological and climatic conditions. Vitic. Enol. Sci. 52 (1): 20-26.

Schwab A.L., Christoph N., Köhler H.J., Gessner M., Simat T.J., 1999. Influence of viticultural treatments on the formation of the untypical aging off-flavor in white wines. Vitic. Enol. Sci. 54 (4): 114-120.

Scrimgeour N., Wilkes E., 2014. Closure trials show volatile sulfur compounds formation can still cause a stink. Australian & New Zealand Grapegrower & Winemaker 602: 62-67.

Scrimgeour N., Nordestgaard S., Lloyd N.D.R., Wilkes E.N., 2015. Exploring the effect of elevated storage temperature on wine. Aust. J. Grape Wine Res. 21 (S1): 713-722.

Segurel M.A., Razungles A.J., Riou C., Salles M., Baumes R.L., 2004. Contribution of dimethyl sulfide to the aroma of Syrah and Grenache noir wines and estimation of its potential in grapes of these varieties. J. Agric. Food Chem. 52 (23): 7084-7093.

Servili M., de Stefano G., Piacquadio P. Sciancalepore V., 2000. A novel method for removing phenols from grape must. Am. J. Enol. Vitic. 51 (4): 357-361.

Shedid S. A., 2010. Chemical composition and antioxidant activity of Maillard reaction products generated from glutathione or cysteine/glucose. World Applied Sci. J. 9 (10), 1148-1154.

Silva M. A., Julien M., Jourdes M., Teissedre P.-L., 2011. Impact of closures on wine post-bottling development: A review. Eur. Food Res. Technol. 233: 905-914.

Silva M. A., Jourdes M., Darriet P., Teissedre P.-L., 2012. Scalping of light volatile sulfur compounds by wine closures. J. Agric. Food Chem. 60 (44): 10952-10956.

Simat T.J., Hoenicke K., Gessner M., Christoph N., 2004. Metabolism of tryptophan and indole-3-acetic acid formation during vinification and its influence on the formation of 2-aminoacetophenone. Mitt. Klosterneuburg 54 (1): 34-55.

Simpson R.F., 1977. Oxidative pinking in white wines. Vitis 16 (4): 286-294.

Simpson R.F., 1978. Aroma and compositional changes in wine with oxidation, storage, and ageing. Vitis 17 (3): 274-287.

Simpson R.F., 1982. Factors affecting oxidative browning in white wines. Vitis 21 (3): 233-239.

Simpson R.F., Miller C.G., 1983. Aroma composition of aged Riesling wines. Vitis 22 (1): 51-63.

Sims C.A., Eastridge J. S., Bates R. P., 1995. Changes in phenols, color, and sensory characteristics of muscadine wines by pre- and post-fermentation additions of PVPP, casein, and gelatin. Am. J. Enol. Vitic. 46 (2): 155-158.

Singleton V. L., 1987. Oxygen with phenols and related reactions in musts, wines, and model systems: observations and practical implications. Am. J. Enol. Vitic. 38 (1): 69-77.

Singleton V. L., Rossi J. A., 1965. Colorimetry of total phenols with phosphomolybdic-phosphotungstic acid reagents. Am. J. Enol. Vitic. 16 (1): 144-158.

Singleton V. L., 2001. A survey of wine aging reactions, especially with oxygen. In: Proceedings ASEV 50th Anniversary Annual Meeting, J.R. Rantz (Ed.), ASEV, Davis, CA: 323-336.

Singleton V. L., Sieberhagen H. A., de Wet P., van Wyk C. J., 1975. Composition and sensory qualities of wines prepared from white grapes by fermentation with and without grape solids. Am. J. Enol. Vitic. 26 (1): 62-69.

Singleton V. L., Kramling T. E., 1976. Browning of white wines and an accelerated test for browning capacity. Am. J. Enol. Vitic. 27 (4): 157-160.

Singleton V.L., Noble A. C., 1976. Wine flavor and phenolic substances. Am. Chem. Soc. Symposium Series 26: 47-70.

Singleton V.L., Zaya J., Trousdale E., 1980. White table wine quality and polyphenol composition as affected by must SO_2 content and pomace contact time. Am. J. Enol. Vitic. 31 (1): 14-20.

Singleton V. L., Salgues M., Zaya J., Trousdale E., 1985. Caftaric acid disappearance and conversion to products of enzymic oxidation in grape must and wine. Am. J. Enol. Vitic. 36 (1): 50-56.

7. Literature

Skouroumounis G. K., Kwiatkowski M. J., Francis I. L., Oakey H., Capone D. L., Peng Z., Duncan B., Sefton M. A., Waters E. J., 2005 a. The influence of ascorbic acid on the composition, colour and flavor properties of a Riesling and a wooded Chardonnay wine during five years' storage. Aust. J. Grape Wine Res. 11 (3): 355-368.

Skouroumounis G. K., Kwiatkowski M. J., Francis I. L., Oakey H., Capone D .L., Duncan B., Sefton M. A., Waters E. J., 2005 b. The impact of closure type and storage conditions on the composition, colour and flavour properties of a Riesling and a wooded Chardonnay wine during five years' storage. Aust. J. Grape Wine Res. 11 (3): 369-377.

Smith P. A., Waters E., 2012. Identification of the major drivers of 'phenolic' taste in white wines. Final report to the grape and wine research & development corporation, The Australian Wine Research Institute (Ed.), Adelaide 2012.

Somers T. C., Ziemelis G., 1972. Interpretation of ultraviolet absorption in white wines. J. Sci. Food. Agric. 23 (4): 441-453.

Somers T. C., Ziemelis G., 1980. Gross interference by sulphur dioxide in standard determinations of wine phenolics. J. Sci. Food Agric. 31 (6): 600-610.

Somers T. C., Ziemelis G., 1985. Spectral evaluation of total phenolic components in Vitis vinifera grapes and wines. J. Sci. Food Agric. 36 (12): 1275-1284.

Somers T. C., Pocock K. F., 1991. Phenolic assessment of white musts: Varietal differences in free-run juices and pressings. Vitis 30 (3): 189-201.

Sonni F., Clark A. C., Prenzler P. D., Riponi C., Scollary G. R., 2011. Antioxidant action of glutathione and the ascorbic acid/glutathione pair in a model wine. J. Agric. Food Chem. 59 (8) 3940-3939.

Starkenmann C., Chappuis C. J.-F., Niclass Y., Deneulin P., 2016. Identification of hydrogen disulfanes and hydrogen trisulfanes in H_2S bottle, in flint and in dry mineral wine. J. Agric. Food Chem. 64 (47): 9033-9040.

Stöckl A., 2013. Einfluss von Lagerzeit und Lagerdauer: Trinkreife abschätzen? Der Winzer 5: 33-35.

Tominaga T., Guimbertau G., Dubourdieu D., 2003. Contribution of benzenemethanethiol to smoky aroma of certain Vitis vinifera L. wines. J. Food Agric. Chem. 51 (5): 1373-1376.

Ugliano M., Kwiatkowski M. J., Travis B., Francis I. L., Waters E. J., Herderich M. J., Pretorius I. S., 2009. Post-bottling management of oxygen to reduce off-flavour formation and optimise wine style. The Wine Industry Journal 24: 24-28.

Ugliano M., Kwiatkowski M., Vidal S., Capone D., Siebert T., Dieval J.-B., Aagaard O., Waters E. J., 2011. Evolution of 3-mercaptohexanol, hydrogen sulfide, and methyl mercaptan during bottle storage of Sauvignon blanc wines. Effect of glutathione, copper, oxygen exposure, and closure-derived oxygen. J. Agric. Food Chem. 59 (6): 2564-2572.

Ugliano M., 2013. Oxygen contribution to wine aroma evolution during bottle aging. J. Agric. Food Chem. 61 (26): 6125-6136.

Ugliano M., Bégrand S., Diéval J.-B., Vidal S., 2015. Critical oxygen levels affecting wine aroma: Relevant sensory attributes, related aroma compounds, and possible mechanisms. Am. Chem. Soc. Symposium Series 1203: 205-216.

Valade M., Tribaut-Sohier I., Brunner D., Pierlot C., Moncomble D., Tusseau D., 2006. Les apports d'oxygène en vinification et leurs impacts sur les vins. 1ère partie. Le Vignéron Champnois 8: 17-28.

Valade M., Tribaut-Sohier I., Brunner D., Laurent M., Moncomble D., Tusseau D., 2007. Les apports d'oxygène en vinification et leurs impacts sur les vins: Le cas particulier du Champagne (2ème partie). Rev. Fr. d'Œnologie 222: 17-28.

Valero E., Moyano L., Millan M. C., Medina M., Ortega J. M., 2002. Higher alcohols and esters production by Saccharomyces cerevisiae. Influence of the initial oxygenation of the grape must. Food Chem. 78: 57-61.

Vela E., Hernández-Orte P., Franco-Luesma, E., Ferreira V., 2017. The effects of copper fining on the wine content of sulfur off-odors and on their evolution during accelerated anoxic storage. Food. Chem. 231: 212-221.

Vela E., Hernandez-Orte P., Franco-Luesma E., Ferreira V., 2018. Micro-oxygenation does not eliminate hydrogen sulfide and mercaptans from wine; it simply shifts redox und complex-related equilibria to reversible oxidized species and complexed forms. Food Chem. 243: 222-230.

Vérette E., Noble A. C., Somers T. C., 1988. Hydroxycinnamates of Vitis vinifera: sensory assessment in relation to bitterness in white wine. J. Sci. Food Agric. 45 (3): 267-272.

Versini G., Rapp A., Marais J., Mattivi F., Spraul M., 1996. A new 1,1,6-trimethyl-1,2-dihydrohaphthalene (TDN) precursor isolated from Riesling grape products. Partial structure elucidation and possible reaction mechanism. Vitis 35 (1): 15-21.

Vidal J.-C., Dufourcq T., Boulet J.-C., Moutounet M., 2001. Les apports d'oxygène au cours des traitements des vins. Bilan des observations sur site. 1ère partie. Rev. Fr. d'Œnologie 190: 24-31.

Vidal J.-C., Boulet J.-C., Moutounet M., 2003. Les apports d'oxygène au cours des traitements des vins. Bilan des observations sur site. 2ème partie. Rev. Fr. d'Œnologie 201: 32-38.

Vidal J.-C., Boulet J.-C., Moutounet M., 2004 a. Les apports d'oxygène au cours des traitements des vins. Bilan des observations sur site. 3ème partie. Rev. Fr. d'Œnologie 205: 25-33.

Vidal J.-C., Toitot C., Boulet J.-C., Moutounet M., 2004 b: Comparison of methods for measuring oxygen in the headspace of a bottle of wine. J. Int. Sci. Vigne Vin 38 (7): 191-200.

Vidal J.-C., Moutounet M., 2006. Suivi de l'oxygène des phases gazeuse et liquide de bouteilles de vin à l'embouteillage et en conservation. J. Int. Sci. Vigne Vin 40 (1): 35-45.

Vidal J.-C., Guillemat B., Chayvialle C., 2011. Oxygen transmission rate of screwcaps by chemoluminescence and air/capsule/headspace/acidified water system. Bull. de l'OIV 84: 189-198.

Vivas N., Glories Y., 1996. Role of oak wood ellagitannins in the oxidation process of red wines during aging. Am. J. Enol. Vitic. 47 (1): 103-107.

Vivas N., 1999. Les oxydations et les réductions dans les moûts et les vins. Éditions Féret, Bordeaux 1999.

Viviers M. Z., Smith M. E., Wilkes E., Smith P., 2013. Effects of five metals on the evolution of hydrogen sulfide, methanethiol, and dimethyl sulfide during anaerobic storage of Chardonnay and Shiraz wines. J. Agric. Food Chem. 61 (50): 12385-12396.

Voilley, A., Lamer, C., Dubois, P, Feuillat, M., 1990. Influence of macromolecules and treatments on the behavior of aroma compounds in a model wine. J. Agric. Food Chem. 38 (1): 248-251.

Walther A.-K., Durner D., Fischer U., 2018. Impact of temperature during bulk shipping on the chemical composition and sensory profile of a Chardonnay wine. Am. J. Enol. Vitic. 69 (3): 247-257.

Waterhouse A. L., Laurie V. F., 2006. Oxidation of wine phenols: a critical evaluation and hypotheses. Am. J. Enol. Vitic. 57 (4): 306-313.

Waterhouse A., Frost S., Ugliano M., Cantu A. R., Currie B. L., Anderson M., Chassy A.W., Vidal S., Diéval J.-B., Aagaard O., Heymann H., 2016. Sulfur dioxide-oxygen consumption ratio reveals differences in bottled wine oxidation. Am. J. Enol. Vitic. 67 (4): 449-459.

Waters E. J., Peng Z., Pocock K. F., Williams P. J., 1996. The role of corks in oxidative spoilage of white wines. Aust. J. Wine Grape Res., 2 (3): 191-197.

Waters E., Williams P., 1997. The role of corks in the random oxidation of bottled wines. Australian Wine Industry Journal 12: 189-193.

Wegmann-Herr P., 2015: Ein Peptid auf dem Vormarsch? Deut. Weinmagazin 16/17: 25-27.

7. Literature

Wegmann-Herr P., Ullrich S., Schmarr H.G., Durner D., 2016. Use of glutathione during white wine production – impact on S-off-flavors and sensory production. BIO Web of Conferences 7, 02031, https://doi.org/10.1051/bioconf/20160702031: 1-3.

Wildenradt H. L., Singleton V. L., 1974. The production of aldehydes as a result of oxidation of phenolic compounds and its relation to wine aging. Am. J. Enol. Vitic. 25 (2): 119-126.

Williams R. L., Duvernay J. M., Recht J., 1995. Influencing polyphenols in white wines. Seed enhancement studies. *In:* Proceedings of the 4th Internat. Symposium "Innovationen in der Kellerwirtschaft", Stuttgart, Germany, 1995: 233-239.

Wilson S.M., Duitschaever C.L., Buteau C., Allen O.B., 1993. Hyperoxidation of Seyval blanc and Riesling musts and the effect on the quality of the wine. Paper presented at the 44th Annual Meeting of the ASEV, Sacramento, CA, 1993.

Winterhalter P., Sefton M.A., Williams Ö.J., 1990. Volatile C_{13}-norisoprenoid compounds in Riesling wine are generated from multiple precursors. Am. J. Enol. Vitic. 41 (4): 277-283.

Yuan F., Qian M.C., 2016. Development of C13-norisoprenoids, carotenoids and other volatile compounds in *Vitis vinifera* L. Cv. Pinot noir grapes. Food Chem. 192: 633-641.

Zironi R. Buiatti S., Zelotti E., 1992. Evaluation of a new colourimetric method for the determination of catechins in musts and wines. Vitic. Enol. Sci. 47 (1): 1-7.

Zironi R., Celotti E., Battistutta F., 1997. Research for a marker of the hyperoxygenation treatment of musts for the production of white wines. Am. J. Enol. Vitic. 48 (2): 150-156.

Zoecklein B.W. et al.: Wine analysis and production. Kluwer Academic/Plenum Publishers, New York 1995.

White Wine Enology

INDEX

1,1,6-trimethyl-1,2-dihydronaphthalene, 207
2-aminoacetophenone, 191, 195
absorbance at 280 nm, 29
absorbance at 420 nm, 24
absorbance measurements, 29
absorption, 107
accelerated aging tests, 28, 137, 204, 212
accelerated browning test, 30
accelerated reductive aging test, 177
acetaldehyde, 15, 18, 66, 73, 77, 80, 100
acetic acid esters, 9
acidic hydrolysis, 212
active must oxidation, 56
aeration, 155. 162
aeration in the tasting glass, 124
aging on the lees, 94, 104
air pockets, 116
alcohol levels, 25
amino acids, 11
analytical markers, 60
anthocyanins, 28
antioxidants, 66
argon, 112
aroma losses, 115
aroma profile, 125
aroma thiols, 62
aromatic thiols, 93, 143
ascorbic acid, 19, 80, 164, 179, 203
astringency, 22, 38, 86
atypical aging, 63, 84, 191
autolysis, 102
ß-glucan, 49
ß-glucanase, 49, 106
ß-glycosidase activity, 210
barrels, 21, 108
bâtonnage, 105
bench scale trials, 38
bentonite, 55
bentonite fining, 45
benzaldehyde, 11
benzene methanethiol, 149
benzyl mercaptan, 149
bisulfite, 67
bisulfite adducts, 13
bitterness, 24, 36, 38
binding of DO, 123
bottle closures, 162, 169, 215
bottle headspace, 84, 128
bottle storage, 140
bottling, 84, 126
bound SO_2, 15
browning, 23, 52, 58, 83, 105
browning potential, 24
caftaric acid, 21, 50, 53
canopy microclimate, 209
carbon dioxide, 112
carotenoids, 208
casein, 40
caseinates, 16, 40
catechin, 22, 27
catechin equivalents, 28
centrifuges, 45, 117
charcoal, 16
chemical markers, 27, 60
citric acid, 160
clarification, 102, 122, 146, 203
closure OTR, 170
CO_2, 104, 121
cold settling, 43
cold soak, 33
cold stabilization, 121
colloidal silica, 39
colorimetric measurement of flavonoids, 31
commercial tannins, 21, 26, 86
complexed copper, 182
container materials, 107
copper, 17, 42, 85, 104, 153, 158, 193
copper additions, 179
copper citrate, 159

copper complexing compounds, 182
copper fining, 85, 104, 155, 184
copper levels, 185, 163
copper management, 179
copper requirements, 158, 178
copper solubility, 182
copper stability, 181
copper sulfate, 159, 163
copper uptake, 184
copper-sulfhydryl complexes, 168
corking machines, 131
coupled oxidation, 10, 17
cross-flow filtration, 117
crusher-destemmer, 33
cyclic aldehydes, 31
cysteine, 10, 88, 151
degree of polymerization, 41
dehydroascorbic acid, 81
destemming, 36
dialkyl disulfides, 151
dicarbonyl compounds, 10
diethyl disulfide, 147
dimethyl disulfide, 147
dimethyl sulfide, 147
dimethylaminocinnamaldehyde, 31
dissociation constant, 14, 17
dissolved oxygen (DO), 54, 198
disulfides, 85, 152, 190
DO, 54, 68, 131, 198
DO consumption rate, 82, 100, 124
DO decrease, 70
DO level at bottling, 80, 114, 137
DO meter, 112
drought, 200, 210
dry ice, 131
egg albumin, 38
ellagitannins, 21, 86, 102
enzymatic oxidation, 50
epicatechin, 22
esters, 14
ethanethiol, 147
ethyl thioacetate, 147
evaporation, 111, 115
extraction of flavonoids, 36
Fenton reaction, 14, 18, 77, 86
filters, 116
filtration, 45, 79, 103, 107, 122, 168

fining, 32, 37, 122
first-order reaction, 99, 123, 155
flavan-3,4-ols, 22
flavan-3-ols, 22
flavonoid concentration, 29
flavonoid extraction, 33
flavonoid phenols, 20, 26, 34, 78
flavonoid precipitation, 55
flavonols, 22
flintstone, 149
flotation, 57
Folin-Ciocalteu's reagent, 28
free acetaldehyde, 15, 79
free SO_2, 14, 19, 30, 67, 72, 75, 78, 83, 134
free-run juice, 35, 202
fruit ripeness, 36
FT-NIR, 29
functionalized liner, 186
furfural, 11
gallotannins, 86
gas-injection unit, 56
gelatin, 38, 46
gentle wine treatment, 107, 114
global climate change, 199
glutathione, 20, 53, 88, 203
glutathione disulfide, 88
glycerin, 18
grape processing, 33
grape reaction product (GRP), 53, 60
grape solids, 102, 106
grape-derived aroma, 33
gravity flow, 34
H_2O_2, 28, 68
H_2S, 144, 164
headspace, 115
headspace blanketing, 80, 111
headspace inertization, 80, 108, 118
headspace oxygen, 128, 137
heat exposure, 139
heat tests, 177
heavy metals, 17, 30, 42, 153
higher alcohols, 9
higher aldehydes, 11, 16, 18
homogenization, 42
hydrogen disulfane, 149

hydrogen peroxide, 18, 52, 68, 88
hydrogen sulfide, 94, 144
hydrolysis, 9, 21
hydrolyzable tannins, 21, 86
hydroxycinnamates, 21
hydroxyl radicals, 18
hyperoxidation, 51, 58, 203
immobilized copper, 185
inactivated dry yeast, 62, 88, 93, 160, 203
indole, 194
indole-3-acetic acid, 194
inert gas, 79, 111
influence of juice treatment, 37
injection pump, 40
instantaneous DO concentration, 100
iron, 17, 73, 85, 166
iron instability, 48
isinglass, 40
juice browning, 52
juice clarification, 43
juice clarity, 43
juice oxidation, 56, 203
kieselguhr, 120
kieselsol, 39, 48
laccase, 53, 58
lactones, 10
laminar flow, 117
level of juice clarification, 43
light-struck flavor, 152
liners, 173, 186
liquid movement, 109
liquid surface, 114
Maillard reaction, 178
mannoproteins, 107
masking effects, 32
matrix effects, 25
measurement of flavonoid phenols, 30
measurement of must turbidity, 44
measurement of total phenols, 29
mechanical harvesting, 33
mechanical impact, 35
membrane press, 35
mercaptans, 146
metal-complexed sulfhydryls, 155

methanethiol, 147
methional, 11, 27
methionine, 152
methionol, 45
methyl thioacetate, 147
microbial risks, 59
microbial stability, 79
minerality, 148
minimal treatment, 121
mixers, 119
mixing of wine, 42
molar ratio of $O_2:SO_2$, 69
molecular oxygen, 19
molecular SO_2, 67, 71, 78, 137
mouthfeel, 25
must bottoms, 49
must oxidation, 56
must turbidity, 63
natural corks, 133, 210
negative pressure, 118
nephelometric turbidity units, 44, 94
nitrogen, 112
nitrogen dropping, 131
nonflavonoid phenols, 20, 28
non-oxidative aging, 9
norisoprenoids, 14
NTU, 44, 94
nucleophilic addition, 20
oxygen during fermentation, 60
oak, 86, 102
oak alternatives, 21, 86
orange wine, 26, 34
OTR, 133, 155, 169
overfining, 39
oxidation of juice, 50, 54
oxidation of phenols, 17
oxidation products, 69
oxidation rate, 42
oxidative aging, 9, 15, 34, 57, 90
oxidative juice processing, 51
oxygen, 50, 68, 126
oxygen acceptors, 17
oxygen consumption, 82, 94
oxygen consumption capacity, 54, 98
oxygen consumption rate, 56, 94
oxygen diffusion rate, 108

oxygen exposure, 90
oxygen measurements, 89, 130
oxygen meters, 112
oxygen radicals, 88, 197
oxygen saturation concentration, 54
oxygen solubility, 108
oxygen transfer, 111, 133, 148
oxygen uptake, 19, 56, 79, 106, 113, 123
oxygen uptake through bottle closures, 133, 169
oxygen-related reactions, 66
passive must oxidation, 56, 58
passive oxygen uptake, 52
pasteurization, 139
pectolytic enzymes, 45
peroxide, 74
petrol flavor, 207
pH, 25, 67, 71, 78
phenol oxidation, 17, 71
phenolate anions, 17, 71
phenolic composition, 17
phenolic taste, 38
phenol-reducing finings, 26, 37
phenylacetaldehyde, 12, 27
physiological ripeness, 198
pinking, 28, 85
plant proteins, 40
polyfunctional thiols, 14
polymerization, 23
polyphenol oxidase, 50
polysaccharides, 25, 102
polyvinylpolypyrrolidon, 39
post-bottling reduction flavor, 143
post-bottling SO_2 losses, 126, 135, 169
post-fermentation yeast lees, 94
potassium ferrocyanide, 166
premature oxidative aging, 26
pressing, 34
pressing fractions, 35
pressing quality, 36
pressing systems, 35
pressure, 34, 117
pressure difference, 104
pressure relief, 117
propeller mixers, 42, 166

protein haze, 39
protein stabilization, 47
protein-based fining agents, 41
proteins, 47
pump capacity, 120
pumping cycles, 33
pumping over, 42, 56
pumps, 115
purging hoses, 119
PVI/PVP, 168
PVPP, 16, 28, 39
quinones, 17, 19, 50, 68, 77, 88
racking, 102, 104
radical scavengers, 197
radical scavenging capacity, 86
random oxidation - 134 -
redox potential, 143, 157, 170, 182
redox regimen, 50
reducing agents, 66
reducing amino acids, 88, 94, 105
reduction flavor, 85, 103, 104, 125, 145
reductive aging, 143
reductive must processing, 65
regenerative polymerization, 20, 71
residual copper, 104
residual flavonoid phenols, 55
residual turbidity, 43, 59, 61, 63
Riesling, 209
S-amino acids, 152
Saranex liner, 174
Sauvignon blanc, 14, 61, 90, 143, 184
S-containing amino acids, 144
screening test for free acetaldehyde, 16
screw cap liners, 169, 173
screw caps, 10, 85, 133, 169, 211
seeds, 22, 33
self-clarification, 104
sensory bias, 16, 193
sensory evaluation, 63, 137
sensory terms, 26
separating pressings, 35
shading grapes, 211
silica dioxide, 48
silver chloride, 161

skatole, 194
skin contact, 22, 33, 202
skins, 22
smell of free acetaldehyde, 15
SO_2, 96, 144
SO_2 additions, 105
SO_2 consumption, 90
SO_2 determination, 83
$SO_2:O_2$ ratio, 69, 72
SO_2-losses, 131
sotolon, 12, 27
sparging, 121
sparging stone, 56
sparkling wine, 36
specific surface area, 111
spectrophotometric measurements, 31
stems, 22, 33
stirring, 104
storage containers, 108
storage temperature, 9, 137, 213
Strecker aldehyde, 11
Strecker reactions, 10, 20
strenuous treatments, 42
sulfate, 18, 68, 144
sulfhydryl group, 148, 161
sulfhydryls, 148
sulfides, 148
sulfur dioxide, 13, 50, 66
sulfur-containing amino acids, 20, 88
surface-area-to-volume ratio, 108
suspended yeast lees, 30, 94, 163
synthetic corks, 133, 211
tannin additions, 26
TDN, 207
technical corks, 133, 211
temperature, 97, 108, 121, 124, 137
temperature loggers, 141
terpenols, 14, 93

thioacetates, 151, 189
thiol-disulfide equilibrium, 154
thiols, 85, 146, 186
tin foil, 174
tin-Saran liner, 136, 173, 186
topping, 118
total acetaldehyde, 16
total flavonoids, 34
total pack oxygen, 129, 146
total phenols, 20, 28
TPO, 129
transition metals, 86, 181
tube diameter, 117, 120
tubings, 119
turbidity measurements, 44, 94
turbidity meter, 45
turbulence, 110
turbulent flow, 114, 116
typical aging, 9
tyrosinase, 52
UV radiation, 200
vacuum evacuation, 131
variable capacity tanks, 112
varietal thiols, 14, 90, 169
volatilization, 42
VSCs, 143
whole-bunch pressing, 36
wine movements, 121
wine surface, 108, 111
wine treatments, 113
wines without added sulfites, 16, 58, 79
YAN, 45, 144
yeast, 194
yeast autolysis, 102
yeast cells, 94, 103
yeast lees, 88, 101
yeast nutrients, 202
yeast strains, 96, 144, 202, 210
yeast survival factors, 45

Board and Bench Publishing

BOARDANDBENCH.COM

WINE FAULTS
JOHN HUDELSON
$39.95 ISBN 978-1-934259-63-4

ACIDITY MANAGEMENT IN MUSTS & WINES
VOLKER SCHNEIDER
$45 978-1-935879-18-3

PRACTICAL FIELD GUIDE TO GRAPE GROWING & VINE PHYSIOLOGY
SCHUSTER, PAOLETTI, BERNINI
$45 ISBN 978-1-935879-31-2

THE VITICULTURE & ENOLOGY LIBRARY

VIEW FROM THE VINEYARD
CLIFFORD P. OHMART
$34.95
ISBN 978-1935879909

UNDERSTANDING WINE TECHNOLOGY
DAVID BIRD
$44.95
ISBN 978-1-934259-60-3

CONCEPTS IN WINE TECHNOLOGY
YAIR MARGALIT
$45 ISBN 978-1-935879-80-0

CONCEPTS IN WINE CHEMISTRY
YAIR MARGALIT
$89.95 ISBN 978-1-935879-81-7

THE BUSINESS OF WINEMAKING
JEFFREY L LAMY
$45 ISBN 978-1-935879-65-7

THE BUSINESS OF SUSTAINABLE WINE
SANDRA TAYLOR
$45
ISBN
978-1-935879-30-5

WINE MARKETING AND SALES 3RD ED.
WAGNER, OLSEN, THACH
$75 ISBN 978-1-935879-44-2

THE WINE BUSINESS LIBRARY

ARTISAN PUBLIC RELATIONS
PAUL WAGNER
$29.95 ISBN 978-1-935879-29-9

HOW TO IMPORT WINE 2ND ED.
DEBORAH M GRAY
$29.95
ISBN
978-1-935879-40-4

WINE BUSINESS CASE STUDIES
PIERRE MORA, EDITOR
$35.00
ISBN
978-1-935879-71-8

www.ingramcontent.com/pod-product-compliance
Lightning Source LLC
Chambersburg PA
CBHW082003150426
42814CB00005BA/209